Let us now praise men of renown
And our fathers in their generation.

ECCLESIASTICUS XLIV: 1

Boasting, as beggars will,
that their grandfathers were rich and great.

JONATHAN SWIFT

Francis Kernan

Francis Kernan, circa 1882

Karen Clemens Kernan,

John Devereux Kernan,
and Robert P. Forbes

Francis Kernan

The life and times of a
19th-century, citizen-politician
of upstate New York

Oneida County Historical Society / Utica, NY

Published in the United States by the
Oneida County Historical Society
1608 Genesee Street, Utica, NY 13502-5425

Printed in the United States
by Phoenix Press Inc., New Haven, CT

ISBN 0-9668178-1-8

BOOK DESIGN BY BARBARA MARKS

ENDPAPER ART:
Tilden receives the news of his presidential nomination
Governor Samuel Jones Tilden (left of table) formally
receives the 1876 Democratic nomination. Senator Francis
Kernan (continuing left) and New York State Lieutenant
Governor W.E. Dorsheimer, stand ready to campaign hard
for the Irish and German votes. Next to Dorsheimer is
Charles O'Conor, a family friend of Kernan and the man
who provided legal counsel both for the ex-president
of the Confederacy, Jefferson Davis, and against New York's
corrupt political boss, William M. Tweed.
Artist unknown. Reprinted from Alexander C. Flick's biography, *Samuel Jones Tilden*.

To the family of Francis Kernan,
that we can all know our connection to
American history—from our oldest
current member, Thomas Spratt Kernan,
now ninety years of age, to our youngest,
Anna Bythiner Kramer, not even
ninety days. To every one who came
before, and to all who will follow.

KAREN CLEMENS KERNAN

If she will accept, I dedicate my part
of this book to Karen Kernan,
without whose help it would have
been written in half the time—
and not been half as good.

JOHN DEVEREUX KERNAN

# ontents

CONTENTS

List of Illustrations

Acknowledgments

W E A R E I N D E B T E D to many people for their interest, suggestions, advice, and help:

To Gilbert Butler, who suggested the project in August 1993, and made it possible through his subsequent generosity and encouragement; and to Fred Butler for his enthusiasm in response to each chapter as it was produced;

To the Oneida County Historical Society for its support of this project. We are sure that such support would please Francis Kernan, who was a member of the Board of Councilors during the 1870s when Horatio Seymour was its president.

In the beginning of this project we divided it into two parts, Book One, in which John Devereux Kernan covers the family life and legal career of his great-grandfather, and Book Two, in which Karen Kernan writes of his political life. We are both especially grateful to historian Robert P. Forbes, Ph.D., of New Haven, for his valuable participation in this endeavor. He wrote the opening chapter and the section on Francis's years in the United States Senate, and wove additional commentary throughout the text to provide the historical context necessary for modern readers. Rob's comments on the work in progress helped us balance the pro-Democratic leanings of most of our primary source material. He pointed us to relevant scholarship and deterred us from factual errors.

We were particularly gratified to find someone of his knowledge and impartiality coming to the same conclusion as we had drawn regarding Kernan's upright character. It was never our intention to idealize our ancestor, and it was a concern when, after many months of research, we could find none of the shadows that humanize a personality or provide the necessary contrast and conflict for a good story. But the fact is that Francis's integrity was fully acknowledged by his contemporaries. Their appointment of Kernan to the U.S. Senate after a decade of corruption and scandal in both the Democratic and Republican parties served to unify and purify the New York legislature. Rob's disinterested and well-researched conclusions are stronger statements than we could have made ourselves without seeming to boast.

Then there are the many members of the family who have answered our queries, and sent us their recollections, pictures, and documents: Mary Angela, Jimmy's Susan, Kitty, Tom, Henry, Frank, Jim Sedgwick, Leslie, Bill, Corinne Sevigny, Winifred Metcalf, Natalie Barringer, Ellen Miles, Eleanor Penniman, Effie Louise Kraft, Clifford Lewis, Peter Savage, and Lawrence Stubbs.

Many outside the family have also helped greatly with answers to our questions with patience, willingness, and cooperation—

Professors: Beekman Cannon, Robert Gordon, Paul Kennedy, John Langbein, William Nordhaus, Cynthia Russett, Peter Schuck, Gaddis Smith, and Harry Stout, all at Yale (for whose libraries D.G.); Kerby Miller of the University of Missouri, Paul Carrington of the Duke Law School, Eben Moglen of the Columbia Law School, and Geoffrey C. Hazard Jr. of the American Law Institute; Mr. and Mrs. Ammon Hoover, who now live on part of the Kernan homestead in Tyrone; Judge John J. Walsh, of Utica; The Reverend R. Emmett Curran, Lynn Conway and John Reynolds, Archivists, of Georgetown University; Douglas Preston and Bea White of the Oneida County Historical Society, and Dr. Paul D. Schweizer of the Munson-Williams-Proctor Institute; The Reverend Donald McIlvride of the Dundee Presbyterian Church; James R. Greenfield, Esquire, of Hamden, Connecticut; Mrs. Barbara H. Bell of the Schuyler County Historical Society; Tammy Love of the Oneida County Surrogate's Court; Frederick A. Muller, State Reporter of the State of New York; the Reverend Michael Gosselin, former Catholic Chaplain at Yale; James C. Campbell, Librarian, the New Haven Colony Historical Society. Sister Mary Virginia Brennan, Archivist of the Visitation Convent, Washington, Sister Catherine of Saint John's Church, Utica; Donald Arthur Rowland, Historian of the Town of Wayne; Marion Springer, of the Steuben County Clerk's Office, and David Herbert Donald, author of *Lincoln*.

Our researchers, Ann Brokaw of Utica; Laura Stabinski and Lisa Weinberger of Yale University, Michael Cronin Jr., now of Denver, and Susan Stein, of Middletown, Connecticut, were all thorough and interested, and gave us outstanding service.

Thanks to Suzanne Kelley and John Cox for their editing and very careful final readings and for catching the little errors that would have haunted us forever.

We are particularly grateful to Professor Michael Gordon of the University of

Connecticut and to Edward Ahearne, Trixie Kernan, and Anita Halton for reading the manuscript, and being kind about it in their comments.

Finally, Karen would like to acknowledge her favorite Kernan, her husband, Sean, who has been so very supportive throughout this time-consuming project; and John thanks his wife, Una, for her patience and support during these last, often difficult years.

Our heartfelt thanks to you all!

KAREN CLEMENS KERNAN   JOHN DEVEREUX KERNAN

A Personal Foreword

by John Devereux Kernan

My introduction to Francis Kernan happened in Utica probably sometime during the middle months of 1916, in its railroad depot. In those days, his portrait hung there, and as my mother and I walked by, she told me that the gentleman on the wall was my great-grandfather. I turned, doffed my panama hat, bowed and said "How do you do, great-grandfather." Do I really remember this? No, but I do recall my mother telling me of it on several occasions.

Francis Kernan was always spoken of in the family, especially by his son Uncle Joe, in proud tones as "The Senator." I selected his name as one of my confirmation names at the age of eleven, with the assurance of my mother (a staunch Protestant—"Plymouth Rock," my father called her) that he was no doubt in heaven, from where, I deduced, he could do me some good. Like all his great-grandchildren, I was brought up to admire, respect, and be proud of him—not that I was ever told much very specific. I knew that he was a lawyer and a Democrat, that he had been to Georgetown, traveling there on horseback, that he opposed parochial schools taking money from the state, and that he was a statesman, not a politician. I gathered from other than family sources that he was called by some a "Copperhead," that is, one opposed to the Civil War.

We have had to reconstruct Francis Kernan fact by fact, searching through family scrapbooks and rusty memories, visiting county courthouses and historical societies, researching archives in Washington, D.C., scanning various collections of letters from other prominent men of his day for Francis's handwriting, wearing our eyes on reels of microfilm and microfiche to spot yet another newspaper story, examining church records, and inspecting indices for the name "Kernan" in hundreds of yellowing books on dusty shelves in the quiet, dark, and wonderful stacks of Yale University's libraries.

Let us consider for a moment should a descendant be involved in writing his forebear's biography, or will the result be too hagiographic, or be overloaded with irrelevant family stories? If I am careful to tighten the reins on those hazards, I may get by and, if not, forgiven. However, there are other problems that any historian faces, such as the unfortunate gaps in the sources. No one can put himself so completely in Francis's shoes as to give a wholly truthful picture of his life and times. It will always be obvious in what period the writer is working by his allusions, and by the very language, grammar, and spelling he uses. His own interests will be revealed by what is included, or omitted.

Fortunately, my co-author is not by blood a Kernan, nor so immersed in the Kernan milieu—Utica, Alder Creek, Hart's Hill, the Sadaquada, the Red House, Boonville, Constable Hall, North Pond, etc.—as to face the same hazards. While I admit to certain tendencies as the family historian to wander from the main tale, I trust that she has seen that we, like James Boswell, "have written, not a panegyric [or a bore] . . . but a life."

There are not many of his great-grandchildren still around, but if you add three more greats, and cousins and collaterals, there will be hundreds to meet him.

Ladies and gentlemen, behold your eminent ancestor!

JOHN DEVEREUX KERNAN
July 1999

The Electoral Commission

The Electoral Commission, created to determine a winner in the disputed 1876 election, took until the following March to give the presidency to Rutherford Hayes over Samuel Tilden. Democrats looked on with horror as an election that the whole world thought their leader had won, slipped away by a single vote. Though detesting the results, Kernan preserved intact his fundamental political principle: to the states alone belonged the prerogative of determining their voice in national affairs. And he had accomplished something still more valuable: his presence on the commission helped the nation to accept peacefully the results of the electoral process, flawed though it was. (Francis sits to the far left, directly below the dais, indicating his late appointment to the commission. He is recognizable by his trademark "Collier" beard.)

By Cornelia Adele (Strong) Fassett (1831–1898). Oil on canvas, 61" × 75" Cat No 33.00006 (Originally named, by the artist, "The Florida Case before the Electoral Commission, February 5, 1877.")

$\mathcal{I}$ntroduction

by Robert P. Forbes

AMERICANS BEGAN THE year 1877 in a nightmare of indecision. On election night the previous November the Democratic candidate for president, Samuel J. Tilden, had apparently scored a decisive victory, winning the popular vote by a quarter of a million and reportedly capturing "a very considerable majority of the electoral vote."[1] Democrats celebrated their first victory in twenty years, and Republicans, by and large, faced the loss with equanimity because the victor was sober, responsible, and tested—a man of sterling character and proven ability, who shared the reformist views of their own candidate, Rutherford B. Hayes, on most questions.

In fact, Americans had reason for pride, since for the first time since the Civil War, indeed perhaps for the first time in the century, the political system had offered up two candidates in whom most of the country could feel substantial confidence. The Democrats had made reform of government and uprooting of corruption their chief campaign issues, and the Republicans, as a matter of survival, had chosen to fight fire with fire. They had rejected more colorful, but morally compromised candidates for the bland but unobjectionable Hayes. Although the Republicans did not break free entirely from demagogic appeals to wartime emotions—"waving the bloody shirt"—the campaign was the most elevated and issue-oriented in years, offering hope for a new civility in American politics.

How ironic, therefore, that this peaceful contest between two sober candidates should embroil the nation once again in fractional and sectional conflict. The faintest chance remained for the Republicans—Hayes himself at first discounted it. Tilden had an undisputed claim to 184 electoral votes, one short of a majority. Hayes had 165. Only if every one of the disputed votes was awarded to him, would he become president. Yet that is just what the Republicans sought to achieve. It was a desperate calculation seized on by men who hated the Democratic Party with a passion. For men such as these, the war was still not over, and a Democratic victory would mean the triumph of treason. Moreover, they had at least a shaky moral leg to stand on, since Democratic intimidation of black voters in several Southern states had undoubtedly kept down the Republican tally. The strategy, then, was to overturn the electoral votes in Louisiana, South Carolina, and Florida.

For his part, Tilden faced the prospect of losing his grasp on the White House with a strangely stoic, almost sullen, passivity. Tension and exasperation mounted among his lieutenants and the party faithful as they waited, in vain, for leadership from their chief. Tilden had adopted a policy of calculated delay, of "watchful waiting"; waiting for what, however, was left unclear. As the days stretched into weeks, and the weeks into months, without any apparent progress toward resolution, the mood of the country grew increasingly frayed. "Another civil war may be the consequence of this state of things," a Tilden adviser wrote in his diary, "and we may enter upon the next century under a difft. form of govt. from that of which for nearly a century we have been boasting."[2]

The Constitution provided little guidance in such a situation, and the politicians—more accustomed to maneuvering for control of patronage and personal power than to exercising statesmanship—stumbled hesitantly toward a resolution. With the Democrats holding a majority in the House and the Republicans controlling the Senate, no one wanted to be the first to "blink." A strategy of naming General George B. McClellan as Tilden's "adjutant" was rejected as too provocative; the proposal of a House caucus to impeach President Grant received more support, but was eventually tabled by more cautious members.

Finally, while Northern politicians and Southern railroad executives met behind closed doors in obscure negotiations, a crack opened in the wall between Democrats and Republicans and a plan for a bipartisan Electoral Commission began to gain momentum. The *ad hoc* body would consist of senators, House members and Supreme Court justices, who would have the power to rule on the credentials of the electors. Like the plan to bell the cat, however, it was one thing to establish such a commission, another to find statesmen to serve on it. A half-dozen senators, including Roscoe Conkling, the dashing, imperious Republican leader from upstate New York whose independence had helped to make the commission possible, now balked when asked to serve on it. Two other Republicans declined as well, as did the supposedly nonpartisan Supreme Court Justice David Davis whom everyone had expected to provide the critical deciding vote but he eagerly seized the exit provided by his unexpected election to the Senate. For anyone with greater political ambitions, this post of responsibility on the electoral commission seemed to be the kiss of death.

As the commission began its work, the outcome became clear: by a party-line vote of eight to seven, every important vote came down in support of Hayes. The Democrats looked on with horror as an election that the whole world thought their leader, Tilden, had won, slipped away from them, pried from their grasp one electoral vote at a time.

But this was not the end of it. When one of the Democratic commissioners resigned because of failing health, the Senate had to find a Democrat to replace him. The choice was Francis Kernan—elected by a vote of 46 to 0.

Who was Francis Kernan, and why was he selected to fill this vexing, thankless role? Surprisingly, in view of the inevitable outcome, he was one of Samuel Tilden's closest allies—the man who had placed Tilden's name in nomination for the presidency at the Democratic convention, the man whom Tilden had successfully supported two years earlier for the U.S. Senate and, five years before that, the man to whom Tilden had first turned when he began his crusade to rid the New York Democratic Party of corruption. For half a generation Kernan had been the New York Democracy's standard of honesty, integrity, and consistency, often chosen for symbolic or sacrificial roles when victory was difficult or impossible. In 1861, in his first term in the New York Assembly, Kernan had received his party's nomination for speaker, to provide a sharp moral counterpoint to the dishonest Republican incumbent whose reelection was a sure thing. In 1872 the Democrats had chosen Kernan as their nominee for governor, as the man best able to dissipate the odor of corruption caused by the flagrant excesses of Boss William M. Tweed and his Tammany ring in New York City, an uphill battle that paid off only two years later. Finally, in 1874, the party had anointed Kernan to be U.S. Senator, to pave the way, like John the Baptist, for the coming of Tilden and Reform. In the campaign of 1876, Kernan's *bona fides* had done much to insulate Tilden from embarrassing disclosures of unpaid income tax and profits from unsavory railroad deals. Even in the current chaos over disputed electoral votes, Kernan's word alone was enough to quash rumors that Tilden's cash had been used to corrupt the count. When Americans of the Gilded Age were willing to heed the "better angels of their nature," it was to men like Francis Kernan that they turned.

And now it was to Kernan that the Senate turned to fill the vacant seat on the electoral commission during its final week of existence. There was no drama to this role, which is overlooked in virtually every history of the era. But it was an appointment fraught with symbolism and significance. Although the count of the commission had gone against them, Democrats still had one card to play, if they chose: to filibuster until inauguration day, to force a new election. Others insisted that the Democrats should walk out and refuse to ratify an unjust process. Kernan's acceptance of the seat on the Electoral Commission, a position which many more

famous men had shunned, lent its decision in favor of Hayes a credibility that perhaps only Kernan could have brought to it both as a personification of integrity and
as the most upright of Tilden's allies. Moreover, by taking the seat, Kernan was
burying his own ambitions—he almost certainly would have had a cabinet position
in a Tilden administration—and thereby also sinking his hopes of lasting fame. His
role cost him dearly in the esteem of many of his fellow Democrats—including
Tilden himself—who were deeply incensed by his willingness to give his *imprimatur*
to a decision they felt was patently unfair.[3]

But Kernan had preserved intact his fundamental political principle: to the
states alone belonged the prerogative of determining their voice in national affairs.
And he had accomplished something still more valuable: he had helped the nation
to accept peacefully the results of the electoral process, flawed though it was. As had
been said two years earlier when Francis received the senatorial nomination, "The
quiet influences have prevailed."[4]

History, it has often been observed, is written by the victors; and with hindsight one
can be grateful that the party of Abraham Lincoln and the cause that he led, won.
But we should not fall into the trap of believing that the losers were necessarily
bad; or that they have nothing to teach us. The overarching theme of American history since the Civil War has been the struggle for equality, the epic effort of the
nation to implement the promises of the Declaration of Independence and the
Constitution; or as the Rev. Martin Luther King Jr. put it, to "live out the promise of
our creed." But the controlling narrative of the previous century was different: it
was not to implement equality, but to defend American liberty.

Francis Kernan was born into and nurtured by an America that no longer
exists.

To Francis and many of his fellow Democrats, it was an infinitely precious
republic whose independence often seemed a fragile thing—more threatened from
within than from without. They deeply believed that the Union that had given
them so much was the chief hope of freedom in a world ruled by despots. They also
believed, correctly as it turned out, that the Union could only survive peacefully if
each state retained the power to control its own institutions—slavery included.

To the Federalists and their descendants, the National Republicans, Whigs, and
Republicans, liberty was power, as John Quincy Adams asserted. America's liberty
conveyed the promise, indeed the responsibility, of pursuing great public undertak-
ings to extend the benefits of the nation's resources as widely as possible. To Francis
Kernan's Democrats, and their predecessors, the Jeffersonian Republicans, power
was the greatest threat to liberty, and had to be checked decisively. Ironically, the
most patriotic Democrats were the most strenuous defenders of the sovereignty of

the states and their independence from central government control. With this belief went a set of corollaries: that government must be kept small, taxes kept low, and individual freedoms given precedence over larger and more abstract conceptions of the public good. Any deviation from this standard imperiled the fragile Union, and thereby endangered liberty itself. The United States began as a tiny island of republicanism in a sea of monarchies, all of them anticipating America's failure and ready to exploit its weaknesses. Is it not possible that Kernan and his fellow Democrats were right, at least for their time?

What can we learn from the life of such a man as Francis Kernan? In the first place, we should probably not look to him for political perspectives, since the conditions of his day were so fundamentally different from ours. Nor will we find in Kernan's biography unusual drama; he was spared the extremes of fortune that make a life gripping to read, and difficult to live. Nor will we find in him a "representative" man, or even a "representative" Democrat; his contemporaries were clear that he was nothing of the kind. Instead, we may find in Francis Kernan an exemplar of political virtue to his contemporaries. He was the man his party inevitably called on when they wished to put their best foot forward; the man they sent up when they sought to convince the electorate that they were the party of principle. By studying the life of Francis Kernan, we can better come to understand the qualities Americans of the mid-19th century found most valuable, even if they did not always possess them themselves: character, honesty, integrity, judgment, honor. And we may even find, perhaps, that the life of Francis Kernan has a similar value for Americans living today.

NOTES

1. *Chicago Daily News,* November 8, 1876, in Keith Ian Polakoff, *The Politics of Inertia: The Election of 1876 and the End of Reconstruction* (Baton Rouge: Louisiana State University Press, 1973), 200.

2. John Bigelow Diary, November 11, 1876, in *ibid.*, 206.

3. Alexander C. Flick, *Samuel Jones Tilden: A Study in Political Sagacity,* 408.

4. *Utica Daily Observer,* January 18, 1875.

Francis Kernan

At Home
and At the Bar

* The epigram *I am no fool—I know my ancestors* should be read in the light of Irish and English law: under Brehon law, only sons, grandsons or great-grandsons of a chief were eligible to succeed him, hence the widespread interest in genealogy; under English law, the deliberate degrading of the Irish by depriving them of education and the right to own land served to remind the many reduced to the peasantry of their descent from former chiefs and dispossessed landowners, thus also fostering the interest in genealogy. Most of the old Irish chieftainships have disappeared. The last known MacKernan, for instance, Bryan Bane, died in 1622. There are in fact only about seven still recognized as such, and the chiefs, no longer having any sept organizations to elect them, now take their positions under English rules of primogeniture. Some, such as the O'Conors Don, managed with good luck to maintain something of their status throughout Penal times, even though remaining Catholics; some, such as the MacDermots, Princes of Coolavin, also still Catholics, managed to regain their former status after a period in reduced circumstances; and some, such as the O'Briens, accepted English titles (Inchiquin) and the Established Church, and some, such as the McGillycuddys of the Reeks, maintained their ownership of land by conforming to the Established Church.

*I*rish Origins

I am no fool—I know my ancestors.*
AN ANONYMOUS IRISH PEASANT

FRANCIS KERNAN'S FATHER, William, exiled himself from an Ireland whose citizens were treated like pariahs in their own country. Ireland's British rulers subjected Catholics to a draconian set of Penal Laws that constituted almost a form of religious apartheid. "Under these laws," wrote William V. Shannon, United States ambassador to Ireland,

> [The Irish were] deprived of civil rights, mercilessly exploited, and subject to hanging or deportation for trivial offenses. No Irish Catholic could vote, serve on a jury, enter the army or navy, teach school, carry a gun, or own a horse of the value of more than five guineas. No Irish Catholic could enter a university, become a lawyer, or work for the government.... [The effects of the Penal Code] were deep, severe, and lasting. The Ireland of the Penal Code formed the modern Irish character. The majority of Irish settlers in America carried this background with them.[1]

William Kernan was a scion of an ancient sept, MacKernan of Tullyhunco (sometimes referred to as "of the Breifne").* The sept had been seated for hundreds of years at Croaghan, near the village of Killeshandra in County Cavan, once part of Connaught, but, after the shiring by Elizabeth I of England, of Ulster. It was a branch of, and originally tributary to, the O'Rourkes, but under the sway of the O'Reillys by Elizabethan times.[2]

Croaghan in Gaelic is *Cruachan mhic Thighearnain* meaning "MacKernan's Round Hill." It was the place where the O'Rourke was inaugurated head of his clan, as well as the seat of the MacKernan.

The area, the central part of what was anciently called the Breifne, was so saturated with Kernans that Queen Elizabeth called it "M'Kernan's country" in a 1590 letter appointing John Kernan, gentleman, to be seneschal during good behavior; an additional duty was "to induce and persuade the rude inhabitants of those parts by example of good husbandry, civil living, buying and selling, and such like usages, to a more humane, sure, and gainful trade of life, more answerable to the laws and their duty of allegiance."[3]

The family name in Gaelic, "Mac Thighearnain," derives from Tigearnain, a tenth-century chieftain, whose name comes from "tigearna," meaning "lord"; and is counted one of the earliest patronymics in Ireland. The tribal name, Tullyhunco, "Tellach Dunchadha" in Gaelic, means "family, or tribe of Dunchadh," a chieftain who lived in the 17th century.

William's father, John, and his grandfather Bryan, both called "gentleman" in 18th-century documents, lived under 31-year leases on Ned and Cornagee,[4] a townland of some 180 Irish acres (almost 350 of our acres) lying a few miles west of Croaghan. It had been confiscated, along with most of the province of Ulster, from the Gaelic inhabitants late in the reign of Elizabeth I, after the rebellion of the O'Reilly. In the early years of the 17th century most of Cavan was granted by James I to Scotsmen and settled by their countrymen, but Ned and two adjoining townlands, Durey and Laraghmoght, were granted in 1611 as a "small estate" to Wony MacThomas MacKernan, one of but three MacKernans to receive direct grants from James.

These lands had been occupied, but not individually owned under Brehon law, by MacKernans for centuries previously as part of their sept lands. However, ownership under English law, acquired in 1611, was lost 30 years later as a result of the 1641 Rebellion, and thus they occupied the lands during the rest of the 17th and 18th centuries under leases from English or Scottish landlords that were limited

---

* The prefix Mac is used also in its abbreviated forms, Mc, Ma, and M', and the rest of the name appears in some sixteen different spellings, including Kiernan, Keernan, Keirnan, Tiernan, and even as MacQuiernan. For a time pursuant to law, no prefixes were allowed. The chief of the clan was addressed simply as "MacKernan," and was referred to as "the MacKernan." References to a particular chief in the Irish Annals are transcribed, for example, as "MacKernan, namely Brian." Occasionally in the Annals, MacKernan was called "Dux of Tullyhunco" in the sense of "leader," not "duke," for there was no such Irish title.

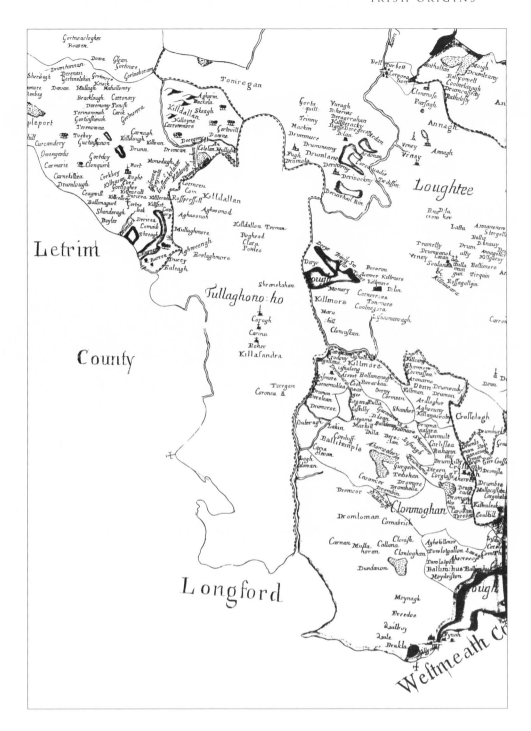

1690 Map of The County of Cavan

The ancient sept, MacKernan of Tullyhunco (sometimes referred to as "of the Breifne"),
had been seated for hundreds of years at Croaghan, near the village of Killeshandra in
County Cavan, once part of Connaught, and later, of Ulster.

From Sir William Petty's *Hibernia Delinatio.*

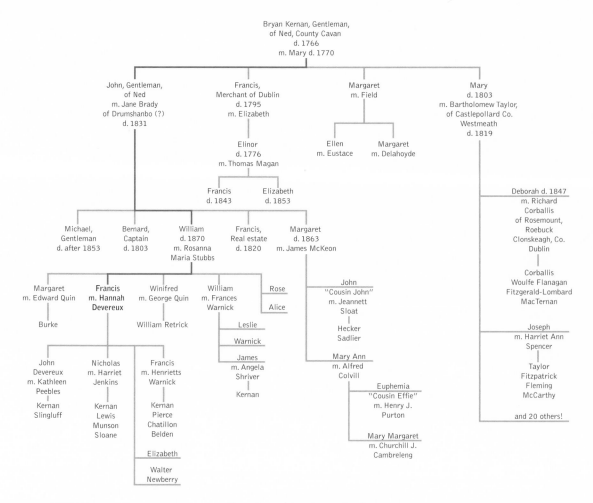

Bryan Kernan, Gentleman,
of Ned, County Cavan
d. 1766
m. Mary d. 1770

John, Gentleman,
of Ned
m. Jane Brady
of Drumshanbo (?)
d. 1831

Francis,
Merchant of Dublin
d. 1795
m. Elizabeth

Margaret
m. Field

Mary
d. 1803
m. Bartholomew Taylor,
of Castlepollard Co.
Westmeath
d. 1819

Elinor
d. 1776
m. Thomas Magan

Ellen
m. Eustace

Margaret
m. Delahoyde

Deborah d. 1847
m. Richard
Corballis
of Rosemount,
Roebuck
Clonskeagh, Co.
Dublin

Francis
d. 1843

Elizabeth
d. 1853

Corballis
Woulfe Flanagan
Fitzgerald-Lombard
MacTernan

Michael,
Gentleman
d. after 1853

Bernard,
Captain
d. 1803

William
d. 1870
m. Rosanna
Maria Stubbs

Francis,
Real estate
d. 1820

Margaret
d. 1863
m. James McKeon

John
"Cousin John"
m. Jeanett
Sloat

Joseph
m. Harriet Ann
Spencer

Margaret
m. Edward Quin

Francis
m. Hannah
Devereux

Winifred
m. George Quin

William
m. Frances
Warnick

Rose

Alice

Hecker
Sadlier

Taylor
Fitzpatrick
Fleming
McCarthy

Burke

William Retrick

Leslie

Warnick

Mary Ann
m. Alfred
Colvill

and 20 others!

John
Devereux
m. Kathleen
Peebles

Nicholas
m. Harriet
Jenkins

Francis
m. Henrietts
Warnick

James
m. Angela
Shriver

Euphemia
"Cousin Effie"
m. Henry J.
Purton

Kernan
Slingluff

Kernan
Lewis
Munson
Sloane

Kernan
Pierce
Chatillon
Belden

Kernan

Mary Margaret
m. Churchill J.
Cambreleng

Elizabeth

Walter
Newberry

Short chart of the Kernan family

by the Penal Laws because of their religion to 31 years. The last known lease of Ned to Kernans was the one dated May 24, 1763, to Bryan and John Kernan. The latter, after the death of his father, demised the remainder of the lease to his brother, Francis, in 1772.

John Kernan married Jane (Brady) Kernan. Living on a remnant of the dispossessed family's estate, they raised ten children. Although Roman Catholics and in reduced circumstances, the couple was apparently on friendly terms with the Irish gentry of their neighborhood, most of whom were in much the same, or worse, condition. They were connected by marriage, however, with a number of well-to-do families. John's brother Francis had been fostered by Charles O'Conor* of

---

* Fostering was an ancient Gaelic custom whereby a youth was sent off to be raised for a few years by another family. We are not aware of the extent to which this was still being done almost two centuries after the Flight of the Earls had destroyed the old Gaelic society. Perhaps Francis merely meant that Charles O'Conor had befriended him in his youth.

Mount Allen[5] and left the leased land to become a successful merchant in Dublin; John's sister Mary was the wife of Bartholomew Taylor, of Nonsuch, Castlepollard, County Westmeath, and her daughter, Deborah, had married Richard Corballis, of Rosemount, Roebuck, Clonskeagh, County Dublin.

The Kernans' oldest sons, Michael and Bernard, were "college educated," meaning they had received formal schooling up to, but not including, university. As Roman Catholics they could not attend Trinity College, Dublin, under the Penal Laws, described by Sir George Macartney, an Ulster-born diplomat as that "most complete code of persecution that ingenious bigotry ever compiled, . . . made for the preservation and security of the Protestant establishment" in Ireland, with the express purpose of driving the Catholic Irish into poverty and ignorance.[6] Most likely the Kernan's could not provide further private instruction for their sons, nor send them abroad, which latter course was, in any event, illegal under those laws. Michael, the oldest, worked in Dublin for a few months after the troubles of 1798, but, resolving "to die the gentleman he was born," he survived the rest of his life presumably in genteel poverty without other occupation. Bernard was commissioned an ensign in the English army,* and died in India from a wounded knee on October 2, 1803, after the Battle of Assaye. John Kernan, the family patriarch, died, and the 31-year lease expired in 1794, leaving the oldest son, Michael, with his mother and two eldest sisters, Mary and Jane. They moved from Ned to somewhere near Edgworthstown, County Longford. Their third son, William Kernan, would be the first of his clan to set sail for the United States.

America offered a haven to the disinherited Irish on many levels. They could own land, pursue any career, engage in politics and, above all, worship freely. As well, there was great satisfaction in holding citizenship in the nation that had defeated Britain. No wonder Irish emigrants such as the persecuted United Irishmen of the crushed movement of 1798 viewed the United States as an almost magical antidote for their pains: "The blessings of America/Will make amends for a' that."[7]

However, the reality of America proved less inviting than the romantic image of it held by Erin's expatriates. To be sure, the American rebels had stood up to the hated John Bull and created a nation whose constitution proclaimed freedom of religion as a basic right. Still, most Americans were Protestants of English ancestry who held fiercely to the religious prejudices of their homeland. The often-merited

* At this period, a commission could usually be purchased for several hundred pounds but only by those acknowledged to be gentlemen. Bernard was promoted to lieutenant quite soon, and, after his death but before news of it reached London, was advanced to a captaincy. His will is recorded in Dublin, and his service records are in the Public Records Office in London. His name is spelled "Keernan" in the dispatches from India of Arthur Wellesley (later the Duke of Wellington), perhaps a clue to its pronunciation there.

reputation for radicalism of Irish of both religions made them feared and resented by the ruling Federalists, who passed the notorious Alien and Sedition Acts largely in response to Irish immigration. "I do not wish to invite hordes of wild Irishmen, nor the turbulent and disorderly of all parts of the world, to come here with a view to disturb our tranquillity," thundered a Massachusetts senator of Anglo-Saxon stock in 1797.[8] The United States to which William Kernan emigrated still harbored much hostility toward his countrymen.

There was one haven for the Irish in America, however, where they were welcomed, where the promise of equality seemed to become real. That haven was the Democratic Party.* Begun in 1792, when the Virginians Thomas Jefferson and James Madison made common cause with the political leaders of New York against Alexander Hamilton's Federalists, the party referred to by Martin Van Buren as "Southern planters and plain republicans of the North" expounded a doctrine of inclusion and acceptance. In contrast to the conservatism and aristocratic haughtiness of the Federalists, the party of Jefferson proclaimed the equality of Catholic and Protestant, of immigrant and native-born, of Englishman and Irishman, indeed, of all men—of all white men, that is. Tragically, the expansive egalitarianism of the Democracy rested on a firm foundation of white supremacy.

There were important structural reasons for the racist orientation of the Democracy, many of which would not become fully evident until the breakdown of the party system on the eve of the Civil War. First, while the party counted on the support of urban Northern artisans and workers, Western farmers, and disaffected Northern-state elites, its core strength came from the Southern slaveholding planter class. For reasons both tactical and practical, Southern slaveholders relied upon the racism of non-slaveholding whites as a critical component of their power. Slavery, so repugnant to the sensibilities of the freeborn American, seemed far less discomforting when it was restricted to blacks—and indeed, all free white men were graciously invited to partake vicariously of the privileges of belonging to the master race. Northern politicians, for their part, mobilized this racism to whip their followers into line and blunt the attacks of their political enemies with charges of negrophilia. For Westerners and other Americans in close proximity to Native Americans in possession of desirable lands, the assertion of racial superiority conveyed a license to expel them couched in a specious doctrine of historical "inevitability." Finally, for the Irish and other marginalized groups, the assertion of whiteness signified an inalienable badge of membership in a privileged class, a crude but powerful claim to that status of equality that so many Americans of Eng-

---

* The political party founded by Thomas Jefferson in 1792 has undergone many permutations and name changes in the more than two centuries of its existence; it began, confusingly enough to modern readers, as the "Republican" party. For purposes of clarity, it will be referred to here consistently as the Democratic Party, or the "Democracy," although this should not be interpreted to imply any greater degree of historical continuity than actually exists.

lish background sought to deny them. Manipulated by cynical defenders of slave-holders' political power, many white voters came to believe that every blow struck in the cause of black liberty was a blow aimed at the dignity and honor of non-elite whites.

The proverbial racism of the Irish was not an ingrained feature of their character, however. On the contrary, Irish immigrants and African Americans, sharing the same poor economic conditions and comparable social status, frequently lived in close proximity and relative equanimity amid the rough, rude, and earthy turf of the taverns, bawdy-houses and oyster bars of the slum districts of many American cities through the mid-1830s and beyond. Earlier, the colonial record is replete with examples of alliances, political and romantic, between Irish servants and African slaves, and indeed, the anti-miscegenation laws of the Southern colonies were largely drafted to resist such unions. It may be here, in fact, that the "privilege" of whiteness had its origins. It is an unfortunate aspect of human nature that suffering under oppression does not always engender sympathy for others who are similarly oppressed. A frequent response is the desire to "do unto others" what was done to ourselves. Particularly when manipulated by leaders with ulterior motives, an unsophisticated group will often turn on another "lower" than themselves. How else to explain the tragic irony that a people who had suffered discrimination and shame under the hated Penal Laws should loudly champion the imposition of almost identical disabilities for free blacks? The Irish leader Daniel O'Connell was heartsick at the contradiction, declaring to the emigrants, "if you remain, and dare countenance the system of slavery that is supported there, we will recognize you as Irishmen no longer."[9] At any rate, the race hatred of the American Irish was carefully cultivated over many generations. Economic competition with blacks for low-skilled jobs and the contempt of Protestant "nativists" set the spark of racism, and demagogues and politicians fanned it into a flame. By the early 1840s, when Francis Kernan was entering politics, racism had long been an intrinsic part of Democratic Party dogma, and voters of Irish descent were among its most devoted adherents.

There was, however, a better-founded, if still unpalatable, case to be made for the racist outlook of the Democratic Party—or more precisely, for its seemingly immoral stance of *laissez faire* toward Southern slavery. From the time of Jefferson on, Democrats recognized that whatever the morality of slavery, the Union could not survive an attack upon it. In this conviction, the Democrats were proved correct. The intricate, delicate system of shared sovereignty between the states and the federal government, the "Union as it was," was destroyed forever in the crucible of war.

That a new, stronger union could emerge from the wreckage of the old was something few Democrats, or any Americans, could imagine. In classical political theory, republics were fragile, easily subject to collapse into anarchy or tyranny; every republic of the ancient world had succumbed to one or the other fate. An extended republic was particularly at risk, according to the greatest modern authority, Montesquieu; only a small, homogeneous state could hope to survive for long. A nation with such radically conflicting interests as the United States—above all, those of slave states versus free—would seem to have no chance at all.

What gave the United States the possibility to escape the fate of other large republics was its unique federal system. By dividing sovereignty between the close-at-hand governments of the states and the central authority of the federal government, the liberty of the people could be maintained and the divergent interests of the states could be respected. It was clear to most Americans that their liberty and security could be maintained only so long as the Union lasted; it was equally clear to Democrats such as Kernan that the Union would last only as long as the states retained their right to administer their own institutions as they saw fit. If this meant tolerating slavery as the price of preserving the republic, so be it.

Francis Kernan, an American scion, engaged in politics and life holding most of the beliefs, assumptions, and prejudices common to his time and station. Among the many encomiums showered on him by his colleagues, none ever described him as a pathbreaking or original thinker. Yet Kernan's contemporaries regarded him as a model of integrity, honor, and decency: Americans' beau ideal of a public servant. Kernan was a highly partisan politician whose positive legislative achievements were few, and whose record on such issues as slavery and states' rights, including a vote against the Thirteenth Amendment which ended slavery, seems indefensible to a modern observer. It might be enough to explain such a record by pointing out that, in all these instances, Kernan acted within the mainstream of the Democratic Party. (It is also important to stress that he appears never to have engaged in the race-baiting, name-calling, and low humor that formed the stock-in-trade of many of his fellow Democrats.) Yet while Kernan never wavered in his loyalty to the Democracy, he clearly lived by the axiom of Rutherford B. Hayes, the man who defeated Kernan's colleague Tilden for president: "He serves his party best who serves his country best." Whether he was right in his convictions or not, it seems certain that in his every action, Francis Kernan sought first and last to serve his country.

Parentage

When tillage begins, other arts follow.
The farmers therefore are the founders of human civilization.
DANIEL WEBSTER

WILLIAM KERNAN

FRANCIS KERNAN'S FATHER, William, was already a man of enterprise at age 19, for then, with no more than a hedge school education,* he determined to find a better life than Penal Ireland could afford him as a leaseholder, and he set sail from the port of Sligo in April 1800 for the New World fired with the ambition of becoming a landowner as his forebears had been. He knew exactly where he was headed. Family friend Thomas O'Connor [*sic*], son of Charles O'Conor, had already left, settling in Steuben County in the western New York wilderness, where he had bought 4,000 acres of the Pultney lands, naming it "Roscommon" after his home county in Connaught, with the intention of founding a colony for his coun-

---

* A hedge school education is an Irish expression regarding the practice of instructing students out of sight from English eyes, that is, holding classes behind a big hedge.

trymen. Reaching New York in August of the last year of the 18th century during a yellow fever alarm and quarantine, William jumped ship with the help of the captain. He quickly found employment with William Weyman, clothier, at 39–41 Maiden Lane, by answering an advertisement in the *New York Mercantile Advertiser*:

> "Wanted immediately a YOUNG MAN to attend a dry goods store—none need apply but those who have a knowledge of the business.
> Apply at this office Aug 22, 1800."*

William worked for almost two years, no doubt adding to the small nest egg he must have brought with him. At the same time, he also found favor with a childless Quaker couple who wanted to adopt him and make him their heir, which he declined.

In the spring of 1802, William became a citizen and left New York City. He sailed up the Hudson, traveled by boat up the Mohawk to Utica and continued by foot out Genesee Street another 100 miles through Geneva to the wilderness colony of Roscommon. There William became the landowner he had longed to be by buying 455¾ acres of forest in the then-Town of Frederick in what had been the favorite hunting grounds of the Seneca Indians. He speedily built himself a birch-bark cabin, a task for which he could have had no previous skills, and gradually cleared his woods and prepared the land for cultivation, becoming in due course a plain dirt farmer.†

William learned quickly, for a letter dated July 8, 1803, from O'Connor (signed "Affectionately yours"‡) requesting his advice about building a house in Roscommon for five boys newly arrived from Ireland, asked could a cow be easily got, should she be paid for in ready money, and how could she be supported in winter. O'Connor also told him to walk over the three lots he had reserved for himself and say how he could lay out farms of 100 acres each; and finally to describe the situation on maps of the farms that were marked or occupied, adding "you can guess pretty correctly without the assistance or expense of a surveyor"—all this to a young man of 22 who had been in the wilderness barely a year.

---

* The New York directory adds to the listing for Weyman: House 1½ stone Bowery, meaning at the 1½ milestone on the Bowery. This is the only advertisement we have found that could possibly have been the one that William read. Possibly William had spent some time with his uncle, Francis, in Dublin, or with his uncle-in-law, Bartholomew Taylor in Castlepollard, both merchants of some sort, and thus actually had some of the required qualifications for the job.

† From JDK: "The story comes from my father through my brother Henry that a brother of William's, after visiting in Tyrone, was asked how the General was doing. He answered: "The last time I saw him he was hoeing potatoes in his bare feet." The story is suspect inasmuch as William was not a general until after his brother Francis died, and he was the only brother ever in this country. The General and the brother part may be inaccurate but the hoeing and the bare feet probably are not."

‡ We assume that this was more than a meaningless formula like "Your humble and obedient servant."

Life during the first few years was hard, so much so that all but William of the Irishmen who came under O'Connor's wing left the colony, discouraged by the fierce labor of clearing the forest for farming, the cold winters, the dangers from the wild beasts, the lack of amenities,[1] and the absence of anyone to minister to their religious needs. Of William, it was said that he was too poor to leave and too poor to stay.[2] For the next few years he labored on his land, spending the first winters with a friend named Minor near Seneca Falls, or with his family in New York after their arrival in 1804. William's youngest brother, Francis, had also left Ireland, taking their mother and four youngest sisters, Winifred, Margaret, Elizabeth, and Alice.*

It was soon apparent to his neighbors that William had the temperament to take part in both local and state government: his first public service was as an ensign in the state militia in 1807 and his last was as a delegate to the state constitutional convention of 1846. In the intervening years, he was commissioner of highways in 1808, 1810, and 1820, justice of the peace in 1812, 1813, 1816, 1817, 1819, and 1820, inspector of elections 1813–1817, commissioner of common schools 1815–1817 and 1820–1822, supervisor (the highest executive position in the town) 1817–1818 and possibly 1823–1832, and delegate to the New York State Assembly at Albany in 1834.[†]

Although he can have had no previous military experience, William must have had a recognizable commanding presence, for, in 1807, as "William Kearnan, Gentleman," he was commissioned by Governor Morgan Lewis an ensign in the Company of Light Infantry in the Regiment of Militia in the County of Steuben.[3] Ever enterprising, he acquired a 378-page book on military tactics so as to be able to fulfill his new responsibilities.[4] By the War of 1812, he was a major on the staff of General George McClure, but saw no action. Eventually, on January 10, 1825, he was appointed by Governor DeWitt Clinton brigadier general of the First Brigade of Infantry of the state, with rank from October 23, 1824, hence becoming known in the family as "the General."

In 1806 or 1807, William's brother Francis spent the winter with him, and by 1810 he had made life sufficiently comfortable so that, according to family lore, his mother, then over 70 years old, traveled by horseback from New York City to spend the summer with him. The census of 1810 indeed lists him as head of a household

---

* The Irish-born Francis made a home in New York City for his mother and four sisters and was successful in real estate ventures. He died accidentally in 1820 at age 37, from being hit by a brick falling from a building under construction He left his gold watch to his American born nephew and namesake, Francis Kernan.

† The printed sources do not agree as to when he was supervisor. Much of the information to which we were led by Donald Rowlandson of Hammondsport, New York, is to be found in the Wayne Roads Book, the Town Clerk's Minute Book, the Poor Masters Book, the Commissioner of Common Schools Book, and the Inspector of Elections Book. William also served on at least one grand jury, the one held on the third Tuesday of June 1808 that held Amaniah Hammond for assault and battery, such service being then considered a mark of acceptance as a substantial citizen. The county clerk's office at Bath has some of the original records pertaining to his services as inspector of elections and commissioner of highways, and as grand juryman. See also Civil List, pages 307, 308, 346, and 392.

with one female of 45 years or upwards and one female between 16 and under 26, most likely his younger sister, Alice.[5] The Town by 1810 had 1,047 inhabitants and had been renamed Tyrone. William probably made contact with the Stubbs family soon after their arrival in nearby Wayne, and thus was able to introduce to his mother the young lady who would be his bride.

ROSANNA STUBBS

Francis Kernan's mother, Rosanna Maria Stubbs, had been born in Dublin, Ireland, to William and Margaret Mary (Read) Stubbs.[6] The Stubbses, an English family of Norman extraction,[7] had gone to Ireland in the late 17th century and settled first in Ballyboden, County Dublin. William Stubbs had been born at Whitewood, County Westmeath; the Reads were Dubliners. Dublin records show that William was a woolen draper there and had experienced some financial problems; but the couple was able to endow their daughter Rosanna with a good convent education.

Woolen drapers were notorious in 18th-century Britain for their radicalism. William Stubbs, a devoted United Irishman, was involved with Lord Edward Fitzgerald and the other leaders of the Rebellion of 1798, and some of their meetings were reportedly held in his house. These connections got him into such trouble with Dublin Castle that he determined to leave Ireland with his wife, four sons, and two daughters. He chartered the ship Osage, Captain Dupliex, solely for his family, a servant, Ann Ross, and all their belongings, and sailed from Dublin on November 1, 1806, reaching New York on January 1, 1807.

Four months later, in April, William Stubbs took off for the town of Wayne in Steuben County, leaving the rest of his family to follow. In due course the family set out, traveling by boat to Albany and, failing to receive there a letter from William advising them to go no further, proceeded some 200 miles west by horse-drawn wagon. Though discouraged and dismayed by the wildness of the surroundings, they took possession of the only house to be had, situated on the west side of Little Lake.

Apart from the facts that Rosanna came from a substantial merchant family in Dublin and had received a good convent education there, we know little about her. She and the rest of her family had become friendly with Elizabeth Seton (canonized in 1975) during their stay in New York City, and the saint's letters to Rosanna urging her to join her in the founding of the Sisters of Charity were at one time treasured family papers which are now at the mother house in Emmitsburg, Maryland.[8]

WILLIAM AND ROSANNA

William and Rosanna were married on May 31, 1812, in the Stubbses' house. Possibly the two merely declared their intentions before witnesses with the expectation of receiving the Church's blessing at some later time, a course of action that would have had its approval inasmuch as there were no Catholic churches in the vicinity and itinerant priests were rare. The family tradition is that some years later a priest blessed the marriage and baptized several children on the same occasion.[*]

For a honeymoon, William brought his bride on horseback to the three-room-and-attic log house he had built in Tyrone and there their first child, Margaret Mary, was born in 1813, followed by her brother, Francis, in 1816. Shortly after his birth the family moved across the road to the beginnings of the house that still stands—its rear kitchen is believed to have been built in 1815 and the rest about five years later.

Within a few years, Rosanna's mother and Ann Ross, the servant, died and were buried in the little graveyard on the hill behind the house. The other Stubbs children had married comfortably and settled around the county. By 1828 they had all left the area for Ann Arbor, Michigan, and elsewhere, except for Edward, who moved to Washington in 1830, taking his father with him, to become a disbursing agent in the State Department and eventually a generous uncle to Francis and his sister, Margaret Mary.

William meanwhile cultivated his ample estate and, thanks to his proximity to the new Erie and Seneca Canals, was able to market his produce very profitably. He was an enterprising and innovative farmer, introducing an outstanding breed of horses through an Arabian stallion said to have been given to President Andrew Jackson by the bey of Egypt, and being one of the first raisers of black Berkshire pigs and merino sheep. Within a few years he had become, according to one observer, a prosperous country squire, well able to support his family of four boys and five girls. By 1830 he had fully paid for all his lands and was able to assist his old friend Patrick Quin when he latter fell on hard times [see Appendix II]. He was also prosperous enough to undertake some land speculations on his own account.

During these years William did what he could to practice his faith. His well-worn prayer book printed in Dublin and his family Bible attest to this. With a mother and four sisters living in New York City, he no doubt attended religious services in Saint Peter's or Old Saint Patrick's Cathedral during his visits. According to

---

[*] The first Catholic churches were in Hammondsport and Watkins, both founded in the 1840s and some 20 miles distant. County histories, as well as diocesan archives at Rochester, report that priests occasionally visited on horseback, but the archives have no records of what rites they performed. The archives also note that some Catholics traveled to New York to obtain religious ministrations. There is no certain tradition as to who performed the 1812 marriage; conceivably it was performed by the minister of another faith. We deduce this from the fact that William showed his ecumenism by buying a pew in the Presbyterian/Baptist meetinghouse in Wayne [see Appendix II] and, on the advice of Professor Harry Stout of the Yale Divinity School, that it was not uncommon for Catholics to avail themselves of such services in frontier settlements. As to a later ceremony, JDK vaguely recalls that Warnick Kernan once showed him the family portraits in his house in Bleecker Street, Utica, and said that one of them was of the priest who had blessed the marriage of his grandparents. Could it have been the one that Aunt Alice recorded as one of her Read relatives, the Reverend William Russell, a number of whose letters from the 1790s are at Cornell?

oral tradition, he took his son Francis to New York to be baptized.* His home in Steuben County became known in the neighborhood as a mass house where Mass was celebrated whenever a peripatetic priest came from Rochester, and there is a record of a Bishop Timon's having confirmed three persons in the Kernan house on February 1, 1848, while visiting from his see in Buffalo.[9]

William continued to serve the county in many capacities, and as his acquaintance and popularity grew, he was entrusted with various personal and legal matters by his neighbors as well.[10] As one of Steuben's leading citizens, he must have had a part in welcoming the Marquis de Lafayette to the area during the Revolutionary War general's triumphant return visit to America in 1825, for oral tradition asserts that the marquis presented him with a brace of dueling pistols in a leather carrying case.†

In Tyrone, as landholder, militia officer and public servant, William rapidly assumed a standing that would have been impossible to attain in his native land, where his faith would have kept him out of all public offices and positions of leadership.‡ It is small wonder then, that he never looked back to Ireland with regret,§ and smaller wonder that he had no love for England, as shown by his eradicating the prayer for the English royal family from his prayer book. His love for the new home that had been so good to him was the basis of his heartfelt toast at an 1828 Rochester celebration of Independence Day, where he was a special guest from Steuben County: "America, my adopted country. The liberality of her people, the equity of her laws have afforded us a sanctuary from the persecutions of our native clime. When her liberties are invaded, may the conduct of Irishmen ever prove they are not ungrateful recipients of her favors."[11]

---

* We have been unable to find any record of Francis's baptism in any New York church. However, in the Zweierlein biography of Bishop McQuaid, the bishop of Rochester, it is written at page 4 that "the Kernans of Steuben County are said to have submitted to such hardships of pioneer life (i.e., 'push[ing] on to New York for spiritual administrations') in order to have a child baptized." See ibid. at page 124 for record of the confirmations.

† We have been unable to verify the truth of this tradition. The only place the two would have met would have been in one of the villages between Rochester and Syracuse, such as Canandaigua or Geneva, through which Lafayette traveled by carriage. But a meeting alone would not explain the wherefore of the gift. The only gifts mentioned in records of this part of his trip are of cash to several Indians whom he had known during the Revolution. Perhaps a more logical explanation was the not uncommon and thoroughly practical custom of traveling dignitaries who were frequently presented with gifts to dispose of some of them by presenting them to their hosts at a later stop. From JDK: "My father gave me this explanation for the condition of one pistol: years ago some of the Kernan boys, including him, got hold of the pistols and decided to fire them. Being ignorant of the use of such flintlock weapons, they overloaded it with gunpowder, with the obvious disastrous results."

‡ His father had been able to sign the Catholic Qualification Rolls in 1778 and thereby relieve himself of some of his disabilities as a Catholic; but this was only the beginning of the lifting of the disabilities—they could not vote until some years later, and were forced to support the Church of Ireland, that is, the Established Church, until 1869.

§ From JDK: "John Quin, William Kernan's grandson, told my brother Henry that William had no interest in Ireland. This is understandable inasmuch as with the persecutions and disabilities there was little chance that he, a younger son of a Catholic family, could make a decent life for himself other than in trade, in which he was apparently not interested."

In 1857, William and his family moved to Utica, where many of his descendants then lived. He sold the remaining part of his homestead at Tyrone in 1865, reserving ownership of the half-acre burial ground (still there), a right-of-way to it from the public highway, and the right for him and his descendants to maintain it.[12]

He is listed in the 1860 census in Utica, at 55 Elizabeth Street, with his wife, Rosanna, two daughters, two sons, and two domestics. His real estate was valued at $13,000 and his personal property at $10,000, the total purchasing power of which today would be in the range of over $2 million.[13] Rosanna died on April 12, 1862, at the age of 74, but William lived on with his children, Alice, Rosanna, William, and Michael, until the latter two married. He died on March 20, 1870. He, his wife, and many of his descendants are buried in Saint Agnes Cemetery in Utica.

Early Years and Education

The very spring and root of honesty and virtue lie
in the felicity of lighting on good education.

PLUTARCH, OF THE TRAINING OF CHILDREN

IN A LOG cabin, in 1816, the first American son of the Kernan clan was born, and
in stark surroundings, Francis began his education, acquired his faith, and learned his
politics. In general outline Tyrone, New York, at the time of Francis Kernan's birth,
must have looked much like Templeton, the fictionalized version of frontier Coop-
erstown portrayed in James Fenimore Cooper's *The Pioneers*. As a friend of William
Kernan recalled in a letter, "about the commencement of this century, we were all
denizens of a wilderness in the Western part of this State with little else of animated nature for our nearest neighbors other than Savages and wild animals of the
forest."[1] Much of the land was heavily forested and full of game and dangerous
wildlife, such as bears, wolves, wildcats, rattlesnakes and copperheads. While the area
had been the hunting ground of the Seneca Indians, by 1816 they were no longer to
be feared. Francis, even as a little boy, must have done what he could around the
house and, as he grew older, helped his father clear the land, chop wood, plant and
harvest crops, round up the domestic animals from the woods, and tend them.[2] No

doubt he also hunted for small game, and fished to help feed the growing family, and as the oldest boy, he probably had his share of keeping an eye on his siblings.

Francis's arrival in 1816 coincided with a period of hard economic times for the nation, particularly for settlers in lands such as western New York, whose initial fertility was now increasingly depleted. The decline of the agricultural market in Europe, now recovered from decades of war, sharpened the problem and helped to trigger the Panic of 1819, a shattering blow to the exuberance of the early American economy. But while thousands of his neighbors were ruined by plummeting prices of staples and land, William Kernan appears to have weathered the storm without undue hardship.

Francis began learning his ABC's in a nearby log schoolhouse, where presumably he learned according to the then prevalent Lancastrian method, with the older children instructing the younger.[3] His playmates came from a wide variety of ethnic and religious backgrounds—the town's residents included settlers of German, Dutch, Scottish, and New England stock. Francis must have learned when young that tolerance was desirable in a heterogeneous society.

The school year was organized around the agricultural cycle, with the demands of the farm taking precedence over classes at planting and harvest times. Francis worked his father's fields alongside local boys hired to bring in the harvest. William Kernan's farm proved to be a veritable nursery of statesmen, for six of them were to meet again some 50 years later—as members of the United States Senate.

It is not known how far Francis attended public school. Education in America up to the War of 1812 had been largely a local religious concern. The numerous sects and groups—Baptists, Congregationalists, Episcopalians, Quakers, Huguenots, Mennonites, Dunkards, Lutherans, Dutch Reformed, Roman Catholics—all claimed the right to teach their children their own beliefs and values. But the nationalist fervor engendered by the war gave currency to the idea that universal, free, and state-controlled instruction was desirable to mold a diverse population into a homogeneous one and essential to realize a workable democratic state.

New York was among the first of the states to provide for education at public expense. As early as 1787, it had established a plan of public education under the regents of the University of the State of New York, and in 1795 the state assembly created the office of commissioner of common schools. In 1812 a bill divided each town into school districts and set up a complete and effective organization to provide buildings, teachers, and tax money.[4] Consequently, when Francis was ready for instruction beyond what his family could offer him, there was a school nearby in the village of Wayne, reportedly a good one. For education beyond the three R's, he could have attended any one of several nearby academies. However, these institutions were generally run by the Protestant sects, whose doctrines and tendencies to proselytize, and even to control family life,[5] would probably have excluded them from his parents' consideration.

One may suppose, then, that Francis took what secondary education the local school offered, supplemented by what an educated mother and a father intensely interested in self-improvement could give him,* and by the early 1830s he was ready to go further.

GEORGETOWN

When Francis was 14 years old, his older sister, Margaret, went off to finish her education at the Visitation Convent in Washington, D.C., where, according to its archives, "her uncle is accountable for her." This could only have been Edward Stubbs, her mother's brother. A few years after her return home, Francis left to take her place under the wing of the Stubbs family and to attend Georgetown College. According to family tradition, he rode his horse down through Pennsylvania, reporting back that the people there burned black stones to heat their houses.[6]

In 1832, the year before Francis's arrival, there had been a cholera epidemic, and on opening day of the school year only 50 students appeared; it was early December before the full complement of students showed up. Francis enrolled on December 9, 1833, as a half-boarder, no doubt prepared to take some meals with the Stubbses and spend the weekends there.

Georgetown was very different from that institution today.[7] Only about a quarter of the 170 students were there for higher education; the rest were younger boys preparing for it. Entrance procedure was simple: the aspiring scholar presented himself, was examined by the prefect of studies and was assigned to the class to which his prior achievements fitted him. The other requirements were modest: that he be of good moral character, be able to read and write, and be provided with the appropriate books. He was also required to dress "genteelly"—Francis's uniform would have been a blue cloth coat and pantaloons with a black velvet waistcoat in winter, and white pantaloons and a black silk waistcoat in summer. He had also to bring a silver spoon engraved with his initials.

While each student paid his personal expenses, there had been no charge for tuition until 1833. That summer the Jesuits began to ask the modest sum of $90 for a half-boarder, chiefly because they found that the lack of a tuition made Georgetown seem like a charitable institution and hence distasteful to some parents as implying social inferiority. Moreover, the Jesuits reluctantly realized that their estate could not support the instructors.

The exercises of religious worship were, of course, Roman Catholic, but members of other denominations were received with the requirement that they

---

* William owned *A History of England, From The First Invasion Of The Romans* by John Lingard, D.D., first American edition from the last London edition, Baltimore, published by Fielding Lucas, Jr., A. Waldie, Printer, Philadelphia 1827–1831. All but two of the 14 volumes are bound in leather and inscribed "William Kernan Steuben Co." It is unlikely that these were his only worthwhile books for Francis to read.

perform the public duties of their own religions. Thus Andrew Jackson's nephew and ward, "an unruly lad," attended in 1829 to benefit from the strict discipline. But his career, as at three other schools, "was interrupted at the request of the faculty."[8]

Hours were rigorous: up at 5 o'clock in summer and 5:30 in winter, breakfast at 7:30 after washing out of doors, Mass and a short study period, followed by classes from 8:30 until 11:15; then formation in single file in order of merit to walk to the midday meal. Recreation lasted until 2:30 and classes to 4:30; Rosary recital at 5:15 preceded more study; to dinner at 7:00 and the dormitories at 8:30.

In August 1833, to preserve economic equality among the students, the president, Father Thomas F. Mulledy, decreed that their weekly spending money could not exceed 12½ cents, that is, "one bit" or "one shilling" in popular parlance. The students had to write home once a week. Corporal punishment was occasionally meted out. The discipline, or homesickness perhaps, was unbearable for some, and the roster above also records that several students "ran away in a few days."

The six-year curriculum, extended to seven years in 1835, was essentially classical, being the Jesuit *Ratio Studiorum* adapted to contemporary conditions, with more emphasis on science and the vernacular literatures.[9] In the first year the scholars studied Latin and English grammars, reading, spelling and parsing, and read in Latin select letters of Cicero—all under the term "Rudiments"—as well as Old Testament history and geography; they were also exercised in Latin and English composition and began Greek grammar. In the second year the students read more letters of Cicero, Plato's *Phaedrus,* and *Graeca Minora*—under the term "Humanities"—continued composition in three languages with emphasis on English composition, and took more Bible history and North American geography. In the third year readings and composition in Latin and Greek were pursued, and particular attention was given to English; ancient history and more geography were studied.

During the last four years more difficult texts in the same subjects were studied, plus rhetoric, logic, metaphysics, ethics, and philosophy, lectures in these years being in Latin. Mathematics up to calculus were studied for several years, and there was instruction in chemistry, physics, and astronomy. It was a matter of pride that, in 1833, the College had the largest electric machine ever seen by Henry Barnard, later principal of Saint John's College in Annapolis—but he failed to record just what it did.

Typically of education of the period, the instructors laid great emphasis on composition, memorization, and public speaking throughout the entire curriculum. The College Prospectus also announced that there was a bookkeeping course "for those who wished to learn it." Italian, Spanish, and German were taught "if required," as well as music, drawing, dancing, and fencing—surely this was a place for gentlemen. Catholicism was not neglected; in addition to philosophy and Bible history, there was catechism on Saturdays for "all schools." This would have been Francis's first exposure to extensive Catholic doctrine aside from what his parents had given him, there being no Catholic churches near Tyrone until after he had moved to Utica.

The schedules were not unbending and there was time for recreation during the day and on the frequent holidays. Handball and fencing were the favorite sports. As in most colleges of the era, debating held an important place in student life, often imparting more useful knowledge than the somewhat turgid classes. Francis was an active member of Georgetown's Philodemic Society, founded just three years before his arrival, and now the oldest such organization in the country.

Occasionally the students made excursions on the Potomac to nearby plantations such as Mount Vernon. The Jesuits also encouraged walks to the city to hear the debates in Congress, and this must surely have been one of Francis's activities. The congressional sessions during the years of his attendance at Georgetown were among the most tumultuous of the early republic. In the fall of Francis's arrival, Andrew Jackson stunned the nation by ordering the removal of government deposits from the Bank of the United States, earning him an unprecedented censure from the Senate. The open warfare between Jackson's supporters and the B.U.S. forces constituted the trial by fire of the Jacksonians. Many deserted the Democratic party. Those who remained loyal gained a place in the pantheon of Democratic heroes. New York's Senator Silas Wright and Representative Samuel Beardsley of Utica were among the most steadfast and effective of Jackson's lieutenants. It is likely that Francis heard these Democratic champions from his own vicinity more than once in congressional debate, along with their general and chief, Vice President Martin Van Buren. It would hardly be surprising if Francis met Andrew Jackson himself, since the Old General regularly greeted the public at the White House each Thursday, gamely greeting each comer until his right hand throbbed. To be a young Jacksonian in the nation's Capital during the heat of Jackson's greatest battles must have been exhilarating indeed.

During Francis's second and third years at Georgetown, a still more ominous controversy convulsed the nation and the Federal District. Britain's abolition of slavery in the West Indies in 1833 brought the issue to a head in the United States, forcing many institutions and individuals to take a stand that was often uncomfortable. The District of Columbia, as federal territory, served as one of the principal symbolic battlegrounds of the slavery struggle.

In 1830, out of a total population in the District of 30,200, blacks constituted about 12,000, almost evenly divided between slave and free. While the white residents' sympathy for emancipation was surprisingly strong, the District also served as a major hub of the domestic slave trade, and coffles of manacled blacks destined for cotton and sugar plantations in the Old Southwest were a common sight on the streets of Georgetown. The College itself had substantial holdings in slaves, and faced a moral dilemma in 1835, while Francis was still a student, when the fathers in charge of the College's Maryland Mission, a Jesuit plantation, proposed selling off the plantation's slaves, whom they had been training in the Catholic religion. The proprietors listed three reasons: the Negroes neglected their spiritual obligations; they were unprofitable, and the farms would command a greater profit if rented to tenants. After a year of deliberation, the Georgetown Fathers agreed to sell the blacks, while stipulating to a series of conditions:

I. That they have the free exercise of the Catholic religion and the opportunity of practicing it.
Therefore,
a) They are not to be sold except to proprietors of plantations so that the purchasers may not separate them indiscriminately and sell them;
b) it must be stipulated in the sale that the negroes have the advantage of practicing their religion, and the assistance of a priest,
c) that husbands and wives be not at all separated, and children not from their parents, *quantum fieri potest,*
d) if a servant, male or female, have wife and husband on another plantation they are to be brought together, otherwise, they are by no means to be sold to a distant place,
e) that those who cannot be sold or transported on account of old age or incurable diseases be provided for as justice and charity demand.[10]

The final bills of sale to Louisiana planters, however, completed in 1838 and 1839, have no such conditions attached to them.[11]

Perhaps it was as a student at Georgetown that Francis began to form his negative views of the abolitionists, who trained their fire on the slave trade in the District of Columbia, seeing it both as an exemplary horror and as one over which Congress had complete jurisdiction. Beginning in February 1835, petitions poured into the House and Senate calling for the suppression of human commerce in the capital. Southerners responded with outrage, demanding that such petitions not be received and that all discussion of slavery be forbidden—the so-called "gag rule." Andrew Jackson's handpicked successor, Martin Van Buren of New York, inoculated himself against Southern Whig attacks by adopting a strongly proslavery position and requiring his party chiefs—Francis Kernan's future political mentors—to do the same.

Congressman Samuel Beardsley publicly instigated a riot against an abolitionist meeting in Utica in October 1835, asserting that "the disgrace of having an Abolition Convention held in the city is a deeper one than that of twenty mobs, and that it would be better to have Utica razed to its foundations, or to have it destroyed like Sodom and Gomorrah, than to have the convention meet here."[12] After disrupting the abolitionist meeting, the mob ransacked the offices of the antislavery *Oneida Standard and Democrat* and scattered its type in the street—an act triumphantly reported on the floor of the Senate by Silas Wright, Democrat of New York, as further proof that New Yorkers would not tolerate any hint of abolitionism.

We do not know what Francis, as a student, heard of these excitements in the town that would soon become his home, or what his reaction was to the abolitionist and anti-abolitionist activity swirling about him. The Dean's Book in the College archives shows only that Francis at various times was studying 2nd Class of French, 3rd Class of Mathematics, 3rd class of Arithmetic, 2nd Humanities and 3rd Humanities. There is no other evidence in the archives of his ability as a student; at the end of two terms, he was placed ahead of his "associates."[13] His later industrious habits suggest that he was a hard-working student.

In June 1836, in his 20th year, Francis left college and returned to Tyrone and his father's farm. His expenses for the three years totaled four hundred forty-seven dollars and ninety-seven cents, seven and a half mills, itemized for sundries, books, and mending. He was possessed of a splendid classical education whose studies and procedures extended back many centuries through the University of Paris to Quintilian. But it is likely that his exposure to national politics at a critical juncture of the nation's history proved more educational than anything he learned within the walls of Georgetown.

eading Law

Six hours in sleep, in law's grave study six,
Four spend in prayer, the rest on Nature fix.
SIR EDWARD COKE

FRANCIS RETURNED HOME from Georgetown with no degree.* This was not then uncommon—either he or someone on his behalf decided that he had had enough education for his future occupation. He came back, not to resume life as a farmer or budding squire, but rather to study law. Perhaps his exposure to the sophistication of Washington left him with no interest in, or taste for, the rigors of farming. Visits to the Capitol congressional debates and hearing arguments before the Supreme Court were no doubt his first opportunity to observe the advantages of a career in the top echelons of politics and law.

These experiences must also have made him aware that, at that time, as observed by Alexis de Tocqueville, "the aristocracy of America occupies the judicial bench and bar," and that "[t]he profession of law is the only aristocratic element which can be amalgamated without violence with the natural elements of democ-

---

* The Georgetown archivist so reports. The suggestion in an obit in the *Albany Times-Union* that his father's growing family required him to earn his own keep seems unlikely, inasmuch as he did not do that, but rather studied law for four years; moreover, his father was prospering in these years.

racy, and which can be advantageously and permanently combined with them."[1] A cousin back in Ireland, Francis Magan, had been one of the first Roman Catholics to be admitted to the bar after the abolition of the Penal Law that had forbidden it for 100 years, and Francis may have decided to follow his example.

In 1836 there were not only some nine law schools in the country where an aspiring lawyer might matriculate but also three other ways to become a lawyer. Francis could have studied on his own whatever books, statutes, and reports came to hand (as did Patrick Henry and Abraham Lincoln, to name only two); or worked in the office of a clerk of a court of record; or, as was most common, served as an apprentice in the office of a reputable lawyer—that is, "reading law." Francis chose the last.

The quality of education obtained in this way depended largely on how seriously the lawyer and mentor took his responsibilities, how interesting and active his practice was, what he demanded of his apprentices,* and whether his library consisted of more than five or six books, such as Coke's *Institutes of the Laws of England* ("*Coke on Littleton*"), and Blackstone's *Commentaries on the Laws of England*.† For some years following the American Revolution the laws of England were considered responsible for the tyranny of George III and hence highly unpopular, so much so that serious proposals were made to abolish the common law altogether and adopt the civil law of the continental countries. However, the impracticality of such radical steps came to be recognized, and Chancellor James Kent's *Commentaries on American Law* came along to give an American flavor to the grist.

In addition to his reading, the student was expected to attend the office of his mentor, copy documents, serve and file papers, and do other simple tasks.[2] He might accompany his mentor to court, carry his bag, and learn how to conduct himself there *vis-à-vis* the judge: to stand when the judge entered and at the call of "*Oyez, oyez,*" to say "May it please the Court," and "Yes, Your Honor" at appropriate moments, as well as *vis-à-vis* the other lawyers: "Yes, Counselor," or "Will the Counselor do so and so?" At Georgetown, Francis would have learned to understand "*De minimis non curat lex*" or "*Actio personalis moritur con personae,*" and to pronounce "*prima facie,*" though his pronunciation might have been Italianate in the beginning because of his use of Church Latin at Georgetown.

Neither the reading nor the copying was edifying; in fact, complaints about the tedium of the former and the uselessness of the latter abounded. Thomas Jefferson said of Coke: "I do wish the Devil had old Cooke [sic], for I am sure I never

---

* James Wilson, a New York lawyer and later a Supreme Court Justice, was complained of thus: "Mr. Wilson devoted little of his time to his students in his office . . . and rarely entered it except for the purpose of consulting his books. . . . As an instructor he was almost useless to those under his direction. He would never engage with them in professional discussions; to a direct question he gave the shortest possible answer and a general request for information was always evaded." Quoted in McManis, at pages 604–605.

† Other texts might have been J. Comyn, *Digest of the Laws of England* (1740); M. Bacon, *Abridgement of Cases in Equity* (1667); M. Hale, *Pleas of the Crown* (1736); and J. Lilly, *A Collection of Modern Entries* (5th ed. 1791).

was so tired of an old dull scoundrel in my life." Daniel Webster read *Coke on Little-ton* "without understanding a quarter part of it. . . . There are propositions in Coke so abstract and distinctions so nice and doctrines embracing so many distinctions and qualifications. . . . Why disgust and discourage a young man by telling him he must break into his profession through such a wall as this."[3] Whatever Kernan thought of his reading during his early years, Kent apparently had a lifelong influence, for an obituary reports that Francis continued to read his *Commentaries* at least once a year.

Francis already had a nearby lawyer in the family. His sister Margaret's husband, Edward Quin, was practicing in the nearby village of Watkins (now Watkins Glen).* In 1836 it was a growing and prosperous town, about to become the seat of a new county, Schuyler; it was a sensible place to begin. Evidently Edward did not require a fee from his brother-in-law: he gave him a place to live and even paid him something for his services.

Francis stayed in Watkins for three years. Of what his legal work consisted, nothing is known; the only case uncovered in the New York Reports in which Quin appeared is an action in the Chemung circuit to replevy a yoke of oxen,[4] after Francis may have left. After about three years, Francis decided to move on to a bigger pond and chose Utica.

In 1839, Utica was a thriving town, with a population of nearly 13,000. Since the beginning of the century it had been a jumping-off place for the movement of settlers to the West, and so it was to continue for many years. It was located not only on the Erie Canal, which ran from the Hudson to Buffalo and via the Chenango Canal south to Binghamton, but also close to the railroads, which were just coming into being, stretching to the east, west, north and south. Its contemporary inhabitants and many others since the 1780s firmly believed that it was a future metropolis of the East. Timothy Dwight, president of Yale College, recorded after his visit to Utica in the late 1790s that: "Their expectations of future prosperity were raised to the highest pitch, and not a doubt was entertained that this village would at no great distance of time become the emporium of all the commerce carried on between that ocean [i.e., the Atlantic] and a vast interior."[5]

---

* Now Watkins Glen, the Village of Watkins was originally the Indian settlement known as Catharines, or Queen Catharine's, then Jefferson.

Francis Kernan, Esquire

Good counsellors lack no clients.

WILLIAM SHAKESPEARE. MEASURE FOR MEASURE, ACT I, SCENE 2, LINE 97

Arriving in Utica in May 1839, Francis began his work in the office of Joshua A. Spencer, one of the leading lawyers of that city and of central New York State, to finish his law studies. Spencer's office was located at 53 Hotel Street, and Francis, listed in the Utica directory as "law student," boarded conveniently nearby at 16 Broad Street. Francis lived there for four years, then moved to Kent Street, and lived there or across Chancellor Square for the rest of his life.

Spencer had a large, varied, and interesting practice that took him on circuit north to Saint Lawrence County, west to Niagara County, east to Albany, and south to Binghamton. He appeared for plaintiffs and defendants, argued appeals for appellants or respondents, and for a time represented the state as district attorney in both criminal and civil matters. He acted in all sorts of cases—land claims, libel suits, trespass, trespass on the case, assumpsit, conversion and trover, and other ancient common-law forms of action now long since discarded; he defended murderers and other criminals. He appeared sometimes with and sometimes against such present and future political leaders as Congressmen Samuel Beardsley and John McKeon

(Francis's first cousin); Attorney General Benjamin Franklin Butler (not to be confused with the demagogue U.S. Civil War general of the same name); Charles O'Conor (the family friend of the Kernans who was to become an influential proSouth Democrat) ; the future president of the United States, Millard Fillmore; and Ward Hunt, a future justice of the U.S. Supreme Court. Other local luminaries included Hiram Denio (judge of the Court of Appeals), Theodore Sedgwick (scion of a distinguished family with noted lawyers), James Clapp (uncle of Francis's future wife and sometime-Chenango County district attorney), and Benjamin Clapp Butler (cousin of his future wife). Francis rubbed shoulders with these and other prominent lawyers of the time in the New York Supreme Court of Judicature and the U.S. Supreme Court. Francis's thoroughness, reliability, and sound judgment would have opened doors for him in any circles; the doors opened to him in Spencer's law firm provided a view of power and influence on a national scale. Spencer's office was, in short, an ideal place for Francis to finish his studies and from which to seek admission to the bar.

Admission to the bar in the 1840s was much simpler than now. In some states anyone could practice law. In states where some admission procedure was required, the sponsoring lawyer might take his apprentice before a judge, introduce him, and assure the judge the candidate was qualified by virtue of reading in his office; thereupon he was admitted.[1] New York law required that an attorney "be found to be duly qualified," but there were still no written examinations to determine that. Four years' practice as an attorney gave the right, *ipso facto,* to admission to the higher courts.[2]

It so happens that the well-known diarist George Templeton Strong was admitted to the bar in 1841, a year after Francis Kernan, and he traveled to Utica to do so. Doubtless Francis's experiences were similar.* Strong, who had been reading law in his father's office in New York since the fall of 1838, recorded in his diary that on June 9, 1841, he "(c)ommenced studying for that beastly bore of July."[3] On July 13 he set out for Utica where the "bore" was to take place, boarding a steamer to Albany and then the train, known as "the cars." Between Schenectady and Utica, he noticed "several palpable law-students in the cars, recognized by a certain hang-dog expression and the assiduity of their applications for brandy and water and other drinks at the various grogeries at which we stopped to wood, water and liquor." At Utica, he strolled for a smoke on the Genesee Bridge and spat into the gentle river, having grown "courageous on seeing the gang of shakebags who are to pass the ordeal with me."

On Thursday, July 15, he went to the courtroom and witnessed the entrance of His Honor, Chief Justice Samuel Nelson, who announced to the gathered victims

---

* The reason Francis had to go to Utica was because the Supreme Court of Judicature (then the highest court in the state); though based in Albany, happened to be on circuit in Utica at the date set for the examination and admission ceremony.

the names of the three-man Inquisitorial Committee. The committee's first oral question, "What is an action and into what are they divided?" drew varied answers: "civil and annual," "legal and equitable," "*ex contracto*," even a quotation from Blackstone and the *Revised Statutes*. Strong was asked: "Mr. Strong, how do you serve a dec[laration] in ej[ectment]?" to which "hideously entangling and horribly recondite query I thereupon made a great effort and answered. He put some two or three questions to me as to the pleadings in proceedings to settle claims to real property and I answered them, and that was the extent of my examination." Those less well prepared were helped through more questions, and this, wrote Strong, "was the richest part of the affair. Such a farce of an examination, such an asinine set of candidates, and such prodigiously uncomfortable timber benches I never met with before."

While waiting to hear the results of the exams, Strong walked along the banks of the Mohawk, "stripped and took a grand swim." The next day brought "News from the Court—All passed. . . . Went up to court and signed the Roll, and after dinner went up again and took the oath—imposing ceremony—cost $1.50 and cheap at that."

Back in New York, Strong took the steps required to become a solicitor in chancery by going to "that amiable old swine [Vice Chancellor William T.] McCoun to arrange for an examination. . . . This is bore No.2." On July 27, "Went to the Vice-chancellor's after dinner, at five, and spent half an hour with him. His examination was fair enough—little to it but what's to be found in the rules—and I went through without any mistakes and very comfortably, to my surprise, for except for what I've picked up during the last week, my knowledge of chancery practice might be put into a pill-box without squeezing." On July 30 he went to Saratoga to see the chancellor himself, Reuben Hyde Walworth, at his residence.[4] After several calls, he found him at home and the deed was done: "He was very civil and made a solicitor of me in no time."[5]

The original minute book of the United States Circuit Court for the Northern District of New York from 1839-1850 (now in the National Archives, Northeast Region, in New York City) contains no record of Francis's admission to its bar, although one would have expected it, especially as Spencer was frequently before the court as United States District Attorney and moved the admission of many others. Perhaps Francis was admitted while the circuit court was on vacation by presenting proof of his state admission to the clerk of that court under a procedure that became possible after October 1841.*

Whatever the political power and influence Francis witnessed in his years of study at Spencer's firm, the Utica group's prospects shifted precariously with the plummeting political fortunes of President Van Buren. By early 1840 it was clear to

---

* The papers for Francis's admission to the Supreme Court of the United States should contain the information as to the exact date but these cannot be found either.

all informed observers that the luckless president, whose administration commenced with the financial Panic of 1837 and was capped with the diplomatic debacle of the Amistad Affair, would be defeated for re-election by the slickly packaged team of William Henry Harrison and John Tyler—"Tippecanoe and Tyler, too." The campaign newspaper was the *Log Cabin* edited by the irrepressible reformer Horace Greeley, most famous for his counsel, "Go West, young man, go West." It is likely that the impending electoral calamity that Greeley helped to organize played a role in young Francis's decision to do just that, because on his admission to practice in July 1840 he asked Spencer for a letter of recommendation, telling him that he had in mind to settle somewhere in the West.

Spencer persuaded him to remain in Utica, however, by offering to make him his law partner. The position would involve significant responsibility. Spencer was so often on circuit all over the state, trying and arguing cases, that Francis would frequently be alone in the Hotel Street office. This opportunity coupled, perhaps, with evolving, romantic persuasions was enough to keep Francis in the East.

In Francis's first year of partnership Spencer became involved in a notorious case growing out of the Mackenzie-Papineau Rebellion of 1837 in Canada. That fracas, and the aftermath better known as the *Caroline* affair, almost led to war between Great Britain and the United States. The case involved one Alexander McLeod, a British national who was arrested and indicted at the Niagara General Sessions in February 1841 for the murder of Amos Durfee on December 30, 1837, after foolishly boasting of his part in the encounter. The colonial authorities of Canada had ordered an expedition to destroy an American steamboat, the *Caroline,* that was suspected of having conveyed war stores to Navy Island in the Niagara River, then occupied by the Canadian insurgents. The vessel was captured and burned while moored on the American shore, and in the *mêlée* Durfee was killed. Great Britain demanded McLeod's release in a *habeas corpus* proceeding in which he was represented by Gardner & Bradley, with Spencer as counsel and in the employ of Great Britain.[6]

The affair aroused great excitement throughout the nation, and diarist Strong put in his two cents' worth. On January 4, 1837, he wrote: "There's a great deal of excitement about this affair of the *Caroline,* and I don't wonder. It's infamous— forty unarmed American citizens butchered in cold blood, while sleeping, by a party of British assassins, and living and dead sent together over Niagara; it is one of the most high-handed outrages I ever heard of. I shan't be surprised if the feeling it gives rise to produces a war. I shall not be sorry if it does . . . ."[7]

McLeod lost in the *habeus corpus* proceeding* and was then sent to trial by jury

---

* The case involved abstruse matters of *nolle prosequi,* public, private, and mixed war, the right of a sovereign to compel a subject to commit an unlawful act in a neighboring country, and questions about the court's jurisdiction over a subject of diplomatic negotiation. McLeod lost in the *habeas corpus* proceeding, which is reported in *The People v McLeod,* 25 Wendell 483, and occupies one hundred twenty-one pages, including lengthy excerpts from the diplomatic correspondence between Webster and Palmerston.

in Utica, where he was again represented by Spencer with the consent of the United States government even though Spencer had by then become United States Attorney for the Northern District of New York. Judge Gridley grandiloquently charged the jury, "If you believe that this man is guilty of murder then, fearless of the consequences, whatever those consequences may be—though they shall wrap your country in a flame of war—whatever the result, look to the God of Justice and say whether the prisoner be guilty or not guilty."[8]

Counsel established an alibi for McLeod, and the jury deliberated for only 20 minutes. McLeod speedily returned to Canada, and there was no war. The decision of the Supreme Court, 1 Hill 377, affirming the result, is but 60 pages long.

For his services Spencer was reported to have received $10,000 from the British Government, a sum equivalent to between $1,000,000 and $1,500,000 today. It was a great case for Francis to be involved in so early in his career because of its notoriety, complexity, and fee. In addition, it may well have brought him into the Devereux circles; and possibly a share of the fee financed his wooing of Hannah Avery Devereux.

Thereafter the office returned to lesser matters.* One of the first cases in which Francis appeared alone was *Averill v Williams & Sage,* 1 Denio 501, tried at the St. Lawrence circuit in May 1843: "Francis Kernan, for the plaintiff."[9] The trial judge declined to charge the jury to the effect that the plaintiff was responsible for the sheriff's actions in seizing and selling the defendants' property under an execution, for the plaintiff had not directed or assented to what the sheriff did, and hence was not liable for the damages to the property.

In a criminal case, *The People v Mary Runkle,* both Spencer and Kernan appeared for the prisoner, who was charged with the murder of her husband. After a patient investigation, the jury found the prisoner guilty of murder, and a murder most foul it was. The sentence, that she be "hung" [sic], was carried out at Whitesboro on November 9, 1847, without her having made any revelations "as to the crime for which she was convicted, nor relating to her previous life."[10]

The first reported cases Francis argued in the Court of Appeals were *Crary v Smith,* 2 N.Y. 60 and *Beach v Crain,* 2 N.Y. 86, both heard in December 1848. In the first, his client won specific performance of a contract for the sale of land. In the second, where he appeared for the defendant-in-error, the decision in his client's favor was that the original defendant's covenant bound him to replace a gate at the termination of a right-of-way.

As to how Francis occupied himself when not in the office, there is little

* The lesser matters were no doubt typical of what a young lawyer in a small city of the period dealt with. One of the first reported cases that Francis handled was *Mitchell v Williams & Roberts,* (4 Hill 13), a suit for trover for six cows tried at the Oneida circuit in April 1842: "F. Kernan and J. A. Spencer," for the defendants. On appeal, the Supreme Court, sitting in Rochester, held that the trial judge had erroneously directed a verdict for the plaintiffs, and it ordered a new trial. As often happens, there is no information readily available as to what happened in the second trial, if indeed there was one.

information. There was the newly founded Young Men's Association that bought an old family house and stocked it with a modest library. Most of its members were professionals, predominantly lawyers and law students, who jumped at the chance to perfect their skills as public speakers at the weekly debates. There was also a new literary club, with its own meeting room as a makeshift home in after-hours, whose purposes were "debate and general improvement." It is hard to believe that Francis did not take advantage of such organizations, in both of which young Ward Hunt, the close friend of the Devereux family, was a member. There was in addition a Mechanic's Association, where Francis might have enjoyed the company of other young bachelors. Whether he joined this organization in its early years when it was an association of young men, or later when it had become "merely a handsome public auditorium where the middle and upper classes gathered to hear scientific lectures or view exhibits of technological wonders," there are no records to tell.[11]

During these years the firm continued to take in law students to read law, but without paying them. The young men who studied there knew they were fortunate to be under excellent auspices. Joshua A. Spencer and Francis Kernan were admittedly two of the greatest of upstate attorneys at that time, who sometimes charged, and got, as much as fifty dollars a case.

Francis was known for his kindness and respect towards the firm's students. One of the students reported at the time of Francis's death that "Mr. Kernan was the most courteous man I ever knew. It was his custom always to address the boys in his office as 'Gentlemen.'"[12] One of these aspiring lawyers was Roscoe Conkling, who began his studies in 1846. His friendship with Kernan that began during this association continued throughout their intense rivalry of later years in both the political and legal fields. As a historian of Utica recorded, "Friendly adversaries they were called—the relationship of two gifted attorneys whose encounters in the courtroom and political arena made colorful legal history."[13]

Erastus Clark, another student, wrote from Amherst, Massachusetts, at the time of Francis's death: "My memory of the three years under Mr. Kernan is very pleasant. He was not much older than we were, but he knew a great deal more than we did, aided us in our studies, and gave us the information our many questions demanded. There were wide differences of politics and religion in the office, and many were the blows given and received . . . . He had a keen sense of humor—he loved fun. Amid of all our discussion and studies and political wrangles there was much merriment and laughter, and of it all he took his full share. He would turn from his desk, join in the sport, and turn back refreshed to the hard work on which he built his career. . . . We young men in his office felt for him a respect and regard years have not lessened."[14]

The Kernan Achievement of Arms
Confirmed to the descendants of William Kernan, 1781–1870,
by the Chief Herald of Ireland, on May 1, 1957. "Mac Kernan Aboo" is a battle cry.

Recorded in Volume R. Folio 68. Listed in Hayes, *Manuscript Sources of Irish Civilization.*

The Great Ford of the Mohawk, at Utica
An imaginary scene of 1759. The ford was 1,500 feet east of the present overhead crossing
at the foot of Genesee Street. The watercolor illustrates a trip such as the one made by the
Stubbs family in 1807.

From a booklet by The Savings Bank of Utica.

1804 map of the townships of the Geneseo country

Reproduced with permission from Yale University, from the original in the
Map Collection of the Sterling Memorial Library.

In the spring of 1802, William left New York City and sailed up the Hudson. He traveled by boat up the Mohawk to Utica and continued by foot out Genesee Street another 100 miles through Geneva to the 4,000-acre wilderness tract of Thomas O'Connor, which he called "Roscommon" and where William finally became the landowner he always longed to be. This 1804 map (above) shows the townships of the Geneseo country. William's land lay along the turnpike from Utica, adjacent to township number five.

This map (right) drawn by O'Connor shows William's acres in cross-hatching. Life during the first few years was so hard that all but William of the Irishmen who came under O'Connor's wing left the colony.

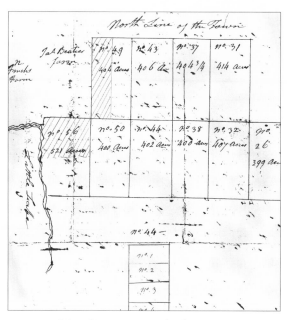

Map of Roscommon, Schuyler County

Reproduced with permission from the original in the Kernan Papers, #722,
Division of Rare and Manuscript Collections, Cornell University Library.

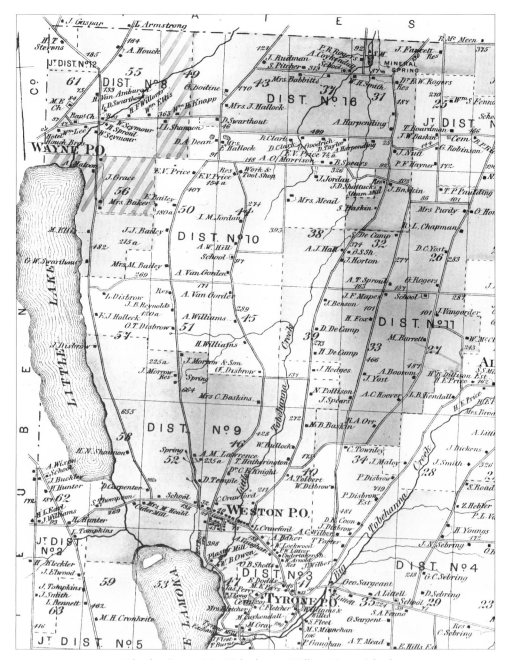

Schuyler County, New York, showing William Kernan's land

This map of Schuyler County gives a larger view of the area encompassing Roscommon colony. Although it was said of William that he was too poor to leave and too poor to stay, he was soon amply able to support his family of four boys and five girls—thanks in part to the proximity of the new Erie and Seneca Canals, which gave access to markets. By 1830 he had fully paid for all his 455¼ acres.

Reproduced with permission of Sterling Memorial Library, Yale University, from an atlas by Pomeroy, Whitman & Co., Philadelphia, 1874.

Record of marriages and births from the family Bible

In the family Bible, William only recorded two marriages: his own, to Rosanna Maria Stubbs
in 1812, and that of their first born, Margaret Mary Kernan to Edward Quinn in 1831.
He was more conscientious when it came to recording births, including his own in 1781 and his
wife's in 1779, both in Ireland. He dedicated the left column to their children, making a new
entry every two or three years for 20 years, beginning with Margaret Mary on April 20, 1813;
Francis on January 14, 1816; Edward Joseph on April 5, 1818; Jane on July 31, 1820; Winifred Eliza
on August 4, 1822; Alice on November 14, 1824; Rosanna Maria on August 4, 1827; William
Kernan Jr. on February 4, 1831; and Michael John on September 18, 1833.

Courtesy of William Kernan, 1947– , of Wescoville, Pennsylvania.

William Kernan's log house near Wayne, built in 1802

For a honeymoon, William brought his bride on horseback to the three-room-and-attic log house he had built in Tyrone (now Wayne), New York. This is the birthplace of Francis Kernan, 1816, and his older sister, Mary Margaret, 1813, the first native-born Americans of the Kernan clan.

By F. Farney Eilers Jr., from a copy of a photograph belonging to Donald Arthur Rowland, historian of the town of Wayne.

William Kernan's house, built between 1815 and 1820

Shortly after the birth of Francis, the family moved across the road to the beginnings of the house that still stands—its rear kitchen is believed to have been built in 1815 and the rest about five years later. The house still appears much as it does in this turn-of-the-century photograph.

Photograph courtesy of Clifford Lewis 3rd of Fourtown, Pennsylvania.

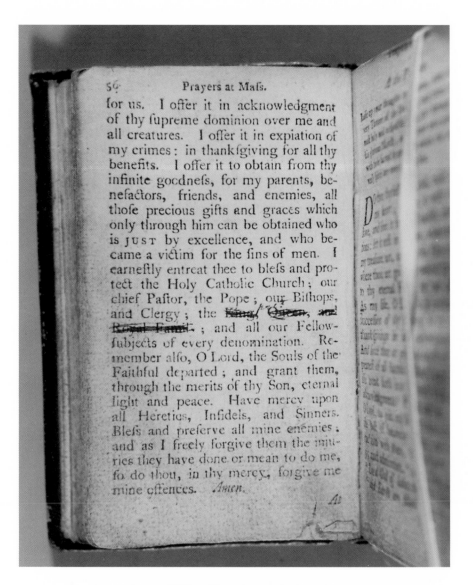

William Kernan's prayer book
During his early years, with no nearby church,
William did what he could to practice his faith. His well worn
prayer book printed in Dublin and his family Bible attest to this,
and his elimination of the English royal family from its pages
attests to his opinion of the oppressive rulers of his kinsmen.

Photo courtesy of Katherine (Howard) Kernan of Utica, New York.

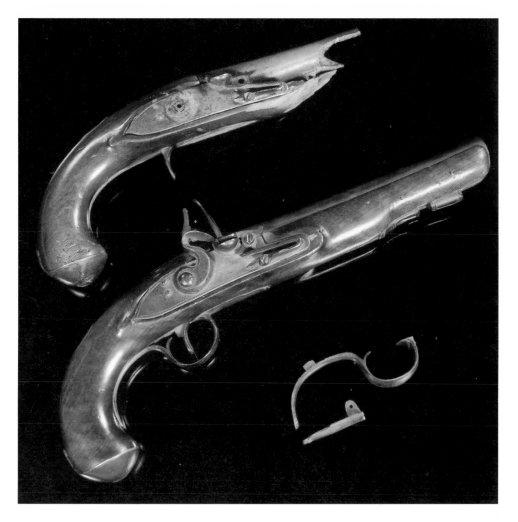

Brace of dueling pistols

This brace of dueling pistols, according to family lore, was presented to "General" William
Kernan by the Marquis de Lafayette during the Revolutionary War general's triumphant return
visit to America in 1825. Perhaps a more logical explanation was the not uncommon and
thoroughly practical custom of traveling dignitaries who were frequently presented with gifts to
dispose of some of them by presenting them to their hosts at a later stop.

Courtesy of William Kernan, 1947– , of Wescoville, Pennsylvania.

The family graveyard at Wayne

When William left Tryone (now Wayne) in 1865, he reserved ownership of the half-acre
burial ground, a right-of-way to it from the public highway, and the right for him and his
descendants to maintain it. This is how it appeared at the turn of the century.

Courtesy of Clifford Lewis 3rd of Flourtown, Pennsylvania.

*Gravestones of Margaret Mary (Read) Stubbs
and Margaret Mary (Kernan) Quin*
The family graveyard is still there, though
under sad condition. Under weeping willow
trees—one with the letters IRS and a cross—
are the inscriptions: "Margaret Mary / wife
of William Stubbs / died May 31, 1813. May
her spirit rest in Peace," and on the other
headstone, "Margaret Mary / wife of Edward
Quin / and daughter of William & Rosanna
M. / Kernan / born Apr. 20, 1813 / Died
Dec. 23, 1844. May her spirit rest in Peace!"
Karen Kernan

William Kernan, 1781–1870, and Rosanna Maria (Stubbs) Kernan, 1789–1862
From *carte de visite* photographs, *circa* 1860. In 1857, William and Rosanna moved
from Tyrone to Utica, where Francis and other descendants lived. Rosanna
died on April 12, 1862, at the age of 74, but William lived on with his children,
Alice, Rosanna, William, and Michael, until the latter two married.
He died on March 20, 1870.
From photographs belonging to co-author John D. Kernan.

Francis Kernan, Esquire

Francis likely occupied himself outside the office at the newly founded Young Men's Association where members practiced their public speaking skills at the weekly debates. There was also a new literary club, with its own meeting room as a makeshift home in after-hours, founded for the purposes of "debate and general improvement." Utica also offered a stimulating Mechanic's Association, where Francis would have enjoyed scientific lectures, exhibits, speeches, and the company of other young bachelors.

From an oil panting, circa 1845, belonging to Corinne (Kernan) Sevigny.

Utica, Washington and Genesee Streets, 1838

When Francis arrived in 1839, to work in the office of Joshua A. Spencer, one of the leading lawyers of that city and of central New York State, Utica was a thriving town with a population of nearly 13,000 inhabitants. Because of its strategic location on the Erie Canal and proximity to the railroads, which were just coming into being, Utica was considered a future metropolis of the East. But the town was also a jumping off point for those following Horace Greeley's famous dictum, "Go West, young man, go West." Francis intended to do just that, but Spencer persuaded him to remain in Utica by offering to make him his law partner.

Engraving after a painting by William Bartlett, courtesy of Beekman C. Cannon.

Nicholas Devereux' 1830 house on Chancellor Square, Utica

Francis called upon "Miss Devereux" at her family's house on Chancellor Square. Hannah had recently returned from several years' schooling in New York at the academy at 40 Beach Street run by Madame Binsse de Sainte Victoire, an elegant establishment where pupils were taught that "a sweet smile" was preferable to outright laughter—a rule Hannah happily admitted she had trouble following.

From a watercolor by Egbert N. Clark, belonging to The Savings Bank of Utica.

Saint John's Church and Orphan Asylum
This drawing on wood by Hannah Avery Devereux shows the church which had recently
been built with large contributions by her uncle and her father, and which she and Francis likely
both attended. Hannah was the oldest daughter of the leading Catholic family in the city, and
Francis was a young man of the same faith with a good education and fine prospects in
the office of Joshua A. Spencer, the leading lawyer of the area.

Courtesy of Thomas Spratt Kernan of Utica and of Springbank, Alder Creek, New York.

Francis and Hannah with their two oldest sons
Nicholas (middle) and John dressed in matching clothing for a rare photograph, *circa* 1850.

From a photograph belonging to the Oneida County Historical Society, gift of Thomas Spratt Kernan.

Senator Francis Kernan and his seven sons
In a photograph taken in 1876, the year of his senatorial election, Francis poses with his
seven sons (from left to right), Joseph Francis, Francis (junior), Nicholas Edward, the senator,
John Devereux, Thomas Philip Neri, William, and in front, Walter Newberry.

From a photograph belonging to co-author John D. Kernan.

*Hannah Avery
(Devereux) Kernan,
circa 1901*

From an original photograph
belonging to co-author
John D. Kernan.

The Kernan daughters
Elizabeth Butler (Lizzie) 1851–1920 (left), and Rosanna Maria (Rosa) 1849–1874 (right).
Lizzie enjoyed playing hostess in Washington during her father's Senate years. The third daughter,
Mary Agnes, 1847–1870, became a Sacred Heart nun.

Francis Kernan, circa *1882*

Reproduced with permission from the original in the Kernan Family Papers,
Division of Rare and Manuscript Collections, Cornell University Library, Ithaca, New York.

Francis Kernan

This portrait, dated 1892, hangs in the Fort Schuyler Club in Utica,

of which Francis was the second president in 1886.

By Benoni Irwin. Photo of the original oil painting taken by Ed Mickaels.

Reproduced courtesy of the Fort Schuyler Club.

*M*iss Devereux

*[Time] trots hard with a yonge maid, between the contract
of her marriage and the day it is solemnized.*

WILLIAM SHAKESPEARE. AS YOU LIKE IT, III, II, 332

AMONG THE FAMILIES of Irish extraction in Utica when Francis Kernan arrived in 1839 were those of John Corish Devereux and his youngest brother, Nicholas. They were descendants of a Norman who had settled in County Wexford, Ireland, in the 12th century, and come to be known in local folklore as "Proud Devereux."[1] They were reportedly descended from an uncle of William the Conqueror, the Comte d'Evreux and archbishop of Rouen, and distantly related to Queen Elizabeth I's favorite, Robert Devereux, Earl of Essex. The relationship was acknowledged in 1599 when the earl, then Lord Lieutenant of Ireland, visited the head of the family, Sir Nicholas Devereux, at his seat, Ballymagir, and knighted his oldest son, James. The entertainment tendered to Essex was extravagant and legendary—Sir Nicholas had to sell three townlands to pay for it. The great hall built for the occasion today stands roofless at Ballymagir.[2] In disobedience to his queen, who wished him to remain in Ireland, Essex returned to England and to his beheading.

John Corish Devereux had come to the United States via France in 1796 where family tradition tells that he answered General Bonaparte's query with ready wit by saying that the Conqueror had gone to England with the Devereux—"Proud Devereux" indeed. He settled in southern New England for a few years, and, having no ready occupation, put his gentle upbringing to use by teaching, according to his advertisement, "plain and fancy Minuets, Cotillons and Pettycotees, Irish Jiggs and Reels in their various figures, the much admired Scotch Reele, first, second and threeble Hornpipe, Country-Dances &c. in the most modern and elegant stile."[3] After "dancing two thousand dollars out of the Yankees," as he said, he moved to Utica in 1802. With that Yankee money, he opened a store and was on the way to making a fortune as a merchant and banker. In Utica he won a reputation as a prince among men, was a generous public benefactor, and served as mayor of the city.

Nicholas Devereux, who meanwhile had arrived in 1807 at the age of 16 from The Leap, the family's home near Enniscorthy, joined his older brother at first in merchandising but later branched out into banking, manufacturing, land speculation, railroads, and insurance, in which he too was eminently successful. He also was a public benefactor.

In 1817, Nicholas married Mary Dolbeare Butler, born in New London, Connecticut, and then living in New York City, on Hester Street. Her parents were Benjamin Butler, son of a Tory of Norwich, Connecticut, and formerly a medical doctor, but by then a stockbroker, and his wife, née Hannah Dolbeare Avery, daughter of Colonel William Avery, a soldier in the Revolution, of the Avery Clan of Groton, Connecticut. Dr. and Mrs. Butler also had a house and large landholdings in Oxford, New York, and possibly first made contact with Nicholas when traveling to or from New York. Or perhaps it was John Corish who had first come to know them, for he had given dancing lessons in and around New London and Norwich.

Mary—or "Grandmother Devereux," as she was later referred to in the family—proved to be a very good wife to Nicholas. In addition to bringing him a share of her father's considerable fortune and some handsome personal property (much of which is still scattered around the family), she made a happy home for him and bore him six children who lived to maturity. Though of delicate health in the early years of her marriage, she nonetheless lived to the age of 84. She was described by her great niece, Julia Newberry, in her diary as "very kind, but fearfully formal & particular"; adding that she should have "a long black satin gown, trimmed with lace about the neck, she would look so handsom [sic] in it. She thinks men are as unselfish as women; I don't!"

"Madam Devereux," as she was known outside the family in the fashion of the day, was called in an obituary in the *Utica Observer* "a lady of magnificent presence and courtly manners," and "one of the most charming of women, . . . a lady of brilliant accomplishments, a great reader, easy and agreeable in conversation and manner . . . [who] took great pleasure in the society and enjoyment of her family and friends." She and her family were ardent Episcopalians, but in October 1846 she

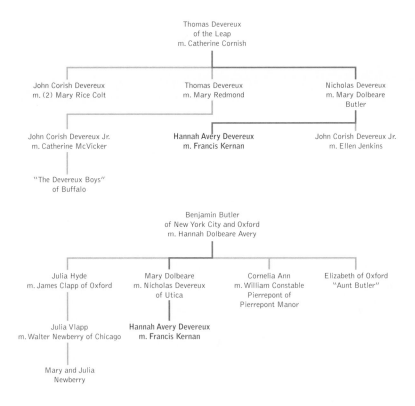

Short chart of the Devereux and Butler families

joined the Catholic Church, to the distress of her Butler relatives. Throughout her life she was a leader in works of charity and benevolence.

On September 20, 1820, the Devereux's first daughter was born in the Hinman house,[4] on the corner of Whitesboro and Hotel Streets, and was named Hannah Avery after her maternal grandmother. In 1823 Nicholas bought the Van Rensselaer house, which stood on seven acres of land and faced 416 feet on the east side of Genesee Street, running south from a point just below Elizabeth Street. There Hannah lived in considerable luxury for seven years—the family kept a carriage "drawn by one horse, a splendid animal"—until her father built a large brick house on Chancellor Square that remained in the family for nearly 90 years.[*] There the Devereux were living in 1839 with four daughters and two sons when Francis Kernan came to town.

Hannah had recently returned from several years' schooling in New York at

---

[*] From JDK: "I barely remember being there for the annual Christmas party (it must have been in 1916), and hearing Grandfather Kernan, 1844–1922, lead the singing of *Go Ye to the Forest,* the carol that was, traditionally, brought over by the Devereux. In the English baronies of County Wexford, Bargy, and Forth, in the 1970s at the Christmas Midnight Mass, they were still singing the traditional carols composed by Father William Devereux (*obit* 1771), but this one was not known to the John Devereux who was then leading the singing in the village of Kilmore."

the academy at 40 Beach Street[5] run by Madame Binsse de Sainte Victoire, where she enjoyed herself "quite as much, if not more than [I] expected to." Mme. Binsse ran an elegant establishment, she being, as Hannah wrote her grandfather, "a perfect lady . . . possess[ing] in a high degree all the politeness and gaiety of the French," and teaching her pupils that "a sweet smile" was preferable to outright laughter—a rule Hannah happily admitted she had trouble following.[*]

During these years, Hannah spent much time with her Butler grandparents, then living in a house on the north side of Wall Street, third door west of William Street. She was able to shop at Stewart's, and take her purchases of beautiful dark silks to the mantua-maker's for a hat to be trimmed with fur or velvet. She went driving "in the country, so they term the Fifth Avenue," and "up and down Broadway gazing and admiring the beauties as we passed"; she "laughed heartily at the witticisms of Tom Moor at the theatre." She made or received calls on or by friends, such as the Pierreponts, Judge Ruggels [sic], Charles and Hetty King, and Messrs. Weston, Barry, Peck, Beekman, and Cannon (of whom she wrote: "His name, Cannon, sounds rather awful, but he is as soft and mild as possible.") and countless others, in the city and in nearby towns, such as "Brooklin" [sic] and Jamaica.[6]

The most moving image of Hannah comes from the pen of her father in a letter to her mother, in 1837. In New York on business, Nicholas had stopped to see his daughter, who was enrolled at that time at Mme. Binsse's school. Although Nicholas had arrived exhausted at three in the morning after a terrible trip in a small steamer from New Haven carrying 650 passengers, he was up again at six and "went to see my dear Hannah and when she heard the bell and I got in the house, down she came three steps and half from the upper story. Oh, what a meeting! My dear child, poor girl, she is all heart and affection. We remained in each other's arms for several minutes unable to speak. I was never more overcome in my life. We talked an hour and made arrangements that H. should meet me at three at Runkey [perhaps a livery establishment] and drive with me. She came in time, fixed for din-

---

[*] Madame's billheads advertised that, for $75 per quarter, she offered "Board and Instruction, providing French and English Languages, Writing, Arithmetic and Geography, Astronomy (with the use of Globes), History, Belles Lettres and every kind of Needle work." The young ladies were required "to be furnished with Bed and Bedding, Towels, silver Mug, Knife and Spoon." (It is not know if these items of silver still exit within the family.) Hannah's bills show that she incurred further charges for books, theater tickets, music and dancing lessons, music paper, winter fuel and extra fire in her bedroom, use of piano and harp, pew rent at St. Joseph's, as well as for washing, stationery, crayons, drawing paper and postage. Hannah was a good pupil, and in a Reward of Merit, dated July 1837, she received twelve "Premiums" and six "Accessits" (short for "proxime accessit," meaning "She has come very near). She could also "converse entirely in French" with Mme. Binsse, though she had found it very difficult at first. She must have excelled also at drawing, for at least one of her works, a charming picture of Saint John's Church and Orphan Asylum, survives. Saint Joseph's Church is on Sixth Avenue at Washington Place, a two-block street running west from the western edge of Washington Square that in the 1830s was called "Barrow Street." The original Greek Revival building is the oldest Catholic Church building in New York City still in use for its original purpose. On the nearby side streets there are many buildings that might well have been there in Hannah's school days. The oldest congregation in the city is Saint Peter's, Barclay Street, where at least two Kernan weddings have taken place, that of Alice Kernan to Lackey Reynolds in 1812, and of Linda Hill to Charles Burck in 1966.

ner and there we were as grand as possible. After dinner we went to Brooklin [*sic*], had tea at Mr. P[ierrepont's]. . . . I felt as grand as the Lord of the Manor."

By 1838, Hannah was back in Utica, "finished" and ready for matrimony. In February of that year she gave a large party, "Miss Devereux' ball," which she described in a letter to her aunt, Elizabeth Butler, in Oxford: "We wrote eighty invitations and Mr. and Mrs. Hunt were the only married persons in the room. The company assembled at eight o'clock and a minstrel (of whose complexion I am sorry to say was not of the fairest hue) played most enlivening tunes, and the good folk danced most merrily. . . . Would that I could have seen my good Aunt tripping the fantastic toe with the gallant Dr. Hunt or his more favored namesake Ward."*

While it is improbable that Francis Kernan was one of the dancers at the ball, as he was then still reading law in Watkins, his and Hannah's paths must have crossed soon after he came to Utica in 1839. Hannah was the oldest daughter of the leading Catholic family in the city, and Francis was a young man of the same faith with a good education and fine prospects in the office of Joshua A. Spencer, the leading lawyer of the area. They probably both attended Saint John's Church, which had recently been built with large contributions by her uncle and her father, on land donated by Morris S. Miller and his wife, both Protestants. As the correspondence between Hannah and her cousins in Oxford and Pierrepont Manor, and her friends in New York and Brooklyn, bear out, Utica in these years was a very active place socially, and there were numerous parties and gatherings of all sorts, where eligible young men would have been in demand and welcome.

Francis's first known letter to Hannah, dated Tuesday evening, September 20, 1842, while florid and formal to a degree, shows more than tentative interest; clearly the two had known each other for some time. Addressing his letter to "My dear Hannah," he wrote,

> Much would I enjoy a chit chat with you this evening either at your own pleasant home or with your fair cousins at Oxford, but as this may not be, I will console myself in spending an hour in writing you. I hope your visit [to Oxford] is passing agreeably, and am happy in believing it will pass none the less so from knowing that your absence is not a matter of indifference to me, or even without producing a little selfish regret. Indeed I feel it much, and particularly, as when, as tonight, I find a leisure hour or two on my hands. The very agreeable manner in which my leisure evenings have of late been passed has spoiled me for spending them alone. There was a time when a crackling fire and an entertaining book was enough for an evening, and my steps did not stir from the one nor my thoughts from the other, no matter who was in Utica, or who visiting from it. But it is so no more, nor is the change regretted. But let this pass, it will do to talk of when we meet. . . . But all has passed on very quietly. . . . Not even a

* Ward Hunt sat on the Supreme Court of the United States in the 1870s and 1880s.

43

party, except a small one given by Miss Stewart last week. I was not able to attend. Do not imagine that "no invitation" was the cause however, but take the credit of my industrious habits that evening to yourself. . . . The weather has been too bad hitherto. Indeed sunshine departed Utica with you. This I can say truly as well as expressing my personal condition, by a bit of figure of speech, as that of our citizens who have been drenched with daily rain.

[Your mother] allowed me to read a few lines of your letter received Sunday. Your "friend" with far warmer than mere friendly feelings read them, and thanks you for enumerating him among those to whom affectionate greetings were sent. To your cousins he would gladly in person make thanks for their kind inquiries.

And now, my dear Hannah, and surely I may thus call you without offense, when you do return, not that a selfish wish of mine would have you shorten your visit with friends so admirably endowed to render it very happy to you, but of course to me it will appear long, and I will be happy to know when we may expect you, and should you find any inconvenience as to a suitable escort, you will know to whom it will a pleasure to be yours, on your suggestion.

Please make my regards to your friends at Oxford, and wishing you health, happiness, and a safe return, believe me,

Yours very truly

F. Kernan

Toward the end of the year curiosity was obviously afoot in the family, and Hannah knew she was an object of it, but on October 18, 1842, she warned her cousin, Mary Clapp, at Oxford:

. . . do not indulge on too much romance these cold afternoons. Do you recollect the sad fate of Kathleen O'Moore, who looked at the moon one cold afternoon, and dropped alas! from that hour. Probably she exerted herself too much in milking the dear cow, which was not over and above gentle. But would you like to know some news? Of course you would, but prepare yourself for a disappointment for I have none to tell you.

By Christmas morning, 1842, Francis had hopes:

Miss Devereux will allow Mr. Kernan to accompany his "Merry Christmas" and warm good wishes with the enclosed slight token of his esteem, and a memento of the many happy hours for which he is indebted to her.[*]

---

[*] A handwritten note accompanying a bracelet given to Hannah's granddaughter, Hannah Devereux (Kernan) Chatillon, states that it had been given to Hannah by Francis before their marriage. Possibly this was the "token of his esteem."

Sometime between Christmas and late February, an engagement was agreed to, for on February 28th, 1843, Hannah's mother informed her sister Elizabeth:

Hannah is very busy preparing for her future. She does her own sewing, which is a very serious undertaking. Mr. K. has rented a neat house,[7] and we are already thinking that the time for parting with one we so much love will come only too soon. The Month of May is the one fixed upon, but the day not decided.

She added plaintively:

I have not received any money from Mr. Hyde the last year, altho' I want some very much [Hannah's father had died in January of 1839 and Mr. Hyde was one of the executors of his estate]. . . . Furnishing a house in the plainest manner, and marrying a daughter are very expensive, & we need all our resources to meet the demand. Will you be able to come up to the wedding, or would you prefer visiting us in the summer when Hannah is settled & our house quiet?

On a subsequent Sunday afternoon, in late April, she wrote her sister again:

. . . I flatter myself that at the present time me & mine occupy a share of your thoughts. We are very busy cleaning house, in fact two houses. Mr. Kernan has rented a house on the square which the Landlord (himself a single gentleman of no particular age) is papering and painting, & quite desirous that it should please.

I suppose you would like to know all our plans, and I only wish that you were able to participate in them. The Wedding is to take place on the 23rd and will be in church & private. The party will be the next evening, similar to Julia's arrangement.[8] After a few days Mr. Kernan will take his bride to visit his father's family near Bath in Steuben county. . . . We do not wish these particulars known for they as yet are only hinted at in Utica.

It is a solemn & serious thing to marry a beloved daughter, particularly one who has proved herself so worthy of all our care as Hannah. I sincerely hope that Mr. Kernan will prove to her a faithful friend & protector.

The earliest surviving account of the wedding and subsequent events was written by Hannah's brother John Corish Devereux Jr., to his uncle, William Constable Pierrepont[*] at Pierrepont Manor, Jefferson County on May 27, 1843. "Dear Uncle," he wrote,

. . . The wedding took place on Tuesday evening in the midst of a Utica shower. It was intended to be very private the doors only to be opened a few minutes

[*] He was the husband of his aunt Cornelia Ann Butler.

before the ceremony but on going in the Church we found every seat full. At least fifteen hundred present, a pretty good number for a private wedding.

A very few besides the relatives came over to the house and spent the evening but on Wednesday the whole town and their wives were visible with their best foot forward.

The preparations mother made although they may seem a little extravagant were none too large for the occasion. The rooms were dressed with flowers & greens, 100 candles burning besides lamps and 170 pound cake disappeared in two days, 30 quarts of ice-cream melted in a twinkling and lemonade was made by the tub full. The whole passed off very pleasantly and seem to give satisfaction. Mr. Newberry owing to a delay in the cars did not arrive until a few moments after the ceremony. Mr. N. with Julia & Mary started for Chicago on Thursday. Hannah and Mary D. with Mr. K., Mr. K.'s father and sisters* left on Friday. Mr. and Mrs. K. expect to be in Jefferson Co. in about two weeks. . . .

Mother will write to Aunt in a few days and give her the particulars of the wedding. . . . Hoping to hear from you soon, believe me to be.

Your affectionate nephew,

J. C. Devereux, Jr.

Hannah's mother, Mary Dolbeare Devereux, wrote to "My dear sister," a week later, on June 3:

It is with pleasure that I improve the first leisure moment to sit down and write to you of the wedding.

We felt sorry that you and Mr. Pierrepont could not be with us. Mr. Clapp also declined, and would not allow James to come up. However, Mary & Julia were here, also Mr. Kernan's father, two sisters, quite pretty girls, plain & simple in their manners and delighted to be at their brother's wedding. Mrs. J. C. Devereux† kindly entertained them. Cousin John from New York‡ was here and in great spirits, very agreeable & displayed much taste in decorating the rooms. . . . The bridal party looked beautifully. Hannah appeared just as a bride should, with quiet dignity and modesty. She wore a handsome watered silk, with my Irish veil fastened in her hair. It completely covered her person and formed a rich drapery. The four young ladies were dressed in white muslin with trimmings in the hair, ornamented with silver fringe. The Gentlemen of course looked their best. We

---

* These were probably Alice, aged nineteen, and Rosanna Maria, aged sixteen.

† This was John Corish Devereux' second wife, née Mary Rice Colt, of Paterson, New Jersey, of the Colt Arms family.

‡ This was either John McKeon, Francis Kernan's first cousin, son of Margaret (Kernan) McKeon, and at one time New York District Attorney; or still another John Corish Devereux, first cousin of Hannah, son of her father's brother, Thomas and his wife, Mary née Redmond, who had been sent over from Ireland to be raised by his uncle, the first John Corish Devereux.

intended to have the wedding very private, but the curiosity of the good people was not to be restrained. It rained hard, but notwithstanding more than a thousand people collected to see it. It was a solemn & impressive ceremony and to me one of surpassing interest, deciding the happiness of a daughter. After the company returned from church, we had coffee (no wine) & at ten o'clock supper. Mrs. Newberry came in from New York about an hour after the ceremony, having been detained in Schenectady about seven hours.

On Wednesday evening we exerted ourselves to have a brilliant party, & everything in the way of lights & flowers were put in requisition. The company was numerous all elegantly dressed. The refreshments consisted of lemonade & Ice-cream. The Boquets [sic] of the Bride & her party were much admired. The rooms & hall were decorated with tulips & white lilies intermixed, they formed a pretty contrast.

Mr. Kernan kindly invited Mary [Devereux] to accompany them on their journey. She is so delicate that I gladly accepted the invitation and hope it will be of service to her. . . . They spent this week in Steuben county with Mr. Kernan's friends, & on Monday will leave for Niagara. They will return by way of Oswego & intend to spend a day or two with you, and on the 11th & 12th will be at the Manor. . . .

Your affectionate sister

Francis and Hannah settled into their "neat little house, it is not so small either," as she described their "humble little home." She dived into the mysteries of the cellar and kitchen with the help of a maid, Catherine, and he attended to the hurry of business. She complained gently that he rushed off to the office in the mornings, declining to tinker about the house or work in the garden before breakfast. They attended numerous parties, until Francis demanded more evenings at home to rest himself for his growing practice. According to a student in the law firm, Francis worked from 12 to 16 hours a day.

In due course, Hannah's letters suggested a coming event. On February 13, 1844, she confided in her Butler aunt in Oxford: "I am very well, quite encouraged and hope to do well. I have been able to go over to Mother's, ride out, my walks are very limited and do not extend beyond my suite of apartments upstairs, and once a day I descend." Twelve days later, on February 25, she was the proud mother of John Devereux Kernan, the first of her seven boys and three girls. He was baptized at Saint John's Church with his maternal uncle and aunt, John C. Devereux Jr. and Catharine Devereux, as godparents. Thus began the family still known today as the "Utica Kernans," (although most of those still residing in the area are also descended from Francis's brother William and his wife, Frances Warnick Kernan).

The house on Kent Street was their home until 1848. In that year, Francis, for $5,000, bought from Charles A. Mann a house that stood on about a half-acre of land,[9] and thereafter for a few years he was listed at 2 Kent Street.[10]

There is unfortunately little record of either Francis's or Hannah's physical appearance in these years—only a small portrait of Francis painted according to family tradition by G. P. A. Healy and a photograph of the two of them with their two oldest boys. In both, Francis appears with a great head of hair, shaven lips and chin, and whiskers in the style termed "collier" that he kept throughout his life and whose whiteness became so striking a feature. Perhaps at this period it was light brown like his father's.[11] It would appear that Francis was almost six feet tall, with the fine physique, large, loose frame, and great length of arms and hands remarked on in later years. He had his father's fine, fresh color and fair complexion and probably already had the upright and distinguished carriage of his later years, which could have been likewise a carryover from his father's military bearing. In the Healy portrait, his eyes appear dark. However, an 1892 portrait in the Fort Schuyler Club in Utica shows him with blue eyes although, perhaps as described at least once, also dark and brilliant. Opinions vary as to his voice that was called variously "harsh," "sweet," "of an almost feminine tone," or "clarion," by reporters who either favored or scorned his later political speeches. His pictures bear out that he continued to dress "genteely," as he had reportedly done at Georgetown.

*K*ernan and Quin

IN LATE 1852 or early 1853, Francis, now 37 years old and father of five children, began to consider organizing a new firm, seeing that his sister Winifred had married George Edward Quin, the son of his father's old friend from pioneer days, Patrick Quin, and his wife, Elizabeth, *née* Wolcott. George had probably read law in the Watkins office of Edward Quin. Being already the father of three boys (with five more to come), George was seeking better prospects than Watkins offered. Francis discussed the proposed change with Joshua Spencer, and they agreed to dissolve their firm on the following July 1. Francis then wrote to George on February 14, 1853:

> Dear George:
>
> Your letter of a long time since, in which you expressed solicitude lest our proposed arrangement would be detrimental to myself, & that I was influenced in making it by a desire to be of service to you & yours was recd. and I intended to answer it earlier. Now I believe that the arrangement will be one profitable and pleasant to both of us & I go into it on this basis. But even if I did it to make life to you and Winny pleasanter it would be no objection. I would

be doing nothing but what I know you would do for me. But I am fully persuaded that the change will not be detrimental to me and I trust that it will not
be to you. At any rate we make it with good motives and for good objects and
when we thus act, taking all needful precautions, we should not be uneasy about
the result....

Francis said he would secure rooms for their office to be opened on July 1, and
he asked George for a list of what law books he could bring, and when, after July 1,
George might be able to arrive. He leased offices in the Devereux Block—a trian-
gular-shaped building in the heart of Utica on Genesse Street that had been built
by Nicholas Devereux—and George Quin and his family moved to Utica sometime in 1853. The firm of Kernan and Quin was on its way.*

Before the following year was out, Francis was appointed by the governor to
be state reporter of the newly created court of last resort, the Court of Appeals. The
appointment made Francis a constitutional officer of the state.†

The job called for exacting work: it required Francis to attend the sessions of
the Court of Appeals, and, if so directed by the court, to study the briefs, arguments, and opinions of the judges in each case, and to prepare them for publication
in the official reports as a record of what was done. The annual salary was $2,000.[1]
Francis's service as reporter lasted three years and resulted in the publication of four
volumes of reported cases. Originally denominated 1, 2, 3, and 4 Kernan, they are
now printed and cited as 11 through 14 New York. Their original title pages read:

"REPORTS OF CASES / ARGUED AND DETERMINED / IN THE / COURT OF
APPEALS / OF / THE / STATE OF NEW YORK / WITH / NOTES, REFERENCES, AND AN
INDEX / BY FRANCIS KERNAN / Counselor at Law." Volumes 1 and 2 are dated 1855,
Volume 3, 1856 and Volume 4, 1857. The original printings of all four are hard to
come by, especially in their original leather bindings. These volumes show that
Francis not only argued his firm's cases before the court, but also reported them. He
also reported the cases of his former partner, Spencer, as well, and, of course, was in
frequent contact with other noted lawyers of those years, all eager to see their own
cases in print.

---

* The firm remained in the Devereux Block until the 1950s and continues in Utica to this day; there are no longer
any Kernans active in the firm, although two are "of Counsel," in effect, retired. Many other Kernans have succeeded Francis, but only one other Quin has followed George, his son William Patrick. See Appendix IV, which is
a brief account of the firm written in 1963 by Warnick J. Kernan, a nephew of Francis, to Francis's great-grandson
Francis Kernan Kernan (1902–1986).

†The duty of the court reporter was "to report every cause argued and determined in that court, which it shall
direct him to report, and such others as the public interests shall, in his judgment, require to be reported. To enable
him to perform this duty, the judges of that court shall deliver to him their written opinions in all cases, in which
their oral opinions in deciding the same shall not be delivered in open court....And the reporter shall prepare for
each volume such digest and tables of contents as are usually prepared for similar reports." See *Reports of Cases in
the New York Court of Appeals* 1847, c. 280—The Judiciary Act of 1847. New York had been very early in providing
for official reporting, doing so by statute passed April 7, 1804.

Only the reports of the first three New York State Reporters (Comstock, Selden, and Kernan) were cited to any extent by the reporters' names, and the practice persisted in the opinions of out-of-state courts for some time after it had ceased in the home state.[2] Kernan's work as reporter was considered to be "distinguished by accuracy and good judgment,"[3] and his reports have been useful over the years. Many of his cases have been cited hundreds of times, and one has been cited in some 480 cases (see Appendix V for a discussion of its interesting subject, prohibition of alcoholic liquors).

In Kernan and Quin's first four decades, younger members of the Kernan family entered and left the firm, as did one William Patrick Quin, George's son. The first to join was Francis's younger brother William Jr., in 1857; and the first to leave was George Quin, who died in 1863, survived by a widow and seven sons. In 1865, Francis's eldest son, John Devereux Kernan, came into the office, probably to read law, as he was only 21 and just out of college. Subsequent comings and goings in the firm over the next 110 years are recounted in Appendices IV and VI.

During the many years when Francis was also pursuing political and business activities, the firm was able to build an impressive list of clients, including local railroads, such as the New York Central, and those further afield; numerous insurance companies; banks located all over the state; nearby counties, cities and towns; and many Utica manufacturing establishments. Individual clients were not neglected, and there are many of all races and religions. The lists in the Kernan Papers at Cornell cover 87 pages, and 90 years.*

A notorious matter back in Utica in which Francis had but a minor part was that of the Loomis Gang. The criminal activities of this infamous family—house and store burglaries, robberies of wayfarers and stagecoaches, systematic horse thievery, and bribery, for none of which they had ever received any punishment— terrorized Oneida County from the 1850s until the fiery end in the burning of their house and barns near Sangerfield in 1867 by a vigilante group that included some county officials. The penultimate legal proceeding in their story was the dismissal of the indictment of James Filkins for his part in that episode, procured by Roscoe Conkling. The last was an action brought by the family's matriarch, Rhoda Loomis, against Madison and Oneida Counties for the $20,000 damages suffered in the fire. She engaged the services of Francis, who won the case but only to the extent of a

---

* Francis or his firm handled numerous matters for members of the Devereux and Kernan families,[4] principally wills, estates, and lawsuits. One was the estate of Nicholas Devereux, who died suddenly in 1855, leaving a large estate that included some 40,000 acres of land in western New York.

verdict for $1,000, explaining to her that there was not much sympathy in the courts for her family's troubles.[5]

In November 1869, Kernan and Conkling were opposing attorneys in a suit for damages brought by a New York Central railroad engineer for injuries suffered in a crash at the Oriskany railroad station. His claim was that, at the demand of a party of the Road's officials, the train was going 60 miles per hour so that they might reach Utica in time for a banquet at Bagg's Hotel. In a courtroom packed with spectators for the final arguments, Kernan on behalf of the Central appealed earnestly to the jurors to disabuse their minds of the common prejudices against corporations, but Conkling followed with a two-hour harangue portraying heartless, diamond-studded directors, forcing the honest, hard-working, teetotaling engineer to speed them to dinner and nearly to his own death. Cornelius Vanderbilt, then president of the railroad, accepted the $18,000 verdict, the largest of its day, rather than risk a retrial and even higher damages.[6]

Francis's growing reputation was such that he was retained to argue before the Supreme Court following his admission to practice there on December 9, 1863. Particular attention to the names of counsel appearing before the Supreme Court suggests that certain lawyers were retained solely to argue there because they had become noted for excellence in that activity; the same names appear over and over again. Francis's was one of them.

Thereafter his renown as a lawyer spread far beyond New York. In one case, Orchard v Hughes, 68 U.S. 73, he and a lawyer named Woolworth from Nebraska successfully appeared for the appellants from a decision of the Supreme Court of the territory of Nebraska. In another, known as The Bank Tax Case, 69 U.S. 200, he appeared unsuccessfully with several others on behalf of the United States Tax Commissioner. The reports show that he argued cases in the United States Supreme Court during the years he was in the Senate, and also in the New York Court of Appeals. In at least one case in the latter, he was joined by his son Nicholas.[7] No cases in which he appeared after the October 1882 term have been found.[8]

Francis was engaged in many prominent cases in the United States Circuit and District Courts as well. Among civil cases, two are noted by the *Journal of the American Bar Association,* including "The long continued litigation growing out of the failure of the Ontario Branch bank, and the defense of Thomas Buchanan Jr. in the suits brought against him by Charles S. Symonds, receiver of the People's Safe Deposit and Saving Institution of the State of New York, otherwise known as the Beehive Bank."[9]

In 1870, had Francis not "promptly declined" to run as judge of the New York Court of Appeals, he would have easily been elected, according to his friend Charles O'Conor of New York, who wrote, " His present is equal to that of any gentleman in the land; his future, as he is not aged, is full of promise."[10]

Though he left no record of cases that made a major contribution to American legal thought, the one consistent philosophy that he sought to push throughout his career was his devotion to the Constitution of the United States, and his belief that the people of a state should be free to create their own rules—political ideals born of his family's suffering in Ireland and their success in America.

Francis Kernan, Ward Hunt Jr., William J. Bacon, and Roscoe Conkling were the only lawyers from Utica invited to meet in August 1878 at Saratoga Springs to consider the feasibility of establishing a national bar association; the meeting resulted in the foundation of the American Bar Association.[*] Francis was unable to attend the organizational meeting, but became an original member and in 1881-82 was the vice president from New York. When President Clarkson N. Potter died on January 23, 1882, Francis was selected by the executive committee to fill out the term.[†]

[*] The association's constitution required its president, in his annual address, to "communicate the most noteworthy changes in statute law on points of general interest made in the several states and by Congress" since the preceding annual meeting. The address Kernan gave on August 8, 1882, at Saratoga Springs was not, perhaps, the liveliest, but it included with approval two items of interest regarding the status of women: "Massachusetts has authorized women to be admitted to practice as attorneys at law on the same terms as men"; and, "In Connecticut a married woman may now be an executrix, administratrix, trustee or guardian the same as a feme sole." . "*Feme sole*" is defined in Black's Law Dictionary as "a single woman, including those who have been married, but whose marriages have been dissolved by death or divorce and, for most purposes, those women who are judicially separated from their husbands." Kernan also reported a matter of special interest to some present-day members of the family involved in forestry: "Maryland and New Hampshire have appointed commissioners to examine and report as to the destruction of forests." See the *Albany Law Journal,* vol. 26, pages 146-148; and IV *Journal of the American Bar Association.* pages 169–170.

[†] As acting president of this association, he was in august company: among other presidents have been Simeon E. Baldwin of New Haven, Joseph H. Choate of New York, William H. Taft of Washington, Elihu Root of New York, John W. Davis of New York, and Charles Evans Hughes of New York.

Book Two

*I*n Politics

$\mathcal{F}$ree Soil!

Whigs, Democrats, we'll all unite,
and Liberty boys—for our cause is right,
Hurrah! Hurrah! Hurrah!
RALLY SONG FOR THE ELECTION OF 1848

FRANCIS KERNAN GREW up in the period when the modern system of party politics in the United States took shape, and in the very state of its creation. It was a system that had raised his father from a disinherited outcast in his native land to a respected public servant in his adopted one. And Francis had seen with his own eyes during his three critical, formative years at Georgetown, within walking distance of the Capitol, the party struggles that made national figures of such New York Democratic stalwarts as William Marcy, Samuel Beardsley, and Silas Wright, and that raised Martin Van Buren from a humble publican's son to the presidency of the United States. The party system was based on loyalty and merit rather than family connections, and it offered talented and ambitious young men a straight path from a log cabin to the Executive Mansion. It is little wonder that Francis believed fervently in the Democratic Party. And with the presence of so many nationally known figures in the region, a local election for Utica's aldermen could inspire the same level of passion and debate as a presidential campaign.

❖

In 1843, Francis assumed his first elective position, that of school commissioner in Utica and in the following year he was elected aldermen. His victories were in spite of his Catholic faith, and they did not rely upon the Irish vote, since most Irishmen lived in the eastern part of town. For four years he served as one of the city's four aldermen, while his law partner, Joshua Spencer, served as mayor. Reports of their council meetings show that they handled endless matters, routine but important to the booming city, such as new streets, box drains in a gutter, removal of nuisances, laying of plank or brick sidewalks, repairing of bridges, and construction of new buildings. Francis headed the committee on legal proceedings. These years were an apprenticeship in administrative and governmental activities, but he was no doubt glad to get into politics of a more interesting kind, as he soon did.

Though Francis had moved to Utica at the zenith of Democratic influence, party unity had ended soon thereafter. Without solidarity, the Democrats lost control of the state; then, in 1840, they lost the presidency and their political stranglehold on federal patronage.

The two factions were known as the Barnburners and the Hunkers.* Kernan was a Barnburner, a member of the progressive faction of the party guided by Van Buren. In the presidential election year of 1844 the Barnburners worked furiously to regain the White House, promoting Van Buren once again. His nomination seemed sure until shortly before the convention, when he announced his measured opposition to the annexation of Texas. This stand—essential to maintain his support at home—angered most Southern Democrats, who, with the votes of Western delegates, gave the nomination to James K. Polk, the original "dark horse" candidate. Adding insult to injury, the maladroit Polk bestowed the top federal jobs in New York exclusively on Hunkers.

To stalwart party men, patronage and principle were already synonymous; being cut out of the spoils was principle enough for the Barnburners to launch a crusade. But in 1846, Barnburners and their Northern allies had the occasion to fuse

---

* The Barnburners were so named by the Hunkers, who compared them to the legendary Dutch farmer who burned down his barn just to get rid of the rats. The implication was that Barnburners were needlessly ending public improvement projects just to get rid of some financial abuses. "Hunkers" comes from the Dutch word "hunkerer," meaning one who seeks office for himself. Both nicknames were derogatory, but both factions bore them with proud defiance. The initial dispute had been over the use of public loans to expand canals, which were hugely important to the state economy, but the rival factions continued to fight over just about everything. Hunkers (or conservatives) wanted to continue using state loans to fund canal growth. Barnburners (or radicals) suggested a new pay-as-you-go policy of using the canals' toll revenues. The pay-as-you-go policy finally prevailed after the state debt rose by 225 percent. Barnburners earned respect for their philosophy of living within one's means. Barnburners were most influential in Buffalo, Batavia, Rochester, Albion, Canandaigua, Utica, Herkimer, Clinton, Rome, and Watertown.

The County Election

The act of casting the ballot is depicted in near-mythic proportions, while not ignoring the
rough edges of the new nation's ideal of universal (male) suffrage. From the "whiskey cider"
influence, to the thoughtful discussions, to the silk-hatted candidate resisted by an
independent thinker, to the smiling farmer swearing before the judge, to the prayer-like
moment on the porch between the voter and the recording official.

By John Sartain, after George Caleb Bingham, ca. 1954. Engraving, mezzotint, and etching, with stippling.
Reproduced with permission of the Yale University Art Gallery, New Haven, Connecticut.

their anger at lost patronage with the more edifying goal of combating the expansion of slavery—a cause that could stir the electorate. The Northern Democrats'
opportunity came when President Polk asked Congress to approve $3 million to
wrap up the Mexican War. He sought funds to use both for a quick negotiation and
for a bid on California, which was also part of Mexico. If all this territory were to
be organized as slave states, it would tilt the precarious sectional balance in the Senate decisively toward the South. Even more important, it would put the nation's
stamp of approval on the abhorrent institution, making slavery a national, not just a
local practice.

Congressman David Wilmot, a Van Buren supporter from Pennsylvania, consulted with New York congressmen to add a proviso to the bill that said "neither
slavery nor involuntary servitude shall ever exist" in any territories acquired with
the money.

Predictably, when the Wilmot Proviso was introduced, Southern leaders exploded, and demanded that their Northern allies repudiate it. The motion passed in the House, but was narrowly defeated in the pro-Southern Senate. In New York, the Hunkers obligingly withheld their support from the Democratic governor, Barnburner leader Silas Wright. With the Democratic party still divided, Wright lost decisively to the Whig candidate.

This was a serious matter. Although his name is virtually forgotten today, Silas Wright held a revered place in the hearts of his contemporaries. Much like Francis Kernan in a later period, Wright was universally esteemed for his decency and rectitude.* A staunch opponent of slavery expansion, Wright was the *de facto* leader of what might have been called the "Conscience Democrats" if such a term had been coined. Northern Democrats looked to Wright as their next presidential nominee, but he died unexpectedly in August 1847—a martyr, in Barnburners' eyes, to Hunker vindictiveness. Walt Whitman, then editor of a Democratic newspaper in Brooklyn, lamented: "Our hopes, in common with nearly all the Democratic party of this state, and indeed of other states, were so identified with this man—relied so much upon him in the future—were so accustomed to look upon him as our tower of strength, and as a shield of righteous virtue—that we indeed feel pressed to the earth by such an unexpected blow!"[1]

Wright's sudden death prompted the movement to draft Van Buren once again, mainly for his connection to his late loyal lieutenant. The election of 1848 became, for Barnburners, a struggle for spoils, a moral crusade and a passionate grudge match of the highest order.[†]

The Wilmot Proviso became the acid test of its day: the one-question trial of anyone's political and moral convictions. The proviso moved practical issues of land and tariffs into a realm of morals where people were unwilling to compromise. In homes, family members pounded their fists on dinner tables, while at political conventions, the banging gavels could barely be heard over the angry noise of delegates. Southern congressmen from both the Democratic and the Whig parties were alarmed at the North's righteous hostility and began to demand a federal slave code in the territories, an idea as obnoxious to most Northerners as the Proviso was to Southerners. Personal alliances formed along geographical lines as the national political parties and religious institutions were pulling apart, dividing North and South.

The parties did their most vicious fighting in New York, especially in the "Burnt Over District" of central New York, which was at once the mother lode of evangeli-

---

* "Mind, manners, morals, temper, habits, unified in him to form the character that was perfect, both in public and private life, and to give the example of a patriot citizen," Thomas Hart Benton panegyrized. See *Thirty Years' View; or, a History of the Working of the American Government for Thirty Years, from 1820 to 1850,* two volumes (New York: D. Appleton and Company, 1858), II:701.

† Just as Hunkers had been willing to see a Whig governor elected over a Barnburner Democrat, the Barnburners were willing to help elect a Whig to the White House in order to stop the Democratic nominee, Lewis Cass, whom they detested both for his acceptance of the extension of slavery and for his role in securing the nomination for Polk in 1844.

cal abolitionist fervor and the chief battleground of the bitter affray within the New York Democracy. For much of the debate, Francis Kernan held a front row seat.

The New York Democracy blew apart over the Proviso at its state convention in Syracuse in September 1847, and by the following year the fighting was at fever pitch. The centrally located town of Utica was the host site for much of the controversial debate, and Kernan, as a city alderman helping to organize events, gained the attention of two leaders of the opposing Democratic factions: ex-governor Horatio Seymour and the Hon. Samuel J. Tilden. These two men would play prominent roles in Kernan's political life, and Kernan would help both in their close presidential races. Seymour was a Hunker and one of the few party leaders capable of hammering out compromise. It was he who had found a way around the canal-money abuses while still expanding the waterways. Seymour most certainly already knew Kernan professionally and socially, since Seymour had his law office in Utica and was mayor in 1842. Samuel Tilden led the Barnburners. A close associate of Van Buren, he helped the candidate write the "Cornerstone Resolution" of the new Free Soil party.

Francis Kernan was a Democrat, it is true, but the essence of his loyalty was personal, not abstract. He belonged to that wing of the party that followed Van Buren, and revered the memory of Wright; and who helped to form the Free Soil party. Party loyalty meant loyalty to these men, not to any cadre of officeholders who might take control of the machinery of the convention.

Debates over free soil in the Southwest took place in the office where Kernan practiced law, as well as in public meeting halls. Kernan's law partner, Joshua Spencer, was the Whig mayor, and Roscoe Conkling, a law student at the firm. This handsome (some said magnificent) young man certainly added his arrogant oratory to the office fervor. He would soon be Utica's youngest mayor, then Congress's youngest representative and later the head of the national Republican Party, serving in the Senate along with Francis Kernan. For now, he was studying law under Francis, making public antislavery speeches for the Whig candidates—and courting Horatio Seymour's sister.

Indifferent to the damage their continued rivalry was inflicting on party strength in New York, the Barnburners and Hunkers staged a showdown at the national convention in May 1848 and dragged the horrified delegates into their fight. The Barnburners wanted a vote for the Wilmot Proviso; the Hunkers did not. Each sent their own delegation to the convention, and each delegation demanded to be seated as representing New York's real Democratic Party. For the national organization, choosing either delegation would have meant taking a stand on slavery and thus destroying a fragile national unity. Party leaders offered a compromise: both delegations could be seated with each delegate having half a vote.

The Barnburners, realizing they would not be able to press the Wilmot Proviso or hold their own against the unified Hunker contingent, bolted the convention, keeping their free soil principles intact. The remaining delegates nominated Senator Lewis Cass of Michigan for president—the man who had led the congressional fight to kill the proviso. A terrific scene interrupted the proceedings the following morning when an alarm was given that the gallery was giving way, that the building's pillars were sinking. None of the 3,000 participants knew exactly what was happening, but hundreds jumped out of the windows or jumped from the gallery to the floor and rushed the doors. Many were badly injured. After much confusion inside and out, it was determined that the alarm had been caused by the breaking of a bench. The crowding and the tensions were at such a height that the incident had set off a calamitous chain reaction.

Although the Barnburners were defeated, they claimed higher moral ground. Freed of party constraints and supported by popular antislavery sentiment, they called for their own Free Soil convention in Utica on June 22, 1848. The first goal was to mobilize popular opinion, and this is when Kernan began to be noted in the press.[2]

While Democratic rallies for and against the nomination of Cass took place, the Whigs added fuel to the fire by howling down the Proviso at their national convention in June and offering up the Southern slaveholder and Mexican War hero Zachary Taylor as their presidential nominee. Many New York Whigs, chagrined by their party's choice, joined forces with abolitionists and pro-Proviso Barnburners in the state to nominate Martin Van Buren for president. The announcement caused a national sensation. Parties were splitting in every direction, and New York once again was setting the nation's agenda. These New York Barnburners and Whigs formed the core of a new national Free Soil party which convened in Buffalo that year for one of the most spectacular and historic conventions of the period.[*]

Under a mammoth tent, in sweltering heat, the brilliant assemblage of orators and entertainers inspired a spontaneous, near-religious enthusiasm. (Many historians cite this gathering as the seed of today's Republican party.) They reaffirmed New York's choice of Van Buren for president. Barnburners, including Kernan, abolitionists, and Liberal party members milled in the tent and sought refuge from the heat outside. When Frederick Douglass was spotted in the audience, the convention cheered for a speech from the ex-slave and leading abolitionist. But recent throat surgery had left Douglass able to wish only "God Speed." He did, however, endorse the platform in his newspaper, recognizing the Free Soil party as the only national party that was openly antislavery, even if it did not go as far as the abolitionists.[3]

Not everyone shared Douglass's satisfaction that slavery was now part of the

[*] The list of party leaders indicates the prominence of this convention. It includes John Van Buren, Churchill C. Cambreleng, Samuel J. Tilden, Samuel Young, Dean Richmond, Sanford E. Church, William Cullen Bryant, Henry W. Van Dyck, David Dudley Field, and John A. Dix.

nation's political process. Most likely, Kernan embraced a combination of feelings common among members of the Free Soil party who saw the question of slavery not so much as "whether black men should be made free, but whether white men would remain free" [to determine their own destiny].[4] The fearful premise of most party members was: if the nation contained more slave states, the increase would add to the South's unequal power in Congress. Eventually, the South would domi-nate the nation and force all states to accept slavery.* The Wilmot Proviso, com-monly called "the White Man's Resolution," could prevent the spread of a Southern slave culture in the territories.[†]

The fear that an alien Southern slave culture would eventually affect and over-whelm the North was apparently the idea Kernan put forth during the campaign season that followed the Free Soil party convention. In putting forth this argument, Kernan probably followed the line of such reluctant Free Soilers as John A. Dix, a long-time Van Buren loyalist, who argued: "I would preserve for free white labor a fair country, a rich inheritance, where the sons of toil, of my own race and color, can live without the disgrace which association with Negro slavery brings upon free labor."[5] However, it is difficult to know exactly what Kernan said, since our first view of his early political life is through the eyes of a scornful Hunker. The *Utica Daily Observer* on July 28, 1848, refers to Kernan as "the eloquent Humspun," an amusing combination of compliment and insult. "Eloquent" is certainly a compli-ment and Kernan was known as an articulate speaker. "Homespun" refers to some-thing local, perhaps plain, and "hum" connotes a continuous drone.

"We should not allude to the remarks of our friend Kernan," writes the edi-tor, "did we not feel the greatest alarm lest he should die through fear that the black people in the new territories will make slaves of our white brethren! It is a duty we owe to our fellow man, to assure Mr. Kernan that there is no danger of the black people doing any such thing; and if he wishes to go to California, he can do so without being alarmed as to his freedom. This is said officially. Mr. Kernan's illustra-tion, intended to prove that the people of the territories are not to be trusted with self government, is very fine. Suppose, said he, 1000 Catholics should go and settle one of the new territories, establish the Catholic religion and forbid any other, would the people of New York stand it? Mr. Kernan forgot that the Constitution guaranteed religious freedom to every one, and his illustration for this and manifold other reasons amounts to just nothing at all."[6]

We should not take this editorial to mean that the Hunkers were against free soil or that they supported the negro population. Blacks were excluded from society

---

* The South argued the opposite fear.

† Some scholars in the turbulent era of the 1960s, determined to prove that all white Americans have always been racists, argued that any antislavery activity (except by Garrisonian Abolitionists) was really just anti-black activity, and lumped the Free Soil party in that camp. While the Free Soilers had their share of racist leaders and support-ers, they were in fact more genuinely antislavery than racist—and their platform was highly idealistic. It was drafted by Salmon P. Chase, later known as the "Attorney General of Freed Slaves."

in Utica, and the *Utica Daily Observer* was no advocate for their advancement. Rather, the paper reflects its readership's general concern that "up until the last few months, the subject of slavery was never made an issue by any party, except that miserable mischief-making body, the abolitionists."[7]

The conflict over self-government resonated among the Irish population, which saw parallels in Europe, where the Irish were subjected to detrimental English rule, and where the Irish were agitating for independence. This perception may help to explain why such leaders of Irish extraction as Kernan's friend Charles O'Conor identified so strongly with the South. Although Francis's father, William, took little or no interest in the affairs of his native land, Kernan joined his Irish-born father-in-law, Nicholas Devereux, as a member of the newly formed Utica Confederate Friends of Ireland. Its purpose was to raise funds to aid that most distressful country, then in the fourth year of the potato famine.*

In later notices the newspaper wrongly lumps Kernan and his fellow debater Ward Hunt (later of the U.S. Supreme Court) in the same category as the generally disdained "abolitionist agitators," and in an October 17 article, the editor scorns Kernan as "one of the three contemptible fizzles who has dared to challenge Horatio Seymour to a debate." The editor compares the challenge of these "intellectual infant Abolitionists" to that of "Benedict Arnold daring George Washington to discuss the propriety of his course in sustaining the cause of this country against traitors." He escalates the insult, saying, "Arnold had not had the face to do this but the apostates of the present day are his equals in treachery and superiors in impudence."

Whatever the outcome of the debate that night between the Hunker Seymour and the Barnburner Kernan, we can only presume it helped sell papers the next day, for none can now be found to show us more of Kernan's reasoning or explain why he and Seymour were to become so closely aligned in future endeavors. Kernan's stump speeches during these agitated months put him in a favorable light with not only party leaders, but a wider voting public.

To the beat of bands, drums, and cannons the campaign of 1848 was a kaleidoscope of contentious speeches, righteous sermons, emotional slogans, personally venomous accusations, and equally rancorous countercharges. Audiences wanted to

---

* Francis was elected one of the three vice presidents, and his father-in-law, Nicholas Devereux, was elected treasurer. Reacting to the many recent rebellions in Europe, the meeting passed a resolution rejoicing "as republicans and philanthropists, at the success of the French and other European people, in their late struggles for freedom" and lamenting exceedingly "that the rightful heirs of Erin yet writhe and groan upon their native soil, under oppressions and afflictions more grievous and protracted than any of those which the people of France or Prussia have been provoked to cast off and abolish." Other resolutions urged the Irish people to follow their sacred duty and "to break the chains which English usurpers of their inalienable rights have long riveted upon them, and to hurl their oppressors from their soil, whenever and however they may be enabled to do so." Noting that the current Irish leaders represented the prominent sects of Catholics, Episcopalians, and Presbyterians and were encouraged by an attitude of revolt among the Chartists in England, the meeting "hailed the present as the most auspicious period of their history for Irishmen to declare and maintain their independence." .See the *Utica Daily Observer*, May 19, 1848.

hear of nothing but the slavery issue, it finally being a respectable topic in public politics.

> *The North is ripe for the Proviso*
> *Hurrah! Hurrah! Hurrah!*
> *She'll back the names from Buffalo*
> *Hurrah! Hurrah! Hurrah!*
> *Whigs, Democrats, we'll all unite,*
> *and Liberty boys—for our cause is right,*
> *Hurrah! Hurrah! Hurrah![8]*

The election results in New York and throughout the country provided a lesson still repeated by today's political pundits: third parties are spoilers. Taylor won by only 140,000 votes. The "Free Spoil" party drew most of the Democratic votes, but those 300,000 ballots would have gone to Cass, who would have become president. Once more, a divided North had given the Executive Mansion to a united South.* Although the Free Soil party never regained its momentum and failed to develop a national organization, it had provided an opportunity for dialogue among like-minded men who did not return to the arms of their parties. These men would form the core of the modern Republican party.

The bitter election of 1848 articulated the basic division of American society. Great congressional debates followed and resulted in Senator Henry Clay's Compromise of 1850, which would retain an uneasy peace for the next decade. In that compromise, gold-rich California was admitted as a free state; the territories of New Mexico and Utah were to be organized without mention of slavery; the slave trade was outlawed in the District of Columbia; and a draconian new Fugitive Slave Law was passed giving vastly expanded federal support to the return of suspected runaways, and making every black in the nation a presumptive slave.

The election defeat was a wake-up call for the Democratic rivals to stop their self-destructive feuding and unite their forces. The membership called a truce, and Horatio Seymour and Martin Van Buren brokered the peace. Their efforts, along with the Compromise of 1850, allowed men like Tilden and Kernan to return to the Democratic party mainstream. There was no more talk of Barnburners and Hunkers.

The Compromise of 1850 temporarily saved the Union and marked the beginning of the end of the Whigs. Zachary Taylor died in office and was replaced by his vice president, Millard Fillmore. Although Fillmore was from New York, the state's Whigs had split over the Proviso and over Fillmore's endorsement of the Compromise of 1850, and were unable to reunite. Although they would run one more presidential candidate, as a national party the Whigs were finished.

---

* President Taylor, however, proved to be far less an appeaser of the South than Cass, who remained so until the guns were fired upon Fort Sumter.

The Democrats, battered and bruised, managed to restore their national fortunes; but the struggle to find candidates acceptable to a broad enough electorate in both sections of the country resulted in the election of two of the least successful presidents in American history. The North and the South each contained honest and honorable men; but the gulf between them over slavery was now so wide that no one who was honorable could honestly appeal to both sides. And for all the ethical questions that marked the public debate and private conversations during this agitated campaign of 1848, Frederick Douglass was correct in his belief that moral arguments alone would never end slavery.

Rum, Romanism, and Slavery

For almost four years, the Compromise of 1850 kept a lid on the issue of slavery. While it simmered, most Northerners focused on problems closer to home—alcohol and Catholics. While "Rum, Romanism, and Slavery" defined both the Democratic party and the new Republican party, they also helped the young lawyer Francis Kernan define his own vision of America.

Kernan served as Utica's city counsel for several years. He also served on Democratic party councils, including the nominating committees that selected and promoted candidates for elective office such as district and Supreme Court judges. In 1852, when his political mentor Horatio Seymour became governor for the second time, Seymour awarded Kernan his first significant political appointment. The job of court reporter was a perfect match for the young lawyer's abilities, and Kernan's reputation for accuracy and solid judgment spread throughout the state's legal and political networks.

Utica boomed during these years. Francis joined the Mechanic's Association, which expanded its hall twice to contain the crowds at lectures, fairs, balls, and political events. In these days before organized sports and entertainment, lectures and political rallies constituted the main entertainment of 19th-century America (other than churches and bars). Mechanic's Hall's new balcony was redesigned with a wrought-iron bar that rested on iron brackets and could support 300 people! *

The same audience who came to laugh at speeches about women's suffrage or to hear a scientific lecture on the benefits of frequent bathing, might come the next evening for a temperance meeting, or the next night be shocked and titillated by speakers such as the popular "Monk of La Trappe." Appearing in monastic dress, the "monk" read "Popish documents, proving that Priests, Monks, and Bishops cannot be lawful citizens of this country without violating the oath taken by them at their ordination."[1] He described how the pope had released him from his solemn vow of celibacy, how he had married in Philadelphia, and how his wife had been "dissevered from him by Priestcraft." For another 12½ cents, gentlemen could come back the next evening alone and get the details.

The anti-Catholic, anti-Irish mood had grown after the largest wave of Irish immigration, which came in the wake of the Great Famine of 1846-50. In the years between the beginning of the Famine and the Civil War, about 1,700,000 Irish came to the United States—starving, largely uneducated, and nearly devoid of marketable skills. It was the newly arrived Famine Irish, recruited right off the boat into the Democratic party at the height of the sectional crises of the 1840s and 1850s, who competed with blacks for jobs and survival and who became the shock-troops of the extreme anti-black racism that became a hallmark of the urban proletariat.

Utica felt the strains of immigration, but this canal town always had had a large Irish contingent and was known for its tolerance. According to demographics of 1845, a full 25 percent of the population was Irish-born. Kernan chose a good place to raise his family and develop his legal practice, because elsewhere in the state and country an Irish background was a distinct social disadvantage. Anti-immigrant and anti-Catholic sentiment had become so intense it crystallized into the "American" party, nicknamed the "Know Nothing" party for the way its members responded to police investigations of riots and church burnings. Even Utica had a small American party contingent.

Perhaps some of the town's reputation for tolerance was due to the courtly charm and warm personality of Utica's chief Irishmen, John C. Devereux and his brother Nicholas (Hannah Kernan's father). They were highly successful merchants and two of the greatest benefactors of the Catholic Church and its various institutions in the entire diocese of western New York. John Devereux had arranged for Utica's first St. Patrick's Day celebrations in 1824 (and probably footed most of the bill). Until he died, he was the parade's green-sashed grand marshal. He was so well liked that in 1840 he became the town's first popularly elected mayor—never mind

---

* Francis was a member of the Utica Mechanic's Association, when it owned Mechanic's Hall on Hotel Street. It eventually foundered over the project of building a large opera house, and passed out of existence. See Walsh, *Vignettes of Old Utica* for a history of the association.

that he was a Democrat in a Whig stronghold.* This public admiration for his in-laws certainly translated into votes for Francis, who as a first-generation American, was a role model for Utica's Irish.

Horatio Seymour was another reason for Utica's reputation. Born into a long-established family of English extraction, Seymour had a deep appreciation for the cultural complexity of New York State, which was an unusual attitude for his day. He loved to recount the contributions of the overlaying populations of Dutch, English, New England Yankees, and Irish. It was Seymour who supported Kernan's political rise and would later rely on him to help court the Irish vote, even beyond New York.

On March 7, 1843, the same year Francis married Hannah, he won his first public appointment as school commissioner, despite mistrust of the Irish Catholics regarding public schools. Kernan's appointment as a Utica school commissioner was a notable occurrence. The office had been created a year earlier when then-Governor William H. Seward signed legislation establishing an elective board of control for public schools. The new law created so much anxiety about Catholics taking over the schools that on election night in April, New York City mobs raided the Irish areas and stoned the residence of Bishop Hughes. The mayor called out the militia to protect Catholic churches.

Free public education had been a high priority of the Yankees, but even as the school system was forming, it became the strategic battlefield for America's cultural and religious clashes that it remains today. At issue in Francis's day was the controversy over public money and religious schools. Governor Seward had recommended that special schools be created for foreigners so the students could get instruction from a teacher who spoke their language and shared their faith. Roman Catholics liked the idea and asked for part of the public school funds, which caused a huge and bitter public reaction. The issue of public education crystallized the anti-immigration backlash, yet strengthened Kernan's beliefs about not using public funds for religious education, beliefs for which he is still remembered in state history.

Utica's new school commissioners had their hands full. "The common schools of the city were worse than useless," according to a Utica historian.* "Little beneficial was learned, while the children when collected were ready to receive and practice lessons in mischief and crime," with the result that they "were patronized by none who felt any interest in the education of their children, or who could do otherwise." Kernan shared the responsibility for the city's schools with Commissioners Hiram Denio, Spencer Kellogg, J. Watson Williams, Rudolf Snyder, and Robert T. Hallock. By 1851 the same historian was able to record that "a new and healthy spirit was soon infused in the schools—they were soon patronized by all classes of citizens, and placed on a respectable footing. Competent teachers were employed, new school houses were erected or fitted up, which were filled with furniture, too

---

* Before 1840 the mayor was selected by the Common Council.

good to be whittled and marred, new and improved text books introduced, and a spirit of pride and ambition inspired in the pupils. The school system matching the city's growth, with ten primary and two intermediate schools, a large three-story building on the corner of Charlotte and Elizabeth Streets for advanced and intermediate departments, and a library of 3,000 volumes. . . . For all this progress the city is mainly indebted to the energy and judgment of the Commissioners."

While anti-Catholic sentiment continued to spread, the mania for compulsory temperance also swept through the valleys of upstate New York. Kernan became a "teetotaler," though he may have been under the heavy influence of his mother-in-law when he took the pledge. His certificate from the Irish Total Abstinence Society is signed by the famous Father Theobald Mathew, "the Apostle of Temperance," who after convincing 5 million of his fellow Irishmen at home to follow his example, went to the United States for an extended two-year visit, continuing his wildly successful moral crusade. Mary D. Devereux, in a letter to her like-minded sister, Elizabeth Butler, described the temperance meeting at her home that she held for Father Matthew, who diverted more souls from a path of rum and ruin. "More than 1,000 persons took the pledge in my parlors and hall, from one to twenty at a time," she wrote. "It was very solemn & impressive & the good old man never too tired or weary to be called upon to give the pledge or speak a word of comfort and encouragement to the poor. . . . [His] innocent cheerfulness and anecdotes reminded me so much of my dear Father that I was often overcome by the feeling."[2]

Other family members were not impressed, particularly Mary's eighteen-year-old niece, Julia Clapp (later Newberry).[3] In a letter to another family member, Julia declared her aunt's view of temperance "entirely too complimentary." The young woman had just witnessed her first—and last—temperance meeting and declared "it is a disgrace to the age that these people should be allowed to rail at thousands of excellent and pure minded persons who have lived in the moderate use of wine and harmed no one, while these poor fanatics are hardly worthy to brush their shoes. . . . The speaker was a native from 'Auld Scotia's hills and plains,' and he gave a history of his life which had been passed amid the lowest scenes of vice. The details were shocking and yet the house was crowded with people whose gaping eyes and ears told of the same interest with which they would have looked at a 'hanging.'"

Taking the pledge had political as well as social and religious implications. In 1854, Governor Seymour fell victim to the temperance mania and lost his reelection by just 300 votes—votes he might have captured had his tolerance of alcohol not matched his tolerance for Catholics. Not only had he vetoed a popular anti-alcohol

---

* Kernan served as a school commissioner until he entered Congress in 1863, but his interest in education continued throughout his life. In this, he was following in his father's footsteps. The quotations regarding Utica's school are from Pomeroy, pages 623 to 624. Francis's brother, William, and his nephew Warnick also served as members of the board in later years, and in 1925, the board voted unanimously to name a new school on Warren Street the "Kernan School" in recognition of their long and faithful service that had then lasted almost continuously since 1843. See the *Utica Daily Observer,* June 10, 1925.

bill he considered unconstitutional; he had hosted a reception at his home for a papal nuncio, Monsignor Bedini,[4] following the dedication of a new altar at St. Peter's, in Albany. The press considered the monsignor tactless, and although some Protestant clergy had also attended, the affair was reported as a near scandal—further evidence of the threat of Rome.

That same winter of 1854 the U.S. Congress ignited a political explosion by passing the Kansas-Nebraska Act. Complex political and economic forces (such as the irresponsible ambition of Stephen Douglas and the powerful railroad interests) inspired the bill. It blew the lid off the slavery issue again by repealing the Missouri Compromise, which had barred slavery in the Louisiana Territory north of the line of thirty-six degrees thirty minutes north latitude.[*]

The new act split the Nebraska territory into two parts, Kansas and Nebraska, and allowed the white settlers in each to decide for themselves whether to allow slavery. This enraged the North, and set off a civil war in Kansas between free- and slave-state partisans. The hostility gave birth to the Republican party in the North and West, whose members were Free Soilers, Abolitionists, Whigs fed up with straddling the slavery issue, and Democrats who refused to stay in a party dominated by slave owners. In New York the new Republicans were of New England (Yankee) origin. By the presidential campaign in 1856, they had cobbled together a regional party large enough to nominate a slate and champion John C. Frémont. Their slogan, "Free speech, Free press, Free soil, Free men, Frémont," announced their agenda, while their cries of "No Compromise, No Concession!" broadcast their righteous fervor.

Democrats in turn defined freedom as freedom from government. Government should not intrude upon private behavior—meaning freedom to stock a wine cellar, freedom to say the rosary, or freedom to keep slaves. The policy of nonintervention was a common bond between Northern and Southern Democrats: even if they disagreed about slavery, they could all agree that people should mind their own business, and their own business did not include dictating rules for those settling in the new territories. "Popular Sovereignty" was the term given by Stephen Douglas for this policy, reminding everyone that the government had been created as a sovereign nation of sovereign states. Any other arrangement, Democrats believed, would make it impossible to sustain the Union.

This is the policy Kernan advocated as a Democratic stump speaker when he returned to active public speaking during the campaign of 1856. Democrats feared the regional new party of Republicans as the first step toward disunion, and they had a point: Kansas broke into civil war while legislators in Washington went armed

---

[*] Although the Compromise, adopted in 1819, was but an ordinary piece of legislation without any special constitutional standing, it had taken on the status of a sacred covenant between the sections. No less an authority than James K. Polk had presciently asserted that any attempt to repeal it would "alienate the people of different portions of the Union from each other; and…endanger the existence of the Union itself." (See Benton, 2:713.)

to their sessions. In the Senate Chamber, South Carolina's Representative Preston Brooks caned Senator Charles Sumner of Massachusetts into near-unconsciousness in retaliation for characterizing Brooks's cousin, also a Senator, as bedding the "harlot Slavery." Martyred by his bloody beating, Sumner was unable to resume his Senate seat for more than three years.

The Republicans also had a valid point. How could Democrats advocate compromise with those who had shown they would not be satisfied? There was good reason for resisting Congress's Fugitive Slave Act, in which a simple affidavit from a judge or commissioner from a slaveholding state was all that was needed to identify (often falsely) black people as runaway slaves and force them back to their masters. The right to a presumption of freedom was stripped away, with no recourse to trial or appeal. In practice, the Fugitive Slave Act amounted to declaring open season on all blacks in the North, who had little or no formal basis on which to verify their freedom. Even those citizens who cared little for free blacks nevertheless cared very much that the act sacrificed the judicial principles of *habeas corpus* and due process. As Daniel Webster put it, the act required Northerners to "sacrifice their consciences on the altar of the Union." The new Republicans, under the standard of the flamboyant Frémont, generated more passion, more debate, and more favorable press in the election campaign than did the Democratic stump speakers. Most blacks remanded by the Fugitive Slave Act were accosted in coastal cities, not in upstate New York, but the national debate played out in every village. Exactly how Kernan, a strict Constitutionalist, perceived the Fugitive Slave Act in these early days of his political career is impossible to know because there is no record of any speech or reference to comments he might have made. However, considering his later, impassioned defense of *habeas corpus,* his silence at seeing this essential civil right denied to blacks might be interpreted, at best, as a firm belief that the Southern states had a right to make, and uphold, their own laws, and, at worst, a view of blacks as a problematic category apart, not worthy of or subject to the principles of liberty he so consistently defended for whites, both North and South.

A newspaper article in the Republican *Herald*[5] dismisses a rally for James Buchanan in Boonville for attracting a smaller crowd than the Republicans had garnered the previous week, and is less concerned with reporting Kernan's words than in stereotyping his audience as lower-class, rowdy immigrants: "The Hon. Charles A. Mann and Francis Kernan did the talking, while the 'crowd'—with some exceptions—'did' the rum. The order of exercises was somewhat varied by the 'short boys' of Utica engaging now and then in a plug-muss and an occasional hurrah for Buchanan." The reporter's use of "plug" refers to carpenters' awls, and connotes hoodlum violence, much like the later brass knuckles, or today's box-cutters. "Short boys" is likely a demeaning name for the Democratic marching clubs that attended all rallies. They were normally called "Little Giants," in honor of the Little Giant himself, Stephen Douglas. (The Republicans' drill teams were called "Wide Awakes.")

Americans have always loved vivid nicknames, but never so much as in the 19th century. Even the term "stump speaker" is nearly a treatise on American English, with its delight in humorous imagery and contempt for formality. Kernan rode an "iron horse" and "stumped" the "boom-towns" to speak at "mass-meetings" or "pic-nics," where he promoted a "straight-ticket" vote for the candidates "running" on the Democratic "plank." Political parties held innumerable local rallies, synchronized with county fairs or barbecues—the news and entertainment of their day. Elections were won by "grass-roots" efforts of organizing precincts and by convincing the electorate to come out on election day.

James Buchanan won in 1856, and for the first time a president was elected without New York's popular vote. Although Democrats still controlled New York City, John A. King became the state's first Republican governor, and for the next four years leading to civil war, the Republican Party continued to gain strength. Its economic platform supported Northern business interests, lower tariffs, and more railroads.

Several years later Kernan would come forward as a voice of dispassion in the national crisis and as the party's hope against corruption in the state government. Perhaps he received some encouragement to run for office from his father, who was now living in Utica. Shortly before moving in 1857, William Kernan declined a nomination to run for state senator from Tyrone. He had a small handbill printed to spread the word to the electors of that district, saying, "I have reached that age when I am admonished to relinquish the active duties of political life, at least those required of a candidate for office." William's son, however, was at a perfect age.

Francis Kernan might have also been spurred by the election of his former student Roscoe Conkling, who in 1858 at the age of only 28 was elected Republican mayor of Utica. For years he and Roscoe Conkling had been rivals at the bar, where Conkling's ability to badger witnesses and move juries to tears was legendary. His style of magnificent thundering was exactly the opposite of Kernan's. By the end of his mayoral term, Conkling was elected to the U.S. House of Representatives, making him in 1859 the youngest man in Congress.

Kernan's increased involvement in politics was clearly inspired by a personal determination to help prevent calamity. In 1860 the Democratic Party split apart at its national convention, unable to nominate a ticket. Unionists and Southern sectionalists reconvened separately. The Unionists nominated Illinois Senator Stephen Douglas. The South championed Kentucky's John Breckinridge and threatened secession if Abraham Lincoln, the Republican presidential candidate from Illinois, won.

Kernan worked hard for Douglas, for the Democratic party, and against the rising passions. Party leaders sincerely felt that "the Empire State must save the Union and keep the rail-splitter out of the White House." Shortly after the divisive national conventions, Utica held an almost spontaneous mass meeting to ratify the nominations of Douglas and his vice-presidential candidate Herschel V. Johnson, former governor of Georgia. They hoped to garner the votes to fend off disaster. With little time for advance preparation, the organizers of the rally of July 24, 1860, stunned themselves with their results.* It was the largest meeting the town had ever seen. The program included a mile-long procession, banners, cannons, bands, and a large bonfire in front of Mechanic's Hall, where local luminaries Horatio Seymour, Francis Kernan, and Dr. D.P. Bissel were to speak for two and a half hours. Only a small portion of the 5,000 could cram into the hall, so a rude platform was hastily erected outside for other speakers and entertainment. Bissel had been a delegate to *both* national Democratic conventions. His mission had been to convince Democrats of the legitimacy of Douglas's nomination over Breckinridge's. Every state had been represented, he explained, even after the disgruntled delegates left. "The voice of the people is the voice of God, and should be so regarded." Leaving to address the crowd outside the hall, Bissel deferred to "far more eminent speakers," and the men shouted for Kernan and Seymour. Kernan spoke for nearly an hour. He warmed the crowd by chiding the Republican paper for what he considered a preoccupation with Douglas's religious views, noting, to the crowd's amusement, that the *Herald* was "charitable enough to say that a man may be a good citizen, *although a Papist.*" He supported Douglas's principle of "Popular Sovereignty" and disagreed with Lincoln that the Union was a house divided against itself, doomed to fall.

"The institution of slavery came here through circumstances beyond our control—and we must deal with it practically," said Kernan.[6] He warned of the men in the South "who say that Congress shall intervene to protect slavery in the Territories while similar men in the North argued that Congress should intervene with the opposite intention, and claimed the right to use physical strength." Under these circumstances, "our Union cannot exist." That is why, he explained, the Democratic party advocated the principle that "this question shall be taken from the halls of Congress and let the people decide for themselves."

He argued that "it is the very foundation of our government [that] it is the people's right to say whether they shall have slavery or not. . . . Each state must deal with it as they see fit. . . . It is their curse or blessing." Take the issue out of Congress, he said, "and the wrangling and agitation, North and South, will end." Otherwise, "our Union will crumble in dust."

Seymour then attacked the meddling policy of Republicans, who, he queried, would ask a Congress to govern the new territories when it could not even govern itself? While worrying about the territories, the state of New York had ignored its own corrupt legislature and nearly bankrupted its treasury. "There is a mock and false hypocrisy of philanthropists sighing and weeping tears over the pious African on the plantation [while they] suffer the poor blacks of our own city to rot in degradation. How we crush him beneath the heel of our prejudice, grinding him down in the dust." Seymour pointed out another hypocrisy regarding New York's

* George Quin, Kernan's brother-in-law and law partner, served on the committee on resolutions.

almost savage aversion to the Fugitive Slave Act, noting that "the states most rabid against having a slave to be taken out are the very states most determined to keep foreigners from coming in." He reiterated Kernan's point that self-rule was the foundation of the country, the reason Americans had overthrown the English crown.

The following day the *Herald* accused Kernan of playing on the religious prejudices of his Catholic listeners, but the spontaneous rally established Kernan as a popular speaker in the next few months of the spirited campaign and resulted in his own inclusion on the state ticket.

Stephen Douglas was the first presidential candidate to go on a national campaign tour, a journey made possible because of advances in steamboats and railways. Many people considered such overt self-promotion as unbecoming and beneath the dignity of the office. While touring New York, Douglas pretended to be en route to see his mother in Clifton Springs. Lincoln remained silent, allowing Republican leaders to run the campaign, and avoided making statements that would have alarmed the South or riled the North.

Kernan was among the dignitaries that September day in 1860 when Douglas spoke in nearby Syracuse, where approximately 40,000 people crowded into the four-acre parade grounds to hear the dynamic "steam engine in britches." Several women and children had earlier stationed themselves near the platform, with dire results, reported the *Utica Daily Observer.* "Some fainted and had to be lifted out, passed along over the heads of the packed audience. One was separated from her child and commenced shrieking until the child was lifted to the platform where she could see it was safe." Douglas was not able to begin until those men and women who could not stand the pressure had been hoisted out to the fringes. When he did begin to speak, thousands who could not see or hear him, left the field.

The editor of the *Herald* wrote that Douglas seemed worn and jaded and lacked the fire of his earlier days. "His face had a hard look—as if he had lived intensely—and suffered no common mental and physical pain within the past few months." Yet traces of the lion remained in the bold warrior. "One listens in spite of himself, and no less intensely when he doesn't believe a word of what is said."[7]

On the local circuit, Kernan spoke in New Hartford, Rome, and Floyd, while Utica's Little Giants drilled, rehearsed on their instruments, registered voters, ordered smart new uniforms, and enlisted their female relatives to sew flags and enormous banners. Kernan traveled by train, boat, and buggy to his engagements throughout the county, campaigning for popular sovereignty in the territories and noninterference in the South. He spoke at halls, churches, and ward houses to worried crowds hungry for information. At South Trenton the throng was so large he stood in the middle of the hall, rather than at the one end, so everyone could hear him shouting over the deliberately disruptive Wide-Awake procession outside. (One location where Francis would not have campaigned was nearby Madison County, an antislavery stronghold to the southwest. It was the home of Gerrit Smith, perhaps New York's largest landholder, a former congressman and a radical abolitionist who backed John Brown's raid on Harpers Ferry.[*]

On September 19, 1860, Kernan was unanimously nominated to run for the U.S. House of Representatives against Roscoe Conkling. It was not a great offer. It would be nearly impossible to beat Conkling, who had established himself as the darling of his new party on his second day in Congress, when he crossed his arms and placed himself solidly in front of a furious Southern representative about to trounce a Northern representative for yet another insulting remark. Conkling may have been a "stuffed shirt," but he filled it with a muscular torso.

In a letter to the nominating convention, Kernan replied simply that "I am so situated that I should be compelled to decline." He might have more accurately replied that he was so situated as to have a far better chance of election that year to the state legislature. There, the incumbent assemblyman James McQuade had so shamed his party with outrageously corrupt behavior that even Republican voters were willing to put aside party loyalty and elect someone with a reputation for honesty. At a Democratic district convention weeks later, Kernan accepted the nomination to run for state assemblyman.[†]

In this 1860 campaign, and in all others, Kernan's major appeal was his integrity and spotless reputation. He would always run as "the people's guarantee against corruption." The worst that his opponents could find to say was that he was a firm and unyielding Democrat. "Democrats nominate no other kind—this is the gospel truth," reported the *Herald,* finding an ingenious way to get truth on the Republican side while simultaneously managing a religious reference. "Let it be remembered that Mr. Kernan is one of the leading ROMAN CATHOLICS in this city!" warned Utica's Welsh-language paper *Y Drych* (The Mirror).

The best that Republicans could say on behalf of their own candidate was that McQuade would vote Republican. Rumors had it that McQuade had won his election the previous year because men from New York City had come into town with railroad money and purchased his close victory. Once in the state legislature, McQuade pushed a bill through over the governor's veto that granted to eighteen of the state's most prominent businessmen and politicians a tax-free monopoly[‡] of

---

[*] When upon his capture a canceled check for $100 from Smith was found in Brown's pocket, a warrant was issued for Smith's arrest. His neighbors, many of them blacks to whom he had sold farms at nominal cost, stood guard at his Peterboro home to defend him against possible arrest by federal marshalls. Smith's mental health snapped under the pressure of the moment, and he was committed temporarily to the New York State Lunatic Asylum at Utica, an institution that Kernan had supported with his philanthropy. Smith initially found Lincoln far too moderate for his tastes, and upon recovery from his breakdown, he ran against him in 1860. Although Smith did not receive many votes, Stephen A. Douglas did not get many votes from Madison County, either.

[†] George Quin was chairman of the First Assembly District Democratic Convention.

[‡] The monopoly was granted to 18 people: Charles W. Durant, Myron S. Clark, John Butler Jr., Henry Rigley, Orson H. Sheldon, Warren E. Russell, Robert B. Van Valkenburgh, John Myers, John De La Montaigue, William R. Stewart, James S. Leach, James S. Sluyfer, John A. Cooke, James C. Kennedy, Thomas C. Durant, Benjamin E. Bruce, Edward R. Phelps, and Augustus L. Brown.

the passenger traffic on two major railroads, through the most populous streets of New York City.

McQuade's bill was also backed by the speaker of the State Assembly, DeWitt C. Littlejohn, otherwise known as "the Grand Master of Corruption." Abuse of the public trust was a fully bipartisan affair and not unique to Albany. Governmental bodies, at all levels, all over the country, were coming under the influence of money. Newspapers and preachers and honest politicians everywhere bemoaned the loss of idealism. The lure of money had begun to distract the attention of ambitious young men who were suddenly amassing unheard-of wealth. Land values soared and trade prospered with each new public works project or private development. A legislator's salary might be a pittance, but the office provided a perfect opportunity for greedy men to serve themselves quite nicely—at the taxpayer's expense. In New York, the state tax deficit increased from $6,000 at the start of the decade to nearly $100,000 by its final year.

On the 1860 Democratic state ticket, Kernan's experience as a fiscally conservative Barnburner put him in good graces with the electorate from his First District. He earned praises from all sides for his dispassionate explanations of the legal issues facing the state and the nation, appearing in North Bay, Clayville, Holland Patent, Clinton, McConnellsville, and Oriskany. Newspapers referred to his "clear, able, fair and convincing manner," and his "calm" demeanor, or his "pleasing and convincing" argument. In these days of grand oratory, the speaker's performance was often considered more newsworthy than his words, so exactly what Kernan said in his stump speeches is not known, only that he said it "in the most logical and convincing style," or that the audiences enthusiastically applauded until dark, or that he gave "one of the best speeches in relation to this slavery question, and in favor of the people of the territory governing themselves." The most detailed review appeared in the *Utica Herald* on October 11, 1860. It noted the large number of Republicans in the crowd and said Kernan "went over the whole ground of the slavery discussion, calmly and candidly reviewing the positions of both parties and showing incontestably that the Democratic principle of referring the whole matter to the people of the territories was the only sage, constitutional, and just mode of disposing of the question and the troublesome and dangerous agitation to which it had given rise." Given the *Herald's* intensely Republican orientation, the neutrality of this review indicates Kernan's bipartisan support.

At the height of the campaign vice-presidential candidate Herschel V. Johnson appeared at a rally in Rome, where Kernan was also featured. "COME ONE! COME ALL!" proclaimed the posters. "GRAND TORCH-LIGHT PROCESSION! One hundred men on horseback with torches! A string of 33 oxen drawing a wagon on which is a BLAZING BONFIRE!"

Early on the day of the rally, participants began arriving on special trains reserved by the party with half-price fares. The rally began with smaller afternoon processions of horse-drawn wagons and brass bands greeting the speakers at the train station. Johnson stepped out of his private car to a cheering crowd and was escorted by a team of Little Giants through the town, past flags and under banners of the Stars and Stripes which had been strung across streets to proclaim "Let the People Rule" and "Non-Intervention by Congress."

Mounting the outdoor platform, Johnson told the waiting crowd that everywhere he had gone he had addressed the voters' concerns about the great peril to the nation. Republicans had accused him of creating fears of secession, he said, but national Democrats were fighting for unity, not to arouse fears. He reminded his audience of the Republican desire for "political and social equality of the negro race." And for the next hour or so he raised the specter of such "sweet-scented association"; the threat of millions of black people coming North and competing with their cheap labor; the threat of negroes voting and holding public office; and the ultimate threat: "Take notice, fathers and mothers, that your daughters . . . may be led fashionably to the marriage altar by a sweet-scented buck-nigger fellow." After the crowd's reaction of screams of laughter and cries of "that's true!" Johnson pointed to the cotton clothing worn by individuals in the crowd, the tobacco they smoked, and the sugar and rice they enjoyed. These are products of slave labor; he said; if you don't like them, "take off your shirts!" Stop eating rice or using sugar to sweeten your breakfast wheatcakes, he urged; "and the North will end slavery in ninety days!" Johnson concluded with an assessment of the monetary value of the South's slaves and asked how meekly the North would willingly submit "to being robbed of such an amount of property."*

Kernan was to speak as part of the evening program, which was given over to music and a parade. "Day-trippers" continued to stream into the train station, until the crowd was estimated at 7,500. The triumphal march halted in front of the American Hotel, where the evening speeches began. Colonel Clinton of Mississippi spoke for two hours about how the South had never infringed upon the North and now only wanted her constitutional rights. The crowd was so large that another platform was put up near the post office, where Kernan spoke for nearly an hour. But it was almost midnight, and this was not the age of soundbites. Holding his pad under a torchlight, the newspaper reporter finished writing his final paragraph on the day's events. Kernan spoke, he said, "in a strain of eloquence and convincing argument that we have rarely heard equaled by any man." The reporter still had to get back to Utica and file his story in time for the lead type to be set for the next day's edition.

The final Democratic rally of the 1860 campaign was held in Utica on November 2, right before the election, and Francis had the support of his younger brother, William, who helped organize the event, and of his brother-in-law and law partner, George E. Quin, who was one of the event's vice presidents. The afternoon

---

* Southern politicians played upon white fears of what would happen to all the emancipated slaves. Even Lincoln at that time shared the fantasy of The American Colonization Society that freed negroes could be shipped to Liberia.

before the rally, contingents of men on horseback gathered from surrounding towns, despite the strong winds and a threatening storm. They rode toward Utica wearing sashes with "KERNAN" in large letters. Francis was one of the few candidates on the state ticket with a good chance of winning, and major party leaders joined in this last effort to inspire a Democratic victory.

By the next afternoon thousands of men, women, and children lined the principal avenues, or sat on porches or roofs to get a good view. It was the largest crowd that had ever gathered outside of New York City. The weather lifted into a superb fall day, and the sun shone brightly on the 40-square foot platform, where the Utica Band roused the audience into a holiday mood. At half-past two, the crowd was estimated at nearly 25,000, and stretched far into all the surrounding streets. The speakers included men from the South, flanked by former governor Seymour and Kernan.

Seymour could barely speak, his voice so sore from months of rallies, but he stirred his audience's hearts with an invocation of George Washington and raised them to merriment with a joke about the senseless agitation over slavery in the South. It was like "the telescope man," he said, "who gave you an opportunity to view the moon, and while your mind and eyes were so absorbed with the far distant orb, you didn't notice your pockets were being picked! Seymour also said that his Southern visitors, having heard of Republican philanthropy, had expected to find that every negro owned a house and lot and was happy and industrious. "I did not tell them of Post Street, and you know why!" And judging from the crowd's laughter, they knew well the sorry living conditions of Utica's African American population.

E.C. Marshall of Kentucky followed. He spoke for an hour, deriding Lincoln as a liar and abolitionist and concluding "all the curse of slavery rests on the South. The North enjoys its advantages but don't suffer from it. The North substantially owns the negroes, and the Southerners are only overseers, and are badly treated at that!"

Speeches went on into the evening, and as late as the hour was, the crowd called loudly for Kernan. By then the torches had burned low. Said the *Observer* editor, "He could not have been recognized, save by his voice, a few feet from the stand. Yet there were thousands still present, and they listened with delight to one of the best speeches which our gifted fellow townsman ever made. As an outdoor orator, Mr. Kernan is excelled in no respect by any man we have ever heard. His clarion voice rang out on the evening air so clear and loud that every word was distinctly audible in every corner of the Square." However, the report concludes, it was too dark to take any more notes, so exactly what Kernan said so clearly is—once again—not recorded.

Even in the Republican landslide that followed, Kernan won his assembly seat by 200 votes. (Conkling had an even larger majority than Lincoln and kept his seat in the U.S. House of Representatives.) In New York, Republicans now had a majority in the assembly of 93 to 35 Democrats, and in the Senate of 23 to 9. The election by no means ousted corruptionist influences from the legislature, where Littlejohn won reelection but where state concerns would soon give way to the nation's conflagration.

Despite the election of so many Republicans to office, the landslide had an ominous feature. Lincoln won with only 40 percent of the popular vote, and did not receive a single electoral vote from the South, whose leaders had vowed to secede if he were elected. Francis would soon be one of the thousands of citizens frantically trying to keep united this "sovereign union of sovereign states."

The North Must Talk Something Other Than War

*We shall hold that man to be as much a traitor
who urges our government to overstep its constitutional powers,
as he who resists the exercise of its rightful authority.*
FRANCIS KERNAN, 1861

MOST OF THE state legislators settled into boarding houses in Albany for the three-and-a-half-month legislative session. The trip from Utica now took only one day, and because of the invention of gas-powered headlamps, the trains ran even at night. This was the first time Kernan had lived in separate quarters from his close-knit family. Perhaps he set out the photograph of Hannah and their sons. Perhaps he set out the two-sentence letter from his father, reminding Francis why he was there. It is the only letter from William Kernan that has survived—a letter any son would cherish.

> Dear Francis,
>
> I am highly gratified at your patriotism and disinterested self-sacrificing spirit which prompts you to accept the nomination of Assemblyman. I hope you will get a handsome role and drive the corruptionist scoundrels so far out of sight that they never hold up their heads again.

Whatever the worthy or corrupt ambitions of the 128 representatives answering the roll call along with Francis at the statehouse on January 2, 1861, few could concentrate on the business of the state when South Carolina had just declared its independence! In a special Christmas session, that state's legislators voted to secede from the Union and denounced the North for "its erroneous religious belief that the institution of Slavery [is] sinful." The extreme action horrified most New Yorkers, who blamed the frothing madness of abolitionists as much as the insane provocations of Southern secessionists.

Over the next few weeks individual citizens in both the North and the South would make noble efforts to stop the landslide of secession. But on that cold morning in Albany, the first order of business for the representatives assembled was to elect their Speaker. The minority nominated Francis Kernan and the majority renominated the sitting speaker, DeWitt C. Littlejohn, the Oswego Republican also known as the "Grand Master of Corruption."* That Kernan was nominated for the top position on his first day in the Assembly indicates the high regard in which he was held by his fellow Democrats. Since they had no chance of winning, their choice of Kernan for speaker represented a purely symbolic statement. For the first time—though not for the last—his party placed Kernan's name in nomination as the personification of integrity. Littlejohn won by a straight party-line vote of 90 to 31, and after the count, Kernan escorted him to the Speaker's chair and took his own assigned seat, number 91, as minority leader.†

The assembly then heard the annual message from Governor Edwin Morgan. He outlined the state's economic condition and presented the main issues before the legislature. The message began with an apt warning against the great corrupting evil of special-interest and class-based legislation and concluded with the topic foremost in everyone's mind: secession. Morgan blamed the South for its continuing expansionist pressure to bring slavery into the territories. The South had forced the North to support federal intervention, he said. Morgan accused "a few inconsiderate Northern agitators" for their aggression, "which understandably caused the South to retaliate." His statements reflected the attitudes of most New Yorkers that winter. The governor pleaded for both sides to step back and work out a compromise. Though he advised moderation and conciliation, he offered no solution other than to keep looking for one.

Just the week before, on December 26, 1860, Major Robert Anderson moved his federal garrison under cover of darkness from an indefensible position in Charleston harbor to the well-protected Fort Sumter. There, Anderson held firm

---

* DeWitt C. Littlejohn sued Horace Greeley, editor of the *New York Tribune,* for libel in September of 1861. The case was dismissed because the jury disagreed—nine were for the defendant, two for nominal damages, and one for heavy damages.

† Kernan voted for George Varian of New York County's Fifteenth District.

and waited for reinforcement from Washington. To show support for the Union and express their outrage over South Carolina's rebellion, New York's legislators debated a joint resolution to present Major Anderson an inscribed ceremonial sword "for his bold patriotism" in preventing the seizure of Fort Sumter.

Kernan proposed a less inflammatory resolution. He did not want to introduce a sword, even a ceremonial one, into the tense situation between the two sections of the Union. He believed that war might yet be prevented. Strong moderate elements existed in the South, and many Northerners felt that the South should be allowed to secede in peace. Kernan defended his resolution on the grounds that he "hesitated to say or do anything to increase the excitement existing in the Union, or anything that would seem unkind to those who are unhappily estranged from us at this time. . . . Let us rather do all we can to allay the excitement rather than perform an act that, even under mistaken views, may be misinterpreted into a desire to irritate and gall our erring fellow-countrymen."

Replacing the defiant language of the New York legislature's initial proposed resolution, Kernan's version used language to match that of the U.S. House of Representatives' resolution "approving the Major's bold and patriotic act" and "supporting the President in all Constitutional measures to enforce the laws and preserve the Union." Kernan also included in his resolution an offer to President Lincoln of "whatever aid in men and money from New York necessary to uphold the Federal government's authority." His firm but calm language was in marked contrast to the inflammatory rhetoric of the Albany legislators' debate. A prominent Republican, Lucius Robinson, finally brought the arguments to a close, recommending the assembly present Major Anderson a medal instead of a sword. The whole subject was tabled by a voice vote, as the majority of both parties apparently wanted to halt the escalating rhetoric.

As the Cotton States rapidly followed South Carolina's lead, federal and state legislatures everywhere worked frantically to devise any compromise that would convince their seceding brothers to return. Kernan, attempting to keep communications open with the South, successfully argued against a suggestion that the Assembly return to the sender a series of hostile messages delivered to New York and other Northern legislative bodies: Alabama announced her secession; Tennessee resolved to resist any Northern invasion to the last extremity, and Georgia approved their governor's troops' taking possession of Fort Pulaski.

Not having jurisdiction in national events, the assemblymen debated proposals that attempted to silence the hated Northern agitators in New York State and to stop what they described as their provocative and illegal antislavery activities. The Assembly and the Senate met in joint committees to hammer out a recommendation called the Compromise Resolution, which might settle the nation's crisis.

They worked against time and rising passions to find a settlement at the ballot box rather than on the battlefield. Kernan served on the Special Committee on Foreign Relations, chaired by Lucius Robinson and including moderates of both parties.* The committee's responsibility was to define New York's position in the present crisis.

On the federal level, President Lincoln's advisers urged all states to comply with the Fugitive Slave Act, which required that captured slaves be returned. Although the law was generally hated in the North, better compliance might mollify the South and offer support to those Southerners who wanted to stay in the Union. Kernan sat on the Joint Judiciary Committee that immediately began examining all the state's personal liberty laws. These state laws had been passed in reaction to the federal law as a way of safeguarding free men in New York from being surrendered as slaves, and were often used to resist or even flout the federal law, much to the fury of Southern slaveholders. The federal act denied the Constitutional guarantee of the writ of *habeas corpus* (to runaway slaves or those accused)—the same Constitutional guarantee that Kernan and his fellow Democrats defended so vocally against Lincoln's disregard of this right (for white men) as the war progressed. Still, although no record of Kernan's stance on this issue in committee has been uncovered, it seems likely that he supported the weakening or repeal of the state laws as a gesture of good faith to the seceding Southern states.

On January 18 the Special Committee on Foreign Relations presented a report known as "The Robinson Resolution" that denied the right of secession, insisting that the government and Union be sustained and that all her power, both moral and physical, be exerted to uphold the law and prevent revolution and anarchy.

Although the report was celebrated by both parties and by the press as a potential solution to armed hostilities, it never came to a vote by the full Assembly. A secret caucus of the more zealous Republicans opposed any concession or conciliation toward the South, and bound its members to refuse to speak or even to give their reasons for withholding their support for the compromise resolutions.

The next day Kernan passionately addressed fellow assemblymen. He was incredulous that they "would forego any attempt to address the national crisis, and, in the eyes of the world, now, in this emergency, follow the behests of a [partisan] caucus, rather than the dictates of patriotism and duty."[1] Rather than looking back to blame those who had caused the crisis, Kernan directed the legislators to look to ending the present danger. "Five states have already left the Union, and men are actively urging the formation of a Southern Confederacy. One of three things [will] happen: compromise, war, or a peaceful splitting of the country in two. The Union must not be torn asunder . . . yet [does] anyone believe that coercion [can] prevent dissolution?" He doubted the North's chances for victory "over men who would be fighting to defend their own hearthstones. Even if we could subdue

---

* Republican members also included Frothingham Fish, Wilkes Angkill, and S. Chandler Bull. The Democrats were Kernan and M.C. Dermott.

them, who would desire to see South Carolina desolated by war? Before blood was shed, a resolution must be found and the North must talk something other than war." These Southern states were associates and brothers, he reminded the gentlemen of the Assembly, who, he said, "had not been elected by constituents in favor of concession and conciliation to raise a war cry."

His speech was widely reported and admired. New Yorkers in general were not yet inclined toward war. A mammoth national petition of 38,000 voters urging compromise was presented to the U.S. Senate on January 31. The next day more than 100 bipartisan political leaders, including Kernan, sat on a dais in Utica at a peace meeting called by Horatio Seymour supporting the Robinson Resolutions, and urging Congress to find a peaceful settlement. Seymour asked New Yorkers to "consider which was the greater revolution: Northern coercion or Southern secession?"[2]

Seymour's formulation accurately captured the dilemma facing dedicated Democrats. They staunchly believed that the Union consisted of a confederacy of sovereign states. While secession meant an end to the Union, would not keeping the states together by force of arms put an end to such a voluntary union just as surely? The caucus officially agreed that "Civil war will not restore the Union."

Yet even while Democrats implored Congress to hold the nation together, their own party was splitting into three main camps: those who would agree to restore the Union, preferably by compromise, but by force if needed; those who would bend over backward to compromise; and those who fully sympathized with the seceding South. Kernan himself passionately urged compromise, but—and this is the defining issue—he insisted upon Union.

As the crisis advanced, Kernan held out for compromise while supporting the government's stance against the rebels. He did vote against one appropriation bill for $500,000 for arming the militia, but his motive was not, as his critics charged, to help the secessionists, but to fight corruption. He called the bill "a mischievous measure, too small for war, and too much for peace," and one that only benefited the contractors.*

In Washington, lame-duck President Buchanan fretted, prayed, and stalled as Lincoln's train wound slowly toward Washington. The president-elect had scheduled a 12-day circuitous route from his hometown of Springfield, Illinois, to introduce himself to the electorate and to garner support for his impossible new job. On the trip of almost 2,000 miles, he passed crowds of delighted, curious, disappointed, frightened, and angry voters. He made no major speeches or policy statements, but repeatedly stressed that he had been elected to uphold the law and the Constitution.

The train stopped in Albany on February 19, 1861. This was likely Kernan's first introduction to Lincoln, who was still not a nationally known figure. According to the press account,[3] Lincoln's entourage arrived a bit shaken from an incident in

---

* The bill was passed but never carried into effect, being superseded by war and more appropriate legislation.

Schenectady. As the train had approached that earlier station "a cannon was recklessly fired point blank at the first coach of the train, the concussion bursting in the door, tearing the lock, and breaking to atoms three windows. Several people were covered with broken glass but no one was injured." Arriving soon after in Albany, ten minutes ahead of schedule, Lincoln's entourage found equally lax security. "Mr. Lincoln had to wait in his car for the military escort to arrive while the curious, shivering crowd demanded 'come out, and show yourself.'" Once the escort was in place, the mayor gave a welcoming speech to which Lincoln responded briefly. The party went on to the capitol to meet Governor Morgan, who escorted everyone to the statehouse steps. There he introduced the president-elect to a cheering crowd. The Illinois country lawyer "used less common language" than the sophisticated crowd expected in his short speech before entering the Assembly, where both branches of the legislature were formally gathered to receive him. Another reception later that night at the Delevan Hotel was "crowded to suffocation."

Thus far into its term, the 87th New York State Assembly had spent much more time debating national affairs than tending to the business of the state, and not everyone was happy. Even Utica's Republican paper demanded more than "a dull monotony of stupid harping in exchange for the representatives' three-dollars per diem."[4] The main business of the state legislature, after all, was to vote on taxes and appropriations of money. Kernan had only to glance at his father's letter to remember why he was there and the work before him in fighting the high level of corruption in the state government.

The problem was in part due to the state's faulty constitution, drafted by the Barnburners in 1846. Its framers had believed in Jacksonian democracy, which deeply distrusted centralized authority. They had designed the constitution to prevent any official from wielding too much control. Unfortunately, they overreached their goal. They took the control from those who legitimately needed it to run their cities and gave it to legislators in Albany, men who were accountable only to their own districts and to themselves. The document had become an invitation to plunder. As a lawyer, Kernan had practiced under its law, and now, in Albany, he could see just how easily legislators could be manipulated, corrupted, or simply deceived. The constitutional framers had created a document based on their agrarian experience, but by 1861 the land was not just being farmed; it was being flattened by roads, mined for metals, gouged with canals, and overlaid with bridges, roads, and rails to spur ever more development. Industries were growing faster than the laws regulating them or regulating the banks. Here was booty aplenty. It was much easier to buy a few votes in Albany than to convince an entire electorate to lay sewers along a city block just purchased for speculation. Political power translated into state contracts and jobs. Everyone looked to Albany.

State assemblymen determined city tax rates, borrowing powers, salaries, building rules, welfare expenditures, and much more. Individual legislators presented measures for the benefit—or the looting—of their home districts. Their explanations would be the only information on which the other legislators would decide their votes. They had to trust one another or the committees' recommendations, or just vote along party lines. A few strongly committed men could easily form a coalition, enabling a few corrupt legislators to get free license to loot state or hometown coffers. Albany had more than a few of these "corruptionists," and party affiliation was no barrier. Citizens had to live with the results of Albany's decisions. No local officials seemed to be in charge whom voters could petition, blame, or cast out of office.

Kernan's method of fighting corruption demonstrated his deep belief in the power of law and reason over passion. He never attacked the personal motives of bill sponsors, although he managed to kill many "plunderbund" jobs by swiftly showing that the legislature could not legally make the appropriations asked. Notwithstanding his respectful behavior, however, Kernan was making enemies he would have to face after the horror of the battlefields could no longer distract the public eye from the outrageous abuse of public money.

Against his votes, the state legislature passed several bills that helped pry open New York City's coffers to a small clique, the "Board of Supervisors." In 1861, Kernan resisted a bill authorizing the supervisors to levy taxes, regulate its expenditure, borrow money against taxes owed, and issue bonds. By 1871 this group would be infamous for "the most spectacular bit of looting ever perpetrated against an American city,"[5] and Kernan would be one of the men to help topple it.

For the rest of the short, turbulent legislative session Kernan focused on three issues: he resisted war measures, he opposed corruption, and he pressed for judicial reform. The state constitution, with its system of electing judges, had inadvertently reduced the state's judiciary to a level of incompetence.[6] To be sure, law was a young profession and had few precedents in this land of experimentation. Technical errors were common between lawyers and judges who were still developing professional and ethical standards. The judiciary was subject to partisan control—judges were elected for short terms by popular vote. Turnover was so frequent that judges often were selected less for their ability than their availability. Court of Appeals judges, for example, served on a one-year rotating basis. Judicial inexperience and annual turnover created backlogs and confusion.

The Assembly's judiciary committee drafted constitutional amendments to alleviate some of these problems. In his capacity as a committee member, Kernan began a 20-year effort to reform the government through constitutional change. One of the committee's proposals would increase the number of Appeals Court judges and gradually increase their terms to 12 years, with broadly overlapping terms. Other proposals, aimed at preventing political influence and payoffs, dealt with larger forums and stabilized salaries. But almost all these proposals, like other state business, would have to wait.

In April, President Lincoln dispatched the supply ship *Star of the West* with food and supplies to Fort Sumter, where Major Anderson was planning on surrendering to South Carolina when the last of his food was depleted. Although there were no arms on board, impatient South Carolina staff officers took it upon themselves to open fire on the fort on the morning of April 12. The episode electrified the nation and solidified Northern public opinion against the South. For Kernan the event made him a full supporter of the Union, in favor of putting down the rebellions with whatever arms were necessary. This was the stance he would maintain throughout the war.

Three days later the state legislature adjourned and Kernan returned home to help raise volunteers. The war had begun. Lincoln had a clear mandate to save the Union. Even the leading Democrat, Stephen Douglas, agreed the rebellion had to be put down. Four more states soon joined the Confederacy, and with Maryland wavering, the situation threatened the safety of Washington, D.C., and impressed everyone with a sense of urgency. Lincoln's immediate response convinced Democrats that the new president meant to prosecute the war with little interference from Congress and with little regard for constitutional niceties. His independent and sometimes extraconstitutional behavior would infuriate Democrats in the years to come, and it infuriated many in the congressional wing of his own party who wanted Congress to have the power. In the spring of 1861, Lincoln did not wait for Congress to reconvene before extending the time of military service, expanding the size of the army, and purchasing steamships for the navy. He simply authorized the Treasury Department to advance $2 million to a New York committee headed by John A. Dix to pay "such requisition as should be directly consequent upon the military and naval measures necessary for the defense and support of the government." In essence, Lincoln had entrusted public funds to a private person.

We can surmise some of the attitudes in the Kernan family from a letter dated August 11, 1861. Mary D. Devereux writes of her daughter-in-law's visit. "To Ellen [Devereux] the visit was one of great comfort. Her secession friends in Baltimore are so highly excited it was a relief to find those she loved at the North, full of hope for the future without anger against the South. . . . Mr. Newberry stopt over and sp[e]nt part of a day with us. He was very patriotic and was willing to give all his property to preserve the Union."

Initially New Yorkers rallied in support of the Union. But the patriotism was a shallow, emotional response to Fort Sumter. The first Battle at Bull Run was a bitter disaster for the Union and one-third of its casualties were from New York. Citizens debated two points of view: the Union must be preserved, and the South has a perfect right to declare its independence. One might agree with both positions one at a time, but the two positions could not coexist. The final choice determined one's side in the war.

Kernan chose Union, which made him a War Democrat, though hawkish Republicans would prefer the term Copperhead, meaning a treacherous Democrat who pretended support but demanded compromise and could strike against the Union.

By the fall of 1861, Kernan was a rising star in his party, and was named temporary chairman of the state Democratic convention held in Syracuse that September. It was an off year for elections; only minor state offices were at stake, but the state convention provided an arena to debate the nation's concerns. New York was the most influential of all the Union states, and the national party watched carefully for New York's lead. Kernan's passionate keynote address in the convention hall outlined the position that the War Democracy of the whole country was to occupy. He declared it to be "the duty of the party to oppose equally abolitionism at the north and secession at the south, to protect and to preserve the government, but not to let it be a war for the emancipation of slaves."[7] The *New York Tribune* carried the full text of his speech:[8]

Gentlemen of the Convention—I tender you my thanks for the compliment you have conferred upon me in selecting me to preside temporarily over your actions and deliberations. I could have wished, indeed, that I could have congratulated you on this occasion on the present condition, or even on the future prospects of our country. But it is a saddening truth that our country, its government, its people, and the institutions under which we have so long prosperously lived, are threatened by dangers such as never before surrounded them—not even in the days when our fathers rose up against oppression and vindicated their right to independence. Ah! we could, if a united people, rise up and meet the whole world in arms in a righteous cause. But bitter dissensions have arisen, and deadly enmity has been excited by one section against another, until it has culminated in civil war.

We have before our eyes the saddening spectacle of sons of men who were, but a few years since, banded together in defense of their liberties and their lives, engaged in fratricidal strife and shedding each other's blood. Such a spectacle must fill the breast of every good man with sorrow and alarm. But, gentlemen, it is our duty, if we are worthy of our fathers and of the institutions bequeathed to us by them, to meet these great dangers firmly and wisely, if we can, and to seek by all the means in our power to stay the ruin that seems impending over our beloved country. It is our duty to this end, to oppose abolitionism at the North and secessionism at the South, which are equally making war on our Government and threatening to overthrow our institutions, and I exhort you, (speaking from my heart,) let us as men and patriots, so far as in us lies, endeavor to consign them both to a common grave. Never will our country see peace unless we do so. The abolitionists of the North, through the ballot box, are seeking to obtain power which is as destructive as death to the institutions under which we live. [Loud Applause.] Let us by the unanimity and the patriotism of our action, show to the world that we are ready at this time to take a position which shall effectively put down abolitionism at the ballot box. Secession at the South, instigated by comparatively few men, has availed itself of this excitement against Northern abolitionists, array a host with arms in their hands, beleaguering the Capitol of the Nation, and seeking to overthrow the government. We care not what men are in charge of the government, it is our duty as patriots and Democrats, to protect and preserve that government and resist with arms and if need be, our lives, the men who seek to overthrow it. We will say to everybody, at home and abroad, that this must be no war for the emancipation of slaves, but a war for the preservation of the government and of the rights of all sections of the union. The Democracy will stand up against all comers in support of the Government, and the Constitution. Its history in the past established this fact, but I believe the time has come when the position of a great party must be decisively taken for no negative policy can preserve the country from destruction at this crisis.

It is true that, unhappily for the country, we have not the power at this time to administer the Government; but we can clearly, boldly and firmly mark out the decisive course of action, which we propose in order to rescue the country from the dangers that surround it.

In making these brief remarks, I have desired so far as in me exists the power to evoke a spirit worthy of the crisis in which we meet together. The time and the circumstances that surround us may well lead to conflicting views in relation to the wisest policy to be pursued, but let us in temperate and moderate discussion, compare these views so that we may arrive at the wisest and most patriotic conclusion. Let it not be said that when the government is threatened with destruction, and our institutions are crumbling around us, we deserve the scorn and contempt that have ever been felt for the Jews of old, who, when an army surrounded their capital with the design of destroying their government and blotting it from the face of the earth, wasted their energies, not against the common foe, but in warring with each other until their institutions went down in ruins. If the destruction of our beloved country must come, let it at least be said that we gathered together like a band of brothers, and took counsel like patriots and laid down a line of policy so wise, so far lasting, so patriotic, that all men should, if they do not, join us in carrying it out for the preservation of the country. We can at least give a tone to this war, so that it may be said that it was a war to uphold the Constitution, to preserve the government, to give every section of the country their just rights under the Constitution, and so that it may be known that we have fought to put down this rebellion from love to our whole country, and not from hate to our brethren from the South, and that we are ready to proclaim that as soon as this armed rebellion is over, we are prepared to meet the South again in a liberal spirit and to guarantee full constitutional rights to all.

We only prosecute this war, in a word, in order that we may have peace under the Constitution, and preserve the country from Northern Abolitionism and Southern Secession. Let us then adopt here such a policy and display such a concert of action and such harmony, that the country will gather hope and confidence, and will look to us to lead the states through danger that surrounds them, and restore peace to the Union.

To a modern reader, it seems incomprehensible to equate abolition and secession as equal evils! To most 19th-century Democrats, however, each meant the same thing: the end of the Union. This was true for a number of related reasons. First, Democrats understood that the Southern economic investment in slavery was far too great for them to abandon it unless defeated utterly. Second, Democrats viewed the superiority of the white man over the black as the essential guarantor of white equality, convinced that the emancipation of blacks would reduce whites to their level, both economically and socially, setting them on a race to the bottom with wealthy eastern oligarchs the only victors. Finally, Democrats viewed the crisis over slavery as a tragic distraction of the nation from its true potential and its rightful destiny: to "rise up and meet the whole world in arms in a righteous cause." Two generations of rationalizations and evasions had blurred many Americans' ability to see the bitter irony of seeking to impose their "righteousness" upon the world, when slavery and the poisonous effort to excuse it had so largely vitiated the high moral purpose proclaimed by the Declaration of Independence. Like most of his fellow Americans, Republicans as well as Democrats, Kernan never conceived that blacks could be entitled to equal rights within the Union; for one thing, if they were, it would make the enormity of slavery too great to bear. With its higher purposes obscured, America itself became the vessel of patriotic affection, rather than the principles on which it had been founded. Significantly, Kernan seems almost wistfully to welcome a foreign foe, as a means to restore the nation's shattered unity. The link here to the Democracy's ardent embrace of racism is perhaps the impulse to define Americans by who and what they are not, rather than the more controversial and divisive problem of what they are.

The eloquent vigor of Kernan's speech was magnified by its contrast to the tired tone of the elderly permanent president of the convention, Herman J. Redfield.[9] Kernan's passionate arguments inspired the New York delegates, who had been expecting yet another loss at the polls. He next roused the delegates in the fight over the platform. The issue was whether to support Lincoln's illegal suspension of the writ of *habeas corpus* and other curbs on freedom, such as free discussion in the press. On April 27, 1861, Lincoln had suspended the privilege of the writ of *habeas corpus*. Accordingly, military authorities could make summary arrests of persons they thought to be aiding the Confederacy or attempting to overthrow the government. Men could be detained indefinitely without judicial hearing and without indictment, and the arresting officer was not obliged to release them when a judge issued a writ of habeas corpus.

Because of Lincoln's action, one reporter had not made it to the convention. While boarding the cars of the Hudson River Railroad en route to Syracuse, Henry

Reeve, the Democratic editor of *The Republican* of Green Point, L.I., was arrested for treason and sent to Fort Lafayette.*

Kernan resented such illegal and arbitrary arrests, particularly in a state not yet engaged in actual hostilities and where the courts were open for the regular administration of justice. When a delegate argued in support of Lincoln's war methods, Kernan rose to object. With a few ringing sentences, he threw the delegates into wild cheering:

> Let us not forget that these guarantees of freedom are not alone for peace or war. [Cheers.] All government is established among men to protect civil liberty and individual rights. [Cheers.] . . . no executive should come into New York, into a State not in insurrection, into a peaceful State, and at night seize the person of any individual and put him in prison; that we should not have simply a censorship of the press prescribing by known rules what should not be printed, but that the press should be seized or its usefulness and circulation destroyed altogether. [Cheers.] We will go as far as freemen ought to go, but we protest that upon mere suspicion or secret information, without known charges, without trial, or open proof, any officer should invade my house by day or at midnight, and take me to prison, or that on the information of an enemy, a telegram should be sent forward to put down a press and trample down the rights of property.... [Cheers.] Even in the revolutionary war and amid the great dangers of that fearful unequal war, the people, through their representatives told the immortal Washington, that not even he, except in the camp or military lines, should put a man in prison without the authority of law. We owe it to ourselves, to freedom, to the most sacred guarantee of popular rights as established in all civilized lands, to the liberty of every citizen and of our own prosperity to protest against and rebuke those usurpations against common rights. [Cheers.][10]

In this speech, Kernan eloquently illustrated the noblest tradition of the "negative liberty" championed by the antebellum Democratic party. Immediately after his address the delegates enthusiastically adopted the platform. The next order of business was to name the slate for a series of state offices for the fall election. Kernan, now the champion of the convention, was unanimously nominated for the office of attorney general. Scott Lord placed his name in nomination, declaring "Kernan's words of wisdom and of fire . . . had awakened them to a sense of the right."

Kernan had no time between his nomination and the unanimous acclamation to protest. But even before the cheers subsided, he firmly declined, citing his "pri-

* According to the *New York Tribune*, September 4, 1861, someone had sent the local marshal copies of the publication, asking whether the U.S. Government ought not to arrest the editor. This correspondence was sent on to Washington and the marshal received an order back to arrest, though no charges were stated.

vate business as an insurmountable barrier to accepting the nomination under any circumstances." If they would insist on using his name, he said, he "should be compelled to decline through the press, and therefore begged the convention to accept his declination now, and to allow him to nominate Lyman Tremain of Albany."[11]

Not everyone who had participated left happy. Some of the speeches sympathetic to the South sounded uncomfortably close to encouragement of armed rebellion, and other delegates agreed with the need to restrict the press. Even some Democratic party papers denounced the convention's resistance to Lincoln's war methods as animated by a malignant and traitorous spirit.

Kernan's refusal to be placed on the state ticket had been prudent. A week later all the work of the convention began to unravel. Its nominees soon declined to run or repudiated the platform. The main reason for the nominees' embarrassment was that they suddenly found themselves running not against Republicans, but against a slate of War Democrats! The "Union" slate had been jointly named at the Republican state convention and at the so-called "People's Convention," which consisted of dissatisfied Democratic party members.

Though all knew the regular Democratic slate was hopeless, Kernan campaigned energetically. His speeches supported the war, states' rights, and individual liberties (though not those of slaves). His anger against Lincoln is apparent in a wartime speech he made in Utica. "We shall hold that man to be as much a traitor who urges our government to overstep its constitutional powers, as he who resists the exercise of its rightful authority," he said, contending that "the rights of the States and the General Government are equally sacred."[12]

For Kernan, law was a hallowed trust that was his duty to maintain. His beliefs are evident in a toast on the occasion of the first annual dinner meeting of the Oneida County Bar Association.[13] After the dinner the distinguished company took turns raising their glasses in toast. Horatio Seymour toasted the legal profession, others toasted law and order, the Constitution, and the progress of reform. One credited the recent legislative session for all the mischief they had not done. "To Lawyers:" pledged Kernan, "Imbued with the learning of their profession, actuated by the purity of motive which becomes those who minister in the temple of justice, and rendered firm by a sense of duty which looks not to self and is not measured by gain, they form a bar behind which innocence is safe, and against which the tide of fraud and corruption, prejudice and power rolls in vain."

Kernan was not alone in his dismay over Lincoln's arbitrary acts, and his judgment would eventually be sustained by the Supreme Court in 1866. But this was 1861, and wars begin when law breaks down.

$\mathcal{W}$ar

For Francis Kernan the year 1862 began with a ceremony for a hometown war hero, a Colonel Mullitan, who had arrived in Utica fresh from the Battle of Lexington in Missouri and was touring the lyceum circuit with his account of that defeat and reports of skirmishes in the Virginia peninsula. The public was hungry for news and explanations. Instead of the predicted early and easy victory over the South, there were growing numbers of wounded and dead. The Treasury was bleeding and more states talked of seceding. Gen. George B. McClellan, the man in charge of all the armies, was lying in bed in Washington with typhoid fever.

A quasi-military procession escorted the Colonel from the Utica train station to Bagg's Hotel, where he was met by the sleigh of ex-assemblymen Francis Kernan and James McQuade. This was the same McQuade whom Kernan had unseated the previous year, but now both had reason, personal and political, to be together, blanketed against the cold January wind.

On a personal level, McQuade's parents and Kernan's mother-in-law were close friends with Colonel Mullitan's mother. Both families hosted the Colonel during his three-day stay. On a political level, the Democratic Party suffered constant accusations of disloyalty to the Union, and needed to display bipartisan support whenever possible.

The colonel must have been a convincing speaker, for his influence on Kernan and other leading Democrats would continue throughout the war. Following his tour, the state's Democratic newspapers switched from criticism of General McClellan, whose army in Virginia was making suspiciously little headway, to blind support. Colonel Mullitan passionately blamed Washington politicians for the defeat at Lexington (as had McClellan), although it would have required little to persuade Democrats that meddling Republican politicians were to blame for just about everything. Many Democrats also agreed with McClellan's view that slaves were civilian property that, like all such property, should not be touched by the armies.

Radical Republicans were daily becoming more adamant that this was a rebellion of slaveholders and that Lincoln must attack the issue of slavery head-on, even if it meant destroying the social fabric and economic basis of the South. The president listened carefully, but resisted demands for emancipation. Although he was personally against slavery, his objective was to restore the South to the Union, not destroy it. Besides, the border states still maintained slavery, and he could not afford to alienate them.

Although Republicans denounced slavery, few actually called for the racial equality suggested by only the most extreme abolitionists. By 1860 one out of seven Americans (not including Native Americans) was a slave, and the North deeply feared it would soon be sharing the "Burden of the South"—a code term meaning a huge black population.

One of Lincoln's early attempts to resolve the financial issue of slave ownership was to ask Congress to adopt a resolution obliging the federal government to compensate with money those states that voluntarily adopted policies to gradually abolish slavery. No state was interested in the offer.

In May, Congress forced Lincoln's hand by passing a bill calling for the confiscation of all property of any rebel. Because slaves were considered property, Congress had, in effect, finally ruled on slavery. The Confiscation Act included any officeholder, from the president of the Confederacy, Jefferson Davis, to minor state officers, and included private citizens, North or South, who were aiding the rebellion. There was no clear provision defining exactly what constituted "aiding the rebellion." It was an extreme, unprecedented war measure.

Republican congressmen succeeded in their real intention, which was to push Lincoln into action and defy McClellan's sympathies toward slavery. However, the bill also had the effect of energizing the Democrats and giving them a solid campaign issue against confiscation of citizen's properties. Before the act could take effect, Lincoln secretly began drafting the Emancipation Proclamation and began exercising his role as commander-in-chief. He could hardly do worse than his generals. He had already reduced McClellan's duties to Commander of the Army of the Potomac, and now the Capitol was in danger.

Lincoln requested another $400,000 and 400,000 more men. An impatient, critical Congress voted him $500,000 and 500,000 men, and passed a second Confiscation Act. This one had even more clout.

Had Kernan and other War Democrats known what document Lincoln was so carefully composing, they undoubtedly would not have spent the summer encouraging more volunteers to enlist. Kernan worked vigorously as a private citizen and member of Governor Morgan's bipartisan war committee. Speaking at a large gathering in Steuben Park, Kernan insisted the war was not a party issue in the North, and that everyone must unite behind the president. "Disloyalty is the cause of our danger, and loyalty must be its remedy," he said. "Though we may have a private opinion that all [Lincoln's] orders are not entirely judicious . . . this is not the time for cherishing any other feeling than that of a resolute determination to crush out the rebellion at whatever cost." The armies that held the Union soldiers at bay, threatening the national capitol, "must be annihilated."[1]

The most vocal critics were from Lincoln's own party, and the most openly contemptuous were New York radicals who demanded that Lincoln recognize the conflict as a rebellion of slaveholders and attack the issue of slavery head-on. On August 20, Horace Greeley, the influential editor of the *New York Tribune,* published an impassioned editorial entitled "The Prayer of Twenty Millions," declaring his disappointment over Lincoln's policy and accusing the president of being remiss in his duty in not ending slavery. Greeley dismissed the potential reaction of the border states, saying the government "cannot afford to temporize with traitors or semi-traitors."

By 1862, Lincoln had come to believe that emancipation was a military necessity and had shown his cabinet a draft of his document, but he was waiting for a military victory to make the announcement to a more receptive public. Lincoln replied to Greeley: "If I could save the Union without freeing any slave, I would do it; and if I could save it by freeing all the slaves, I would do it; and if I could do it by freeing some and leaving others alone, I would also do that. What I do about Slavery and the colored race, I do because I believe it helps to save this Union; and what I forbear, I forbear because I do not believe it would help to save the Union."

He waited for a victory, but got another humiliating defeat. The second battle at Bull Run was as crushing as the first had been over a year earlier. Casualties were heavy in the 101st New York Regiment, known as "Conkling's Rifles." The army protecting the capital was near mutiny.

Kernan continued to support the war, though according to sources in his family, dissuaded his 18-year-old son, John, from enlisting on the grounds that "it would kill your mother." Whether the story is true or not, fewer and fewer boys in the North were interested in signing up, except those who wanted to get the enlistment money before slipping out of town. Of those who had enlisted, an estimated 30,000 were absent without leave, or had simply deserted, and were being picked up all over the country. Groups of such young men passed through Utica every day, as reported in the press. In July and August, Kernan and Roscoe Conkling, on recess from the House of Representatives, vied in court over the case of a local deserter, Charles E. Hopson. Kernan lost the case, but local sentiment for deserting soldiers was growing stronger daily. On August 28, just one week before the state Democratic convention, 180 such delinquents passed through town, being conveyed back to their regiments by the chief of police of the nearby city of Elmira.

Something had to be done to end the conflict and reunite the country. The Democratic party believed itself to be the only hope for the nation and looked to the fall elections. In New York the party knew it had enough support to regain control of the state and elect Horatio Seymour governor. The Democrats also had a good chance of regaining the congressional seat held by Roscoe Conkling, whose caustic attacks on the congressional committee that was investigating real abuses in the War Department were backfiring. Conkling was not corrupt, but he knew how important money was to the war effort, and blindly defended the War Department—even while it was knowingly issuing shoddy blankets to its soldiers and paying corrupt suppliers top dollar. By the fall of 1862 the electorate had had enough of Conkling's violent language and passionate harangues. The obvious alternative was the gracious, conciliatory Francis Kernan. He was even more popular than Seymour in Oneida County, and the Democrats needed a strong candidate in a Republican district.

The state Democratic convention met in Albany on September 11 and nominated Seymour for governor by acclamation. The platform called for preservation of the Union, deplored the war that the other side had started, and opposed the unconstitutional arrest of citizens and the violation of their inherent rights. In his acceptance speech, Seymour denounced all proposals for emancipation as making "for the butchery of women and children, for scenes of lust and rapine and of arson and murder, which would invoke the interference of civilized Europe."[2] Several weeks later the county conventions enthusiastically acclaimed Kernan as the nominee for Congress, not only from his own party, but from a coalition "Union" party. There were plenty of Oneida Republicans ready to take an active part in the campaign.[3]

Democrats' arguments spoke to receptive ears. The party had tried to avert the war; it had supported Congress's resolution that the war's purpose was solely to restore the Union and to preserve the Constitution; it was loyally supporting the laws and authorities and giving the president all the money and men needed to end the rebellion and gain an honorable peace. Many voters agreed that Republicans seemed to be giving strength to the South and distracting the North with all their dissension, and they were undermining their own administration with insubordination and corruption.

Conkling was in trouble and he knew it. He stumped the state against his brother-in-law, Seymour. In Utica he waged a personally nasty door-to-door campaign against his former teacher. While Kernan spoke of the need for conciliation at his party's nominating convention, Conkling declared at his that "I would rather see rebel cities smoke, I would rather see New Orleans the bed of a lake where fishes would swim, I would rather see the seats of treason unpeopled from the Potomac to the Gulf, than that one star should be blotted from the flag of our fathers, or one stripe torn from its azure folds."

Even the conservative Republican papers acknowledged that a change in administration was needed. The *New York Post,* which despised Democrats, conceded the faults of the Republicans' arguments defending their abuses of power. The paper did not openly endorse Kernan for Congress, but concurred that "in the present state of the country it is eminently proper and necessary the best men should be heard, and that the Administration, if it has not the ability to carry on the war, should be ruled by those whom the people may choose to send to Congress to devise new measures and infuse a more vigorous spirit."

Democrats were poised to gain ground, but several more events, in rapid succession, clinched the election. On September 17, 1862, McClellan attacked Lee at Antietam Creek in Maryland. It was the bloodiest engagement in American history, lasting only fourteen hours and killing or seriously wounding 20,000 soldiers. McClellan had only checked the Confederate army, but it was enough of a victory for Lincoln to enable him to make his bold announcement.

The news dumbfounded the Democrats. The preliminary Emancipation Proclamation gave a deadline of January 1, 1863, for any state to return to the Union or have its slaves declared forever free. Lincoln had carefully crafted the document as a military measure to strengthen the Union and weaken the South. It contained no language concerning morals or broad principles of freedom; it simply freed the slaves of the Confederate states and welcomed them into the Union army. Despite its careful wording as a military measure, the document changed the nature of the war from one of restoring the Union and defending the Constitution, to one of ending slavery.

Kernan probably first read the text of the Emancipation Proclamation in the evening edition of the *Utica Daily Observer,* September 23, 1862. The editor's exasperation reflected the sense of betrayal shared by Lincoln's Democratic supporters. Why would the president submit to abolitionist congressmen at this time? Lincoln had the support of moderates within his own party who, along with loyal Democrats, had just voluntarily raised "such an army as the world never saw before. . . . Why insult their common sense, why rebuke these supporters now? . . . To gratify the malice and the fanaticism of an insane faction is a mystery defying penetration."

A couple of days later, Lincoln took the extraordinary and unprecedented measure of suspending the writ of *habeas corpus.* Already, over 1,000 citizens had been or were still being held without trial, arrested simply by a word of the secretary of state for behavior considered supportive of rebels. New York Democrats were especially vocal, and Seymour was their most vociferous mouthpiece. He saw Lincoln becoming a military despot. The affront to civil liberties in Seymour's view became an even larger issue than the Emancipation Proclamation and he pledged, if he became governor, "to resist arbitrary arrests in New York, even if the streets be made to run red with blood."[4]

For the next three months, Lincoln would face his greatest opposition. The army that guarded the capital was near mutiny, following a general who considered his commander-in-chief an idiot.[5] The general public was suffering under a shaken economy.

The violation of civil rights was the issue closest to Kernan's heart. It was the reason his father had fled to America, where he flourished under its protective laws and where he had proudly watched his son defend the nation's civil-rights laws in court. The English had deprived the Irish citizens of their rights and had impoverished and crushed the populace. Now, in America, citizens could be subjected to arbitrary arrests and imprisonment. If we allow this, Kernan said, "our Government fails in the great object for which all good governments are constituted."

The war rallies of the early summer became Peace Meetings as the 1862 fall elections neared. In Kernan's speech accepting the congressional nomination, and in his addresses throughout his campaign, he was careful not to directly attack the president in the midst of war. Yet his party was determined to take charge of what they saw as a failed administration. "For eighteen months, the country has been involved in a destructive and devastating civil war, a rebellion, instigated by ambitious men . . . which threatens to overthrow the Government," he said, pointing out that the voters had given fully of men and money to the administration to defend the government. Now it was time for the cabinet and Congress to provide an account.

He described the dissension within the cabinet and the plundering of the Treasury under the secretary of war. "[Simon Cameron] has apparently been more intent on allowing political and personal favorites to plunder the Treasury than on suppressing the rebellion," said Kernan, who was offended that while loyal citizens had been sent to prison without process of law in loyal states, Cameron's punishment was to be given an ambassadorship and sent abroad. Kernan also cited the cabinet's lack of support for McClellan, and blamed the cabinet for McClellan's halting Peninsular Campaign. "Instead of sustaining the general selected by the President, they thwarted his plans, and the gallant McClellan and his brave army were repulsed from Richmond." Kernan was blind to McClellan's gross ineptness, as was his audience that day, which went into wild applause at the very mention of McClellan's name. If the General's battles had been as effective as his public relations, the war would long since have been decided.

As for the actions of Congress, Kernan quoted conservative Republican leaders' denunciation of the "incendiary and infernal" spirit of Congress. Democrats were outraged that instead of working to strengthen the loyalty of the border states, congressmen were making unnecessary and inflammatory speeches about abolishing slavery in the District of Columbia and passing bills to establish diplomatic rela-tions with Haiti and Liberia.

Kernan saw the Emancipation Proclamation as the fault of extreme Republi-can congressmen who overcame a weak-willed president in their clamor to make the war one for the overthrow of negro slavery in the states. Conservative Republi-cans and Democrats, including most of New York City's powerful merchants, wanted the South back in the Union with its economy intact. They did not see the South as an enemy, an alien nation, but as brothers who were suffering at the hands of an ambitious, rebellious contingent.

On October 17, 1862, just three weeks before the election, Kernan appeared with Horatio Seymour and Amasa Parker at a large rally in Utica. Judge Parker spoke first, warning that the Emancipation Proclamation "would bring about the horrors of a servile insurrection against loyal and rebellious owners alike.... It was a policy which releases the negro from control and sets him at the throats of women and children."

Seymour spoke of his opponent in the gubernatorial race, Gen. James S. Wadsworth, who was not a field commander but held a staff-desk postition in Wash-ington. General Wadsworth was responsible for the widely publicized arrest and imprisonment of a Democratic newspaper editor during the 1860 Democratic national convention. Now, according to Seymour, Wadsworth "spent most of his time working against McClellan, arresting white men, and freeing the negro."

Kernan spoke last, promising to "prosecute the war with vigor, to give Lincoln all the men and money necessary, to sustain him earnestly and honestly in the exe-cution of Constitutional authority, and to make the war one of preserving the Union, not abolishing slavery.... Let slavery take care of itself.... Let us take care of the rights and institutions and the government of 20,000,000 of whites, and not now spend our time as to slavery, when we know we cannot better their condition, while we may allow to be destroyed your and my government, so dear to us."

Kernan waited long into the night of November 5 for the election returns. They came by telegraph and train and hearsay to party headquarters. Occasionally, to break the boredom, the crowd demanded another short impromptu speech from the candidates among them. Seymour praised Kernan and Kernan praised Seymour, not having much left from their stump speeches applicable to the occasion.

When the returns were counted, Seymour had won the gubernatorial seat by over 10,000 votes. However, he had lost his own town and county. Kernan had car-ried Oneida County by 200 votes, but won the congressional district by only 98. As close as this election was, it represented a significant victory in a district that two years earlier had given the Republicans a majority of 8,000.

Nationally, the election mirrored New York as a severe rebuke to the Republi-can administration. Even though the party managed to maintain control of Con-gress, it lost some major leaders in the House, including the Speaker, Galusha A. Grow of Pennsylvania, John A. Bingham of Ohio, and Roscoe Conkling.

❖

After the election, Conkling complained that he would have won were it not for all the loyal boys of Utica being at the battlefront and unable to vote. Seymour, conversely ascribed the close victory to the "letters written by our soldiers from the battlefield imploring their fathers and their brothers to put down the wild and bloody fanaticism." Kernan said he had "no partisan spirit, and no unkind feelings towards political opponents, to rejoice over the result of the late election," but exulted in the belief that Democrats had saved the country from devastation and saved the cause of civil liberty throughout the world. They planned now to join with conservative Republicans in Congress, where, together, they could provide Lincoln with the backbone he needed to resist the radicals, repudiate the proclamation, end the rebellion, restore the Union, and uphold the law.

Lincoln carefully observed New York's election returns. The most powerful state in the Union was now to be governed by the most articulate spokesman for the opposition, Horatio Seymour, and Kernan, in Congress would be considered Seymour's surrogate. Conkling, the hawk, had been ousted by Seymour's choice for Congress. Even Fernando Wood, who as mayor of New York City had once suggested the city secede, was now on the way to Washington, where Democrats, though still in the minority, had gained solid control of the House delegations from New York, Ohio, Illinois, and Indiana. Delegations from Pennsylvania and Wisconsin were now evenly split.

Seymour's gubernatorial term began on New Year's Day 1863, a couple of months after the election. Although he had won the popular vote, his supporters were not in control of the state legislature, and legislators were unfriendly. He would spend the next two years, according to his biographer, "in fierce argument and ceaseless anxiety, the hard-working object of unjust suspicion and long-lived slander."[6]

Kernan's term would not begin for nearly a year. By statute, the newly elected Thirty-Eighth Congress did not meet until the first Monday of December 1863, a situation much to Lincoln's advantage. While Kernan waited to take his seat in Washington, the lame-duck Congress gathered in December 1862 for their final session under a gloomy cloud made suddenly darker by the North's crushing defeat at Fredericksburg. The winter months marked the lowest point of the war. Everywhere, Union citizens were losing faith in the ability of their leaders while Congress passed resolutions endorsing the president and the policy of emancipation.

By early spring 1863 heavy casualties, rising prices, and the growing unpopularity of the war stemmed the enrollment of volunteers. In March, in one of its final acts, the Thirty-Seventh Congress passed the first federal draft act. All males between 20 and 45 were to register for military service, and each loyal state was to provide soldiers in proportion to its percentage of the total population, with deductions for previous enlistments. A draftee could commute service on payment of $300 or avoid service altogether by securing a substitute.

The federal draft infuriated New York Democrats and many Republicans as well, who argued that their state was already the leading supplier of men, money, supplies, tax revenue, and contributions to relief organizations for the war effort. Even Lincoln acknowledged Seymour's prompt cooperation in sending nearly 20,000 troops from New York State that summer, troops who played an important part in the victory at Gettysburg, the decisive battle of the war. No federal law had been needed to fill the ranks until now, and the new law was unfair to the poor, who could not afford either to pay the $300 or pay a substitute. Only one year earlier, Kernan had worked hard to encourage enlistment. Now he joined the peace-movement protests against the federal draft and against New York's unfair quota.

On July 4, 1863, the day after the end of the Battle of Gettysburg, Seymour gave "the most unfortunate" speech of his career.[7] The occasion was a Fourth of July celebration at the Academy of Music in Brooklyn, New York, and Seymour unwisely had not edited his opening remarks regarding the "broken promises" of victory to take into account the most recent news from the front: the Union army had just won an important victory in Vicksburg, Mississippi, and checked General Robert E. Lee's invasion of Pennsylvania. The tide had turned, and instead of pointing to New York's important participation, Seymour used fiery language, comparing Lincoln to Charles I of England, who had been beheaded in the English Civil War! His demand that the administration respect civil liberties and freedoms of the press and speech in time of war was equally ominous: "Remember this! That the bloody, treasonable, and revolutionary doctrine of public necessity can be proclaimed by a mob as well as by a government."[8]

The *New York Herald* caustically attacked Seymour, saying "the more these small fry politicians chatter, the firmer becomes our conviction that if a couple of hundred niggerhead and copperhead organs had been suppressed, and about 5000 niggerhead and copperhead leaders thrown into a common prison, long ago, the country would have been in a far better position today and in the future."

Nine days later, when a draft riot broke out in New York City, Seymour was blamed. On Saturday, July 11, names had been drawn in a lottery that was followed by a hot summer evening of grumbling and drinking in the poor Irish sections of town. Many of the unskilled workers saw no sense in fighting to emancipate their chief potential rivals for jobs. By Monday the rioting began and the panicked news coverage speculated that more than 1,000 blacks were killed and that Governor Seymour had incited the crowd with a speech earlier in the week, and during the riot itself he had addressed the drunken rioters as "my friends."

Reports were exaggerated, but the truth was bad enough. For three days a roaming mob controlled the streets of Manhattan. Beginning by torching the building that housed the draft board, the rioters turned their fury chiefly against blacks, destroying the Colored Orphan Asylum, lynching and mutilating more than a hundred African American men, women, and children, and causing $2 million worth of property damage. While not on the scale initially reported, the Draft Riots constituted the most destructive domestic insurrection in the nation's history to that time.[9] The "friends" Seymour addressed were not the rioters—rioters are not known for pausing mid-riot to listen to political speeches—but news-hungry citizens gathered at the steps of City Hall. Nonetheless, Seymour only called out the militia after dozens of people had been killed and hundreds of thousands of dollars worth of property had been destroyed. This, plus the fact that he had spoken out strongly against the draft in a speech a few days earlier, severely damaged his reputation. Thomas Nast, the political cartoonist, immortalized the moment in an inflammatory cartoon of Seymour addressing a crowd of rowdy, drunken Irishmen at the scene of the riots, while the body of a negro hung from a nearby tree.

The draft took place throughout the Union. In Utica it "occasioned great excitement but no rowdyism," according to a letter from Mary D. Devereux to her sister Elizabeth Butler. "More money than men will be obtained here. Most of the young men joined Clubs. There were 100 paid $75, making $7,500. Twenty five names were drawn, taking just the amount. Denis Lalor was one of them. Thos. [her son] & all the Kernans escaped. It is a very unpopular measure here, no one goes with cheerfulness." Of Francis's sons, only his eldest, John Devereux Kernan, would have been old enough to participate.

Although Democrats had initially received a warm response to their arguments for conciliating the South, for condemning the unfair draft quota, and for protesting arbitrary arrests, by the autumn of 1863 public opinion was changing. The war economy was benefiting the North, and the victories at Gettysburg and Vicksburg appeared to mark a turning point of the war. The Union would still face setbacks, but the worst was over. The new nation had passed its first and greatest test. Everyone felt it, and in the polls, they gave back the control of the state legislature to the Republicans. Governor Seymour would soon face the assemblymen's hostility.

As Kernan prepared to leave for Washington, Mary Devereux reported to her sister Elizabeth that "Hannah is always tired & busy with her large family . . . and Francis looks very gloomy at the thought of leaving them all winter."

The Loyal Opposition

Democrats should not present their opposition stance as a counter revolution, but in all their unconstitutional measures, and in their insane policy we should oppose to them a firm opposition.

FRANCIS KERNAN, WASHINGTON, D.C., FEBRUARY 7, 1864

THE CIVIL WAR was the greatest test of America's young Constitution. It was also the most dangerous threat the Democratic party had yet faced. A Pennsylvania newspaper aptly stated the Democrats' position: "[I]n these fearful times," Democrats had "to give up for the time being their party predilections and stand by the government. . . . In assuming this attitude," however, "it requires no surrender of our political principles, no admission of the justness of the war, no acknowledgment of the rights of a sectional party in the North to invade the Constitutional rights of the South—it requires no sacrifice of this sort, it requires us simply to do our duty by our government."[1] Democrats recalled the fate of the Federalists, whose opposition to the War of 1812 had cost the party its existence, and the tepid response of the Whigs to the war with Mexico, which had undermined their popularity with voters. Northern Democrats had extended the hand of peace to their Southern brethren until the last possible instant. Now men who had always looked South found themselves thrown on the defensive as their old political comrades turned their guns on the Union. In tremendous numbers, Democrats had responded to the call to arms, buoyed by the new president's assurances that he, like they, wanted simply to restore the Union, not to abolish slavery and subjugate the South.

Bruised but unbowed, the Democratic party soldiered on in the electoral battlefield as well. The fact of war did not cause them to rethink their bedrock principles. Northern Democrats grew hoarse crying "Constitution!" They demanded that the wartime government simultaneously wage war and treat its citizens according to the law. In doing so, they made a new and vital contribution to the country's political system. They were *the loyal opposition*—a new concept on American soil. These men were loyal to the law of the land while firmly opposing those who administered that law. The world watched in amazement as the United States, in the midst of civil war, continued to hold open debate and free elections.

On the opening day of the Thirty-Eighth Congress, Monday, December 7, 1863, Francis Kernan joined his fellow members as they filed into the House of Representatives dressed in black broadcloth coats and silk hats. Washington had changed since his student days at Georgetown College. Then, the men who occupied these very seats adopted the gag rules that stymied open discussion and criticism of slavery. Today, almost 30 years later, the representatives would vote to strike a medal of thanks to Ulysses S. Grant for recent victories at Missionary Ridge and Chattanooga. Outside, the view from the Capitol dome down Pennsylvania Avenue showed the progress of time with a streetcar line running down its center. Even more striking—blacks were now allowed to ride the line.[2]

The president's message to Congress was in marked contrast to the gloom of 1862, the year Francis Kernan was elected. The war was showing signs of success, with rebel troops pushed back, Tennessee and Arkansas no longer under insurgent control, and the South effectively cut in two and unable to communicate. The Emancipation Proclamation was generally accepted. It had not caused a servile insurrection, and the loyal slave states of Maryland and Missouri (not affected by the Proclamation) were debating their own emancipation plans. Lincoln stated clearly, "I shall not attempt to retract or modify the Emancipation Proclamation; nor shall I return to slavery any person who is free by the terms of that proclamation or by any of the acts of Congress." He asked the Congress to pass a constitutional amendment to ensure that the guarantee of freedom stood on legal grounds. One week later, Republicans in both the House and the Senate offered amendments, and debate began on the proposed final bipartisan draft. The main resistance was from Republicans who were angered that the president's plans offered too much amnesty and too few restrictions on the reconstruction of the South.

Periodically, Democrats tried to negotiate with sympathetic and loyal persons in the rebel states. During his first month in the House, Kernan joined his fellow party members in voting in favor of opening negotiations. Republicans countered with charges of betrayal and offered a resolution that opposed any negotiations "as long as a single rebel is in arms" and recognized only two parties: patriots and traitors. When Kernan voted with the majority against this outrageous measure, the *Utica Herald* told hometown readers that Kernan had betrayed his campaign pledge to support the abolitionists—a pledge he had never made.

Kernan honored his actual campaign promise to support the war when the first appropriation bill came before the House requesting money to pay bounties and raise volunteers. Some Democrats demanded a full accounting of funds already spent before voting to spend more. Kernan chided them to respond immediately to the need for troops and later to demand a careful accounting. Enough Democrats joined him to pass the appropriation, and Kernan was credited with saving the measure.

The issue of the readmission of the seceded states haunted the House throughout the war and the years of "Reconstruction" that followed. Lincoln's controversial plan called for congressional representatives to be seated from the Southern states as soon as just 10 percent of their voters took an oath of loyalty to the Union. Of course, this would mean that the new "rump" representatives would almost certainly be Republicans. The specific concern on the morning of January 29, 1864, was a resolution declaring that Mr. A. P. Fields of Louisiana should not be seated, as he was not elected according to the laws of Louisiana, but elected under military rule. Kernan agreed that loyal citizens in that state had not had a fair opportunity to vote, and he wanted the House to express its condemnation of the military government of Louisiana. Members of Congress held conflicting views of the Southern states. Those who regarded slavery as the essential issue of the war saw them as enemies to be crushed, while those who viewed slavery as of little concern saw the Southerners as brethren in rebellion. This latter group, including Kernan, wanted legislation that would restore "the Union as it was," not subjugate a portion of it. These two views toward the South were reflected in the strident debate over the Second Confiscation Act.

Kernan had been elected to the House campaigning against the injustice of the original Confiscation Act, which threatened to seize property of citizens, and now he could use his practiced arguments to denounce this sudden, unconstitutional measure. The new Confiscation Act declared that all property seized by the Union army would be kept, not only from its owners, but from their heirs. The intent of the proposed law was not merely to prevent slaves from being returned to slavery, but to bar owners and their families in perpetuity from ever reacquiring their seized lands.

Lincoln had nearly vetoed the original Confiscation Act. He cited specific language in the Constitution declaring that punishment cannot extend beyond the lifetime of those convicted. To prevent a presidential veto, Congress had passed an explanatory amendment denying that such a thing could happen. Lincoln reluctantly signed the Confiscation Act, but accepted it only in tandem with Congress's explanation.

Now Republicans wanted to amend the Confiscation Act so that it matched the constitutional language Lincoln had cited. They reasoned that the Constitutional wording was sufficiently vague as to allow an interpretation that would indeed make confiscation absolute. Kernan's protest helped prevent the measure from being voted on when it was introduced on January 10, 1864. His heartfelt response temporarily convinced his fellow legislators to slow their haste and consider the mess they were about to create. His argument that day illustrated the fact that Lincoln's best defenders in the Congress were often Democrats.

"I agree with the President," said Kernan, quoting Lincoln's words that "the true construction of the Constitution is that we have not power to cut off the inheritance of innocent heirs as part punishment of treason." Passing a deliberately vague law would lead to discrepancies in lower court rulings and endless challenges, Kernan argued. He laid out several scenarios, each ending with the imaginary buyer of confiscated property (always a loyal Union citizen) either paying too much or losing his purchases altogether, depending on the outcome of a court challenge. And since passage of this amendment would automatically repeal the older act, all of those rebels whose confiscation cases were currently in the courts would get off entirely, with all their ownership rights intact.

Kernan asked his fellow legislators to consider the larger issue of how the law would affect the masses of people in the South. "Do not take away their own right to their land or their right of inheritance. . . . If we hope to see our people ever again living peacefully under a united Government . . . it seems to me that one great inducement would be that the Government had not taken away from the masses of the people the right of their children to inherit their lands, or their own right, if they lay down their arms and comply with such amnesty as the Government may deem it wise to offer to buy back cheaply the estate they have lost." He pointedly addressed the representative who offered the strident proposition, saying, "No man, I take it, desires to exterminate the great masses."

A vote on the amendment was stalled, giving Kernan time to prepare more formal arguments. During the week that followed, the measure was the subject of great debate among citizens of both the loyal and the rebel states. When Kernan spoke again on February 4, his opening remarks to the speaker of the House suggest he had been selected as spokesman for his party. The fact that the speech was printed and widely distributed further suggests its importance to the Democrats.

Kernan appealed not to wartime emotion, but to logic. He did not attack the motives of the Radical Republicans to punish traitors severely. Rather, he respectfully demonstrated a clear understanding of their goals and passed no judgment upon them. He went on to show how the amendment would simply not accomplish the goal of punishment. Worse, it would create a legal tangle more detrimental to loyal Union citizens than to any rebel. He began on neutral high ground, with a history of English law and the principles embedded in the U.S. Constitution, which prohibits Congress from passing bills of attainder—laws declaring an individual's guilt without a trial. The Constitution also declares that Congress cannot pass an *ex post facto* law. (In other words, a person cannot be made a criminal for deeds that were not against the law at the times they were committed.) The Confiscation Act now before the House was both a bill of attainder and an *ex post facto* law.

Kernan then addressed those legislators who maintained that the act was based on the law of nations rather than on the U.S. Constitution, as it concerned alien enemies. Even if Congress were to recognize the rebels as a foreign government, said Kernan, the law of nations did not permit the confiscation of lands owned by private persons.

After addressing the arguments of his opponents, he then pointed to what he considered the true flaw of the bill—its effect on the rebels. If they believed their lands would be taken from them and their children, he argued, it would be better for them to keep on fighting than to face impoverishment. Such a law would make it harder to end the rebellion or to reconcile the rebels afterward, and would therefore tend to destroy, rather than preserve, the government. It is interesting to note what he did not say, and what surely motivated his own passion. England's confiscation of Irish lands had resulted in exactly the dire end Francis predicted for the United States. The rights to land and inheritance were the very reason for his own father's coming to America, and the reason for the deaths of others of his clan. But on this he remained silent. It would not have helped his argument that day to refer to his Irish background, given the predominance of representatives from English stock.*

Back home in Utica, Hannah wrote that their son John "got some copies of the *Observer* this morning with your speech to send to friends and Grove [the editor] told him there was a great demand for it, it was very much thought of. . . . We are all delighted at the prospect of seeing you so soon. I have been looking over clothes and am very tired and must lay down. I could not let the day pass without thanking you for our kind letters. May God bless you and bring you safely home to us, Your loving wife, Hannah."

Despite Kernan's reasoned pleas, the Confiscation Amendment prevailed in the House and was passed on to the Senate. There, it was recognized as unconstitutional and killed.

Democrats also labored in vain to resist the Draft Act. Debates often turned personal and nasty and even crossed party lines, as when Democrats tried to lessen the severity of the Conscription Bill of 1864. An amendment offered by Kernan recommended that the act exempt clergymen. Ohio's Democratic representative Samuel Cox immediately objected that "the pestiferous clergymen" of the country had fomented the rebellion and deserved no such consideration. When others chal-

---

* While one can identify no direct ancestor of Francis as having died for his lands, there is evidence that the MacK-ernans were among the more forward septs in the county of Cavan in the ten-year rebellion that ended with Cromwell's victory in 1650; some 56 MacKernans were accused of "rebellion, robbery, murder, 'horrid murder', and high Wordes" during those years; and the chief of the name and his brothers were hanged by the English. [See MacKernan of Tullyhunco, John D. Kernan, pages 39–42 and notes 28–29.]

lenged Cox's insult to the cloth and questioned his loyalty to the Union, Cox responded by attacking those who were "singing anthems to John Brown and plotting sedition and revolution." Acrimony continued to escalate despite pleas from members of both parties that the House should not be wasting time in personal disputes when the army was about to enter a potentially decisive campaign. Tension finally ended in laughter when someone suggested that the ministers be exempted only if they agreed not to preach politics. Since "ministers are intermeddlers and stirrers up of strife and mischief, they ought to go to the war. They are more fitted for that than for peace."[3] After the laughter subsided, the vote was called and Kernan's amendment to exempt clergymen was rejected.

A few days later Kernan tried again to lessen the severity of the federal Draft Act, suggesting that the draft be delayed until after states attempted first to fill their quotas voluntarily. "Never, prior to the passage of the Conscription Act, did the State of New York fail to furnish promptly its quota of volunteer soldiers," he argued. His amendment lost by only four votes.

With little ability to shape the direction of the war in Congress, the Democrats placed their best hopes in a quick end to the hostilities and to the fall elections. In one of the very few surviving letters written while he was in Washington to a fellow Democratic representative, Henry G. Stebbins of New York, Kernan gave voice to the desperation felt by the party faithful:

> It seems to me clear that it is of the utmost importance to the Country now for the future that the Democrats and conservatives should unite and gather strength so as to defeat the present national dynasty in the next Presidential election. If not, I fear the present form of Government will be substantially destroyed. Lincoln will be their candidate; in the future as in the past, he will yield in his policy to the radicals who think more of carrying out their one idea [abolition] than of ending the war and having the Constitution and Union.
>
> To this I write and have thought it sufficient that we should occupy these positions: This is our Government. It is essential to our peace and prosperity that we preserve it and we can not and will not allow it to be destroyed. Those Secessionists who with arms in their hands are endeavoring to overthrow it, we must defeat by armed force. Those who are likely to overthrow the courts and present Government by their unconstitutional and unwise policy by political power obtained through the ballot box or its forums, we must defeat at the ballot box.
>
> Those legitimately in power, entrusted for the present with the administration of the Government, we should sustain with the necessary men and means to put down the rebellion, holding them responsible before the people for their proper [conduct].
>
> But in all their unconstitutional measures, and in their insane policy we should oppose to them a firm opposition, discussing them fully but in a spirit of

moderation and patriotism. We are not to talk of getting up a counter revolution against the administration by illegal or violent measures.—This is a remedy
nearly as bad as the [present], & if a last resort, never to be talked of till all else
fails.—Our opposition should not be factious . . . but firm and mainly appealing
to reason. This always wins through.[4]

That even a moderate like Kernan could entertain the option of "a counter
revolution…by illegal or violent measures" shows the depth of the Democrats'
alienation from Lincoln's administration. Such a radical impulse is explicable only
by recognizing that the Union they knew and loved was rapidly being transformed
beyond recognition by the war. Before the hostilities began, the expenses of the
federal government ran to about $70 million a year. Over the five years of the Civil
War the average annual appropriation was at least $800 million. The U.S. House of
Representatives controlled the purse and raised the funds to finance the war and the
growing trade deficit. Kernan's calls for economic caution went unheeded, especially by those who were benefiting from the sizzling wartime expansion. In New
York and other industrial states, production fueled general excitement, if not universal prosperity. Speculation was rampant and fortunes were being made daily in
coal, oil, liquor, and government contracts. By 1865 the trade deficit was $15 mil-
lion.[5] Along with a demand for army supplies was a public demand for foreign lux-
uries. "There is a reckless money-making spirit abroad which, profiting by our
disasters, favors a long war," wrote Thurlow Weed, political boss of New York's
Republican party.[6]

Kernan shamed his fellow legislators into holding back spending on one
short-lived occasion. At issue, January 25, 1864, was an additional $400,000 to cover
the cost of decorating a newly expanded building in the Capitol and continuing
work on the Treasury building extension. The $4 to $6 per day wages being paid in
Washington for frescoing seemed exorbitant, particularly when the government was
working hard to raise taxes and money for the war effort. Kernan urged postponing
the costly decoration while all the resources of the government were being
strained. The expansion could wait until later, he said, "and I think unless we begin
with bills like this, and cut down the expenditures by the hundreds of thousands of
dollars, upon matters which are not of pressing importance, we are hardly doing our
duty to the country in the present state of things." The House voted with him a full
majority, 71 to 37, to limit the expenditure, but overnight many representatives must
have heard some compelling arguments from Capitol lobbyists, because they
reversed the vote the next morning to defeat Kernan's initiative, 78 to 56.

Tensions in the House continued to rise as the Union armies realized some
victories on the battlefields. Representative Kernan concerned himself mainly with
the issue of war debt and taxes, finding little patience for the "humbug" resolutions
that interrupted daily the progress of urgent legislation. On February 16, in
response to yet another typical resolution, this one declaring it the duty of loyal

men to strive to preserve and restore the Union, Kernan rose to protest that the representatives pushing the legislation needed to address the urgent issue of strengthening the government's credit. "We have spent months here uselessly!" he said, and demanded to know "if any member of the House thought we were doing anything to preserve the Union by spending day after day and hour after hour in discussing questions that can be postponed, when questions are pressing upon us which threaten the destruction of the Government and the ruin of this people?" He pointed to a number of critical bills before the House, including the Enrollment Act aimed at increasing the number of troops, and earnestly suggested that "there are practical questions before us; that there is some importance to be attached to trying to preserve this Government for white men as well as for black men. Let us not," he said, "spend all our time upon one subject, when every man knows we are endangering the liberties, the rights, and the Government of the country and are doing no practical good to the unfortunate black man, who is being ground to powder under these circumstances."

He was not unaware of or necessarily unsympathetic to the condition of freed slaves. Eyewitness accounts of the tremendous hardships they continued to face offered evidence to those who wanted to believe that they were better off in slavery. A letter from a Reverend A. S. Fiske, chaplain of the Memphis army, printed in one of Kernan's hometown papers described the calamities taking place where plantations were laid waste and crops destroyed. Everywhere the Union army went, slaves were either freed or fled with their masters further south. Most eventually approached the Union army lines, where the men were recruited as soldiers or workers. Out of approximately 4,000 blacks in Chaplain Fiske's charge at Memphis in February, March, and April 1863, 1,200 had died. "Three-fourths of the women had but one garment between themselves and utter nakedness," he wrote. "Many children were kept night and day rolled in the poor blanket of a family—its sole apparel. They had multitudes of these—no beds. There were no floors in their leaking tents, and no chance for fires. The wonder is not that so many died, but that so many lived. The suffering of these people is our national dishonor. If they were not rescued, history would write something thus: The American people enticed within their lines tens of thousands of slaves, alluring them hither with promise of liberty, took from them all able-bodied men to reinforce their armies, huddled the rest together in great camps, and left them to perish of nakedness by the hundreds. Now, how will that page of history read?"

Still, Kernan's faith in the fitness of blacks only for slavery—a fundamental element of Democratic party gospel—must have received a decisive setback from witnessing their conduct in the war. Hundreds of thousands of supposed "faithful darkies" abandoned their plantations and made for the Union lines, while millions more engaged in what W.E.B. DuBois later described as a massive "general strike" that crippled the South in its ability to wage war. Yet they did not, as another doctrine of proslavery dogma asserted, unleash savage violence against their former masters. Ultimately, as the Northern conscription effort lagged and the logic of combat dictated the revolutionary step, more than 180,000 blacks, most of them former slaves, enlisted in the Union army. Their conspicuous gallantry and military discipline gave the lie to the racist ideology espoused by the Democracy.

The issue of taxes and war bonds was a major focus of Kernan's term. He attempted to ensure an equal sharing of the cost of the war by the entire population. The existing laws allowed wealthy individuals and corporations to purchase tax-exempt war bonds, thereby sheltering their property from state, county, town, and municipal taxation. These bonds had a minimum face value of $500, restricting their purchase to the rich. "Thus they escape their just share of these burdens," Kernan argued. His fellow legislators adopted his resolution "to enquire into the expediency of so changing the laws."[7] He reasoned that the war debt existed as interest-bearing bonds, owned by citizens of the free states. These war bonds were paying high interest as an enticement to the public to take the risk in exchange for uncertain securities.[8] However, at the current rate, so many were being purchased that nearly half of the total property in the state would soon exist for tax purposes as tax-free bonds. The entire state and local tax burden, said Kernan, would fall on those who were least able to afford investing in war stocks and bonds. "Why should the owners of the bonds, receiving a handsome profit on their investment, be exempt from the burden of taxation?" he asked. (Even New York's Republican political boss, Thurlow Weed, had to agree that too much money was being diverted from state coffers.)*

Kernan was not so successful in convincing businessmen in Utica, where speculation fever was in full swing. During a trip home in March he tried to prevent the trustees of the Savings Bank of Utica from investing a disproportionate amount in federal government bonds. Kernan had served as a trustee of that institution for approximately 20 years, and now, speaking first in private to the bank's president, he advised caution and deemed it unwise that the savings bank had invested nearly three-quarters of its funds in United States Bonds and Certificates of Indebtedness. The bank, he reminded the trustees, was not an institution chartered to make money, but to provide financial security for its depositors, with extra profits going toward the guarantee of a stable, annual 5 percent interest. However, the enticement of large, quick profits was more convincing than Kernan's conservative fiscal advice.

That same March two major financial issues concerning gold and whiskey came before the Thirty-Eighth Congress. As might be expected on any argument over money and alcohol, debates crossed party lines and votes represented the personal politics, constituencies, and party influence of each legislator. The Gold Bill was an ineffectual attempt to tame speculation. Its passage in the summer of 1864

---

* Kernan's resolution was adopted and sent to the Committee on Ways and Means, but it was not pursued as it was soon superseded by national events.

only worsened the situation, and gold prices continued their wild climb and fluctuation, dramatically affecting the worth of paper money, or "greenbacks." Citizens had used these greenbacks to purchase government bonds, but now the Treasury had to pay the interest on those bonds with gold, resulting in the government's paying a costly 15 percent on its loans (which exlains why the Utica Bank trustees wanted to maintain their investment in government bonds).

Kernan tried to address the perils of paper money.[9] He called the Gold Bill, which authorized the secretary of the treasury, Salmon P. Chase, to sell surplus gold, ostensibly to shore up the value of the federal government's paper money by buying it back, "merely a proposition to enable the government to use its coin to shave its own paper at an enormous discount." Furthermore, he believed "the bill was sustained by an outside pressure or influence, which had but little care for the welfare of the country and the government." He pointed out that the bill had not come from the Ways and Means Committee, normally responsible for such measures and which had earlier reported against it, nor had the bill been recommended by the administration. The gold was currently pledged to paying the interest on the public debt, with only 1 percent of it going toward liquidation of the debt. Now, said Kernan, Congress was proposing to sell it for depreciated paper. Alluding to the gold flutter in Wall Street, and referring to his consultations "with able and intelligent men, not in gold-speculating cliques," he correctly predicted continued speculation in gold regardless of any actions of the secretary of the treasury. "If [the secretary] sells out, gold will go down, and speculators [will] buy it; and the same speculators will then put up its price." He would never give a vote, he said, "that would give power to the government to dabble in stocks with gold."

Rather than attack the bill's sponsors directly, he simply acknowledged their goal but then explained how that goal would not be gained by passing the bill. "To authorize the Secretary to sell gold on hand, or his making sale of it, will afford no permanent relief against the evils of a disordered paper currency. If we do this we not only incur disgrace, but we fail to accomplish the only desirable object put forth by the friends of this measure, which is the raising of the value of paper and diminishing the value of gold. We will only by this means be able to put it down for a time, and then it will go up again higher than before, causing greater fluctuations in values than are occurring now, and causing them to occur according to the arbitrary will of one man. No legislation of this character," he predicted, "could bring the value of gold—the standard of value throughout the world—to the level of the paper currency which has been created in this country."

The measure nevertheless passed through both houses of Congress and went to the White House, where Lincoln approved it on June 17. Gold continued to climb in value as greenbacks dropped, reaching their lowest point that summer at 40 cents on the dollar.[10] The fall coincided with military defeats. At this point, Kernan tried again to sway his fellow bank directors in Utica. At meetings of the trustees in June and July he recommended they sell $200,000 of the war bonds and invest the money in Utica, New York City, and New York State "stocks." Kernan pointed out that none of the trustees there was willing to risk his own personal future by investing it in such bonds, and that the bank should not thus risk so large a portion of the money of its investors. The majority refused, and Kernan resigned in protest. His detractors viewed his action as a shameful, unpatriotic lack of support for the war effort. Barely two weeks later, on July 2, Congress acknowledged the futility of the Gold Act in preventing speculative sales of gold, and repealed it.

Democrats continued to pressure the administration to prosecute the war without violating constitutional law and to protect the civil liberties of its citizens. Tempers flared constantly in the House, as, for example on March 21, when Democrats resisted an army appropriation bill on the grounds that money was being used to stack elections. Kernan offered an amendment barring use of the money appropriated for transporting civilians to their homes. He said a clerk in the Department of Transportation had informed him that thousands of Republican voters were being sent to Pennsylvania via railroad passes (the same as those issued to soldiers) at public expense. Representative Thaddeus Stevens of Pennsylvania demanded to know the name of the clerk. Kernan responded that the clerk had insisted on anonymity, but he would name the witness if a committee was instituted to examine the matter, "and not a whitewashing Committee," he added, a pointed reference to the Committee on the Conduct of the War, which had been appointed to investigate abuses and scandals in the War Department, but which had so far appeared blind. The debate went on for hours, blending rumor, fact, and dirt. Some members denied that the government had been spending money to send home Republican voters, while others (such as Benjamin G. Harris of Maryland) said they could easily believe this of an "administration which had sent boats into Maryland to steal negroes." William D. Kelly of Pennsylvania denied the allegation and accused another representative of saying "the dividing line between the Union and the rebel states is north of Pennsylvania." The debate went on continuously, as usual, and Kernan's amendment barring the use of army appropriations to transport civilians home lost by 21 votes.

A few days later Kernan introduced an amendment to create a special committee, to be composed of five Republicans selected by the speaker, for the purpose of inquiring whether civilians in the employ of the government had been sent home at government expense to vote at elections. Republicans objected that such an inquiry should be conducted by the existing Committee on the Conduct of the War. Kernan would not consent, and again, his amendment lost.

Early in March 1864, Republicans in Congress, responding to a request by Lincoln, passed a bill to create the rank of "Lieutenant General of All U.S. Forces." Lincoln used the act to bring Maj. Gen. Ulysses S. Grant to Washington to replace the ineffectual McClellan, who had earlier been relieved of his command. Kernan's most heated speech during his entire term in the House was in opposition to a measure proposed later that month, which aimed to discharge from the service

Generals McClellan and Frémont, along with many other Democratic officers the Republicans wanted out. The measure, a proposed joint resolution by the House and Senate, would expel all officers who had not been on active duty for the last three months—a measure which, incidentally, would save Lincoln from having to fire these men and suffer the political consequence. Kernan's passionate protest against the injustice of the act was credited with preventing it from being pushed through that day.[11]

The president, he argued, has the power to dismiss anyone in the military at any time. "It is he who has taken these able-bodied generals out of service. Shall Congress now dismiss them without reason, charge, or trial?" Kernan proposed a substitute bill, which differed in one particular only: instead of dropping all the men not on active duty, the president should appoint a board of military officers to examine the efficiency and capability of these men and report to the president which are competent and which are not. "If the officers are unfit for the rank they hold, the welfare of the country requires they should be dismissed, and it is the duty of the President to dismiss them at once; and if he has not the courage to perform his duty," said Kernan, "I will give him a board of officers to aid him in determining who are unfit to be retained; but I will not consent that Congress shall relieve him of his responsibility by voting them out of office without knowing or having the means of judging who is meritorious and who worthless. I, for one, will not be a party to legislating an entire class of officers out of the Army to relieve the President from the duty of dismissing those of them who are not fit to be entrusted with the duties of their rank, or from the responsibility of retaining men in position and under pay who are not serviceable to the country."

He called it a "cowardly stab" against General Frémont and those soldiers loyal to him "should Congress legislate him out without assigning a single reason." Then, referring to McClellan, he asked,

> [W]hat effect will it have upon the Army of the Potomac [McClellan's former command], which has firm faith in and affection for its old leader? What effect will it have upon his friends throughout the country? It will be said that he was booted out because the President has not seen fit to employ him, although brave and competent, and ready to respond to any duty. The naked injustice of such a proposition is apparent to all. We propose to strike down without cause the man who won this nation at Antietam. . . . What faith will the soldiers and officers we are now calling into the field have in the gratitude of Congress, and the country, when they find that the President, through prejudice, through pressure, through importunities which politicians are ever pressing upon a man in his position, has relieved an accomplished and patriotic General from command; and then Congress, under the pleas that he is unemployed—no other suggestion is here made against him—unemployed when all know he is ready and willing to serve, legislate him out of the Army?[12]

Kernan risked being charged with disloyalty to the Union in defending McClellan, whose political actions had already amounted to insurrection. However, the greatest risk Kernan took in this respect was in defending an extreme Democrat, Ohio representative Alexander Long, against a censure and proposed expulsion from the House of Representatives for a pro-peace speech he had given on April 8, 1864. Long had infuriated members by saying that the war was wrong—unconstitutional—and that he preferred to recognize the Confederacy rather than subjugate it and eliminate its people.

After four years of war Republican congressmen did not need to hear the case that the issue of peace without union should be considered—there was a limit to the endurance of the country and Long's biting speech exceeded that limit. A resolution to expel him was hastily placed before the House, and Republican newspapers had a field day denouncing Copperheads.

Given that Kernan's formal address, delivered a couple of weeks later, was published and circulated by the Democratic press, one can assume he spoke on behalf of the national party. He was careful to distance himself from Long's views, but he directly addressed the issue of the absolute right of free speech on the floor of Congress and alluded with clear disapproval to the rowdy demonstrations of spectators in the galleries of the House as interfering with the principle of free speech and the need for fearless debate. "Without such freedoms," he said, "the Representative who feels bound to advocate unpopular views will not be overborne by reason and argument, but will be expelled and thus silenced. You will have no debate except that which runs in one groove, the majority silencing by mere numerical power all who oppose them." He claimed that the only question was whether the House "could expel a member because he believes a certain policy wise and gets up in this Hall and advocated it." If it should come to that, he said, "we shall have stricken down the honest and fearless discussion which is the life of liberty." Long barely escaped expulsion.

Lincoln's request for a Constitutional amendment abolishing slavery had finally moved through Congress toward a vote. The joint resolution passed the Senate on April 8, 1864, by 38 to 6, but it failed to carry the requisite two-thirds vote in the House. On June 15 the vote was 95 in favor, 65 opposed, and 23 not voting. It is difficult to know just by looking at the vote if representatives were actually opposed to ending slavery, or if they were still holding to the argument that Congress did not have the right to rule on states' domestic institutions. Many members had also argued that such a vote could not be made when the affected states were not represented. Even though the amendment failed, both parties had an issue to use in that fall's presidential campaign.

In the remaining weeks of its first session, Congress repealed the $300 exemption clause in the Conscription Act. Now, if someone was drafted, either he had to join or send a substitute. The armies needed men to complete the work of subduing the South, and volunteering had nearly ceased.

With so little time remaining, Congress focused on the issue of Reconstruction. Radical Republicans in the House and Senate passed a bill providing that rebellious states might form governments as long as they had a majority of white males and prohibited slavery, even though no such laws applied to Union states. Lincoln absolutely infuriated the Radical Republicans by simply putting the bill aside on the day Congress was to adjourn, rather than sign or veto it. Lincoln had already abolished slavery in rebellious states through an executive order justified by military need. Congress had yet to pass an antislavery amendment of its own.

Looking toward the presidential election campaign, the Democrats had a single goal in preventing Lincoln from returning to office, and Lincoln estimated they had a good chance of succeeding, especially as their goal was shared by many Republicans! The outcome of the war continued to be uncertain—the casualty count was staggering, the enormous public debt mounting—and still the president called for more men.

The growing peace movement, headed by Fernando Wood in New York and Alexander Long in the West, promoted an armistice and compromise in its platform and hoped to cast Governor Horatio Seymour as its candidate. In looking toward the national Democratic convention, George Pendleton of Ohio warned Kernan that McClellan's nomination would cause trouble. "I feel so anxious for harmony in our councils at Chicago [where the convention was to be held]," he said, pleading for another candidate.[13] Peace Democrats did not want a war general leading them, especially one some accused of being as tyrannical as Lincoln over the issue of civil rights. Meanwhile, Kernan again faced Roscoe Conkling, who had cleared the way for his own Republican nomination by having his potential opponent appointed to a state office.[14]

The Republican national convention met in Baltimore in early June, and after some hesitation united behind Lincoln and adopted a no-compromise platform that included unconditional surrender and an antislavery amendment. The Republicans also stretched beyond their regional base to nominate Andrew Johnson as vice president. Johnson was governor (under military rule) of Tennessee, and as a senator had consistently denounced secession.

The Democrats postponed their convention date as long as possible, hoping to benefit from the national gloom. Grant, after recapitulating some earlier victories, now found his Army of the Potomac stuck in the trenches at Petersburg. Union forces in the Shenandoah Valley were not doing much better, and the Western armies were only inching forward. People were simply sick of war—a state of affairs that could only help the Democrats' candidates, as it had helped Francis Kernan and Horatio Seymour in 1862.

Finally, with only two months to go before elections, the powerful and distinguished New York delegation headed toward Chicago for the Democratic convention. Slow travel by water and rail gave delegates opportunities to campaign along the way, and time to plan how to unify the peace and war factions within the party.

Although Peace Democrats favored Seymour, the War Democrats (including Seymour) wanted McClellan for president. The New York delegates reflected that same split: while most wanted McClellan and an end to hostilities, some were anxious to achieve a peace with the South that would preserve the principle of states' rights—and slavery—intact.

The *Detroit Free Press* carried the story of their arrival in that city on August 25. The mayor and other city officials boarded the delegates' steamer and about 4,000 people gathered that evening in City Hall to hear speeches. Kernan soberly advised against the kind of fratricidal division that had wracked the border states, counseling the delegates "to be firm in the defense of their rights, but to be law-abiding. . . . Let there be no Kentucky in Michigan," he said, "as we will have none in New York." The same paper carried dispatches from General Grant announcing the capture of Fort Morgan, and dispatches from General Sheridan announcing the enemy was leaving the Shenandoah Valley—good news for the Union, not so good for the Democratic election campaign.

Seymour presided over the convention, which began on August 27. He blamed the Republicans for the war and called for an armistice. His speech was a poignant plea for restoration of "the Union as it was," the complex hybrid of federal and state power founded on collapsed compromises. Since the Republicans' rise to power, said Seymour, they had made the country's history seem like "some unnatural and terrible dream." Even as Seymour spoke, General Sherman's army was beginning the final push into Atlanta, whose capture would seal Lincoln's reelection and put an end to "the Union as it was" forever.

After two days of convention, on the first ballot, the delegates nominated General McClellan, the man Lincoln had fired. To mollify the peace faction, they named Congressman George Pendleton of Ohio as vice president and adopted a strongly worded peace platform. They even included a resolution offered by the maverick Clement L. Vallandigham, who played an important role in creating the platform that would soon stigmatize the party and give Republicans a chance to make treason a campaign issue.[15] The resolution declared the Lincoln administration's "experiment of war" had failed to restore the Union and insisted that "justice, humanity, liberty, and public welfare necessitated making immediate efforts . . . for a cessation of hostilities, with a view to an ultimate convention of the States." Even though the resolution was distasteful to War Democrats, such as Kernan, it was preferable to an even more extreme offer made by Alexander Long for an immediate end to fighting, and recognition of the Southern Confederacy.

No sooner had the convention adjourned, and before Francis Kernan could complete his journey home, than news of a string of conclusive Union victories filled the press, making success all but certain, and turning the tide of public opinion toward Lincoln and the Republicans. Francis heard the news along the way: General Sherman in control at Atlanta, Farragut victorious at Mobile Bay. By the time the New York delegation returned home, they appeared unpatriotic, even traitorous. McClellan immediately repudiated his party's platform, but Grant, the man Lincoln had hired to replace him, now seemed the nation's savior. The South was falling, and Democrats were about to go down in defeat at the polls, but not before a month of futile campaigning.

Francis had to face a gloating Roscoe Conkling, who had already begun his tour of Oneida County, where he would visit nearly every hamlet and crossroads to attack Kernan for having failed to support the war effort. The Democratic campaign began for Kernan at a Saturday afternoon rally in Rome, where he was the main speaker appearing with Governor Seymour, who was ill. Suffering from an ailment of his throat and lungs, Seymour spoke only in greeting. Kernan followed. It didn't matter what he said, or that he tried to focus on the future, or that he spoke to those who held him in regard. As the war headed into its final days, Kernan still failed to see that slavery had been its cause, or to recognize that peace and reunion would be impossible until the whole nation, North and South, acquiesced in emancipation. With his blind spot for slavery, Kernan sought a restoration of the old Union on its original terms, with slavery presumably intact. "The question with us is how shall the Union be restored; and it is more important than to know how it was broken," he said. "We should hold out to them the promise that if they will now return, the Southern people shall enjoy all their rights and their past transgressions be forgotten." Without a hint of irony, he chided the Republicans for seeking to make slaves of white Southerners: "No eight millions, or even six, whether right or wrong, scattered over a vast territory, were ever compelled to be the slaves of twenty millions. Let us sacrifice prejudice and every thing else to secure the Union again, for that alone can give us peace, prosperity, and happiness."

The *Daily Herald,* whose editor was a close friend of Conkling, attacked Kernan's motives during his last session of Congress, painting him as unfaithful in refusing to approve the confiscation bills, and thereby preventing soldiers of the Union from gaining land confiscated from the rebels. But the editor spent most of his time attacking Kernan for attempting to convince the local bank trustees to sell off its government bonds, securities whose value had shot up even more in the wake of the conclusive Union victories.

Kernan spoke at nearby towns and at small rallies such as a pole raising at Deerfield, where the younger men of the Democratic club gathered the morning of October 7 to raise a "one hundred and one feet-high hickory pole, straight as an arrow, donated by a Mr. Getman, of Frankfort, a warm-hearted liberal Democrat." Kernan's speech took place under a leaky sky, and while he was speaking a storm came up and rain fell steadily for over half an hour. The newspaper reported, however, that he held his audience in spite of the weather, and the crowd was rewarded for its perseverance by a concluding song sung by Mr. John Piper, also of Utica.

Of the 22 meeting notices published that day in the *Utica Daily Observer,* Kernan was slated to speak at half of them over the coming 13 days. A letter to the editor complained that overzealous federal employees in their enthusiasm, and in the absence of their respected pastor, had desecrated the Presbyterian church and per-petrated an outrage on the moral and religious sentiment of the community by holding a mass political meeting to beat Mr. Ward Hunt and call for Mr. Conkling's and Mr. Lincoln's election—their stamping and shouting and applauding "alto-gether a profanation of the pulpit."

Despite rain and mud, citizens of Utica turned out again to hear Kernan speak at a rally on October 13. Times were changing, and ladies now squeezed into the galleries' seats. At a second meeting, formed outside in the drizzle to accommodate the crowd, Kernan reiterated his arguments against the Republican policy of con-ducting the war, and pointed to McClellan's greater wisdom and finer character. He introduced a Lt. A. J. Sizer, of Holland Patent, an officer of the 65th New York Vol-unteers and three-year veteran who had returned from the army only a week ear-lier. Lieutenant Sizer had served under McClellan, whose reluctance to commit men to the battle had hastened his downfall, and testified how the soldiers loved him. "If there is a soldier here," said the lieutenant, "I want his hand to go with me and vote for that glorious man on election day." Instantly a one-armed soldier appeared on the edge of the platform and thrust out his hand to clasp that of the lieutenant.

Kernan's final campaign rally took place the following week. The crowd was larger than expected, given the weather and the lackluster campaign, so rally orga-nizers improvised extra stands and speakers. People roamed the town square, alter-nating between politics, picnics, music, and socializing. In the spirit of the elections, the crowd voted one Peter C. Darling a capital singer. Regardless of party affilia-tion, people were buoyant with the prospect of military victory.

According to the *Utica Daily Observer,* "[Kernan] was exceedingly hoarse and spoke with great difficulty, making great accessions to the crowd before him—a stream of people constantly pouring into the Square through its gates." He argued that "the Democrats have only made Union the one condition of Peace, while Lin-coln's administration and the Republican Party insist on the abolition of slavery before there can be peace."

A popular scientific lecturer, a Dr. Morron, followed. He first defined his own position on slavery, which he believed to be an evil, but added that "by the terms of the bond between the states, we have no right to interfere with it." His speech must have been highly interesting to his listeners, because "fewer than a dozen left when the doctor's speech was interrupted by the cry of fire and bells ringing a violent alarm."

Other speakers continued the theme that the election would determine whether the government would be preserved as it was, or whether it would be abandoned to experimentation. Referring to the destruction of the Shenandoah Valley, Jasper S. Thayer, a delegate, proclaimed "desolation is not peace."

The rain began to fall in torrents, and the crowd quickly voted for adjourn-ment to Mechanic's Hall. Even those without umbrellas made their way to the hall rather than seek nearby shelter and end their Saturday's pleasure. But once there, drenched and restless, they disturbed the speeches in progress. The crowd filled the aisles, blocked the doors, and overflowed onto the platform so that even the speakers were hard-pressed to find room to continue with the program.

The topics ranged from slavery to confiscation to the local contest between Kernan and Conkling. Thayer accused Conkling of piling up the public debt, and raised the specter of impending poverty. "It could happen in America, as well as in the old countries which are heavily burdened with debt: the women and the children will indeed have to bear the load with the men in the rudest fields of labor." The example was close to the experience of many immigrants in the audience, and was already the reality for many in the defeated South.

The election, not surprisingly, was a Republican landslide. Lincoln defeated McClellan by 400,000 votes and won 212 electoral votes to McClellan's 21. In New York, however, Lincoln's margin was less than 7,000 out of 730,000 votes. Governor Seymour was defeated by Reuben Fenton, a Radical Republican with a majority of 13,000 votes. The Lincoln administration considered Seymour's defeat a vindication of its policies. Kernan lost to Roscoe Conkling, but only by a narrow margin. It was a testimony to his popularity that even in a district with a Republican majority he could hold voters' loyalty in the most adverse of circumstance. It was a larger accolade to both parties that free elections were held at all, and that the results were accepted in the midst of civil war.

By the time Kernan returned to Washington for the second and final session of the lame duck Thirty-Eighth Congress, public opinion about Lincoln had changed. The Democrats who had attempted to defeat him now found in the president an ally against the Radicals' harsh Reconstruction policies. The war was coming to an end, and many members of Congress were ready to take back control of the federal government from the executive branch. On opening day, Congress received Lincoln's message, in which he looked forward to seeing laws passed that were needed to reconstruct the Union. His single condition of peace was that the rebels stop fighting (a proposition Kernan had supported throughout his own recent campaign). There would be no reconsideration of emancipation; he again urged Congress to pass a constitutional amendment ending slavery forever.

That amendment became the first order of business for the new year. Debate began in the House on January 6, and lasted for three weeks, with nearly a third of the members participating. Democrat William Steele Holman of Indiana spoke for many who opposed the Thirteenth Amendment, saying "the fate of slavery had been wrongly determined by war, by the measures of the war, by the results of the war."[16] Samuel S. Cox of Ohio minced no words in declaring that the loyal slaveholding states were rendering the amendment useless. "Missouri yesterday almost unanimously voted to abolish slavery. Maryland has already done it whether by force or freedom it is not now my purpose to inquire. Kentucky will be forced to do the same. What remains? Little Delaware. She had in 1860 eighteen hundred slaves and the enlisting agents have mostly sold them out to this humanitarian government for soldiers costing $150 apiece in Delaware and selling for $1000 in New York! Surely Delaware will soon be free."[17]

Most Democrats viewed the Thirteenth Amendment as unauthorized by the Constitution, because it was a repudiation of the original compromise upon which the Union was founded. Yet they recognized that emancipation was inevitable, and many began to waver in their resolution to oppose it—particularly lame ducks whom the Republicans wooed with promises of federal appointments. Kernan rejected such blandishments, according to Samuel Cox, who discussed the matter in a letter to *New York World* editor Manton Marble:

> Yours is recd. It is eminently satisfactory. Kernan and Ganson and myself and some others were discussing the amendt [amendment] question yesterday over a glass of wine and some nuts; and with such inspiration as they furnished, we concluded to avoid all other "temptations." The sentiment of our Congressmen has been oscillating on the amendt. question; and I only wished party success, knowing if we had power, all would be well. We must not do anything to give the ne plus ultras of our side a chance to rule out the really dominant and salutary influences. I look upon it, as a question of party policy. Mr. Townsend and other N.Y. men wish to confer about this matter and when we get to N.Y. we will get Mr. Tilden, Mr. Barlow, yourself, and a few other wise men of Gotham, together and afloat on this topic, around a Dinner at Delmonicos. I shall be over at the end of this week.[18]

Historian Michael Vorenberg elucidated, "The 'temptations' referred to are those perks (patronage, etc.) being offered to the lame ducks by Republicans. Cox end[ed] up convincing a number of Democrats to vote for the amendment but then he vote[ed] against it himself. Marble end[ed] up giving the amendment a lukewarm endorsement in the *World* (he release[ed] party members from any obligation and [told] them to vote as they wish), Ganson vote[d] for the amendment, and Kernan vote[d] against it. In other words, Kernan remain[ed] the most principled one of the lot—loyal to old Democratic ideas, consistent in his position, but, unfortunately, a supporter of slavery."[19]

How Kernan viewed slavery personally, is not known. In all his reported speeches there is no evidence of his ever supporting the institution. His silence on the subject, however, carries its own eloquence. It seems likely that for him, as for many in his party, neither the "Negro" nor slavery was a matter of great concern. He only spoke of the issue in terms of the Union and the right of individual states to make their own laws; like his party's presidential candidate in 1860, Stephen A. Douglas, he presumably did not much care "whether slavery was voted up or down." Still, it is noteworthy that Francis appears never to have verbally demeaned blacks, though he often shared platforms with those who did.

It seems likely that Francis, like most Democrats, felt that since the South would never voluntarily remain in the Union without slavery, then slavery would have to stay. Kernan came of age politically in the days of the "gag order" of the 1830s, and had seen the debate over slavery sunder friendships, parties, and ultimately the Union itself; perhaps he can be forgiven for the limited vision that viewed the slavery controversy as the source of the problem, rather than slavery itself. For Kernan, as for Lincoln, the Union was more important than the fate of blacks: "If I could save the Union without freeing any slave," Lincoln had written, "I would do it." But he recognized, as Kernan did not, that the Union could not be preserved without the death of slavery. Kernan and his fellow Democrats correctly regarded emancipation as a radical, untried "experiment." It is worth considering how radical it truly was: the almost instantaneous conversion of 4 million souls from chattel into free American citizens, and the simultaneous liquidation of hundreds of millions of dollars in human "property." But those who opposed the radical experiment of ending slavery were unwilling to face the fact that the *status quo* had failed, and was no longer an option. The nation had no choice but to set off into the uncharted waters of emancipation.

Kernan listened in silence during the three-week debate in Congress, during which the Republicans became more assured and the Democrats less confident as the moral pressure grew to view the war in terms of slavery versus human liberty.[20] On January 31, 1865, the galleries were packed with citizens anxious to witness the historic moment the U.S. House of Representatives passed the Thirteenth Amendment by a vote of 119 in favor, 56 against (including Kernan), and 8 abstained.* The house went wild.

There are only two cases on record in which Kernan and President Lincoln communicated directly, only one of them authenticated. The first was occasioned by Kernan's successful request for a pardon for a young soldier who had deserted his post to see his dying mother. This story was variously reported many years after Kernan's death, but its authenticity is questionable. The most recent telling of this story by the *Utica Observer-Dispatch,* was February 10, 1984.[21] According to Virginia Fehrenbacher, coauthor of *Recollected Words of Abraham Lincoln,* there are too many tales of Lincoln's freeing convicted deserters to credit them all.[22] This particular story follows a familiar pattern, and the boy's name is not known. Supposedly a very young Utica soldier of the 14th Infantry Regiment (called the First Oneida) heard that his mother was dying and so left his post in the front lines to hurry back to Utica in time to be at her deathbed. He was caught, found guilty of desertion and

* The amendment was referred to the Senate and later ratified by state votes.

sentenced to death by firing squad. Even the secretary of war, Edwin Stanton, is said to have declined to intervene. After an appeal to Kernan on the morning of the scheduled execution, the congressman supposedly hurried to the White House and was immediately brought in to Lincoln himself. The president said: "Well, Kernan, what can I do for you?" Kernan recounted the boy's story, and Lincoln responded: "Well, by God, Kernan, it is a shame to sentence a boy to death for going home to see his dying mother. I admire that boy and he shall not die." (The very language is so unlike Lincoln's well documented conversations that this sentence alone would cast doubt on the incident.) The story continues that "Lincoln signed the pardon and sent the necessary telegraph, and the boy was saved." Kernan supposedly commented years later: "These words that Lincoln uttered on that occasion showed his kindness of nature and feeling for the wants of others. He spoke to me on that day very dramatically. . . . I shall never forget the way he spoke. He seemed to forget for the time being everything except that young boy, and when he had telegraphed a pardon to the court, he apparently felt at peace with himself and all others." The purported statement in no way reflects Kernan's linguistic style. However, a very recent discovery of a trove of Lincoln papers in the National Archives, in which the president signed and commented on 570 court-martial documents, validates the oral history of Lincoln's magnanimity, so there may be some element of truth in this story.

The only confirmed record of direct communication between Kernan and President Lincoln regards a similar plea for a young private named Luther T. Palmer, of the Fifth New York Artillery, who was to die for deserting his post. The correspondence is in the Library of Congress among the Robert Todd Lincoln Papers. [See Appendix VIII.]

On February 15, 1865, just two days before the sentence was to be carried out, Kernan received a letter from an acquaintance, A. P. Case of Vernon, New York, explaining that the soldier had deserted after not having heard from his family for three months, and asking Kernan's help in obtaining an immediate interview with President Lincoln for the soldier's wife. Kernan wrote the president; Lincoln granted the interview, and heard the unhappy wife's plea for a pardon. The president promptly telegraphed General Philip Sheridan to suspend the execution, and asked for Palmer's record to be sent to him. He granted the pardon on April 10, one day after General Robert E. Lee surrendered unconditionally to General Ulysses S. Grant at Appomattox, and only four days before he himself was shot at Ford's Theater.

The shock of the assassination, and its martyrdom of the man who led the nation through war, profoundly changed people's perception of Lincoln. Kernan likely appreciated that Lincoln had suffered the war without bitterness toward the Southern states and had remained solemn in the Union victory. Republican congressman James G. Blaine beautifully recorded the sentiments shared by many in the days that followed Lincoln's death. "The gloom which enshrouded the country was as thick darkness. The people had come, through many alternations of fear and hope, to repose the most absolute trust in Mr. Lincoln. They realized that he had seen clearly where they were blind, that he had known fully where they were ignorant. He had been patient, faithful, and far-seeing. Religious people regarded him as one divinely appointed, like the prophets of old, to a great work, and they found comfort in the parallel which they saw in his death with that of the leader of Israel. He too had reached the mountain's top, and had seen the land redeemed unto the utmost sea, and had then died."[23]

Kernan rode on the slain president's funeral train on its solemn passage between Albany and Utica. Just as Lincoln had begun his term by introducing himself to the people of the Union with a slow, circuitous train ride to Washington, his funeral train now proceeded through many of those same towns and villages. All along the route, the people massed in the villages to get a glimpse of the train as it slowly passed the depots. At Palatine Bridge, a band played mournful music; at St. Johnsville, supper was furnished to the entourage; as the train passed Little Falls, minute guns were fired and a dirge played; people of Herkimer decorated buildings near their depot with mourning emblems; and Mohawk citizens held torchlights and tolled the city's bells as the train's occupants looked out the windows on a line of 36 young girls all dressed in white, holding evergreen wreaths—at their center stood a man draped with an American flag.

The Utica depot was covered with American flags, looped up with bands of black. More flags and black banners on the nearby express and telegraph offices were lit by locomotive and other lamps. Hundreds had arrived hours early to observe the arrival of the train, and by eight o'clock in the evening, crowds stretched from the west side of Genesee Street along the track for blocks, waiting patiently and quietly in the slow rain. Kernan was among the small group of dignitaries representing Utica, which included such prominent native sons as Charles H. Doolittle, Hiram Denio, Horatio Seymour, Roscoe Conkling, G.B. Matterson, Ellis H. Roberts, Thomas R. Walker, E.A. Wettmore, Ward Hunt, A.B. Johnson, and E.M. Gilbert.

❖

In the final months of the Thirty-Eighth Congress there was little heart left to do the work that remained. Lincoln was gone; the moderate Andrew Johnson was president. The war was over; 618,000 people had died. There was no agreement in Congress as to how to reconstruct the Union, but the Radical Republicans were determined to reassert control. Democrats, including Kernan and Seymour, were left without an issue to unite the party. The war had not failed, as so many in the party had predicted. Peace had come without negotiation; the South was subjugated and slavery abolished. The abuses to civil liberties in the Union were now only a vague memory. The war had not bankrupted the economy. The moderate new president proclaimed an amnesty for all those who had participated in the rebellion and restored property rights to the rebels, except for the return of their slaves.

Despite the fears of Democrats, and the expectations of other governments of the world, the nation's civil war ended without the execution of a single man who had borne arms against the government, without mass imprisonment and without wholesale confiscation of property. Although the rebels' right to vote was not immediately restored, negotiations were begun.

At the next Democratic state convention, in the fall of 1865, the party turned away from its wartime leaders, including Horatio Seymour and Samuel Tilden. It would be many years before the party's "dark days" would end and Democrats would be able to shake off the Copperhead image or to run in an election where the opposition could not sway the crowd by waving a bloody shirt of a dead Union soldier.

13

Dark Days for Democrats

THE ORGANIZED KILLING of soldiers by soldiers was over. Beyond that, however, Americans were hardly less divided during Reconstruction than they had been during the war itself. As before, the chief point of contention was the status of blacks. The freed people were determined to achieve their full rights as citizens; the former Confederates were equally determined to return them to subordination; and each regarded the others' goal as the height of evil. For their part, Republicans viewed blacks as potential Republican voters, and as their chief tool in holding the white South in check. Whether they saw them as more than this varied from individual to individual.

President Andrew Johnson, a lifelong Democrat whose wartime service as governor of restored Tennessee had elevated him to the national ticket, was a pugnacious man of narrow outlook, little tact, and great stubbornness. Radical Republicans were initially buoyed by his promises to "make treason odious" and to act as the "sincere friend of the negro." Yet Johnson soon reverted to his Democratic roots and what historian Eric Foner called his "unconquerable prejudices against

the African race."[1] Johnson's tactless stubbornness and the Radicals' desire for vengeance and the overthrow of Southern institutions collided violently, destroying civility in the capital and leading the Republicans to take control of government, and of Reconstruction policy, through the sheer strength of their numbers.

The postwar behavior of the Radical Republicans shocked Francis Kernan more than had the bloodshed of the battlefields. "The men who remained home in the day of battle . . . [become] ferocious when the battle is over," he derided, addressing the members of Congress.[2] The South was at the mercy of its victors, whose vengeful acts went against the deepest grain of Kernan's nature and violated the ideals his own life on American soil had validated. "Irishmen understand what it is to be pinned to a dominant power by the bayonet, and bear burdens which they have no part in imposing, and obey laws which they have no part in enacting," he fumed.

What galled him most was Congress's refusal to admit newly elected Southern congressmen. After all, the Southern states had followed the rules of amnesty, accepted emancipation, and pledged allegiance, but their elected representatives came to Washington only to encounter the fury of the noncombatants. Congressmen, no longer constrained to defer to the commander-in-chief during wartime, now fought hard to regain control of government. They insisted the legislative branch, not the executive—and most certainly not the refractory President Johnson—would set the terms for Reconstruction. Congress would say who could be admitted to the Union, how, and when. The radicals persisted in their policy of military occupation of the South while they built up the Republican Party with the help of former slaves.

To Kernan, the threat to America's form of government had not ended at Appomattox, but took a more insidious shape in peacetime. "There is no vituperation too strong [for those] inculcating a policy of hate and vindictiveness," he declared in his keynote speech at the 1866 state convention—the first following the Confederates' surrender.[3] Congress, he said, had "done little else during the whole last term except indulge in incendiary speeches toward the South. "Will we make them love the government by dealing with them in a way that could not be justified by the Constitution we were upholding?" He pledged to "go out among the honest people who are being deceived and deluded" and tell the real story of what Congress had been doing the past eighteen months since the war's end.

Kernan found the legislators' treatment of their own Union soldiers nearly as disgraceful as their treatment of the defeated South. He was livid that they had granted themselves an extra $4,000 compensation while allotting a "pitiful" $100 to Union soldiers maimed for life. The bill raised monthly soldiers' pay a mere $13— and that only after three years of service.

On the campaign circuit that fall Kernan deplored the "monstrous corruption" in national and state government—"the result of centralized power and greed." Even the state's Republicans campaigned against "the corruptionists," overlooking the irony that they had renominated the same slate of men who had earned the title in the first place.

While Kernan contemptuously denounced Albany's and Washington's abuses, Roscoe Conkling, the man who had replaced Kernan in the House of Representatives, spun a very different story. Conkling had been the Republican party's main hawk, and was still its star performer. As a leading member of the House's "Committee of Fifteen," he had been instrumental in legislation blocking the Southern representatives from taking their seats. The committee believed, said Conkling, that the "unseemly clamor of Southern rebels for immediate representation" was aimed at returning the South to its previous position of power in Congress, at obtaining remuneration for emancipated slaves, and at making the federal government pay for war damages and the Confederate war debt. Conkling preferred that Union "graves should grow green, that the cripples should have time to limp back to their homes, that the inky cloak should begin to disappear before the authors of our woes come back into the presence of their surviving victims; and that when they do come, it should be on terms of equality with the rest of us, and with nothing more."[4]

The year was 1866, a terrible year to be a Democrat. Kernan and his fellow party members were in the odd position of defending the Reconstruction plans of Andrew Johnson and Ulysses S. Grant against the radical element of the ruling Congressional party—Republicans who wanted none of the president's policy of forgiveness. To make matters worse, the Radical Republicans didn't even call themselves Republicans in 1866; continuing wartime practice, they called themselves "Unionists," implying total credit for keeping the nation together, and tarring their opponents as "Disunionists." Few voters wanted to call themselves Democrats, at least in public. The party was so isolated that rather than nominate its own slate of doomed candidates, it simply endorsed the nominees of the moderate Republicans, who called themselves "Independent Republicans."

It was at this low point in Democratic party morale, when so many members were leaving, that its demographic base began to shift: departing members were being replaced by new faces from abroad; 1866 marked the first election in which the Irish-American population was recognized as an important political bloc, especially in New York State. The Irish famine, exacerbated by the economic policies of the British, had caused such massive migration that one can hardly imagine the degree of change in and cultural strain on American society. (By 1870, one out of five people living in New York City had been born on Irish soil, the great preponderance having arrived hungry and desperate.)

The Irish population in Utica that year understood Kernan's campaign message all too well, from the newly arrived to those Americans whose parents and grandparents had left Ireland before the great famine. Kernan's political speeches for the first time carried heavy references to his heritage. "Irishmen were not apt to be blarneyed," he said.[5] Irishmen were not apt to believe a Congress that claimed to be too busy to repeal the neutrality law* when that same Congress "had no trouble to find time to pass Freedmen's Bureau bills and other laws to help them spend money."[6] At one rally Kernan read an excerpt of a report from General Grant to President Johnson to show the people of the South had returned to allegiance and would comply with reasonable conditions of Reconstruction. As for Congress shutting the door "against men who had been elected according to law," he said, "We know that we can never perpetuate a government by having a large portion of the people unrepresented and out of the Government." The audience cried no! no! at this reminder of their homeland's troubles. (Few of Francis's listeners were likely to remark the irony of the "unrepresented" white Southerners' unremitting efforts to deny freed people the vote.)

During a more intimate meeting a few weeks later, Kernan spoke of men such as his own father, "who knew what it was to be governed by laws, in making which they had no hand." This was the first time he had spoken on such a personal level, and prefaced his remarks by acknowledging that he was not accustomed to speaking in this way. "The effrontery of these radicals amazes me," he continued, "[expecting] that Irishmen will vote for a system which would make these Southern States worse off than Ireland since the days of Cromwell."

On November 1, 1866, thousands of people came from towns throughout central New York, swarming into the central park of Rome to hear the "Patriot of '48," Richard O'Gorman.[7] Kernan, president for the day, shared the platform and introduced his famous guest, though his story was familiar to all. As a young man in 1848, O'Gorman had raised an armed rebellion against the British, and although it was unsuccessful, his efforts politicized the famine, the British evictions, and the economic policies that led to mass starvation and exile. O'Gorman was forced to flee. In New York City he continued to organize his fellow Irishmen into a voting political bloc that the city government had to recognize. (At the time of the rally, O'Gorman, though eminent at the New York bar, had not yet displayed his ability to be just as corrupt as any native-born politician.)

Kernan introduced O'Gorman as "one who had seen and felt in his native land the policy of proscription and oppression the Radicals advocate," and O'Gorman lived up to his reputation for rousing the passions of a crowd with fiery denunciations of the cruel tyranny he had experienced in the island home which gave him birth. And what was the history of Ireland, he asked, "but the history of just such insane steps of tyranny and proscription as the Radical party urge us to take towards the South? There was a time when England might have said to the Irish people, we will not crush you, when England might have been generous, and

---

* The Neutrality law (passed ca. 1793) barred Americans from training on U.S. soil to engage in military action against a foreign power. Thus, it handicapped Irish nationalists after the Civil War from organizing for anti-British activity in Canada, which some nationalists hoped to conquer and hold as a playing card to force England to give up its rule of Ireland.

then the indelible stain would not rest upon her escutcheon today. But she was vindictive and cruel, and she burned into the hearts of the Irish people a feeling that will yet cause her to roll as low as Ireland was ever rolled in the dust!" He concluded his speech with an appeal to the voters to secure a better form of union for this country than England and Ireland's unhappy form.

The rally was the high point of the 1866 campaign, a rousing speech and picnic social on a glorious fall day. "Aye," one news report reads, "It was a day when men felt strong; when energy seemed a quality of the blood; when life was rich; when hearty patriotism was awake; when men's whole natures were alive and active."

At the end of the rally Kernan led the three cheers, "which the crowd gave with a will," and then read a letter explaining that while Horatio Seymour had been detained elsewhere, his heart was with his fellow citizens of Oneida. In past campaigns Seymour and Kernan had frequently shared the same platform. From 1866 on, however, they tended to split their duties to cover greater territory or, perhaps, to better target their speeches to Irish-based and English-based audiences. In a similar letter that Kernan presented a few days later, Seymour explained that his absence "is not a matter of indifference to the local ticket," but rather that the party chairman "thinks it best" for him to be in Syracuse.

The glorious weather soon turned, and the momentary blaze of optimism displayed in Rome was as temporary as the autumn leaves. Republicans swept national, state, and local offices, even in the South, where Republican "carpetbaggers" and Southern collaborationist "scalawags" controlled much of the voting. New York elected Republican Reuben Fenton to replace Horatio Seymour. Roscoe Conkling, at the young age of 36, returned to the House of Representatives as New York's Republican boss, soon to be nominated for a seat in the Senate. *

Although Congress held much of the South under military rule and carefully controlled its elections, it was somehow patching the rebel states back into the Union. History moved forward, however unjustly, while soldiers returned home and citizens refocused their energies on daily life, local concerns, and private business. Francis Kernan, too, rededicated himself to his law practice, where there was plenty of work to be done. His anger had cooled, but his passion for constitutional law found a perfect focus. In April of 1867 he was a delegate to the New York State Constitutional Convention: a caucus in which "the great political battles of the period were waged,"[8] and in which the foundations of New York's present government began to be laid.

By all accounts, the 160 delegates represented the state's most able leaders. Its vice president, William A. Wheeler, afterward became vice president of the United

---

* The Republicans overwhelmingly controlled the state's legislature and would soon choose Conkling to replace Senator Ira Harris when his term expired.

States and two delegates, Horatio Seymour and Samuel Tilden, later campaigned for the presidency (with Kernan playing an important role in both campaigns).[*]

Kernan was an excellent choice as a delegate-at-large from the Fifth Judicial District. New York's constitutional conventions came in 20-year cycles. The last had been in 1846, when Francis was 30 years old. His father, William, had also served as a delegate-at-large, helping to frame the document that Francis was now called on to reconsider. Francis knew the logic of the document, had practiced law under its rule, had argued frequently before the state's highest courts, and knew the constitution's strengths and weaknesses.

Kernan sat on the judiciary committee. along with 13 others.[†]

Although the convention fell short of its official purpose of securing a new state constitution to put before the voters in the fall, the delegates continued to work on it after the 1867 election. Their articulate debates, which lasted nearly a year (from June 1867 to February 1868), educated voters to the issues of the day: black suffrage, female suffrage, minority representation, taxation, finance, bribery, education, intemperance, canals, and home rule for cities.[9]

It appears from the journal of the convention that Kernan spent most of his time in the judiciary committee rather than attending the meetings in the Assembly chamber in the capitol at Albany, for he is recorded as having made just four motions, and having presented only one petition. He did, however, make one speech that caught the attention of the press, especially because the speaker was a Catholic. Kernan emphatically advocated an absolute prohibition of sectarian appropriations of public money, saying,

> the provision . . . that the legislature shall not donate any moneys or property of the state to any person, association or corporation, is correct and just. According to the theory of our government, all sects and denominations of religion are to have equal rights, and there is to be no discrimination in favor of or against any. The members of one denomination are not to be taxed to support the religious, charitable or educational institutions of the other. This is as it should be. The provision reported by the committee on finance is based upon this princi-

---

[*] Other notables included William M. Evarts, George William Curtis, Charles J. Folder, Charles Andres, Amasa J. Parker and Theodore W. Dwight. Men from Oneida County included George F. Comstock, Hiram Denio, Othneil S. Williams, Thomas D. Penfield, and George Graham.

[†] Judicial reform was the convention's most immediately pressing issue. The state's system of having eight coordinated appellate tribunals in the supreme court created disunity, while the annual turnover of half the members of the Court of Appeals resulted in delays, backlogs, and inconsistencies. The judiciary committee proposed that the Court of Appeals should be composed of six associate judges and one chief justice, chosen by popular vote. At the first election, each voter could vote for the chief justice and up to four associate justices. This system would enable the minority party to elect at least two judges. Judges' terms were extended to 14 years, and the retirement age was set at 70. The convention's recommendations (accepted by the voters in 1869) materially changed the judicial system, increasing the number of judges and creating a commission to dispose of the large backload of cases that had accumulated in the Court of Appeals.

ple and will carry it into effect. It cuts all those institutions off from the public treasury; it placed them, as they should be, on an equal footing; it leaves them to be supported and sustained by the charitable contributions of the individuals and religious denominations which organize and control them. This is in accordance with the principles or our government and is just to all. It will prevent jealousy and sectarian bitterness, which are ever to be deplored, from springing up between the members of the different religious denominations on account of real or fancied inequality in the appropriations made to charitable institutions.

It was a speech that would be cited often during his run for governor in 1872, in which he was attacked as a Catholic and feared for holding just the opposite sentiments.

Another of Kernan's motions concerned voting qualifications. It proposed that a person must have been a citizen for only ten days, rather than the required 30, to be allowed to vote. It passed by 87 to 60 votes and withstood several proposed changes at later sessions. The ten-day requirement was in the final draft of the new constitution proposed by the convention, along with a one-year state residency and four-month county residency requirement. The close vote and debate are not surprising, given the success of the Democratic party in signing up immigrants fresh off the boats and offering patronage jobs in exchange for a promise to vote Democratic. In some elections, thousands of immigrants were signed up in a single day, and New York City's Democratic "Boss" Tweed was known for his ability to guarantee high numbers of votes—higher by far than the voting registries!

It must have seemed ironic to watch Kernan, as a Democrat, arguing to relax the voting qualifications just when Tweed was flouting any and all restrictions. Using fraudulent practices, Tweed had just managed to elect himself to the state legislature in the November election, adding the title of state senator to the long list of 17 municipal offices he already held.

Describing the final draft of the new proposed constitution, Chairman W. A. Wheeler pointed out that it included a "stringent provision to stop bribery and improper influences at elections, [and had] set guards against the making in wicked ways and for evil purposes, of contracts for the maintenance of the canals."[10] The recommendations did not go far enough, however, nor were they approved by the state's voters in time to make a difference in stopping Tweed's rising power. Its provisions addressed local city corruption by preventing members of the common council from holding multiple offices, by preventing city officers from also being members of the state legislature, and by restraining the power of the common council of any city to dispose of public money.

The delegates did not adopt the one reform measure proposed by Kernan that he regarded as the most important of the convention.[11] Had it been adopted, the infamous "Boss Tweed Ring" could not have plundered the treasury of the state and of New York City over the next few years. Kernan proposed that any city with a population of over 20,000 should have a board of audit whose sole job was to monitor and approve financial transactions. The city could contract no debt nor pay any bill without the board's approval. Board members were to be elected by the taxpayers, and no one else; they would have no patronage or pay; and their terms would last three years, with one member entering and one leaving each election.

As a state assemblyman in 1861, Kernan had seen up close how the constitution gave too much control over local affairs to legislators in Albany, who answered to no one but their own party bosses and themselves. The corruption he saw then was a fraction of what the unbridled prosperity of the postwar years was now spawning in both parties.

Kernan's proposal directly countered the structure of New York City's corrupt bipartisan Board of Supervisors, controlled by Tweed, which audited county expenditures, appointed inspectors of elections, and performed other highly important functions. By 1867, the year of the constitutional convention, the board of supervisors was deeply involved with corrupt assemblymen who approved state jobs and contracts, for which the board regularly charged contractors a levy of up to 35 percent on all bills it allowed to be paid. "Boss Tweed" was keeping 25 percent and paying 10 percent to the city's comptroller.[12] While no proof yet existed of this abuse of taxpayers' money, the corruption of city and state government was common knowledge.

Kernan's recommendation regarding boards of audit would have prevented the illegal expenditures of the Tweed Ring; and Samuel Tilden's energetically argued recommendation that the state should run the Erie Canal as a public trust, if adopted, would have made the subsequent scandal of the "Canal Ring" impossible. But neither recommendation passed, and Tweed would soon also hold the title of director of the Erie, along with his comptroller, Peter Sweeny.

The postwar years marked a major change in the nation. The U.S. Constitution had survived its terrible and most crucial test, but could it now survive prosperity? Mark Twain dubbed the era "The Gilded Age." Powerful party dictators, hand in hand with corrupt businessmen, controlled government patronage, and attitudes were changed rapidly from the days when government office represented the highest ideals of the nation. Ambitious young men were now finding more opportunity and prestige in the world of business than in public service, and for the first time the upper classes began to look down on men in political office.

Back in Utica, Francis Kernan practiced law in a world changed by war, a world where governments at every level were more centralized, wealthier, and more powerful, as were corporate clients. Businesses spread beyond state borders, aided by coast-to-coast rail transportation and telegraph lines. Everywhere, and especially for the industrialized North, opportunity abounded.

The firm of Kernan and Kernan benefited from these changes, acquiring more in the way of business and corporate clients, in particular, the New York Cen-

Law office stationery of Kernan and Kernan

tral Railroad; and with the younger members of the family coming along, the firm had plenty of lawyers to manage the increased case load. Francis's years in public service undoubtedly made his firm well known throughout the state and attractive to national clients. He also became an active investor in real estate in the Utica area, purchasing and selling, and lending money on mortgage.[13]

On the national scene, the radical element in Congress drifted even further from President Johnson's policies. Flagrant abuses of freedpeople under the South's newly-passed "Black Codes" spurred Northern support for the Radicals, who were finally able to pass a Civil Rights Act over Johnson's veto. Passage of the Fourteenth Amendment followed, guaranteeing blacks equal protection under law. Johnson's belligerent opposition to this measure backfired, resulting in the election of veto-proof Republican majorities in both houses of Congress. Its power almost absolute, the Republican Congress undertook to run the country, and Reconstruction, on its own. Although Congress easily overrode Johnson's vetoes of their stringent new Reconstruction Acts, the president still had the power to thwart their enforcement. After a series of showdowns, the House finally impeached Johnson in February 1868 by a party-line vote—only afterwards drawing up the charges against him. The House managers included some of the most extreme Republicans in Congress, but the President's defenders outmatched them in legal acumen. After a trial of 11 weeks, the Senate, organized as a court, fell one vote short of the two-thirds majority needed to convict. The event marked the zenith of the Radicals. Most Republicans by now were favoring a more moderate Reconstruction policy, and the public was weary of conflict.

A week after the impeachment vote Kernan participated in the state Democratic convention to help sort out the possibilities for the year's presidential elections. The state's Democratic position as expressed by Samuel Tilden was that the Civil War "caused a fungus growth of centralism in the Republican party, failed to heal wounds or revive industry. Instead, it inflicted on an exhausted people [of the South] the burdens of war's aftermath, established negro supremacy, and packed Congress with black Republican allies' over-representation of blacks in the Senate." Rather than preventing the states from returning to the Union, he argued that restoring the South its rights could instead save the nation $125 million a year, reduce taxes, and liberate industry.[14]

The nomination scene at the convention was to be one of the most dramatic political events of Kernan's career, and no one, not even the participants themselves, could afterward tell the story in a way that made sense or peace among them. It happened at a time in American political history when no one knew who the nominee would be until the convention voted: a time when party bosses and delegates spent days and nights in "smoke-filled rooms" making deals, bending arms, pressuring delegates, and forging alliances.

But this story begins on the state level, in March 1868, with ex-governor Horatio Seymour, Samuel Tilden, Francis Kernan, and others at a meeting in (Boss) William Tweed's room at the Delavan House in New York City to prearrange the state convention's program.[15] The important issue—they agreed with Seymour—was that no candidate for president should be endorsed and all the New York delegation would go to the national convention with their votes unrestricted. This plan was followed out in the state convention, which nominated a delegation to attend the national convention in July. The delegates were uncommitted and the impressive group contained within itself at least six potential presidential nominees, including three men with national followings: Seymour, Sanford E. Church, and George H. Pendleton. Along with Kernan, the delegation also included Augustus Schell, William Cassidy, and three men whose names would become synonymous with corruption: Tweed, Peter B. Sweeny, and A. Oakey Hall.

According to Seymour and his later biographers, he did not seek the nomination. According to Tilden's biographer, the New York delegates had decided to vote for the Ohioan Salmon P. Chase during the initial balloting, but only as a ploy to conceal their intent until they could determine the outcome of the convention. According to Clement L. Vallandigham of Ohio, Chase was the only possible nominee who had a chance to win the national election, but only if he could get a two-thirds majority at the convention.[16] (At a time when the nation was still emotionally divided, it would be difficult to convince voters that the Democratic nominee had the support of the entire national party without at least two-thirds of the convention in agreement.)

On July 4, Tilden's plan for the national convention went off without a hitch. Seymour was made president of the convention (which apparently satisfied his ambitions): Tweed was made a vice president, and the two-thirds rule was adopted. The platform acknowledged that the war had settled for all time the issues of negro slavery and the right of a state to secede. However, it attacked the "so-called" Reconstruction acts as "unconstitutional, revolutionary, and void." California delegates announced it as their patriotic duty "never to submit to be governed by the negro nor by those claiming to be elected by negro suffrage." Other petitions and resolutions aimed at heading off the Fourteenth Amendment and stalling the Fifteenth. (The Thirteenth Amendment had outlawed slavery; the Fourteenth would soon be ratified, giving all persons born in the United States, or naturalized, the right of citizenship; and the Fifteenth would ensure voting rights regardless of color, race, or previous servitude.)

As a delegate, Francis heard two historic petitions presented on the Monday of business. Most probably, he did not recognize their historic importance. Few did. The first petition foreshadowed the Progressive Era, declaring that the producing classes (the workers) were of primary importance; the "distributors, financiers, and statesmen" were of secondary consequence. The petition pointed to low wages, long hours, and the damaging service of "working girls and women" and urged the workers to join labor unions or use any other honorable means to obtain fair treatment from their employers. The second petition came from the Woman Suffrage Association of America and decried the tyranny of taxation without representation. Their objection that sex, as a voting requirement, was an "insurmountable obstacle" was received by the delegates with loud, long gales of laughter. This response only added to their bitterness at seeing 2 million black men given the vote while they had to fight against the insertion of the word "male" into the Fourteenth Amendment. Had that word been added into the federal Constitution, where it had never been, it would have created a further barrier to women being included.* (Although Tilden had serious doubts about black suffrage, he was convinced of the "utter absurdity" of female suffrage.)

However, the delegates were not looking to the future so much as to the pressing question of who "the new man" would be. Who would represent the Democratic party against the nearly mythic Ulysses S. Grant?

Seymour enjoyed the attention and rumors his election as chairman of the convention inspired. Speaking to the press, he seemed to give excellent reasons why he should not be selected and still better reasons why nobody else should be nominated.[17] Yet, despite this false modesty, Seymour spent the evening before the ballot buttonholing each New York delegate to ensure a Chase vote. Not every New York delegate appreciated the suspense. According to Judge W. F. Allen's letters, he complained of being "kept in ignorance long enough! I would like to know now who I am expected to hurrah for then, so that I can make affidavit that he is the spontaneous choice of the people."[18]

Before the balloting began on July 8, Chairman Seymour addressed the gathering, saying it was important that the convention clearly understand the two-thirds rule in effect. Not everyone was happy with the rule, especially those potential nominees who thought they had a chance of winning with a simple majority vote. But the convention needed to show unity and Seymour was "very anxious that no misapprehension should arise after a ballot shall have been taken." He asked for a reading of the rule and invited discussion and a resolution of any doubt.

---

* The first petition went to the Committee on Resolutions, then later went to the Committee on Credentials. It had been signed by Elizabeth Cady Stanton, Susan B. Anthony, Mrs. Horace Greeley, and Abby Hopper Gibbons.

When one delegate suggested the rule not be adopted, Kernan immediately rose to defend it. "For the sake of the country we want not only to nominate but to win," he said, and he hoped "no man would be nominated here who was not voted for by two-thirds of all the delegates." The debate ended quickly, and the two-thirds rule held. The last question put to the chairman before the balloting was whether, after the nominations were closed that day, any new candidate could be brought forth. Seymour replied that the convention could bring forward new candidates at any time; an answer he would deeply regret.

The balloting was crazy. The delegates could not possibly follow the implications or decipher any clues as each ballot came up with a different combination of names, and no one was getting the necessary two-thirds majority. On the 21st ballot, General Alexander McDowell McCook of Ohio set off an unexpected stampede with a stirring speech for Seymour, insisting the chairman's name be placed in nomination. Some say this was probably just to fend off Chase, who was gaining in the ballots, but others say it was part of a twisted scheme of Clement L. Vallandigham's to swing the convention to Chase. The idea was to put Seymour's name in nomination and thereby form a block that would, on later votes, swing to Chase. Whatever the plan, it was too clever by half. McCook's passionate support of Seymour and heat of the hall that summer day combined to spark the fire. "Seymour!" shouted the delegates. "Seymour! Seymour! Seymour!" must be placed in nomination.

When order was restored, Seymour declined, as he had been doing all week to his supporters. But his expressions of gratitude only served to inspire the crowd's determination. "I do not stand here," he said, "as a man proud of his opinion or obstinate in his purposes, but upon a question of duty and honour I must stand upon my own convictions against the world. When I said here, at an early day, that honour forbade my accepting a nomination, I meant it. When I said to my friends I could not be a candidate, I meant it."

Vallandigham responded that Seymour must, in these times of public exigency, put aside personal considerations and yield to the public good. "The safety of the American people is the supreme law!" Kernan, as head of the New York delegation, found himself suddenly standing in the front of the stampede. There was nothing he could do but rise and offer the name the crowd demanded. Disclaiming any lot or part in Vallandigham's motion, he declared that the New York delegation must overcome Seymour's sensitiveness. Seymour ought to abide by the action of the convention, he said. "No one can doubt that he has steadily and in good faith declined; but, now that his honor is safe, his duty to his country, his duty to his fellow citizens, to all that shall come after us, requires that he shall let the judgement of the delegates of this convention prevail if they should select him as the standard-bearer most certain, in their opinion, to win a triumph for the country next November."[19]

When Kernan sat down, another vote began and, amid the growing pandemonium, Seymour rushed to the platform to protest. Horrified, the nominee offered

Chase in his place, but was shouted down. Seymour! Seymour! His friends pulled him off the stage to an antechamber, where Sanford E. Church, Joseph Warren of the *Buffalo Courier,* and other friends urged him to yield to the nomination. Still on the convention floor, Tilden rose to change the vote of the Empire State to match that of her sister states. The voting having concluded, Tilden rushed in to see Seymour waving his arms in distress. "My God, Tilden, what shall I do?" he cried, to which Tilden inscrutably responded, "Your countrymen have called." Vallandigham, who had only wanted Chase, and whose ploy had backfired beyond his imagining, was forced to urge Seymour to put the wishes of the convention ahead of personal considerations.[20] The nominee became the only man ever nominated for the presidency against his will and amid his own protestations.

The only ones who left happy the next day were the Southern delegates and the vice-presidential candidate General Francis Preston Blair, Jr., who gladly accepted the nomination. Chase left believing that he had been deliberately set up and that New York and Ohio had planned it that way all along. Many wondered if Tilden hadn't been angling for the nomination himself, and got caught on his own line. Chase's daughter, Kate, thought Seymour and Tilden had conspired to betray her father and had her suspicions confirmed that "when the South seceded the brains of the party went with it."[21]

Seymour headed back to his Deerfield farm and put himself in seclusion for over a month, not responding officially to the nomination and personally debating how to get out of the situation.

While Seymour maintained his silence, the Fourteenth Amendment was ratified. Then, on May 20, the Republican party dashed any desperate hopes the Democrats still had of winning the coming election by nominating the adored Ulysses S. Grant, "Savior of the Union." The Republican platform demanded full civil rights for freedmen, including voting rights. This would bolster its support among free slaves in the South, but it left the matter of negro suffrage in the loyal states to the white voting population of those states, thereby avoiding alienating Northern voters.

Still waiting for Seymour's acceptance, Tilden began organizing a three-pronged national campaign: courting the labor vote, marshalling the Irish and German vote, and establishing strong communications between state leaders and their counties. Kernan would be important in getting out the Irish vote, but his first duty was to convince Seymour to accept. Tilden insisted to Kernan that it wasn't his fault; he hadn't pressured Seymour, but they could not have a campaign with a candidate declining the nomination. Something had to happen! Fearing the consequence of Seymour's inaction, Kernan and other friends urged him to accept the nomination. Tilden's organizers sent back encouraging opinions from all over the country as to Seymour's prospects. With the state party in such disarray, Tilden begged Kernan "because of his skill and tact" to be permanent chair of the State Democratic Committee when it reconvened after July 8—Kernan declined.[22]

Seymour took until August 4 to write an acceptance speech, a choice he later called "the great mistake of my life." He knew he could not win. Grant could never be beaten, especially by a Northern Democrat so few years after the war. The Democratic nominee kept to himself for the first two and a half months while Tilden maneuvered. Seymour figured if he was going to get buried, the party could dig the ditch without him. Seymour's only hope was that at least New York State could be saved from yet another Republican sweep. The state party clearly realized its mistake. By mid-October there was a groundswell of dislike, and the party panicked. Some begged Tilden to ask Seymour to withdraw. Tilden hurried up to Utica to consult with Kernan and Seymour. Seymour needed no convincing to remove himself as the nominee, but they all saw how damaging it would be for the candidate to bow out to an alternate one month before the election. Instead, Tilden organized a mass meeting to take place in New York City on October 27, both at Tammany Hall and in Union Square, to show support for the nominee and quash talk of his withdrawal.

In the final month of the campaign Sanford E. Church and Kernan accompanied the reluctant candidate on a brief, two-week Western tour, traveling by sleeping-car and making speeches at major stops in western New York, Pennsylvania, Ohio, Michigan, Indiana, and Illinois. Among the press in the entourage was the editor of the *Utica Daily Observer,* who sent back glowing and optimistic reports that contrasted with the gloom of the leaders in private.

The reception in Cleveland took place October 26 at the depot, where, according to the *Utica Daily Observer,* "long into the night, when the party were dozing in their berths, cheering and cries of 'Hurrah for Seymour,' came into the windows of the cars at occasional places, showing that some enthusiastic spirits had been willing to wait up until the small hours of the night, on the bare chance of seeing their candidate."

In Chicago, an editor claimed, "the enthusiasm was unbounded, and the scene in front of the Court House, with thousands of lanterns and illuminations, was simply magnificent." In Pittsburgh, Seymour's voice could not be heard in the open-air arena, and the crowd pressed in on the speakers, causing general confusion and some alarm on the platform. Kernan took over, making light of the situation. "Fellow citizens," he said, "although our candidate cannot be heard to-night by you, I thank God we have got a candidate who we are not afraid to show, and who can talk when his voice is in order."

Seymour campaigned on the issues of taxation, which had risen with the war debt, and the growth of government. "You remember the time was when you did not know what a government officer was, unless, perhaps, it was a postmaster. Now they surround you wherever you go; they find you out in every corner of the land. The structure of our government has been changed by the oppressive system of taxation, growing out of the wanton waste of the public money, and springing from the disregard of constitutional obligations." He complained that Republicans wanted to direct the attention of the people to alleged disorder and violence in the South, to distract voters from noticing the high interest rates due to government borrowing and unfavorable tariffs.

In the final week before the election Kernan campaigned locally, along with fellow Democrats J. Thomas Spriggs, H.O. Southworth, DeWitt G. Ray, and his oldest son, John D. Kernan, making his entrance as a public speaker in a political campaign. Francis addressed a crowd in Utica's Spencer Hall November 1, 1868. Although we have no copies of his campaign speeches, the general Democratic argument was for immediate restoration of all the Southern states and allowing the voting (white) populace to regulate their own elective franchises.

Republicans had an easy time fighting Seymour, using his antidraft riot speech and his war record as a Democrat against him. "Do we want to go back to that and undo everything we have won?" they asked the crowds, who shouted back, "No!" "Shall we turn the war into a farce, win it only to lose it at the ballot?" "No!" The Democrats had little to say except to repeat their long, consistent positions regarding the power of central government.

On November 4, the evening before the national elections, Seymour joined his friends in Utica for his last campaign speech. The reception began—before his arrival—with music, guns, and fireworks. The townsmen crowded into the concert hall, where Kernan led off the evening's speeches, although, after weeks of intense campaigning, he was not in good voice. "We know we have got to meet, in this conflict, an immense army of corrupt office-holders; and encounter the cry of "copperhead," he said, "but we trust to triumph over all these things." He described his journey through the Middle West (then called simply the West) and through Pennsylvania, and the respect and admiration with which Seymour had been received.

After another hour of speeches the crowd left the hall and, accompanied by the band, marched to the depot to greet Seymour and to escort him to the entrance to Bagg's Hotel. There they had formed a procession, headed by the band, and amid the discharge of cannon and the firing of Roman candles, marched Seymour's carriage up Genesee Street to the Butterfield House, where he could address the crowd from a balcony.

He spoke only for a few minutes. "I have just passed through the great States of the West, and through Pennsylvania," he said. "I have seen the fertile prairies of Illinois, Indiana and Ohio, and for the first time, known something of the great mineral resources of Pennsylvania. . . . I have gained much knowledge of the power, the wealth and the greatness of my country, and I have come home possessed of a more profound love for our land than ever before." Seymour had already spoken at various station stops that day and had used up his voice and strength. His last campaign speech was not his best.

At the convention that summer and throughout the fall campaign, Seymour's lackluster behavior assured the outcome. Ironically, however, the eventual election results showed that "the Great Decliner" had had more of a chance than the party leaders imagined. He carried 47 percent of the votes nationwide. To be sure, Grant's 214 electoral votes overwhelmed Seymour's 80, but a passionate campaign might have changed that.

Seymour won in New York, New Jersey, and Oregon, and pulled close to victory in California, Connecticut, and Indiana. Party leaders had failed to notice popular attitudes were changing. The country was tired of talking about the war and tired of antagonistic politics. The Radical Republicans did not know it at the time, but their impeachment of President Johnson had capped their influence. Corruption and scandal would dog their decline, as both parties continued to benefit from the phenomenal prosperity of the postwar economy.

On a state level, Boss Tweed was credited with Seymour's majority vote of 30,000 in New York. It was about equal to the number of fraudulent votes Tweed had corralled by using accommodating judges to naturalize about 35,000 immigrants and sending money to election districts to help convince the populace.

Tweed was actually more interested in promoting the state Democratic ticket than in promoting Seymour for president. Tweed was determined to seat John T. Hoffman as governor so that laws could be passed in Albany to make New York City independent of the state legislature. To find out exactly how many votes were needed to secure the election, Tweed and the mayoral candidate, Oakey Hall, telegraphed a bogus letter to upstate members of the state committee and other local leaders, requesting the estimated returns at the closing of the polls. Signed with Tilden's name and addressed from the "Rooms of the Democratic State Committee," the October 27 missive began,

> My Dear Sir: Please at once to communicate with some reliable person in three or four principal towns and in each city of your county, and request him (expenses duly arranged for at this end) to telegraph to William M. Tweed, Tammany Hall, at the minute of closing the polls, not waiting for the county, such person's estimate of the vote. Let the telegram be as follows: "This town will give a Republican (or Democratic) majority of ____." There is, of course, an important object to be attained by a simultaneous transmission at the hour of closing the polls, but no longer waiting. Opportunity can be taken of the usual half hour lull in telegraphic communication over lines, before actual results begin to be declared, and before the Associated Press absorb the telegraph with returns and interfere with individual messages, and give orders to watch carefully the count.[23]

As a result of these dirty tricks, Hoffman's majority was equivalent to eight percent of the total registered voting population! Tweed soon returned to Albany, where he garnered plenty of bipartisan support, and where his henchman William Hitchman was named speaker of the house. The state legislature got right to work, adding $3 million to the newest budget proposals for New York City. Tweed, serving on the committees of finance and internal affairs, was now in a perfect position to loot on the largest scale the country had ever seen.

Seymour was silent, simply grateful to be the nominee no longer. He planned an overseas tour to get away. Tilden was also silent, in part because, however distasteful Tweed's maneuvering had been over the years, he could be counted on to provide Democratic victories, and in part because Tweed wielded so much power. This was not the first election in which dirty tricks were used, and standard requests for party funds in five- and ten-dollar bills were certainly understood by all concerned. But Tweed had gone too far and too publicly to be tolerated any longer. Tilden now looked to upstate Democrats and Albany as the only hope for reform of New York City politics. With Seymour defeated and in retreat, Kernan became his major upstate ally.

The indignant Republican editor of the *Tribune,* Horace Greeley, was enraged at Tweed's bold theft of the election, and demanded action from Tilden as the only man who could attack the corruption from within the Democratic party. On October 29, 1869, a year after the votes had been fully analyzed and the scandal made apparent, Greeley published his challenge "To Samuel J Tilden, Chairman of the Democratic State Committee:"

> Sir: You hold a most responsible and influential position in the councils of a great party. You could make that party content itself with the polling of legal votes if you only would.... Mr. Tilden, you cannot escape responsibility by saying, with the guilty Macbeth, "Thou canst not say I did it; Never shake those gory locks at me," for you were at least a passive accomplice in the giant frauds of last November. Your name was used, without public protest on your part, in circulars sowed broadcast over the State, whereof, the manifest intent was to "Make assurance doubly sure," that the frauds here perpetrated should not be overborne by the honest vote of the rural districts. And you, not merely by silence but by positive assumption, have covered those frauds with the mantle of your respectability. On the principle that "the receiver is as bad as the thief," you are as deeply implicated in them to-day as though your name were Tweed, [Sheriff] O'Brien, or Oakey Hall.... Now, Mr. Tilden, I call on you to put a stop to this business. You have but to walk into the Sheriff's, the Mayor's and the Supervisor's offices in the City Hall Park, and say that there must be no more of it. Say it so that there shall be no doubt that you mean it, and we shall have a tolerably fair election once more. Will you do it? If we Republicans are swindled again as we were swindled last fall, you and such as you will be responsible to God and man for the outrage.[24]

Tilden made no public response or statement. For the moment, Tweed had reduced him and Seymour to little more than figureheads. Tilden was too practical to attempt the impossible, and Tweed was a dangerous enemy. Despite his cold wit, and brilliant legal mind, "Silk Stocking Sammy" Tilden would never win a New York City street fight against Boss Tweed, and he knew it. By nature, he was so averse to passing judgment before all the facts were weighed that he invented the amusing phrase "see you later," rather than to say "good-bye," politely implying he wanted time for further reflection.

Avoiding an open fight, Tilden quietly plotted, looking for the proof with which to launch a legal assault. Tweed was well aware of Tilden's intentions, and correctly regarded Tilden as his foe. Their animosity was obvious when the two met face to face in private councils. Tilden's effect on Tweed was like a match to a fuse. "Sam Tilden want to overthrow Tammany Hall," the Boss fumed. "He want to drive me out of politics. He want to stop the pickings, starve out the boys, and run the city as if 'twas a damned little country store in New Lebanon. He want to bring the hayloft and cheese press down to the city and crush out the machine. He want to get a crowd of reformers in the legislature . . . who will cut down the tax levy below a living rate; and then, when he gets everything fixed to suit him, he want to go to the United States Senate."[25]

Tilden ignored his outbursts, but Tweed was wrong about Tilden's ambition. He was not looking to the Senate. He was looking to the White House, and he knew he could not get there while Tweed controlled his party.

*B*reaking the Tweed Ring

Can you stop this waste of your money?
Can you draw back the hands that are now
plunged up to the armpits in the Treasury?
JOSEPH W. HALZMAN, LL.D.

THROUGHOUT THE GILDED Age both political parties were split by reform wings that demanded public accountability from those in office; but the officeholders continued to harvest the votes through state and federal patronage jobs. Kernan became a member of the opposition within his own Democratic party. He and Seymour, the national party's nominal leader, represented upstate reformers, while Tilden, the party's state chairman, represented the reform element in New York City.

The leading Republican voice demanding reform was Horace Greeley, editor of the *Tribune*. Greeley longed for public office but embarrassed his fellow party members with his denunciations of their abuses, and he raised the ire of party boss Roscoe Conkling. Senator Conkling was not corrupt, but he was happy to be in control of federal patronage jobs. The U.S. Post Office in New York City had more workers than that of any state, and the Federal Customs House had the largest staff of any in the nation. Roscoe Conkling was one of the biggest employers in the country.

Bosses and reformers alike were trying to deal with the problem of extraordinary growth. They attempted to organize and control the state's transformation from an essentially rural, agrarian economy to an industrial economy concentrated in urban areas. New York City was the biggest urban area, and William Marcy Tweed just happened to be the most capable organizer.

While Conkling controlled federal patronage, Tweed considered the state and city treasuries his own special reserves. Money flowed for public works projects after the Civil War, such as improvement of the city's waterfront, business districts, and tenement houses, and the expansion of upper New York City. These massive projects meant city jobs and Democratic votes. The great thoroughfares on the East Side were redesigned, with sewers, drains, solid pavements, and recreational areas. Sixth, Seventh, and Eighth Avenues were broadened, and a boulevard was built from 155th Street to 59th Street and Eighth Avenue. New parks along Morningside Heights and Riverside Drive were created, while the city's overall transportation systems were improved. The Brooklyn Bridge project and the new Health Department provided plenty of jobs to desperate immigrants who removed sewage from the bulkhead walls along the shore and hauled over 160,000 tons of manure from vacant lots.[1] The city smelled a lot better, but the same could not be said for its politics.

The November elections of 1869 gave a majority in both houses of the state legislature to the Democrats for the first time in 24 years. Tweed controlled votes in both branches, controlled the governor he had helped seat, John T. Hoffman, and even controlled important judicial appointments. From his own seat in the state Assembly, Tweed saw a bright future. His fellow legislators passed a new city charter giving even more local control to Tammany Hall, the venerable social club-turned-headquarters of the city's Democratic political machine. Only 32 state legislators voted against the charter. It was not a cheap victory, however. Tweed, as chairman of the Committee on Cities, spent an estimated $2 million to secure the landslide vote, with the cost of senators between $5,000 and $40,000 each. The new city charter ended Albany's control and limited the governor's power over New York City. Tweed returned home to New York City a hero, ready to work on the fall elections to re-elect Governor Hoffman and Mayor Oakey Hall.

Not everyone was in favor of Tweed's "Black Horse Cavalry," as the corrupt legislators were known. Opposition was developing among disaffected Democrats and Republicans in the City, and members of the bar formed the bipartisan New York Bar Association, calling for judicial reform and declaring that honesty and professional ethics were more important than making money. This was a favorite theme of Tilden's, who gave the association's opening speech, saying that young lawyers should be able to have a successful practice and still preserve professional honor.

Although the judiciary included some enlightened and disinterested jurists, it was largely a political institution. Judges were popularly elected for relatively short terms, and elections were easily manipulated by ward bosses; the resulting turnover in personnel caused confusion in the courts and a severe backlog of cases. The situation in New York City had become so corrupt that Tilden advised a son of Francis Kernan who came to New York to begin a career to "return to Utica rather than confront the degrading competition to which a young man would be exposed."[2]

At the state Democratic convention that fall, Tilden's pocket was picked. The press relished the symbolism. "We hope [Tilden] has a realizing sense of the company he keeps when he opens conventions for Mr. Tweed, Mr. Hall, and Mr. Sweeny," said *The Nation*.[3] It may have been the final insult for Tilden, who, from that time, took on the nearly impossible challenge of purging his own party.

The story of the toppling of Boss Tweed and the ascendancy of reformers in the Democratic party begins in July of 1871, the day the *New York Times* published a list of fraudulent bills and payments made by the city's board of audit. The appropriation for the county court house in lower Manhattan had grown from $250,000 to more than $4 million, not including furnishings. Finally, there were facts to support what everyone already knew.

With the publication of the *Times* article, titled "Secret Accounts," clearly either Tweed or Tilden would have to go as leader of the New York City Democratic party. But Tilden's success would mean weakening the party throughout the state and upsetting the patronage system. As Tilden put it, "a party in power is naturally disposed to allow the continuance of abuses rather than to hazard the extreme remedy of cutting them out by the roots." Even so, he determined to take the fight to the state convention, and for that, he needed allies.

As Tilden later told the story,[4] "the first man I sought was Mr. Francis Kernan. His freedom from all entanglements, whether personal or political, with corrupt interest of corrupt men, his high standard of public duty, his disinterestedness and independence, his tact and eloquence in debate, his general popularity and the readiness of his district to send him as a delegate, make him my necessary ally in the State Convention." After much telegraphing, Tilden found Kernan in Albany on his own professional business. Tilden met him there, on August 4, just six days after the publication of the secret accounts. Kernan was about to leave for the seashore to attend a sick relative. Together they rode by coach to Utica to consult with Horatio Seymour, who had been in correspondence with the two reformers and was in full sympathy with the plan. Seymour saw the corruption of government as a bigger, national problem, rife within the Republican party as well. The question in his mind that should be put before the voters was which of the two parties arraigned its own corruption more plainly.

"I think a spasm of virtue will run through the body politic," wrote Seymour before their meeting. "The farmers are getting poor, with no look ahead of better times. Immigration, railroads, and machinery are crowding the markets with provisions and breadstuffs. Taxes are now felt as they have not been since 1860. The corruption in our party is local. In the Republican Party it is pervading. We can lose nothing by stirring up questions of fraud."[5]

All three agreed they should make the effort, even though they might fail completely. They next sought out Charles O'Conor to help them in their legal tactics. O'Conor had earned some fame for serving as counsel to Jefferson Davis when the ex-president of the Confederacy was indicted for treason. He had also worked with Seymour, Tilden, and Kernan during the 1867 state constitutional convention, and Kernan and O'Conor already knew each other from family connections.* As Kernan was to become Tilden's chief assistant in the political fight against Tweed, so O'Conor was to be his chief assistant in the legal battle. O'Conor agreed to serve as legal counsel for the State of New York against the Tweed Ring without compensation. O'Conor's willingness to lead a commission of inquiry, said Tilden, "led Mr. Kernan and myself to vote for Mr. O'Conor, without his knowledge, as Attorney-General."[6] Having secured the cooperation of Seymour, Kernan, and O'Conor, Tilden next enlisted the support of George Jones, the editor of the *New York Times,* and Oswald Ottendorfer, editor of the state's most influential German newspaper. Tilden returned to Albany to let Governor Hoffman know about the arrangement to have O'Conor institute suits. Hoffman, whether desperate to cut Tweed's controlling strings, or simply recognizing Tilden's threat, joined the reformers' plot.

The secret accounts were followed by more newspaper articles, and soon more citizens found the courage to organize and openly oppose the corruption that extended into the city and state judiciary. A group of lawyers met behind closed doors to discuss forming a "Vigilance Committee," to purge the judiciary, in much the same way a similar body formed in San Francisco in 1849 to drive out the bands of thugs and thieves who had terrorized that community. The volcanic sentiments of Joseph W. Halzman, a respected 20-year veteran of the bar who now supported "extreme measures," jolted the lawyers to their senses. Extreme measures meant hanging the chief malefactors to lampposts, or other convenient scaffolds. The normally peaceful Halzman damned the corruptionists thus:

[Where] can you turn for a remedy? . . . They hold everything within their grasp. Every head of Department in our City is their creature. Every employee of our government is their slave. Fifteen thousand hirelings, who never perform work, and indeed who have no work to perform, are on the City pay-roll, as a praetorian guard around the Chief Boss, to do any act or deed he may command. Can you stop this waste of your money? Can you draw back the hands that are now plunged up to the armpits in the Treasury? Can you stop Tweed, can you stop [City Comptroller Richard] Connolly, can you stop [Mayor A. Oakey] Hall, can you stop [Parks Commissioner Peter] Sweeny, can you stop the coterie of favorite contractors all dripping with the wealth that they have stolen from you and from me? Can you go to the Grand Jury, which is filled with their

* Both Kernan and O'Conor's Irish-born fathers were pioneers of Steuben County. Charles O'Conor served in the state Assembly in 1833 and 1834.

tools? Can you go to the District Attorney, who is their pliant servant? Can you obtain protection from the police, who are these men's bodyguard? Can you call upon the Governor of the State, who extols the virtues of Tweed, the purity of Hall, the brains of Sweeny and the charming simplicity of Connolly? Can you, in fine, appeal to our Courts? If so, where? Get an order from some one Judge—Barnard will vacate it. Get another—Cardozo will vacate it. Get a third, and Ingraham will "modify" it. . . . And long before the case will reach [the Court of Appeals], the City will be in financial ruin.[7]

The implications of Halzman's support of extreme measures scared his companions into taking wiser and more legal action. They planned to temporarily tie the hands of the plunderers with injunctions and, in the coming elections, help elect state legislators who would be willing to impeach corrupt judges.

The reformers, led by Tilden, worked to the same ends, and planned their first open assault against the Ring—a public showdown at the state Democratic convention in Rochester on October 4, 1871. They would bring their own duly elected "reform" delegates, challenging those of Tweed. Tilden knew he must have enough upstate support to hold the balance against Tweed, but he concentrated his efforts in the cities while Kernan and other party leaders worked throughout the state. By the end of September he wired Kernan that O'Conor and Ottendorfer would head the city delegation. He also tried to persuade others to run for the state legislature as well as himself—though O'Conor, Seymour, and Kernan were not willing.

The Boss was well aware of the danger. In an attempt to avert the showdown, he made an offer to Tilden that he would not resist seating the "reform" delegates as long as they did not interfere with Tweed's legislative nominees.[8] Tilden simply ignored the offer. O'Conor and Kernan concurred that "compromise was equivalent to ruin." In a telegram to Seymour, Tilden explained the consensus that "action and not words can save us," and that "public opinion and the many who now accept our lead are strong enough to carry us through." The masses, he said, "expect action from the Democratic leaders, not words," and "we have no danger except in half measures and half-hearted counsels."

The Ring was cracking under the pressure. Shortly before the convention the city comptroller, Richard Connolly, abandoned Tweed and asked Tilden to be his lawyer. He wanted to resign, but Tilden had a better plan. First, Connolly would appoint a deputy with custody of all the documents in the comptroller's office; and second, the city would be prevented from making payments by the institution of a taxpayer suit.

As the showdown approached, the reformers assessed their strength with their own party. It was still not sufficient to guarantee victory. To gain support for reform, while avoiding damage to the party, Democratic leaders began to broadcast the idea that the Ring, not the party, was corrupt. From New York City, Tilden wired Kernan of his progress, but warned him not to underestimate the strength of their

"Let Us Prey"

Thomas Nast depicts the Tweed gang as a band of vultures waiting out the storm
of reform. Boss William Marcy Tweed is still today seen as the epitome of 19th-century
corruption of city government, though he may also be considered the victim of
the power image-making of political cartoonist Thomas Nast.

adversaries.[9] As Kernan saw it, "many were not sore because [the gang] stole the money, but because they kept it all."[10]

With amazing speed and organization (and Tilden's personal financial support),[11] the reformers managed to elect a reform delegation to the state convention.

The morning of the showdown arrived, and most of the delegates filed into the hall ready to support reform. The reformers had managed to pack the convention and challenge the right of the Tammany delegates to be seated. Tweed's representatives were told they would be voted out if they claimed seats, and seeing they were outnumbered, did not ask for them. The reformers were delighted by such an easy victory and proceeded with full assurance, not knowing Tweed was still very much in charge, monitoring the convention from a nearby hotel.

In Tilden's opening speech, he tried to soften the blow he was about to administer to his party by (what else?) blaming the Republicans. The Republicans, he said, had created the circumstances that allowed the ring's growth. "The corrupt centralism of power" that began during the Civil War had resulted in "vulgar millionaires" grasping the highest seats of honor and power. Under Republican control, said Tilden, legislative bodies had become purchasable and the office of U.S. Senator was twice "knocked down to the highest bidder." Albany "must be cleansed by good men of both parties."

Harmony prevailed. After Tilden's speech, the delegate from the first Oneida district, General James McQuade, withdrew his claim to a seat in order that Francis Kernan be invited to participate, a move greeted with sustained applause. Kernan was immediately seated and appointed to the committee on resolutions. The resolutions were then read, and Kernan rose to second them.

The delegates shouted for him to speak, and he mounted the platform, embracing the opportunity. "The Tammany delegation came here feeling that they could not ask [for] seats here until they had cleared themselves of the taint which was resting upon them," said Kernan. "We told them that we would have to vote them out if they claimed seats here, and they, feeling the justice of our determination, did not ask for seats." Kernan told the convention that if delegates maintained this honorable, patriotic spirit, they would "march to certain victory and overthrow the corrupt and cankerous Federal Government." His speech included an attack on the corruption in the Republican party and a thinly veiled threat of jail to the corruptionists in the Democratic party. Tweed's men streamed back and forth from the convention hall to Tweed's hotel suite, keeping him posted on the proceedings.

"The Federal Government is seething with the corruption of its officials," Kernan continued. Doubting that the Republican party could be trusted to reform itself, he pointed as proof to the state Republican convention that had just days before "turned out from its ranks the men who stood up for honesty, including Horace Greeley."

As for the Democratic party's willingness to deal with its own corrupt officials, "Democrats," said Kernan, "will punish with the prison—when legally convicted—their own officers who have plundered the people. . . . As I have said else-where, and so every Democrat says here, by his heart and by his acts to-day, that when such abuses break out among those holding office under the authority of our party's election, we will have acts, and not mere words. We will have acts that tell that we are indignant; acts that tell that we will make men stand out of our ranks until they have vindicated themselves from the suspicion which has been cast upon them."

But the Tweed delegates' seeming acceptance of defeat had been nothing more than a clever parliamentary maneuver. Their immediate withdrawal of any claim to be seated prevented an open discussion between the two forces. Having prevented the big debate, they then went on to ask the convention to forgo seating the "irregularly elected" reform delegation as well. They knew that without those delegates, Tilden, Kernan, and Seymour would not have the votes to sway the con-vention! It would thus be politics as usual. The Tweed forces plan to—as they put it—"save the party" from a debate about reform in the state campaign was really a plan to save themselves.

Standing outside, ready to make his grand entrance, Seymour did not realize the reformers had lost. He entered the hall amid some cheers hailing him as the next president in 1872. There he spotted Kernan seated beyond the rail with the rejected reformers. As soon as the noise abated, he hesitatingly, "and in the hope of arousing no unpleasant discussion," moved that Francis be admitted to the floor of the convention as one "who has grown gray in the party harness . . . and . . . whose very presence was a sufficient credential to his title to a seat." But before the con-vention could respond to Seymour, a waiting delegate rose to block Kernan's read-mission by offering another "who was not only regularly elected, but a "friend of that great Democrat, John T. Hoffman." The first mention of the governor's name set off the predictable roar, and Seymour, the party's nominal national leader watched in humiliation as the convention cried for another delegate over his own friend Kernan. It was a deeply degrading treatment of an honorable statesman who had served through six separate terms as governor, and had held his party together during war.

Seymour understood he would not be elected as presiding officer of the con-vention unless he gave up his tirade against the Tammany thieves. He withdrew his nomination as presiding officer and left abruptly to return home, proud not to be a part of a party assembled in which Tilden and Kernan were not invited.

Tweed was angry. He had expected to defeat Tilden, Seymour, and Kernan, and then control them and trade on their good names. At his hotel room, he denounced the trio as "three troublesome old fools,"[12] while on the floor, the remaining delegates brushed off the charges of party corruption as a mere Repub-lican fantasy, and supported Tweed's hand-picked legislative nominees for the state legislature. Tweed's goal was to maintain his control of Albany.

Back home on his farm, Seymour was aware of his growing years and failing vigor. "All a man does about politics after he is sixty years old is only meddling with other people's business," he maintained. Still, inspired by duty, he urged his younger allies to fight hard. "The Democratic leaders and organizations are dead against us," he wrote.[13] "The members of the Convention went home pleased with the diplomacy of their leaders, but with a lower tone of morality than they had when they left home. The young men we look to with hope in the future are debauched. They were willing to have Tammany coaxed out of the Convention and then to slam the door in the face of the honest men who had unearthed crime in New York. When the leaders had done their work on Thursday noon, the Tammany men stood in the light of having acted in a high-toned, generous way. The Convention was grateful to them for allowing it to say stealing was wrong in a way that hurt no one's feelings. . . . The majority of the Convention wanted to leave matters in that shape, and they were angry when you and Kernan and West and others forced them to do a few decent acts."

"We may forgive others," Seymour continued, "but the men who have left us will not forgive us. . . . They have yielded to temptation, and now they are like church members who have fallen from grace; they not only hate to meet their minister, but they learn to hate him. . . . They were glad to hit us, and the young men would have done more if the wiser ones had not held them back."

Having lost the political showdown, Tilden returned to his law office in New York City to fight on legal grounds. Within ten days, he and his staff produced an affidavit entitled "Figures that could not lie." The document provided a clear picture of the corrupt practices of Mayor A. Oakey Hall, Comptroller Richard Connolly, and William Marcy Tweed. This triumvirate had certified the validity of millions in bills, of which Tweed received between 24 and 42 percent. Others received lesser percentages, but all together, the kickbacks totaled an astounding 64 percent of the total billings. For the city to pay these bills, Comptroller Connolly had issued bonds, the proceeds of which were deposited in the National Broadway Bank, credited to the city treasurer. From this account, the bills were paid. The Ring was so confident of its power that Tweed's percentages were deposited as they accrued, making their discovery easy for investigators.

The legal battle had only begun. As for the political battle, Tilden called on his growing cadre of "militant reformers," for reinforcements and with less than one week before the state elections, the reformers literally created a second Democratic party with its own ticket to run against all other Democratic and Republican candidates. Tilden himself was on the ballot for state assemblyman. He was determined to continue the fight against Tweed in Albany.

The Tweed scandals and the party's internal schism gave the election to the Republicans. Most of the voting public perceived their choice as between the Democratic Tweed faction and the Republican Conkling faction. Conkling made sure the voting frauds of earlier elections were not repeated. The U.S. Congress authorized the Circuit Court of the United States to appoint one person from each

party in every election district to watch voter registration, voting and vote count-
ing, and empowered U.S. marshals to appoint deputies to keep order and make
arrests. Though the federal law was originally aimed at stopping Southern states
from preventing blacks from registering and voting, Conkling considered the law
necessary at New York polls, too. The Democrats protested mightily, as the Republicans were voted back into the majority in Albany.

Although Tilden's reform candidates were badly beaten elsewhere in the state,
they won in New York City by an overwhelming majority. Tilden himself was
elected to the state Assembly, which, given his lucrative law practice, was considered
by many a sacrificial move. Tweed, despite the publicity and legal battles, still managed to win reelection to the state Senate, and expected to return to Albany for
more showdowns with Tilden. Instead, Tweed would languish and die in jail.

In Albany, Tilden "forced the impeachment [of Judge Cardozo], against every
imaginable obstacle, open and covert, political and personal,"[14] though the
reformer's expectations in the legislature exceeded his ability to force change. The
indictments and subsequent legal proceedings against Tweed continued until his
death in 1878. For all the outrage and the accusations of stolen millions, Boss Tweed
was never tried for theft, but was convicted of a misdemeanor: failing to audit
claims against the city—a technicality having nothing to do with what history has
charged.

During the turbulent years in which Kernan worked so fervently to reform the
Democratic party, he was also engaged in another important public service. On
February 10, 1870, the state legislature appointed him to the Board of Regents of
the University of the State of New York, which is still today the governing body of
all the state's public and private schools, colleges, and universities. The appointment
was no small honor. The development of a strong system of public education was a
major accomplishment of the young country. From its beginning, in 1784, the
board had attracted the talents of the state's leading citizens, including John Jay,
Alexander Hamilton, and Stephen and Jeremiah Van Rensselaer. Kernan held the
post for 22 years, serving with such dignitaries as Governors Samuel Tilden, Grover
Cleveland, and John A. Dix, as well as such prominent statesmen as Chauncey M.
Depew and Whitelaw Reid [See Appendix IX]. From the beginning of his membership, Kernan served on a standing committee that reviewed whether applicants
had the necessary financial and physical means and adequate personnel to fulfill
their functions. For most of his tenure, Kernan also served on the committee that
prepared the annual report to the legislature on the condition of the state's educational institutions, and he served on various other committees as well. At times the
supervision got down to such fine details such as reports and opinions about what

textbooks would be used, and even discussion of a proposal to teach not only writing but also how to cut a pen.[*] Francis no doubt took a special interest in the Regents' granting a charter in 1875 to Saint Bonaventure College in Allegany, which had had its beginnings in 1854 when Kernan's father-in-law, Nicholas Devereux, had prevailed on the Brothers of the Minor Order of Saint Francis to move from Italy to America and open a mission, proposing a gift of 200 acres of land and $5,000. By the end of Kernan's active service on the board, the regents were overseeing nearly 20,000 students in public and private high schools, academies, colleges, universities and professional schools in the state and in foreign cities ("Berout" and Constantinople), and more than 1 million students in public grade schools.

[*] In researching this book, a rumor was told to us by Philip Rayhill, of Utica, that Francis Kernan had been responsible for instituting the A, B, C, (etc.) grading system, a system that is still under debate, and for which his descendants might alternately praise or condemn him. We were unable to find any mention of this issue in the official proceedings of the regents' meetings. A grading system is the type of issue that would have been debated by the regents, but, just as likely, it could have been a policy that was instituted in Francis's day and for which he was good-naturedly blamed by those who knew him when grades were first posted in Utica schools.

Kernan for Governor

[Catholics] have been voting for Protestants for nearly
a hundred years, and I cannot bear it to have it said that
Protestants are more bigoted than Catholics, and cannot
vote once for a Catholic in return.

HORATIO SEYMOUR 1872

THE DEMOCRATIC NATIONAL Convention of 1872 marked the only occasion when a national party nominated its arch enemy as its presidential nominee. Horace Greeley had, for more than a decade been one of the most relentless foes of the Democrats, and now Francis Kernan had the misfortune to be on the same ticket. Kernan split his time that year between running for governor of New York and running from any association with Horace Greeley.

How the Democratic party came to nominate a Republican who for over a decade had been one of its most relentless critics requires some explanation. One must step back to the beginning of that year and examine the situation in the Democratic and Republican parties that led to such a debacle.

In New York, Democratic party reformers had managed to expose the Tweed Ring and impeach crooked judges, but the struggle had left the national party's most powerful state party weak and without a potential nominee. While the Democratic party nationally was gaining some respect for its reforms, the Republican party was moving in the opposite direction, largely because of what many Americans viewed as the blatant failure of Reconstruction. "I say to-day, in the face of heaven and before all mankind, that the carpet-bag governments are infinitely worse than Tweed's government of the City of New York," Samuel Tilden fumed.[1] Perhaps even more galling to Northerners than the maladministration of the Southern states was the increasing control of federal patronage by a small coterie of senators close to President Grant, New York Senator Roscoe Conkling being the grandest "spoilsman" of them all. "The last two State [Republican] Conventions were mockeries," seethed Horace Greeley in April, after being thwarted in his own bid for office under the Republican banner by Conkling's supporters. "Some of the delegates [were] bought out of our hands and others driven out of the Convention. . . . I saw numbers, under threats of losing federal office, dragooned into doing the bidding of one man."[2]

Greeley's daily editorial declarations against the spoilsmen in the *New York Tribune* had found a wide audience and, for the coming election, he preferred anyone but Grant for president, just so long as he was not a Democrat. Especially sympathetic to his denunciations were members of the new "Liberal Republican" party. This faction, which had recently coalesced in Missouri around the issue of granting universal amnesty for ex-Confederates, had issued a call in January for a national convention to take place that May, and invited all reform-minded Republicans. The response across the nation had been electric. Support came from all quarters. The Democrats were delighted with the turn of events. Knowing they had no chance alone of beating Grant in 1872, they viewed the large new anti-Grant contingent as allies. They decided to join forces with the Liberal Republicans to champion a nominee they could both live with, and who, with their combined support, could perhaps oust the sitting president.

Greeley was at first lukewarm to the Liberal Republicans, but he had become so much of an anathema to the regular Republican party and to Roscoe Conkling's henchmen that the editor finally accepted an invitation to attend the May 1 convention in Cincinnati. The movement needed Greeley's strong editorial voice, and Greeley needed temporary support. He soon warmed to the group, recognizing its members' sincere desire to end Grant's "military rule," to grant universal amnesty, and to discourage the abuses of federal patronage. More importantly, he recognized opportunity.

The leaders of the gathering, who expected to nominate Charles Francis Adams for president, had neither a national organization nor the necessary experience to conduct conventions. They were hopeless pawns to New York's delegates: political veterans whose skills had been honed by years in ward caucuses. Whatever complaints Greeley had raised back home against Conkling's methods of control, the New Yorkers stunned the crowd with their expert use of offensive parliamentary tactics in blocking certain delegates, substituting others, and, just to be sure, silencing one-third of those delegates who managed to hold on to their seats. Even as it was happening, convention leaders believed these maneuvers would not come to anything more than a polite, complimentary vote showing some support for Greeley, before the delegates could get down to the serious business of nominating Adams. They were wrong.

On the sixth ballot, amid an equal blend of cheers and hisses, Greeley took the nomination. "I have concluded," said the stunned temporary chairman, Stanley Matthews, "that as a politician and a President maker, I am not a success."[3] Many delegates left reconsidering their support of Grant, while the Democrats, who had encouraged the liberal movement, read the news and plunged into depression.

Greeley?

How could they keep their pledge to the Liberal Republicans and support Horace Greeley for president of the United States on the Democratic ticket? For decades the man had waged constant verbal battle against their party leaders, hurling epithets at everyone from Van Buren in the 1840s to Tilden most recently. Greeley had assailed Seymour so bitterly during the war years that any conciliation would have been tantamount to humiliation. The *Tribune* had labeled Kernan an "envenomed copperhead." Greeley had called Kernan "the most dangerous Democrat during and immediately following the war period, for Mr. Kernan's candor was such as to impress upon his hearers that every word he uttered he really believed was true."[4] He had classed Kernan with most New York City Democrats, whom he had characterized as blacklegs, thieves, burglars, gamblers, and keepers of dens of prostitution.[5]

Seymour, Kernan, Tilden, and Sanford E. Church all conveniently found they had more pressing business elsewhere that prevented them from attending the party's national convention. New York was represented by delegates such as John T. Hoffman, who played an important role at the national caucus, and discovered that the Southern Democrats had appreciated Greeley's wartime vitriol against Lincoln and had not forgotten his graciousness in helping pay the bail for Jefferson Davis when the president of the Confederacy was arrested. They also appreciated the editor's more recent attacks against the Republican Reconstruction policies. Another important delegate from New York who helped organize support for Greeley was the man who had succeeded Tweed, "Honest John" Kelly.

The national Democratic leaders agreed that they must support the Liberal Republican movement. The reaction to Greeley's nomination was described by *The Nation* as how one might react to a dish of "boiled crow,"[6] adding a new phrase, "eating crow" to the American lexicon. In 1872, Democrats ate a lot of it, including Greeley's platform, which diametrically contrasted with ten years of Democratic policy. It supported "negro enfranchisement" and opposed any reopening of the issues settled by the Thirteenth, Fourteenth, and Fifteenth Amendments. Even the ex-slaveholders in attendance swallowed hard, agreeing with the Greeley platform to "recognize the equality of all men before the law, and the duty of the government to act without concern of nativity, race, color, or religious or political persuasion."

Seymour chose to avoid the state convention as well as the national convention, although he consulted Kernan and Tilden before the latter gathering, and supported Tilden's choice of Kernan as the gubernatorial nominee. The major qualification for the leading position in the state, following the years of scandal, was that the nominee be of absolutely impeccable reputation, acceptable to both the Democrats and the state's Liberal Republicans. On September 5, Tilden placed Kernan's name in nomination and within two ballots the delegates made it unanimous.

U.S. Senator James G. Blaine of Maine noted in his memoirs, *Twenty Years in Congress,* that "Kernan's nomination alarmed the Republicans because he was a man of spotless character and great popularity." The Republicans were sufficiently concerned as to arrange for Grant himself, as the guest of Roscoe Conckling, to visit Utica right before the state Republican convention. According to Blaine, "the Republicans responded [to Kernan's nomination] by nominating the seventy-five-year-old Civil War General, John A. Dix." To add to the irony of this election year, Dix was a Democrat.

But there was another aspect to the selection of Francis Kernan besides his reputation—his religion. Anti-Catholic sentiment, particularly anti-Irish-Catholic sentiment, was becoming a divisive political issue.* Kernan, who enjoyed the confidence of all classes, was uniquely qualified to counter the prejudice that Catholics could not be trusted in public office. The traditional argument against Catholics in politics was that they owed their allegiance first to Rome, not to the U.S. Constitution, and because of that allegiance, they sought to abolish freedom of speech, freedom of the press, and religious toleration. According to Seymour's biographer, "Kernan accepted the nomination specifically to counteract partisan appeals to religious feelings."[7] The two men spoke frankly on the likelihood of a Catholic being defeated at the polls, and Seymour reported their conversation and their resolve to Tilden. "The kind of fight made upon [Kernan] puts him in a place where if he yields, he does so for reasons which not only say that he can never be Governor, but which also make the rule that none of his family or faith can hold that office. It will not do for a Democratic Convention to lay down that rule. It will be better he should run and be beat than to have our party fall into this fatal error."

The highest ranking Catholics in Kernan's day included Roger B. Taney, fifth chief justice of the Supreme Court (who died during the last year of the war), and

---

* Before the American Revolution, Catholicism was proscribed by law in most of the Thirteen Colonies. However, during that conflict, Catholics had proved their loyalty as citizens in spite of the religious allegiance they owed to the pope; and thus they became accepted as full citizens when their religious freedom was guaranteed by the Constitution. One Catholic, Charles Carroll (of Carrollton), signed the Declaration of Independence, and two laymen, Daniel Carroll of Maryland and Thomas FitzSimmons (Pennsylvania), signed the Constitution. Others in the Revolutionary generation included Oliver Pollock "Financier of the Revolution," John Barry, of Philadelphia, "Father of the American Navy," John Fitzgerald, of Virginia, friend and neighbor of George Washington.

James Campbell of Pennsylvania, who served as postmaster general (beginning in 1853) during Franklin Pierce's administration.[*] By the Civil War, Catholics found more opportunities in state legislatures than in federal offices, and some found opportunity as generals and as statesmen: the best known being Philip Sheridan, William S. Rosecrans, Pierre G. T. Beauregard, Stephen R. Mallory, and Raphael Semmes. By 1872, the year of Kernan's gubernatorial race, no Catholic had served as governor of any state, and only two laymen had reached the U.S. Senate— including Maryland's first senator, Charles Carroll, and the truly exceptional James Shields, who was elected to the Senate three times, each time from a different state.[†] The fact that the country's high ranking Catholics during a 100-year period can all be cited in a single paragraph is the best indication of how rare it was for a Catholic to participate in the nation's political councils.[‡]

The prejudice was not merely due to political differences. Many New York Protestants looked upon the Irish as a blight, a disease killing their state. The Catholic population in the United States had grown enormously, from approximately 25,000 during the American Revolution to 3 million by the end of the Civil War.[8] They concentrated in large industrial centers. As these cities grew and as the old Dutch-English villages of prewar days declined, rural Protestant elements saw only masses of uneducated, impoverished, and dangerous immigrants, living in slums, debauching in saloons and gambling houses, breeding unwanted street orphans, and corrupting Democratic ideals with their dishonest political machines. Some envisioned another, more bloody civil war: an Armageddon between virtuous Protestantism and the rapacious forces of Catholicism.

However, Kernan's experience as an American Catholic was very different from that of the recent immigrants. In 1800, when his father William Kernan arrived from Ireland, there had been too few Catholics to excite any fear. There was no country-wide church organization and too few members to build local churches, as well as too few priests to serve the scattered flock.[§] This situation

[*] Not until well after the Civil War was another Catholic to achieve cabinet status. President McKinley appointed Joseph McKenna attorney general in 1897. In 1905, President Roosevelt appointed Charles J. Bonaparte as secretary of the navy, and later, to the position of attorney general.

[†] A general in both the Mexican War and the Civil War, James Shields was elected to the U.S. Senate from Illinois (1848), Minnesota (1858), and Missouri (1879).

[‡] Theodore Roosevelt wrote in his legislative diary in 1882, "The average Catholic Irishman of the first generation as represented in this Assembly, is a low, venal, corrupt and unintelligent brute." [Elting E. Morison, ed., *The Letters of Theodore Roosevelt* (Cambridge, Mass.: Harvard University Press, 1951), vol. 2, page 1470.]

[§] By 1800, scarcely one in a hundred of the white, non-native population was a Catholic, and those were scattered throughout the nation, mostly in the larger cities of New York, Pennsylvania, Maryland, Virginia, and Kentucky. There were French from Quebec, and refugees from France and the West Indies, Irish in the coastal ports, and Germans in Pennsylvania, along with the original English in Maryland, such as the Plowdens and Brents. What priests there were—perhaps 35 for the enormous area from Illinois in the West to Boston in the East, and from Savannah in the South to Albany in the North—were for the most part former members of the then-suppressed English province of the Society of Jesus, with a few from the old Maryland Catholic families, and a scattering from among the refugees from revolutionary France.

resulted in an unprecedented mixing of Catholics and Protestants not only in everyday life but also in the amicable sharing of meeting places and houses, and of liturgical events, such as preachings, funerals, and marriages. The American Catholic Church was under the leadership of its first archbishop, John Carroll (of Maryland). Native-born, Bishop Carroll was fired with the idea of forging an American Church under the exciting new American conditions of freedom, and without European connections other than allegiance to the pope.

The beliefs in freedom of religion, of separation of church and state, and of legal toleration of others' doctrines were both the religious inheritance and the political inheritance of Francis Kernan. There had been no separate building for Catholic worship during his early childhood in Tyrone, New York, and his father had been a leader among a local populace that practiced toleration and ecumenism. He was later fortunate in moving to a community that was singularly free of prejudice, and he was also fortunate in marrying into a family, the Devereux, with many Protestant and old American connections—Butlers, Pierreponts, and Clapps. In his own Catholic family, Kernans had married Protestant Quins, Pattens, Colvills, Purtons, and Cambrelengs. There appears to have been no evidence of prejudice and bigotry among them.

Francis's life embodied the American ideals of religious tolerance. Even to those who tried to stereotype him in the coming campaign, he clearly sprouted neither horns nor tail. Even the German population delighted in his nomination. The popular *Staats-Zeitung* reported that "the state of New York could not possibly have a governor more honest and more energetically opposed to corruption than Francis Kernan. We must confess that this nomination altogether surpasses the expectations which we had cherished of the Democratic State Convention."

Francis had accepted the nomination with reluctance. He knew his chances were slim. He would have to face the public embarrassment of endorsing Horace Greeley while enduring the more personal, ugly attacks against his religious life.

In Utica at least, the campaign started with jubilation. The announcement of his nomination was posted that day on the bulletin board of the *Utica Daily Observer,* the moment the telegraph arrived. Within half an hour, cannons boomed, and the city hall's bell rang loudly and continuously for half an hour to spread the news. The firemen turned out, cheering enthusiastically as they assembled on Genesee Street. The streets were crowded that evening with ladies and gentlemen ready to celebrate. Utica's Old Band was engaged, and by nine o'clock an extensive procession began its march about town, receiving additional recruits on every block. A half-hour later the crowd marched toward the depot, where the First Atlantic Express brought home delegates from both the state Democratic and the state Liberal Republican conventions. Fortunately, the train was on time, and entered the depot as a two-gun salute echoed over the Deerfield hills.

The delegates stepped from the sleeping-cars to cheers. The handshaking and personal congratulations went on for another half-hour until the speeches began, with Samuel S. Cox (of Ohio) eulogizing the distinguished gubernatorial nominee. "With the Honorable Francis Kernan to lead us, bearing not only the standard of Democracy but the white flag of peace and conciliation borne by Horace Greeley, with mutual good will on all sides, Heaven and even saltpetre will aid us, and we can count upon 50,000 majority in New York City and 100,000 in the State."

After the speeches the procession went, arm-in-arm, to Kernan's house in Chancellor Square, to serenade the nominee and hear his acceptance speech. Kernan expressed gratitude for his nomination by both parties, viewing it as a call for reform in public affairs. He lauded those Republicans who had "stepped out of their party to stand by their convictions, whether they meet with victory or defeat. . . . This was a movement of the people, not of the leaders. We must not forget that men who are elected to office should not and must not be the creatures of any party; they should be faithful to all the people."

A couple of weeks later, at a ratification rally held in the opera house, with a second meeting organized for an overflow crowd outside, Utica heard the nominee's full campaign speech, which he would continue to hone throughout the next month's campaigning.

Kernan began by pointing out the failure of President Grant's stated policy of restoring peace and concord, which "serves for personal aggrandizement and to keep alive asperities and antagonism which unfortunately existed so long between the people of different sections of the North and South. . . . Blacks have been made free, but denied opportunity, and duped by carpet-baggers," he argued, and the "Southern states are under crushing debt, with their citizens suffering still from the angry passions of the war and their economies plundered by men of the North.

"I submit to you as intelligent men whether the colored men have not been exasperated against the whites for the mere object of securing political power through the colored men's vote; for the mere purpose of perpetuating the power of those who hold office and keeping up internal strife, and fanning and keeping alive the ignorant prejudices of the negroes for the purpose of securing their votes, and for massing the negro voters of North and South Carolina to assist them in the Presidential campaign of 1872. They will fail!"

Kernan also attacked the failure of Grant's postwar promises of an honest and economical administration of public affairs and a lightened tax burden. "Friends of Grant," he said, have been "plundering the merchants of the Union and levying private assessments on all property that passed through the ports of the country." The problem was not just with the New York Customs House, but in New Orleans as well, where Grant's brother-in-law was in charge. "If [another] brother-in-law cannot be found," said Kernan, "put an honest colored man in his place and he will not plunder or rob the government as Casey has done."

He pointed to the army of "office-holders" that had replaced the armies of wartime, and who would resist reform. As for members of Congress, the last session was a "triumph of the lobby, who have aimed to push through private jobs and get possession of public lands." Instead of retaining public lands "as the heritage of the people, so that the people of the country could go to them and build up homes, and that they should be reserved as rewards for our brave soldiers . . . Congress has persisted in . . . voting the largest share of these land grants to railroads which have had subsidies from the Government sufficient to build the road, without requiring one foot of public land." Particularly galling was Congress's franking privilege, which allowed members of Congress to use the postal service free of charge, for which Congress had resisted demands for reform. "The mails have been overburdened by the tons of worthless trash sent out by both parties, if you please, with the hope of hoodwinking the people on the eve of an election."

It is interesting to note how Kernan seasoned his own dish of crow in endorsing Greeley for president: "If I had fears that Horace Greeley would prove faithless to the people, I would not vote for him. . . . There is no doubt of his personal honesty. . . . The man who as the editor of a partisan paper can find time to scourge the rogues of his own party will not fail to drive plunderers and thieves from public office. . . . Men of all parties, nationalities, colors and creeds in every State have banded together to place Greeley and Brown at the head of the nation and to inaugurate long-needed reforms in the administration of public affairs. . . . We can have an administration which will be faithful to the interests of the people, one which will ensure the perpetuity of our institutions; an administration which will be economical, pure and honest, and one which will bring all States of the Union together to start anew with the slavery canker cut out, and every prospect for future peace and happiness."

Seymour avoided most of the campaign. "How does the canvas go?" he wrote Tilden from his Utica office. "I am not able to work myself into any heat about it. I grow old very fast. Then too, it is hard to go out to speak for Greeley. His abuse has been so gross. As facts stand, I think it was wise to put him up, and I can see my way clear to vote for him, as he can be made of use in driving negroes out of office; but it is hard to speak for him. But for you and Kernan, I would not move this fall. As it is, I will do what I can."[9]

While Kernan strove to overlook Greeley's wartime animosity, and worked to unite factions of religion, the *New York Times* felt no such constraints, warning readers that the Catholic's first object in office would be "to destroy our public school system,"[10] and, "it is not our purpose to breathe a word against that cultivated gentleman's private character; but his record politically is that of an extreme Democrat."[11]

"Extreme" was the key word, loaded with memories of the war, in which "Extreme" Democrats vied with "Radical" Republicans. "He is a man of extreme views on the subject of his religious creed" which is "all that can be said to recommend him to the lower class of Democrats. . . . A more objectionable nomination to decent Republicans could not have been made, for they are asked to vote for a Copperhead and a bigot. Kernan, happily, stands no more chance of being elected

Governor than the man in the moon. . . . Let Kernan come here [to the city], and find out how things are going, and he would sell his chances for a glass of bourbon."

The *Times's* own war record had been less than sterling in support of Lincoln, and the paper used the opportunity of the 1872 election to realign itself with the establishment. It provided a steady stream of epithets against Kernan, a "scheming," "unscrupulous," "demagogue Jesuit," while the Democratic papers countered with the facts of Kernan's past and quotations from Republican papers, which had praised him over his many years of public service. Utica's spirited Republican journal, the *Herald,* could not speak against Kernan's record without arousing indignation among its local readers, who knew Kernan personally. Francis had been educated in public schools, served as a member of the first City Board of School Commissioners in Utica in 1843, educated his own children in Utica's schools, and in 1867, as a member of the Constitutional Convention, favored prohibiting all appropriations of the public funds to private charities (which meant Catholic schools).

This is not to overlook Kernan's deep devotion to his faith, which was shared by his family. Catholics who sent their children to public schools often deeply resented the Protestant Bible-readings led by Protestant teachers. When the American Bible Society refused to print the Douay (Catholic) version of the Bible early in the 1800s, Francis's father-in-law, Nicholas Devereux, responded by purchasing the expensive stereotype plates of the New Testament. The "Devereux" Testament was printed in Utica by another Catholic layman, and the books were distributed freely for the cost of paper and bindings.*

Even the biting political cartoonist Nast, who had characterized Tweed as a thieving vulture, and now drew Greeley as a cross-eyed pumpkin, was unable to turn Kernan's dignified presence into a physical joke. Instead, he pictured Kernan surrounded by drunken Irish constituents—brawling, ape-like creatures—or pictured Francis bowing to the pope. In other cartoons American Catholic clergymen

---

* Madam Devereux presented a copy of the Devereux Testament to her grandson on Christmas Eve, 1878, with a letter explaining the copy was "printed from the stereotype plates furnished by your Grand Father—These plates were originally purchased by Mr. Lewis Wilcox of N. York & Mr. Devereux at a cost of $600. each giving $300.—Subsequently Mr. Wilcox was unfortunate & Mr. Devereux purchased his share—The American Bible Society having refused to print either the Douay version of the whole Bible—or of the Testament—led to this purchase. The Testaments were printed in Utica by the Father of R. S. Williams—who was then in partnership with Mr. Seward. The Books were distributed freely at the cost of paper and binding—the plates were used until the dissolution of Partnership of Seward and Williams. In 1840 or near there the Plates were disposed of to Sadlier & Co. who wrote me in 1868. 'We have printed edition after edition from those Plates and must have sold Forty Thousand copies of them - notwithstanding that three other Catholic Firms published Testaments at the same time'—Pardon me, dear John, for writing you all this—but I wished you to know what your honoured Grandfather had done for the cause of Catholic truth and also that you could refute the oft repeated calumny that Catholics never read or distribute the Bible—Mr. Devereux read it thro' from cover to cover 17 times—I have the dates.

"With my best wishes for a happier year of 1879 I remain—Yr. loving Grand Mother, M.D. Devereux."

[The Testament this letter refers to is now in the library of Springbank, New York.]

OUR FOREIGN RULER (?).

F. K. "I will do your bidding, as you are infallible."

Our Foreign Ruler (?)

The intensely anti-Catholic and anti-Democratic cartoonist, Thomas Nast added to the misinformation about Kernan's stance on public education and played to the prejudicial fears of Protestants. Nast depicts Kernan bowing to the pope and pledging to do the bidding of the infallible foreign potentate. In Kernan's hats are "Orders from the Pope," while a priest stands ready to post campaign banners that cry "Down with the U.S. Public Schools." "Vote as Catholic." "The Bible must be out of the public schools."

Campaign label—Francis Kernan for Governor
The New York Times protested, "We are
above all things anxious to keep religious
questions out of the embittered strife. But
our opponents seem resolved to force us into
it. They raise the cry of 'Catholicism against
Protestantism,' and have sent forth the cross
stamped on their political tickets as a sign of
war.... For Heaven's sake, do not let us import
religious quarrels into it. But if you do, look
out for the consequences."

From a facsimile in the *New York Times,* September 29, 1872.

were drawn as alligators, crossing the Atlantic and rising from the slime of New
York harbor. Seymour, in dismay, pleaded for tolerance. "In looking over the history
of my State, I find that we have never had a Catholic Governor, though Catholics
constitute about one-third of the population and a very large share of the voters,"
he said.[12] "They have been voting for Protestants for nearly a hundred years, and I
cannot bear to have it said that Protestants are more bigoted than Catholics, and
cannot vote once for a Catholic in return. Every public man in the State has asked
Catholics for their votes. I ask them if they cannot reciprocate the favor by voting
for an honest man!"

Seymour and Tilden both campaigned hard for Kernan, but it didn't help Seymour's argument that Kernan's Catholic supporters among the Irish population in
New York City happily mixed politics with religion, and printed campaign labels by
the tens of thousands with Kernan's name in a ring and a cross in the center which
campaign workers circulated in the large cities of the state.[13]

It also didn't help that the day after Kernan's nomination, the *Tribune* proudly
boasted that he was a "severe and earnest Roman Catholic," and during the entire
campaign urged his religious opinions as the reason voters should elect him. "It may
be lamentable that a question of religious opinion would weigh in a canvass, but
that it does weigh cannot be denied," declared the *New York Times,*[14] and no facts
could overcome the prejudice, not even Seymour's passionate pleas for fairness.

Another example of the *Times's* caustic coverage, published the day after an
appearance of Kernan at a meeting at the Brooklyn Academy, compared the Democratic gathering to the "peace meetings" of the early war years. "The same flashing
lights and noisy glitter; the same long array of Irish faces gleaming with native rash-
ness; the same blind throng of uncultured Celts, misguided and led to their own
ruin by their politicians or their priests; the same pretentious harangues that urge
peace with the enemy and hate to the preserver of the nation, that in language of
harmony conceal the deadliest treason, and in swelling sentences of reconciliation

hide a fatal purpose. Almost the same faces and the same men appeared again before their countrymen, unabashed and incapable of reform, and their favorite themes were the same. The same unfounded calumnies were heaped upon the chief of the nation, except that it was now President Grant instead of President Lincoln that was their object."

The campaign of 1872 was a mudshower that no one escaped. Kernan's friend Charles O'Conor had chosen not to go along with the Liberal Republicans' ticket and had accepted the nomination to run for president on a ticket of a small contingent of hard-line pro-South Democrats who couldn't stand Greeley. But a lot of voters couldn't stand O'Conor's Irish background. "So far from being an advantage, the reputation of being an Irishman and a Catholic has been to me a most serious political, social, and professional disadvantage," said O'Conor.[15]

Nor did President Grant escape the abuse of this personal and vicious race, being derided as a "man of no ideas," a crook, drunkard, ignoramus, swindler, and worse. Greeley took the worst battering of anyone. Throughout his long career, his intellectual explorations had temporarily entertained, if not embraced every social and political movement of his times, from temperance, to abolition, to spiritualism, and had managed to offend just about everyone at least once. Now, subjected to the intensely vitriolic response, he wondered aloud if he was running for the presidency or the penitentiary.

Throughout September and October, Kernan traveled the state to make appearances at Democratic and Liberal Republican gatherings. Between September 12 and his return to Utica shortly before election day, he delivered 44 speeches, besides answering numerous serenades and responding to impromptu receptions tendered him along the lines of the railroads.

Local, upstate crowds were always enthusiastic. One rousing meeting at Carton Hall, for example, sponsored by Utica's "Young Men's Kernan Club," and covered fully in the local press, featured "the handsomest [banner] of the kind in Central New York, greatly admired not only for its general appearance but also the correct likenesses which it bears of Greeley and Brown, the People's candidates, and the names of those other honest standard bearers, Kernan, Depew and Sherman, which are so popular with the people." The members of the club determined to "have a little jollification over the raising of the banner," which, they noted, was paid for by honest men and did not come out of the government treasury. The young men made their appearance after dark, dressed in uniforms and carrying torches, and "fired their loud-talking little gun and a large quantity of fireworks." After a short parade with the Old Utica Band, the young men returned to the meeting at Carton Hall, where the crowd continued to admire the banner from the various points of view in the street below it. The crowd waited while the young men disposed of the spent rockets, bombs, and Roman candles and hauled the gun to the curb-stone, before enthusiastically entering Carton Hall "with every manifestation of ardor."

Such ardor was not apparent in the big-city crowds, particularly in New York City, where the end of the Tweed Ring had unwelcome financial repercussions for many in the Democratic party who had enjoyed the Ring's patronage. At a mass meeting on October 27, just weeks before the election, the absence of enthusiasm was apparent in the half-filled Tammany Hall.[16] In the middle of Kernan's speech nearly a quarter of the audience, on hearing music outside, rose and left the building. Samuel Tilden and Samuel S. Cox fared no better. Despite the bands, calcium lights, and fireworks, there were hardly enough spectators to fill an ordinary ward parade.

When Kernan returned home from his campaign tour, a politician from Utica's Fifth Ward advised him that he would have to have about $100 to buy the votes of many "floaters," who he feared were going to vote for Dix.[17] Kernan responded that he was not interested in the votes of men who would sell their liberty, and refused to condone the common practice of handing out $5 bills to help convince voters.

The final rally was in Rome, on election eve, November 5, 1872, at Sink's Opera House, where Kernan shared the podium with Horatio Seymour. The following day his hometown newspaper, the *Utica Daily Observer,* sadly noted the "strange chapter in the history of the Empire State which was written yesterday. Debauched by money, led by partisanship and influenced to some extent by bigotry, the citizens of New York rejected Francis Kernan and elected John A. Dix to be Governor.... Dix is a decrepit man standing on the verge of the grave, bearing on his bent shoulders a load of years freighted with the record of numberless political changes and telling the story of how thrift may follow fawning." Utica was dismayed by the defeat of its hometown hero.

Grant and Dix won in New York City by more than 50,000 votes, Kernan was defeated by two quite independent factors: many Democrats refused to go to the polls rather than vote for Horace Greeley, and many Protestants abstained rather than vote for a Catholic for governor.* Interestingly, the defeat of Kernan, an upstate candidate, was clinched in the cities of New York and Brooklyn, which had a far higher proportion of Catholics than did other parts of New York†

Greeley was so devastated by the personal attacks, and by the death of his wife shortly before the election, that he was confined to a private sanatorium, where he died within three weeks.

---

* No Catholic would be elected governor of any state until John Burke of North Dakota won his nomination in 1906, the year Alfred E. Smith was majority leader of the New York State Assembly. Burke served three terms. Al Smith ran for governor of the Empire State in 1918. Like Kernan, he faced the religious issue. Smith served four terms before being the first Catholic to run for president. He lost to Herbert Hoover in 1928. John F. Kennedy, in 1960, was the first, and only, Catholic to reach the White House.

† The 1872 election was held the same year in which the celebrated Susan B. Anthony was arrested for casting a vote at the polls in Rochester, New York. She voted for Dix—not Kernan—and for Grant, insisting that the Fourteenth Amendment guaranteed equal rights for all citizens, and that included women and their right to vote. She voted Republican, she said, simply because that party was the only one that agreed to include a reference to "their obligations to the loyal women of America" in their national platform.

Tilden had "labored with might and main" for the election of Kernan, but with the defeat of the state and national Democratic tickets he was free to realize a long-cherished plan for a trip to Europe. That same summer Kernan also took a trip to Ireland. Other than the trips he took for his health later in life, to Richfield Springs and Atlantic City, this is the only record of his having taken a vacation. In a letter to "My dear Wife," which he wrote on July 10, 1873, from Dublin's Shelbourne Hotel, he reported that he was having a delightful tour, eating, sleeping, traveling, and exercising "as when I was a boy." He went to Saint Paul's Church on Arran Quay, where he "thought Mother used to attend"* and believed he had "found the house in which Grandfather Stubbs lived. All this awakened many sad but pleasurable sensations."

Thereafter Kernan returned to full-time law practice. John A. Dix turned out to be a fairly good governor, whose notable achievements included a new charter for New York City that removed some of the more obnoxious features of the Tweed charter, and the passage of a series of amendments to the state constitution. On March 13, 1873, the state senate confirmed Dix's nomination of Francis Kernan and James Watson William, of Utica, S. Oakley Vanderpoel of Albany, and Samuel Campbell of New York City as managers of the New York State Lunatic Asylum at Utica, a public-service appointment Kernan held until beginning his term in the Senate. The asylum, founded in 1836 for acute cases of pauper insanity, was the first owned and operated by the state that made a gesture of providing humane treatment to the inmates.†

Shortly before Governor Dix had begun his term, Kernan was appointed by Governor Hoffman to a bipartisan commission that was to propose amendments to the state constitution. Having served at the last constitutional convention, Francis was now able to frame the new committee's proposals. The Constitutional Commission of 1872 made a very important contribution to the constitutional development of the state. Following the ill-fated convention of 1867, it exercised judgment and restraint, and was not influenced by partisanship. The result of its deliberations was a series of well-conceived changes in the government of the state.

Kernan worked for more than a year on the proposals, which were submitted to the voters in 1874 in a unique manner. Voters could simply cross out those they did not agree with. Inspectors were required to count the ballots for each proposition not crossed out. This voting method, and a gradual acceptance of new ideas, was believed to be the reason the amendments that had been rejected in earlier elections now passed by a large majority.

It was sweet compensation for Kernan following the vicious attacks of the

---

* His mother, Rosanna M. Stubbs did, in fact, attend this church, and records show that her parents were married there in 1781.

† Located on a farm of 130 acres in Whitestown and New Hartford, the asylum cared for a revolving group of 1,000 patients a year. Whenever possible, they were taken out of their cells, allowed to work on the land, and provided with amusements.

campaign of 1872 that he could effect the governmental changes he sought, working as a lawyer on the constitutional commission and consulting with Tilden, who was now working in the legislature to the same end. The amendments that passed in 1874 abolished property qualification for Negro voters, instituted electoral reforms, forbade extra payments to state contractors, allowed the governor to veto individual items in appropriation bills, required a two-thirds vote of the full membership of each house to override the governor's veto, permitted the sale of the state's lateral canals, and increased the term of governor from two to three years. (Twenty years later the two-year term was reestablished.)

Although these amendments eliminated many obvious abuses, they did not go far enough to centralize New York's government, or to reflect the fundamental changes from an agrarian to an industrial society. Citizens of the Gilded Age remained subject to corrupt greed and machine rule. "Advocates of honest government had overthrown the Tweed Ring, but they had done little to prevent the emergence of similar organizations in the future. As in the past, New Yorkers would continue to be subjected to machine rule, with brief interludes of honest and efficient administration."[18]

$\mathcal{G}$overnor Tilden and Senator Kernan

THE CRUCIAL YEARS in the political career of Samuel Jones Tilden are inextricably intertwined with those of Francis Kernan. It was to Kernan that Tilden first turned when be began his struggle against Boss Tweed; it was Kernan whom Tilden selected as his champion in his campaign for governor; it was Kernan to whom Tilden turned to represent New York in the U.S. Senate; and it was Kernan who placed Tilden's name in contention for the Democratic nomination for president of the United States. Ultimately, because of his close ties to Tilden, Kernan was appointed to the Electoral Commission that voted (over his protest) to award the presidency to Rutherford B. Hayes.

Kernan's importance to history was not simply as Tilden's surrogate, however. As a key participant in the postwar reconstruction of the New York Democratic party and its rescue from scandal and disgrace, Kernan played a vital role in the reestablishment of a viable and effective two-party system in American politics. If the period of his greatest political ascension, to the ranks of the United States Senate, is correctly viewed today as one of relative quiescence and inactivity, this is perhaps itself no insignificant accomplishment during a period of sectional tension, increasing industrial strife, vastly increased immigration, and the shift from a rural to an increasingly urban society. More than most, the era of the late 1870s and early 1880s deserves the well-worn designation "transitional"; and Francis Kernan did more than his share to ease the transition.

Nonetheless, it is in his relationship with Tilden that the key to Kernan's most important political achievements is to be found. In the story of this affiliation may be traced much of the story of New York politics in the era of reform.

In a period of bipartisan graft and corruption in the nation and the state, Samuel J. Tilden's most valuable asset was his reputation as a man of integrity and a reformer who placed integrity before party loyalty or personal gain. However well established that reputation is today, it stood on shaky ground at the outset of the 1870s. Tilden had passed the Civil War as a railroad attorney—not illegal, but slightly seamy. As Democratic state chairman, he had stood shoulder to shoulder with the Tammany moguls Tweed, Sweeny, and Hall as late as October 1870. He had continued to hold his fire against the Ring for a year after the *New York Times* had begun its assault; and the rest of the "swallow-tails," the wealthy, genteel Democrats who made up the aristocratic segment of the party, increasingly doubted whether Tilden was up to the task of reform.[1]

If Tilden possessed caution to a fault, however, he balanced it with an equal amount of sagacity. Tilden's selection of Kernan as the first man he turned to in his battle with the Tweed Ring was a measure equally of Tilden's acumen and of Kernan's unparalleled reputation for rectitude. While Francis could be counted on for hard work and sound advice, his chief contribution to the cause was his unimpeachable moral standing. In that first fight, Kernan had more than proved his mettle. His high character had lent to Tilden's campaign a tone of disinterested purity; and when Tweed's supporters refused to seat him at the Rochester Convention of 1871, they disgraced themselves in the eyes of the state and made Kernan the frontrunner for the gubernatorial nomination in 1872. His graceful and spirited conduct in that ill-fated campaign, as well as the opposition's complete inability to find any fault with him besides his religion, convinced Tilden that Kernan had an essential role to play on the national stage.

After Horace Greeley's humiliating repudiation in the presidential election of 1872 many observers wrote off the presidential chances of the Democratic party for the rest of the decade, if not the century. Tilden was one of the first to recognize that growing public outrage against the corruption and excesses of the Grant administration would redound to the benefit of the Democracy—if only it could get its own house in order, it would have a clear shot at the White House. Tilden was convinced—probably correctly—that no one else in the party could accomplish the task of self-reform in New York State.[2]

Still, the governorship of New York would not be handed to Tilden on a silver platter. Although the Tweed Ring had been defeated in the City, the Canal Ring still held sway upstate, and its members would do all in their power to deny the reformist lawyer the nomination. Kernan assured Tilden that he "could not fail to carry the state," though ex-governor Seymour held scant hopes. "Reformers are hated," Kernan advised Tilden morosely, "and only bear sway when there is a tempest of popular rage against corruption. . . . I do not see any course for you but to go on and take a defeat." Perhaps thinking of his own disastrous presidential campaign of 1868, Seymour consoled Tilden: "The crown of martyrdom is a glorious one."[3] Kernan had no such pessimism, and goaded Tilden to overcome his congenital diffidence, patiently admonishing him, "You should say 'if nominated I will accept.'"[4] Tilden agreed, and fully committed himself to the realities of a public campaign. To win, he would have to attract substantial Republican support and retain the backing of the Greeleyite Liberal Republicans, while facing down the corruptionists and preserving the fragile Democratic reform coalition he had helped to assemble to run New York City after the removal of Tweed.

Democratic victories in state elections in Ohio in 1873 and Indiana in early 1874 were widely interpreted as the opening of an anti-Republican groundswell. Observers turned to New York to see if the trend would continue, and what it would bode for 1876. It was under such scrutiny that Tilden selected Kernan to play a key role in his campaign. Kernan cautioned Tilden to "let only honest men handle the campaign funds," and the money was watched carefully. Seeing the possibility that they might yet win the election, Seymour advised Tilden about the discontented farmer (Granger) vote, which he believed they could secure, while Kernan held the Irish vote. The campaign, unlike the mud shower of 1872, was conducted on an unusually high level.

Kernan campaigned heavily on Tilden's behalf. Years of political rallies had sharpened Kernan's rhetoric, shortened his sentences, and taught him the power of rhythm and imagery. In a well-publicized speech at Tammany Hall on October 29, 1874, Kernan roused the crowd to a "white heat of enthusiasm,"[5] as he protested the state of the economy and the attempts by some Grant supporters to reelect the president to a third term.

"Nearly ten years have elapsed since the havoc and wasting effects and expenditures of the war ceased," he said.

> We have had bountiful harvests, we have had developments of the resources of our mines and forests, we have had all the elements of prosperity, and yet we are not a prosperous nor a prospering people to-day. All the industries of the country are paralyzed. The business of your merchants is stagnant. Your factories are stopped or running short time. Your mechanics' shops are almost empty. Labor, both skilled and unskilled, seeks employment in vain. We find here, with everything from Providence that should make us a prosperous people—we find at the end of a bountiful season, in a beautiful autumn—large bodies of men in this

city suffering because honest labor can earn no wages for themselves and families. . . . I believe that the administration of our executive affairs for a few years past has largely contributed to the sad and lamentable condition of our country. The deranged, depreciated, and unconvertible paper currency is to the body politic what the disordered blood is to the human body. If the blood is disordered, the whole body becomes diseased, and in the commercial world, when the circulating medium is depreciated, you may be sure your business and industrious pursuits will feel the enervating and destroying effect. To-day we have a currency which is depreciated, which is not convertible into the currency of the commercial world. This country has wealth enough. The people have paid taxes enough to make the credit [of this] government [the best] on the face of the earth. Why have we not returned to specie payments? . . . We all know that while [the Republican administration has] promised to return to specie our unconvertible currency they have issued $24,000,000 more of promises which they have violated. This while they have made pledge after pledge that we should have economy in our public expenditures.

I appeal to your intelligence to say whether we ever had so much extravagance and corruption in the administration of our public affairs as exists under the Grant administration for the last two years. These things have tended to the derangement of our business, for the destruction of our industry, for the lamentable state of things generally, which exists over the country at this time. Does this administration deign to give us a pledge that there shall be a change for the better in these things? Not at all.

At the end of his speech, as he turned to present Horatio Seymour, the excited throng did not wait for him to finish introducing the elder statesman who had served the party so honorably for nearly half a century. As Seymour came forward, they flung their hats in the air and shouted. A pleased, and partisan reporter recorded the excited reception:

[Again and] again the welcome seemed over, and somebody on the edge of the gallery leaned forward and swung his hat in the faces of the crowd below, or some one below there tossed his hat ten feet high, and the whole thing [welcoming shout, three cheers and a tiger] had to be done over again. It all died away, and the white-headed, venerable Governor bowed his acknowledgments, and each of the 3,000 men who stood before him suddenly saw full reason to go over the welcome from the start, and welcomed the old man again, and made each welcome, in spite of the wear of ten minutes' cheering, longer, louder, heartier than the one before. The platform caught the hint; gray-headed men sprang to their feet and swung their hats and lifted them onto their canes, and shouted "Hurrah!" and "Seymour!" and "Tiger!" and "Give him another!" with the wildest and youngest of the audience.[6]

Victory was in the air. The dark days of the Democrats were coming to an end at last. The rally was a vindication for the three "troublesome old fools," as Boss Tweed had dismissed Tilden, Kernan, and Seymour in 1871. And there was no doubt that Tilden's race was intended as a prelude to his presidential campaign. In his forceful speech, Kernan had enunciated the themes that would become the hallmarks of Tilden's later presidential campaign: overthrowing corruption, reforming the currency, and reducing expenses. Tilden himself campaigned as avidly against Grant as against Governor Dix, and blamed the latter for the faults of the former on every occasion.

Tilden's election on November 3, 1874, capped a Democratic sweep of the legislature that returned the party to power in Albany for the first time since the Civil War. Nationally as well, the 1874 elections marked a huge shift to the Democrats. The party captured the House of Representatives and made significant inroads into the Senate, depriving the Republicans of their two-thirds majority. Overnight, New York's governor-elect became a frontrunner for the Democratic presidential nomination. Indeed, in the eyes of many observers, it had been precisely the intention of New York voters to send such a national message. The veteran Republican political operator Thurlow Weed interpreted the victory as the state's judgment of the "incapacity and persistent wrongdoing at Washington." Tilden construed the New York vote as a national mandate for change: "The people are beginning to think that it is time to have a real peace in the United States."[7] The first truly contested campaign for the White House since the Civil War had begun.

Kernan could talk of nothing but 1876. His ambitions for his friend were clear. In a congratulatory letter to Tilden, he stressed the urgency of the reformers' agenda and consoled him not to disappoint.

> I am sure you appreciate how very happy I have been at your triumphant election, and at the success of our friends in the state and elsewhere—the victory in this state under your lead is complete. It places us under great responsibility. If we are faithful to our principles and professions in administrating the state government during the next two years, and our representatives in congress prove by their actions at Washington that we mean when in power to inaugurate the reforms in which we are pledged, our friends will carry the elections throughout the Union in 1876 by an overwhelming majority—so much depends upon the actions of our friends in this state and at Washington during the immediate future, that I am quite solicitous that the active influence of all our best men be united to aid in shaping and directing that action.[8]

Kernan had specific advice in regard to the actions of "our political friends at Washington," and recommended that "during the coming session . . . there should be consultations between the leading Senators and Representatives and they should be fully impressed with the responsibility of their position before the country.

Could not the leading Senators bring about an informal consultation with the leading members of the House at an early date and have such an understanding that their actions in each house during the coming session shall be harmonious and in the right direction on all questions[?] This is very important in my judgement."

Referring to state matters, Kernan felt less solicitous, "for you will be at the helm," he wrote,

> . . . and can and will exercise great influence at Albany with our friends. Nevertheless, all our friends must unite giving a right direction to legislation and the action of the Head of the State departments. The question of the speakership is unfortunate—Mr. [Richard Updyke] Sherman of this county is spoken of and others. Mr. Sherman is disposed to look at the matter in the right spirit. He does not seek this place unless in full consultation it is thought he is the best man for the place. I have said to him, as I now say to you, that there should be an early commitment to the support of justices . . . ; let the qualifications of each be fully canvassed in a fair spirit, and when the proper time comes, let us all go for the man that is believed in all respects best suited for the position. In reference to your self and other appointments, act deliberately; give the candidates a hearing and then select the best men for the position—with a view to an honest and efficient administration.

Kernan had not seen Governor Seymour since the election, he told Tilden. Since the election, Kernan had not been home, and he had just learned that Seymour had been confined to his house. "I intend to ride out and see him this afternoon," he wrote.

Kernan also promised to try and meet with Tilden when he came to Albany, "or what is better, when you come to Albany you can escape from the press of calling by coming up here and staying with us a few nights. Your room is ready."[*]

Tilden faced many stiff demands at home, however, before he could focus on the challenge of winning the White House. In the days leading to his inaguration and thereafter he would have to hold together the party's many factions while undertaking radical, stabilizing reforms—and in the meantime, discharging all the administrative as well as the ceremonial duties of governing. All of Tilden's hopes for 1876 rested on the perceived integrity of the New York Democracy and the efficiency of the state administration. The goal would require an equal measure of principle and tact—and no one else in the state party possessed a greater measure of

[*] A family story characterizes Tilden. Walter N. Kernan, in a 1935 interview with Tilden's biographer, Alexander C. Flick, related an incident in Utica, when he was nine years old and Tilden was visiting. Unknowing, Walter walked into the guest room in the morning to see a stranger in a nightcap and a nightshirt that came only to his knees, swinging his legs over the side of the bed. "In my surprise, and frightened, I rushed out of the room thinking that I had never seen a man with such thin legs." See Flick, Tilden, page 271. The incident took place when Tilden was governor and Kernan was a senator.

both than Francis Kernan. To carry forth Tilden's internal reforms with as few ruf-fled feathers as possible, and to burnish the state party's image in the eyes of the nation at large, Kernan was Tilden's indispensable man.

Throughout the months leading up to his election, Tilden had been con-fronted by the problem of patronage. The reformers had campaigned against the system, but after his inaguration, they were the ones with jobs to fill. Kernan's first service to the new governor was to help him do his work by protecting him as much as he could from the insatiable demands of office seekers. This was in striking contrast to Seymour, who "professed to be fending off applicants for office, yet was continually asking for places for relatives and others."[9] To the great credit of the reformers, they managed to resist the patronage stamp and, in the main, placed men in office on the basis of qualifications and integrity rather than political connec-tions.

Kernan also played an important supporting role in Tilden's relationship with "Honest John" Kelly, the New York City political leader who had assumed control of Tammany Hall after the ouster of Boss Tweed. Tilden and Kelly were strange bedfellows, but without their alliance the cause of reform—and of Tilden—would have stalled before it could have got of the ground. Kelly had been selected by Tilden and a reformist "Committee of Seventy" to lead the cleanup of Tammany because of his freedom from any taint of association with Tweedism; but that good fortune derived principally from the fact that Kelly had been absent in Europe dur-ing the three years of the Ring's worst excesses. Previously, as New York's sheriff, Kelly had grown rich in real estate speculation and had provided jobs for some of Tammany's most notorious demagogues and enforcers. Although no scandals had arisen during his term, his sudden withdrawal for "health reasons" as a reform can-didate for mayor in 1868, followed by his quick departure for the continent, had given rise to rumors of improprieties.[10]

But if Kelly and Tilden now needed each other to govern, each needed Ker-nan as well. Kelly's New York opponents, notably Mayor Havemeyer, denounced Tilden for his ties to the Tammany chief, while the Herald went so far as to dismiss Tilden as "Kelly's cats-paw." It was hard to make such charges stick, however, as long as Tilden had the full confidence of men as unquestionably upright as Francis Ker-nan. Indeed, Kernan used the upstaters' fears of Tammany to good advantage, prais-ing the toughness of his chief in taming the "tiger." Likewise, while Tilden's support for Kelly had been essential to his political rise, Kernan's endorsement had bestowed upon Kelly the moral *imprimatur* that enabled him to win and keep the backing of wary upstate conservatives and the many reform Democrats—and even Republi-cans—who trusted Kernan's ethical judgment implicitly.[11] Kelly owed both men, and he delivered on his obligations with the strong support of Tammany Hall, in belief of Tilden's successful reforms. For the time being, the goals and interests of the three were closely linked.

Nowhere were these mutual ties more evident than in Kernan's election to the U.S. Senate. Tilden had promised Kernan his support for this high trust even before the election, but two others had equal claims: Chief Judge Sanford E. Church, a leader of the reform wing of the party and one of the most popular politicians in the state; and the party's perennial standard bearer, Horatio Seymour. But Church, who had actively campaigned for the Democratic nomination against Tilden, knew he would not get the nod and withdrew his name from consideration, while Seymour, who was feeling the effects of his sixty-five years, had no desire to go to Washington. "The office was his," Seymour's biographer asserted, "not for the asking, but merely for the accepting. Not only did he resolve to decline it for himself; he determined to win it for Francis Kernan."[12] During the weeks before the start of the new term, Seymour worked tirelessly on Kernan's behalf, writing letters to newspaper editors and key political leaders and making an irrefutable case for his upright fellow townsman. (Until the ratification of the Seventeenth Amendment to the U.S. Constitution in 1913, election of state senators was by a majority vote of the state legislatures.)

With Seymour and Church removed as potential obstacles, no serious bar remained to Kernan's election. Throughout the state, the clamor for Kernan, both spontaneous and manufactured, made him not merely the frontrunner for the post, but drove all other candidates from the field—or nearly all. Although New Yorkers as a whole endorsed Kernan's selection, the intricacies of downstate politics, and in particular the long rivalry between Brooklyn and Manhattan, provided a modicum of drama in the decision. It was here that John Kelly had the opportunity simultaneously to discharge his political debt to Kernan and to demonstrate his absolute political control.*

---

* The story of politics in New York City, for most of American history, is the story of Tammany Hall. Founded in the years after the Revolution as a benevolent and patriotic lodge, the Society of St. Tammany, named after a fabled chief of the Delaware Indians, was soon enlisted in the byzantine politics of New York by the pioneering political fixer and adventurer Aaron Burr. A fraternal organization of elaborate ceremonies, analogous to the Freemasons or Oddfellows, the Tammany Society ranked its members in an elaborate hierarchy of Indian-derived titles, offices, and honorifics. Tammany "braves" annually elected thirteen "sachems" to conduct the society's business; these appointed one of their number as Grand Sachem, and the president of the United States was honored with the ex-officio title of Great Grand Sachem, whether he would or no. Martin Van Buren, never himself a Tammany member, fashioned the hall into a potent and reliable division of the national Democratic Party. Tammany's strong-arm tactics frequently led to bloody riots, which on one occasion required a detachment of infantry and two cavalry squadrons to quell.[See Allen, pages 42–43.] Along with muscular political discipline, Tammany became indelibly linked in the public mind with graft, swindling, and peculation on a gargantuan scale. In 1838 Tammany appointee Sam Swartwout set a new standard of public theft when he fled to Europe after having stolen nearly $1,250,000 as New York's Collector of Customs—the jewel in the crown of federal patronage posts.[Ibid., page 49.] By the mid-1850s, when the "brilliant desperado" Fernando Wood took control of the hall and presided over New York as mayor, Tammany had completely shed its early complexion of an association for the advancement of merchants and bankers and had assumed its more familiar role as the political vehicle of the immigrants, the artisans, and the laborers of the city. This was the organization to which John Kelly succeeded as Grand Sachem in 1874.

For as long as Tammany had held sway in New York, Brooklyn had chafed under its domination. The fourth largest city in the United States in 1870, Brooklyn would have wielded tremendous influence in national affairs if

Thus it was from Brooklyn that the only dissent to Kernan's anointment as senator came, and it was a dissent aimed at Kelly, not at Kernan. Otherwise, the proceedings of the Democratic legislative caucus that met in Albany on Saturday, January 16, 1875, were as perfect a display of Democratic unity, as edifying a demonstration of Democratic civility, cooperation, and liberality, and as inspiring a testament to the Democracy's commitment to absolute probity and integrity, as its principal author and chief benefactor, Samuel J. Tilden, could possibly have wished for.

A large crowd filled the lobbies of the Assembly chamber as the members of the Democratic caucus took their seats at 4:15 p.m., and Senator John C. Jacobs of King's County, Brooklyn, turned the gavel over to Senator A. P. Laning as chairman. For the first time in seven years, the chairman began, a man who was in favor of a constitutional and representative government was to be elected. Everyone in the room—indeed, everyone in the state—knew that man to be Francis Kernan; there was no suspense, as a majority of the legislators were already committed. But the representatives from Brooklyn had one more stratagem to deploy in favor of Murphy. In response to a motion to elect the senator by *viva voce* vote, Senator Jacobs introduced an amendment calling for a secret ballot. He had known a time when men could walk into the Assembly chamber and say they owned the legislature that sat there, he said; he never wanted to see it again. Still more pointedly, Jacobs challenged the independence of the members: "If there is a man who has the least patriotism in his heart, he will say to John Kelly if he does own New York he does not own this Legislature."[13] Although he respected Kelly as a man, Jacobs continued, "he must know that as representatives we must discharge our duty ourselves, and not delegate them to any one else."

A pro-Kernan legislator rejected Jacobs's contention that all patriots should vote for a closed ballot, arguing that "the people had their attention fixed upon us at this moment and want to know what we are doing," and thus a roll-call vote should be taken.

This argument brought into the open an unspoken charge that cast a pall over the legislature. Assembly Speaker McGuire rose to address it. "It has been sent abroad," he said, "that this Legislature, especially the Assembly, was such a corrupt and venal body of men that it cannot be trusted with the ballot." As presiding officer of the Assembly, he felt responsible to repel this accusation. "A more high-minded and incorruptible body of men never before assembled here," he insisted, adding "on the authority of Francis Kernan himself that no man more emphatically

only it had not languished under the shadow of Manhattan—or so its political leaders believed. The disruption of the Tammany machine after Boss Tweed's fall had offered a golden opportunity to the politicos of King's County to assert their rightful role in the Empire State. At the time of Francis Kernan's election to the Senate, the King's County machine was itself in a state of confusion. It appears that party leaders saw the senatorial nomination as an opportunity to reunite the organization around the candidacy of their old leader, ex-mayor Henry C. Murphy, while scoring points against Tammany Hall and its new leader, John Kelly.

condemned this charge than he." The best way to "prove false this foul and most unnatural charge" was therefore to proceed with an open vote.

Senator John Fox of New York City correctly divined that fear of Tammany Hall dictation lay behind the accusations. Conceding that Tammany and the New York City delegation had met before the caucus, he said that he "could not see that in their consulting together they had committed any great sin. If in their consultation they should select the right man, he himself would put the collar of Tammany Hall on his neck and go with them."[14]

This conclusion was unanswerable. The esteem in which New Yorkers held Kernan was unrivaled by that of any other figure in public life at the time. By endorsing Kernan for the Senate, the sullied New York State legislature could markedly enhance its own moral standing. A process of redemption was now at work in which Tammany bosses, Canal Ring confederates, white-gloved swallow-tails, and the entire motley assortment of factions and interests of widely varied ethical persuasions that made up the New York Democracy of the Gilded Age could give convincing evidence of their honesty by endorsing the candidacy of Francis Kernan. As the *Troy Press* eulogized: "[he] is of a sturdy nature that cannot be absorbed, and when he takes his stand upon what he believes to be a principle, no power of solicitation or intimidation will turn him aside. Perhaps in this character, in which he much resembles Andrew Jackson, he is the fittest man of all who have been considered for the office."[15]

The process was not quite over, however. Senator Jacobs, on behalf of the Brooklyn delegation, moved that a committee be appointed to investigate charges of fraud that had been mentioned. A committee of two senators and three assemblymen was duly convened and quickly reported that there was no substance to the allegations. The caucus then voted, 74 to 13, to reject Jacobs's secret ballot amendment. The motion to move to a voice vote was then carried without discussion.

Placing Kernan's name in nomination was General Richard Updyke Sherman, longtime parliamentarian of the Assembly and a fellow Oneidan, who had at one time been the assistant clerk of the U.S. House of Representatives. The symbolism of Sherman's selection was strong: a former steadfast Republican, he had passed into the Liberal Republican movement and finally into the Democratic fold over matters of conscience and principle. Like Kernan, he was respected for his integrity and his great legal and constitutional acumen. His endorsement of Kernan underscored the nonpartisan respect in which the nominee was held.

After reviewing Kernan's many public services and accomplishments, Sherman broached the matter of their long political differences. Although the two had "entered on different paths in politics, and [had been] oftener antagonists than comrades in political strife," still, "no differences of opinion at any time have lessened my respect for him as a man, nor my confidence in the sincerity and uprightness of his convictions." Moreover, Sherman continued, "the tide of events has brought us at last together. The utter falsity of the Republican party to the high mission intrusted to it, and the overpowering necessity" to defend abused states' rights, had made Sherman what Kernan had always been—a Democrat—and enabled them to stand on the same platform. That platform was the proper place, Sherman seemed to say, for all honest men.

As a former loyal Republican, and clerk of the House during Kernan's single wartime term, Sherman was uniquely well placed to refute any charges of Kernan's lukewarmness to the Union cause. "I was present at Washington during his whole term of service as a Representative," Sherman noted, "and it chanced to be my office to make official record of his votes." In every case not involving fundamental questions of principle, Sherman reported, Kernan cast his vote "in favor of the most rigorous, practical measures for suppressing the rebellion. . . . Moreover, he had the confidence of Lincoln, and Chase and Stanton often sought out his advice."[*] Sherman's eloquent tribute framed Kernan's strengths perfectly, and definitively quashed his gravest potential weakness.

Of Kernan's other potential electoral "weakness"—his Catholic faith—this was no longer a case. Although this had been the principal issue deployed against him in his gubernatorial contest, it was clear that this time it would not fly. Kernan's liberality, his integrity, and his independence were too well known to have his religion count against him; those who had played the Roman card most strongly in 1872 had exceeded the limits of the public's credulity. Moreover, Catholic voters still seethed with outrage at the treatment of their distinguished standard bearer. Some had blamed Tilden for what they saw as his lukewarm support; and one of Kernan's chief goals in the gubernatorial campaign had been to convince Catholics that he had always enjoyed Tilden's steadfast support. The senatorial nomination made that point eloquently. But this time the public at large had clearly had enough of anti-Catholic demagoguery, at least when directed at Kernan. According to the New York Express, "When men like Talmage, of Brooklyn, struck a blow at Mr. Kernan for his religious faith, the almost unanimous nomination became a foregone conclusion."[16]

Although party leaders had hoped for Kernan's unanimous election on the first ballot, the King's County delegates were determined to register their protest vote on behalf of Henry C. Murphy. After Sherman placed Kernan's name in nomination and Senator Bradley, a pro-Kernan Brooklynite, seconded it, Senator Jacobs again took the floor and offered a backhanded semi-endorsement of Kernan: after

---

[*] *Utica Daily Observer,* January 16, 1875. This is a rare mention of any relationship with Lincoln and Kernan, and may be a convenient exaggeration on Sherman's part in promoting Kernan to the Senate. Sherman's statement that Kernan "had the confidence of Lincoln, and Chase and Stanton often sought out his advice," is quoted in obituaries and comments about Kernan and one must assume this well-publicized speech of Sherman's is the source of those later references, which tend to misquote the original sentence to say that Kernan "had the confidence of Lincoln who often sought out his advice."

deploring the position taken by the caucus, which he said the members would remember tomorrow with regret, he declared that "the gentleman named for this high position would receive as warm a support from the King's County Delegation as from any other." However, "if the King's County Delegation stood alone, it would vote for Henry C. Murphy."[17]

The vote was then taken. Kernan received 77 votes, Murphy 9, and former governor John T. Hoffman 1. As soon as the outcome was announced, Jacobs graciously "arose and moved that the nomination of Hon. Francis Kernan for United State Senator be made unanimous. Adopted amidst great cheering, and the caucus adjourned."[18]

All that remained, in view of the Democrats' overall majority in the legislature, was the formality of a vote of both houses of the legislature, which took place five days later. The Senate, still in Republican hands, voted 17 to 13 for Edwin D. Morgan, a wealthy former U.S. congressman who had used his fortune to prevent Boss Tweed from purchasing a controlling interest in the *New York Times*. The Assembly voted for Kernan 75 to 51, with 8 votes going to Hoffman. In the circumstances, the decision was left to a voice vote at a joint session of the legislature. After each legislator had stood and declared his choice as his name was called, the presiding officer declared, "Senators and gentlemen of the Assembly, Francis Kernan having been nominated by a majority of the Joint Assembly as their choice, I do hereby announce and declare that Francis Kernan, of the city of Utica, in the county of Oneida, has been duly elected as Senator of this State in Congress of the United States."[19]

After the election, all was harmonious in what Kernan now invariably called the "Liberal Democratic" party. His magnanimity to his opponents from King's County underscored the aptness of the party's choice: Kernan was the ideal figure to unify the party. That evening, in response to the Democrats of Albany who assembled at the Delevan House to serenade the senator-elect, Kernan underscored the importance of his statewide support:

Fellow citizens: I am not so vain as to take to myself all the honor of the compliment that is tendered me here, tonight. I recognize and rejoice that you, that the Democrats of Albany have come out to honor the Liberal Democratic party, and to rejoice that they are able to send a Senator to the Congress of the United States. I rejoice with you that while I have thus been honored it has been, by no great section of our glorious party in the State, but it has been by men from the East and the West, who have been partial enough to thus honor me. I rejoice that I can say to you tonight that I am the representative of the harmonious Democracy, from the Erie to Long Island. Such I trust, I shall prove myself. I feel that I am under obligations to men from every part of the State, and I trust that I shall so act that they shall feel that I am under obligations to none in particular but that I serve all as far as I am able.

Touching on the national implications of his election, Kernan continued:

I feel that though time has come when we are to take control, not only of New York, but that the glorious party of the Liberal Democracy will take possession of the Administration and will bring back the blessing to civil liberty untouched by arms in every state of the Union. I trust that the party will bring back the Administration to the old paths our fathers followed, and will administer the government for the whole people, by its Constitution and the laws, leaving them carefully in each state to govern their own affairs in accordance with the wishes of their own people.[20]

The *Utica Daily Observer,* bursting with local pride, offered an astute analysis of Kernan's victory. "After the withdrawal of Governor Seymour," the paper asserted, "any other conclusion was a moral impossibility. Over and above all other available candidates, as the representative of that element in the State which seeks to purify the political atmosphere, and to fulfill all public trusts with honest fidelity, stood Mr. Kernan."[21] In the eyes of most New Yorkers, the Democratic caucus did not so much honor Kernan by selecting him, as Kernan dignified it by accepting its endorsement. "He is one of the few men," observed the *New York Express,* "who have been leaders in politics, but whose skirts have never dragged in the mire of party strife or intrigue."[22] It was clear from the editorial reaction compiled by the *Observer,* particularly from Republican papers, that the selection had accomplished its goal of elevating the Democratic party in the public mind. *The Utica Herald* congratulated Kernan on his election, declaring its belief that "he is worthy of the honor at his party's hands, and that he will represent in Congress the best sentiment of Democracy." "Personally," according to the *Albany Journal,* "Mr. Kernan is a gentleman of character and worth. His life is unsullied and no word of reproach can justly be said against his pure, blameless and dignified bearing." The nonpartisan *Albany Express* described Kernan as "a man of culture and fine attainments" who "certainly possesses enough of ability to make his mark." Even the *New York Times* grudgingly acknowledged that "Mr. Kernan is a man of good repute, and an unusually accomplished lawyer; . . . we can only hope that he will perform with credit to himself and his State the duties of his new position. . . . There is plenty of room on the Democratic side for a really able man," the paper added snidely.[23]

Expressions of dismay concerning Kernan's election were few and restrained. "Two old humbugs will now have a firm friend in the United States Senate," the *Rochester Express* opined archly, "but we don't like to be personal, and we shall not say who the humbugs are."[24]

[The "old humbugs" were presumably the rest of Boss Tweed's trio of "troublesome old fools"—Horatio Seymour and Samuel J. Tilden.] Only the rabidly anti-Catholic *Harper's Weekly* had the effrontery to portray Kernan's election as the result of Tammany Hall dictation, and to raise the ugly brand of religious bigotry that had characterized the 1872 campaign: "As a rule, the denominational relations of public men are not legitimate subjects of consideration. Here a man's religion is his own business. But when Mr. Kernan was nominated for Governor in 1872, the fact that he was a Roman Catholic was prominently put forward by his supporters; and although he was known to be an honorable man, and had declared himself to be opposed to sectarian legislation, there can be little doubt that his connection with an ecclesiastical organization [that] has every where and always, as a Church, sought to control the State, contributed largely to his defeat."[25] The more balanced *New York Tribune* put *Harper's* view in perspective: "Mr. Kernan . . . is incorruptible and unassailed. His religion was a serious disadvantage to him when he was a candidate for Governor in 1872. But the most devoted Protestant will scarcely be ready to deny that Mr. Kernan's faith is better than no faith at all, and that has been the sole religious tendency of too many of our Senators."[26]

In sum, the election of Francis Kernan to the Senate was an edifying spectacle, one that showed the New York Democracy in its best light to a national political audience. Perhaps the editor of the *Saratogian* offered the most telling observation: "The quiet influences have prevailed."[27] That, above all, was the reassuring message the nation wanted to hear from New York.

Who was chiefly responsible for Kernan's election to the Senate? At various times, many figures claimed the credit; success has many fathers. Horatio Seymour certainly had an important role. Not only had he stood aside for Kernan, he had worked strenuously for his nomination, even traveling in midwinter to Albany in bad health to see it through to a successful conclusion. John Kelly also had much justice for his claims to have engineered the victory; his effective coordination of the legislators before the caucus smoothed Kernan's road and warded off any effective competition (as the King's County men had complained). But the real architect of Kernan's victory was Tilden. It was he who had given direction to the party leaders who managed Kernan's nomination; more importantly, the elevation of Francis Kernan to the Senate was a cornerstone of Tilden's strategy to secure the presidency. For Tilden to win the Democratic nomination, the party in New York had to be unified; for him to win the election, it had to be purified. Kernan's election, carefully prepared and flawlessly executed, went a long way toward accomplishing these two goals.

If unity and purity were the national keynotes of Kernan's victory, in Utica the sentiment was elation. The *Utica Daily Observer* reported, in a little story replete with cryptic literary references, on one local celebration: "A party of young gentlemen from 'Pent Up' were in the Salt city last evening. On learning the result of the Senatorial caucus at Albany, they 'sent for' a bottle of soothing syrup—not Winslow's by a long shot. They were just as happy as clams at high tide, all because Utica is to have two United States Senators at one and the same time; [they] declared no town of thirty thousand population, in this country, could make such a show. 'Unbounded' was a term they felt privileged to use, freely, for besides two

United States Senators [Francis Kernan and Roscoe Conkling], an M.C.[member of Congress], a United States Judge, and a lunatic asylum, the young men had bright visions that 'President' would be added to 'Pent Up's' glory. None blamed them for their joy—nor 'Had.' either, later on—they have reason for it."[28]

The enigmatic allusions in this humorous tale are to a long-forgotten poem, the "New Epilogue to Cato," by the American poet Jonathan M. Sewall. One stanza of the 1778 verse evidently struck a nerve with Uticans—or struck a chord with their neighboring rivals: "No pent-up Utica contracts your powers,/But the whole boundless continent is yours."[29]

"Pent Up" stuck as a jocular nickname for Oneida's first city; but with Kernan on his way to Washington as New York's second senator, Utica could be taunted as "pent-up" no more.

The Honorable Francis Kernan

KERNAN WAS SWORN in as a United States Senator in a ceremony on March 4, 1875, and attended a short special session of the Senate. On May 24 he took the time to pen a letter to Governor Tilden to congratulate him on the successful start to his administration. "Real reforms have been inaugurated, and they will be carried forward. . . . We are strong throughout the state; and with a good ticket this fall, which the mass of the party will insist upon, we will carry the state. I think you have reason to be well satisfied with what you have already accomplished, and with what you have been the means of successfully inaugurating." Kernan invited Tilden to visit him in Utica, where, he promised, "neither politics or politicians shall disturb you."[1]

Indeed, the governor was a frequent guest at the Kernan household. If Kernan kept his promise to insulate Tilden from "politics or politicians," however, he did not spare him from farmers, fairgoers, Union Army veterans, and other admiring constituents. Francis sought to keep the reticent presidential hopeful before the eyes of upstate voters by dragooning him to speak at as many ceremonial events, fairs, and festivals as he would allow. At times Kernan had to twist Tilden's arm to induce him to engage in this essential but, to Tilden, dreary aspect of his official duties. "I saw Ex-Gov. Seymour yesterday," Kernan remonstrated on one occasion. "He is of the opinion that you should accept the invitation to attend the meeting of the Representatives of the Army of the Cumberland in Utica on the 15 inst. unless you are precluded by other engagements. He says that as you are the Governor of the state and this meeting is to be attended by the Pres't of the U.S. and others holding public positions of distinction, he thinks there is great propriety in your attending if you can do so. . . . I concur in this opinion."[2]

Besides putting up Tilden in his house, Kernan researched train schedules, provided transportation, and did everything possible to make Tilden's visits convenient and to deprive him of excuses for not going. "Our people in this section of the state of all parties hope and expect to see you at the Agricultural Fair," he reminded the governor in September 1875. "The officers of the Society who invited you long since understand you will be here."[3] The *Utica Daily Observer* told a different story: "Governor Tilden, contrary to expectation, arrived in this city last evening and became the guest of Senator Kernan."[4]

At the urging of Kernan, Horatio Seymour, Charles O'Conor, and other close advisers, Tilden successfully overcame his aversion to campaigning and slogged through a procession of muddy country fairs in the fall of 1875. Hammering home his twin themes of breaking up the corrupt Canal Ring and bringing reform to Washington, he proved a surprisingly effective public speaker. Facing the more routine duties of his office, however, Tilden continued to display a worrisome deficiency of tact. Writing to Tammany's John Kelly about a backup in filling relatively minor appointments, Tilden acknowledged the problem, sort of: "when there was no haste [required], more important matters claimed the earlier attention. It is very likely I have not been altogether wise, as the world is largely made up of fools, in this respect. I am so formed constitutionally that I concentrate on what seems of first importance, and defer with almost contemptuous indifference what can as well or better wait."[5]

While Kelly may have appreciated Tilden's frankness, it would have been hard for him not to take offense at the governor's "contemptuous indifference" to issues of patronage, the *raison d'être* of Tammany Hall. In fact, relations between the two men and their allies were always fragile, as Kelly's credentials as a reformer increasingly clashed with the grubby realities of governing the nation's largest city. Behind closed doors at Tammany Hall, Kelly had problems keeping the alliance between reformers and old Tweed allies. Unhappiness on both sides simmered ominously.

For the moment, however, harmony prevailed between Kelly and Tilden, since both were focused on the tremendous benefits that each could expect to derive from continued cooperation. Tammany's guarantee of New York's electoral votes virtually assured Tilden's nomination for the presidency in 1876; and the patronage the Tammany chief would be able to dispense under a Tilden administration would be tremendous. In part for these pragmatic reasons, and also out of a genuine sense of mutual regard, the two men worked closely together in the early months of the term. Kelly was a frequent guest at Tilden's home, often accompanied by Kernan. According to historian Alexander Flick, the governor and the Tammany leader "had a cordial understanding about party matters and patronage. It was to Kelly that Tilden unbosomed himself about appointments and rumors of his 'softening of the brain,' 'stroke,' and excessive drinking. And to Tilden, Kelly wrote: 'May God spare you . . . until you have finished your tasks. Most men would have become disheartened at the many repulses.'"[6]

In the long run, however, it seems likely that conflict between Tilden and Kelly was inevitable. "Both of these potentates," observed historian Oliver E. Allen, "were fiercely proud, ambitious (Tilden for himself, Kelly for the Hall), jealous of their prerogatives, and likely to be unyielding if put to a test."[7] Despite shared goals and interests, moreover, the two men could hardly have been more different in their backgrounds and styles. Samuel Tilden's well-to-do first American forebear had reached American shores more than 250 years before, and in his "Notes on the Origin of the Tilden Name and Family," he traced his ancestry back to the "yeomanry of Saxon Kent." Kelly's parents had left grinding poverty in Ireland in 1816, six years before his birth in the squalid tenements of New York's Lower East Side. "Silk Stocking Sammy" had been born to power, wealth, and gentility; Kelly, orphaned at eight, had had to claw his way to a position of power, education, and a not insignificant portion of refinement. Along the way, he had tenaciously clung to the integrity that had earned him his moniker; but no urban leader could dispense with what the veteran Tammany sachem George Washington Plunkett called "honest graft." Kelly must have chafed at the lofty expectations of the "respectable citizens" who had called him to service after his return from Europe to take the helm of Tammany from Boss Tweed. His opponents made hay by painting Kelly and his lieutenants as dandified swells who had risen above their station—and their constituents. There was enough truth in the charge to rankle, particularly, perhaps, when his "high-toned" colleagues sought to slash the taxes of the affluent while advocating "retrenchment" of the city budget—in other words, cutting the contracts and patronage that were the lifeblood of urban political management.

For his part, it is likely that much of Tilden's discomfort with the likes of Honest John Kelly stemmed less from their differences than from their similarities. Despite his reputation for integrity, Tilden was, after all, a professional politician since his teens; and while the calling is an honest one, it is inescapably enmeshed in the often-grimy toils of favors, patronage, and pull. Tilden, schooled at the feet of the Little Magician, Martin Van Buren, in the New York political tradition of "to the victor belong the spoils," was no innocent.* Alternatively, Kelly knew well, even if

---

* "Despite Tilden's subsequent reputation as a reformer, he was a total political realist. . . . More than anything else, Tilden was a disciple of Martin Van Buren, a broker-politician, a compromiser, a patient man, who never anticipated public opinion." See Mushkat, *Reconstruction*, page 157.

the *New York Times* chose not to remember it, that Tilden had postponed his attack on the Tweed Ring until almost the last minute possible, and that, on pragmatic grounds, he had allowed many of the "little fish" to go free.[8] Moreover, for all his aura of genteel incorruptibility, Tilden had earned his substantial wealth and independence as attorney to the powerful railroad interests—to many Americans, no more savory companions than the hoodlums and grafters with whom Boss Kelly consorted.

In many ways Francis Kernan may have seemed the perfect intermediary between these two unlikely allies. An experienced politician since his youth, and consistently a staunch party man, he was nonetheless always an advocate of reform within his party. An American Catholic of Irish extraction like Kelly, Kernan, like Tilden, was the scion of a distinguished family who took considerable pride in his heritage. Personally upright and uncompromisingly ethical, Kernan eschewed moralizing and had no tolerance for cant. A lawyer's lawyer of formidable skill and finesse, he nonetheless enjoyed a reputation for straight dealing and honorable conduct among the electorate at large. Kernan could speak the languages of both Tilden and Kelly with fluency, and interpret between them when needed. In short, as long as he maintained the confidence of both, it would seem unjust of either to entertain any suspicions of the other.

The Boss broke with the Governor shortly after the 1875 local elections. Although the elections were a stunning sweep for the Democrats, they included some embarrassing victories of several old Tweed allies in New York City, men picked by Kelly. Many reform Democrats, including Seymour, stayed away from the ratification meeting at Tammany Hall on October 28, 1875, called to reaffirm Kelly's leadership in the face of an internal challenge. Although Kernan spoke, he restricted his comments to the national scene. The *New York Times* two days later interpreted Seymour's absence as "conclusive evidence of the utter collapse of Tammany Hall," claiming that the ex-governor was "too cautious a man to risk his future career, or compromise his reputation, by appearing on the same platform with Boss Kelly. Even Senator Kernan, who did present himself," the *Times* tittered, "dared not say a word about City affairs or politics. . . . Fancy the chief Democratic speaker at the great Democratic meeting of the year avoiding all reference to the sole issues which are now before the people of the Metropolis! It is one of the queerest things recorded in political history," the paper taunted. "Tilden brings down his great guns to New York, and they can't be got to go off. Kernan is afraid to talk on any local subject."[9]

Under the circumstances, Kernan found it hard to celebrate the Democratic victory. He wrote Tilden that although "[a]ll things considered," he was "proud of the results in this state," he "greatly regret[ted] the defeat of our friends in N.Y. City."[10] Well he might. Kelly was livid at what he considered Tilden's treachery, and he blamed Kernan personally as well: "He was particularly aggrieved by Mr. Kernan's speech at Tammany Hall," reported a confidant to Tilden, "and his feelings

Tilden receives the news of his presidential nomination

Governor Samuel Jones Tilden (left of table) formally receives the 1876 Democratic
nomination. Senator Francis Kernan (continuing left) and New York State Lieutenant
Governor W.E. Dorsheimer, stand ready to campaign hard for the Irish and German votes.
Next to Dorsheimer is Charles O'Conor, a family friend of Kernan and the man who
provided legal counsel both for the ex-president of the Confederacy, Jefferson Davis
and against New York's corrupt political boss, William M. Tweed.

Artist unknown. Reprinted from Alexander C. Flick's biography, *Samuel Jones Tilden.*

towards him are no warmer than towards you."[11] This was unfair, since Kernan had
gone about as far for the unsavory Tammany slate as he could without endangering
his reputation, and undermining Tilden's reputation for reform.

But even Tammany's opposition could not slow the Tilden juggernaut as it
headed toward 1876. Collaborating closely with Kernan, Seymour, and Lieutenant-
Governor W. E. Dorsheimer, Tilden mapped out a masterful campaign for the nomination at the St. Louis convention.

Kernan's speech placing his friend's name in nomination there was so "splen-
didly done," according to one account, "that it electrified the whole great assemblage."[12] Once again, Kernan's central role in Tilden's political advancement testified
to the symbolic power of his upright presence. Stressing Tilden's accomplishments

in breaking up the Tammany and Canal Rings, Kernan urged the convention to nominate the man who would do in Washington what he had done in New York.

The convention's one moment of drama came after Kernan finished his speech, when John Kelly, "hot and flushed," took the floor like a stage villain amidst the hisses and boos of the delegates. Only when Kernan intervened did the convention subside sufficiently for the wrathful Tammany sachem to declare that Tilden did not have New York City's full support. Kelly played the spoiler to no avail, however; Tilden received the nomination on the second ballot, with Indiana's senator Thomas Hendricks unanimously selected for the vice-presidential slot.

The real excitement came at the Republican convention in Cincinnati, where Sen. Roscoe Conkling thwarted the favored candidate, the "plumed knight" James G. Blaine, and dark-horse Rutherford B. Hayes secured the nomination.

According to the stilted traditional formula, Tilden remained at home during the convention, to receive the "official notification" of his nomination on July 11, almost two weeks after the event. Twenty days later he offered his letter of acceptance—a dense tome three times the length of the party's platform. When a newspaper editor complained to Tilden that it was too long for people to read, he replied testily, "It was not intended for people to read."[13]

Though clearly not a populist, Tilden launched a dynamic and effective campaign. The reformer's organization nevertheless lacked many experienced politicians, and the contributions of longtime party leaders such as Kernan were thus particularly critical. Kernan's hand may perhaps be seen in the grass-roots "Uncle Sam Union Clubs," which were initiated in Utica and soon had 600 branches in New York State alone.[14]

The Democrats sought to make the election a referendum on the Grant administration and the sorry state of the economy; the Republicans, having nothing better to offer, returned to their traditional theme of the bloody shirt: "a solid South, rebel rule, etc., etc., etc.," as their candidate referred to it in cynical shorthand.[15]

These mechanical appeals could no longer sway the nation. The campaign was hard, acrimonious, and tight. Kernan, one of the speakers most in demand, worked tirelessly for the ticket, being dispatched to trouble spots as far away as Ohio.[16] On election night in November, reports came in giving Tilden the contested states of New York, New Jersey, Connecticut, and Indiana, leaving only the South in question. The Democrats rejoiced in what appeared to be a clear-cut victory, and most Republicans gloomily conceded defeat.

On November 8, from his home in Utica, Francis Kernan wrote a congratulatory letter to Tilden:

> My Dear Sir,—Assuming, as I do, that you are elected, I greatly rejoice. I congratulate you, and I congratulate the country. I have never felt so much solicitude as to any political matters as in reference to the result of this election. The welfare of the people and their govt. demanded a change. The entire people will

be blessed by the restoration of economy and honesty in the administration of the Federal govt. Under you I am confident we will have the greatly needed reforms.

We did not do as well in this county as I expected and believed we would. But your young men, especially, worked hard and deserved success. But the Republicans made a very great effort to and did hold their people pretty well; and a good deal of money, wherever it came from, was used in the country, and they, with this, got most of the purchasable vote. I hope you are well. Take care of your health.

Reliable returns gave Tilden 184 electoral votes to 165 for Hayes, with 20 from South Carolina, Florida, Louisiana, and Oregon still in doubt. The Republicans would have to secure every contested vote—an unlikely scenario—to carry the election.

Such a scenario was unlikely, but not impossible. The first indication came from Oregon, where state authorities awarded its one disputed electoral vote to Hayes. In the three Southern states still at issue, the Republicans controlled the state governments—including the election boards. The nation held its breath over the next few days, as the remaining contested votes were awarded to Hayes. Nerves were frayed on both sides. From Louisiana, a frazzled campaign worker telegraphed Tilden that his "friends in La. need moral support and personal advisement," and urged him to send "Kernan and others . . . to New Orleans at once."[17] Meanwhile, the Republicans proved ready to play hardball. "Florida must be made Republican," the party's national chairman wired the state's governor. "Troops and money will be furnished."[18]

Hot-headed Democrats demanded action, a "bloody revolution," urged one high-strung Tennessean. Cooler spirits, including Kernan, remained "firm in the faith" that "right will prevail."[19] In the heat of crisis, Tilden himself appeared beyond calm: disconnected, indecisive, and apparently unconcerned about his own fate. The fearsome slogan "Tilden or Blood!" seemed wildly incongruous in connection with the passive, reserved, lawyerly figure. Nonetheless, the nation faced real danger during the tense month of January 1877.

The Tilden forces, argued a Virginia senator, had but three options: "We can fight; we can back down; or we can arbitrate." Forthrightly, Tilden ruled out any recourse to violence; thus arbitration was the only option.[20] Unfortunately, the Democrats operated at a disadvantage on such a course, since the Republicans held the levers of federal power. After weeks of protracted, delicate negotiations, Congress authorized the Electoral Commission described in the introduction of this book, made up of five senators, five representatives, and five Supreme Court justices, four to be appointed on the basis of the circuits to which each was assigned, and the fifth to be chosen by these four.

The uncompleted commission, evenly split between Democrats and Republicans, was expected to be rounded out by the appointment of Supreme Court Justice David Davis, a political independent and a known friend of reform, who would likely hold the balance of power in its deliberations. His single vote would tilt the election to Tilden, who had, after all, won the popular vote. This hope was dashed, however, when the Illinois legislature elected Davis to the U.S. Senate, and Justice Joseph P. Bradley, a Republican, was chosen instead. With this appointment, the die was cast. By one vote, on every important issue, the commission awarded the decision to the Republicans, eight to seven.

On February 26, after the decisive votes had been tendered for the Hayes electors, one of the Democratic commissioners, Senator Allen G. Thurman of Ohio, resigned from the commission on account of ill health. The Senate, by a vote of 46 to 0, selected Francis Kernan to replace him.[21] It was a symbolically important choice, suggesting the acquiescence of Tilden's closest supporters in the selection process; for this reason, Kernan faced some bitter recriminations for his decision to accept.[22]

At this stage, there was one strategy left to the Democrats: a Senate filibuster. They could simply threaten to shut the government down. Historians are divided over whether Democratic and Republican leaders negotiated the removal of federal troops from the South in exchange for acquiescing in the election of Hayes, or whether the Republicans would have taken that step anyway.

In any case, on March 2, the commission issued its decision in favor of Hayes, and Kernan, in his capacity as senator, spoke forcefully against its ratification. "I solemnly protest against it," he thundered, "and I do so from a higher motive than for the success of any man or any political party. I do not want it to go into the world without protest, that a false and fabricated certificate is to be counted, and I am deeply pained that such a principle should have been affirmed by a vote of eight to seven."[23] After a tumultuous, rancorous debate, Rutherford B. Hayes was sworn in on March 4, 1877, as the 19th president of the United States, in a decision which the historian Paul Johnson has called "legalized fraud." It is impossible to say in what ways the American story would have been different had the will of the majority prevailed in this election, but it is certain that the story of Francis Kernan would have been dramatically different.

After the chaotic, unorthodox process of selecting a president, many Democrats faulted Kernan for lending his moral authority to an outcome they considered patently unfair. Tilden himself appears to have shared some of this bitterness for a time. On March 12, the "level-headed and wise" Kernan wrote to his disappointed leader to place the event in perspective. "You were clearly and fairly elected by the people and Hayes has been counted in," Kernan counseled. Those Democrats in Congress who had acquiesced in this unfair result had "acted patriotically and wisely," since in the event of a deadlock, the Republican-controlled Senate would have declared the election of Hayes, while "the [Democratic-controlled] House would have elected you President and civil war would probably have been the result.

... My judgment was and is that what seemed a reasonably fair tribunal to decide the question involved was better than the risk of evil to our people and our system of government. Civil war is the last remedy of a people for political wrongs."[24] At a time when, as a Tilden partisan later remarked, "[u]nder the lash of party spirit . . . men did what they would not do in saner moments," Kernan kept his sanity, and remained true to higher principles than fealty to party, loyalty to Tilden, or personal ambition. A lifelong adherent to the doctrine of states' rights on constitutional grounds, Kernan believed that Congress had no right to invalidate the electoral authorities of the states even if that meant that the man he felt to be the far superior candidate should be denied the White House.[25] Moreover, Kernan was willing to lend his moral authority to a process he knew would produce an outcome he detested because it would help to spare the nation the horrors of civil unrest.

There is a certain irony in Tilden's irritation with Kernan for lending his prestige to the Electoral Commission. Since his assault on the Tweed Ring in 1872, Tilden had relied on Kernan's support to give a color of disinterested patriotism and honor to all his projects and ambitions. Kernan's unequivocal support secured for Tilden an absolute presumption of integrity during his national campaign that warded off his opponents' charges of railroad interests, Tammany connections, and tax evasion. When confronted with an accusation of using his fortune to bribe electors in February 1877, Tilden turned to Kernan to issue his denial.[26] Tilden could not well now complain that his upright colleague placed the good of the nation above his friend's electoral fortunes. It has been well said that Tilden may have saved the republic by his acquiescence in the results of the 1876 election; it would be hard to overstate Francis Kernan's invaluable contribution to that outcome.

No other event in Kernan's senate career, naturally, matched the Tilden-Hayes contest in excitement. Francis Kernan served in the Senate during "a very sterile period," as historian J. Herman Schauinger accurately noted; and "if he was unable to make any great contribution during his term, neither did anyone else."[27] The late 1870s was a high-water mark for cynicism, as historian Robert Wiebe observed: "Never had so many citizens held their government in such low regard." Out of the unsuccessful experience of Reconstruction "had come a haunting sense of the war's failure, a vague feeling of political betrayal," a perception to which the Hayes election lent painful clarity.

The election of 1878 gave the Democrats control of the Senate as well as the House; but President Hayes routinely vetoed all new initiatives. There were few enough of those in any event, in the "Do Nothing" Congress. The United States was entering a period of massive social and economic transformation, without the political or conceptual tools to confront change. The Republicans futilely endorsed the *status quo;* the Democrats called for reform, but offered chiefly "retrenchment," less government, and a return to the purity, austerity and supposed honesty of the old Democracy of Jefferson and Jackson. "Little wonder that Americans everywhere were crying out in scorn and despair. Unable to comprehend that they had heaped impossible tasks upon officials with woefully deficient means, they explained all crimes in the time-honored manner of unique failures in leadership and public morality."*[28]

In such an environment, Francis Kernan, serving as the second-ranking member of the Senate Finance Committee, must often have seemed out of place. Among the personal stories that remain from his days in the Senate is one that Kernan in his retirement delighted in telling. Shortly after taking his seat, he was approached by a constituent who was working hard to get a personal claim for compensation through Congress. He wanted a senator's vote and influence, and because he could not get the ear of Conkling, he wanted Kernan to get his fellow New York senator interested in his claim. Kernan listened patiently and attentively and promised he would do all he could to get the claim allowed, providing he found it to be a just one. The constituent then asked Kernan where his overcoat was. Kernan told him it was in the cloakroom, but wanted to know why the man asked. "I have an envelope here which I wish to put in one of your pockets," he said. Kernan, growing suspicious, asked to see it then and there and was handed an envelope containing several crisp bills. Kernan handed back the claim and the money and told the claimant to "get out of this room and never come in while I am here." The story sounds almost naive, given the level of corruption that surrounded Kernan in Washington.

In the Senate, Kernan's course remained consistent with the basic principles and beliefs that had characterized his earlier career. He continued as a champion of states' rights, on large issues and small. He argued against a national board of health, believing that such matters belonged exclusively to the purview of the states. He spoke for the Democratic party in calling forcefully on May 14, 1879, for the removal of the army from all polling places. Republicans argued that troops were necessary to ensure the voting rights of Negroes in the Southern states. (And troops could be helpful in the North to prevent Democrats' use of dubiously naturalized immigrants to pack the polls.) Kernan had engaged in a heated colloquy with his colleague Roscoe Conkling over the use of troops in New York City during the draft riots of 1863. Conkling now used the example to prove the need for troops, but Kernan pointed out that there had been no election riots in New York, and the army had never been required to keep order on election day. Defending voting rights with military force seemed to Kernan a contradiction in terms, asserting that

---

* The blunt-spoken Tammany Hall ward boss George Washington Plunkett may have had a point when he argued that if modern politicians had a tendency to steal, it didn't mean they were, "as a class, worse than them of 1835. It just means that the old-timers had nothin' to steal."

it was a new idea to station bayonet-wielding soldiers at the polls to "enforce the right of the one to vote and to prohibit the other." Kernan's speech contributed to the success of a bill to revoke the juror oath test, one of the last vestiges of Reconstruction.[29]

Kernan battled Conkling on patronage issues as well, voting to sustain President Hayes's efforts to remove Conkling's cronies from the lucrative New York Customs House—the issue that would ultimately end Conkling's political career.

Congress was deeply concerned with questions of finance and the currency during most of Kernan's term in office. The official exchange rate between silver and gold had long been 16 to 1, but major silver strikes out west after the Civil War had lowered the market price of the metal, so that investors could pocket a tidy profit by trading their silver for U.S. gold coins. Leery of draining the Treasury of bullion, Congress had eliminated silver currency in 1873—just in time for the great panic of that year, which many blamed on the government's action. Throughout four years of depression, the money supply fell by 50 percent, and prices dropped precipitously. The Bland-Allison Act of 1877 authorized the resumption of limited silver coinage at a level of between $2 million and $4 million a month. Passage of the bill—over Hayes's veto—coincided with bumper harvests in the Midwest and the end of the depression, bringing a cascade of gold into the nation in exchange for exported American grain. Kernan, a hard-money man in the tradition of Tilden, consistently opposed any measures to water down the currency, but reluctantly supported the relatively moderate Bland-Allison Act. "An honest currency should be one convertible into coin at the will of the man who earns it and holds it in his hand," Kernan asserted. "The working man don't want a currency to speculate in. He wants a state of things that will give him steady employment at fair wages, paid in a currency that will not cheat him."[30]

During his Senate term, Kernan expressed deep compassion and respect for Native Americans both through his votes and through his speeches. Defending a bill that would give the government the power to prosecute whites who commit crimes on Indian reservations, Kernan argued: "I think that if some Indian speaker could rise on this floor and give us the views of his people from their stand-point, he would claim that it was they who had been crowded and wronged by irresponsible parties, in violation of their rights, and that they had been thus wronged because our government . . . has failed . . . to prevent our people going in there when the thirst for gold, or the thirst for anything else in the way of making money, sends a crowd there, unless we prevent it."[31] A few months later Kernan angrily objected to the government's policy of supplying the Osage Indians with Quaker missionaries paid for out of the Indians' own trust accounts. The tribe, which had embraced Catholicism in the 1840s, had recently been relocated to Indian Territory (later Oklahoma), and Catholic priests were barred from living on the reservation. Kernan had learned from an Osage's agent that "while the treaty provided that they should have their own clergymen and teachers as they desired, they were deprived of that privilege; that while their own money supported them they were compelled to have others dictate what class of schools they should have, as well as what teachers and what class of persons should instruct them religiously." Kernan urged that the government fulfill its treaty obligations to the Osage "and permit them, so far as they indicate, the teachers, both secular and religious, that they prefer."[32]

Kernan's objections failed to gain religious liberty for the displaced Osages, who had to wait almost a decade before the establishment of a Catholic church on their reservation through the philanthropy of a devout Philadelphia heiress. (They were compensated for their trials, though, when oil was discovered on the barren reservation to which they had been exiled.) In 1880, Kernan introduced a bill to give all religious denominations equal rights and privileges on Indian reservations, but Congress refused to pass it.[33]

Kernan served in the Senate with five other men who, in their boyhoods, had all worked on his father's farm! All had left their childhood homes, and all had reached the U.S. Senate from different venues, some as Republicans, some as Democrats. On March 4, 1879, immediately after Jerome B. Chaffee and Henry M. Teller had been sworn in as Senators of the new state of Colorado, they were greeted by James B. Beck of Kentucky, who had entered the Senate two years earlier. According to one account, Beck grasped Teller's hand and asked, "Is this the same old Hank who worked with me in the harvest field on Kernan's farm away back before the war?"

Just then up stepped Angus Cameron of Wisconsin and behind him Rhoderic McPherson of New Jersey, accompanied by Francis Kernan of New York. The group adjourned to an office in the Capitol for a reunion and to recollect their work as harvest hands through several seasons on William Kernan's farm before they scattered to separate states and territories. At that moment, "the world's most exclusive club" must have seemed small indeed. The six reunited farm boys remained close friends during their days together in Congress.

Although few private letters or other artifacts have survived from Kernan's life in Washington, it is evident that he and his family were well received in Washington society. The Kernans were among those families of "outsiders" who were cordially embraced by the famously insulated sect of "Old Washingtonians"—the socially prominent permanent residents of what was, beneath the veneer of politics, a small Southern town. "Francis Kernan, the junior senator from New York, with his wife and daughter, was seen everywhere," reported Marian Gouverneur, a longtime resident and descendent of James Monroe; and their son Thomas "was a great dancer and a general favorite."[34] The fact that Kernan was a Democrat, plus the Catholic strains of the old Maryland colony, may have figured in the Kernans' acceptance in Washington society. During his Senate term, his living quarters were at the Arlington Hotel, where many fellow Democratic congressman, particularly after the 1874 elections chose to live.

On January 10, 1878, Francis had the pleasure of writing from the Senate Chamber a note of congratulations to his eldest son on the birth of Francis's grandson John Devereux Kernan Jr. [father of coauthor John D. Kernan]. "Your telegram just rec'd in my seat—God bless the boy & the mother. I congratulate you & Kate. Your mother inquired as to Kate's health as soon as I arrived yesterday eve—She will be very happy with the news—Make my most earnest congratulations to Kate & may the blessings of Heaven be with her and you and all your children always."

During the last two years of his Senate term Kernan served as chairman of the committee on patents, precisely the kind of unglamorous but highly useful occupation in which he took pleasure, and in which his superior knowledge of the law could be applied.

Kernan also devoted close attention during those years to the health of the state Democratic party, which remained precarious because of the split in New York City. Tilden's successor as governor had been Lucius M. Robinson, a moderate who did not arouse the antagonism of any faction but did not generate much enthusiasm either. At the state convention in Syracuse on September 10, 1879, Kernan made a plea for unity (which the *New York Times* characterized as a "prosy and incomprehensible harangue in favor of Democratic misrule"), which went unheeded, as Tammany Hall's John Kelly bolted the ticket and ran against Robinson. Kernan was one of the few figures in the party who was able to keep ties to both factions. Although he "acknowledged that he was biased in favor of the 'regular' organization," he spoke, to great applause, at a Tammany Hall meeting on October 30, delivering an address in favor of honest money and striving to keep his fellow New York Democrats focused on national issues, such as the upcoming presidential election.[35] The split in the party cost the Democrats the governorship, with Kelly taking enough votes from Robinson to ensure the election of the Republican, Alonzo B. Cornell. It also helped return the state legislature to Republican control. Thus, although the Democrats in Albany renominated Kernan without opposition, he was defeated for reelection in 1880 by the Republican majority. His seat was given to the complacent tool of Conkling, Thomas C. Platt. It would be hard to imagine a more striking contrast than that between the outgoing and incoming junior senators from New York.

How should the political career of Francis Kernan be evaluated? Not in terms of legislative achievements; these were necessarily slender, not only because the opposing party held the White House, but more fundamentally because Kernan did not accept the premise that the chief business of politicians was "lawmaking." A Democrat of the old school, Kernan genuinely believed that a free people were able, for the most part, to govern their own affairs, and that laws were most acceptable when passed closest to home, at the local or state level. The most important function of a senator, Kernan believed, was as a steward of the public trust. He stood at all times for his nation's honor: in its treaty obligations with foreign nations and Indian tribes, in its fiscal responsibilities to its creditors and bondholders, in its pledges of fair dealing to the readmitted Southern states.

It is not in the details of his career, but in the picture of the man as a whole, that Kernan's true contribution to his country may be found. The very spotlessness and consistency of character that offer to the biographer so little in the way of spice and contrast are precisely the keys to the high, perhaps unique place of honor he held in the eyes of his contemporaries. Kernan's support of Tilden served as a kind of moral shorthand to the public: if Kernan vouched for Tilden's integrity, that was all they needed to know about the subject.

In that capacity, Kernan was a vital figure in the process that historian Jerome Mushkat has called "the reconstruction of the New York Democracy," which he correctly portrays as an essential step toward the post-Civil War restoration of a healthy, functioning two-party system. By the mid-1870s a substantial segment of the population had concluded that the Republican party could not reform itself. When they were convinced that the Democratic party could reform itself, they recognized it as an acceptable alternative. Kernan helped to make that case in New York, the most important Democratic state. His contribution served to make Tilden a convincing candidate among supporters of reform, and opened the door to those "mugwump" Republicans who helped to elect another New York governor, Grover Cleveland, to the presidency.

If Kernan served to restore the Democratic party to full partnership, he broke new ground for American Catholics as well. As a senator, he never shrank from the defense of Catholic rights and prerogatives, as we have seen; but he did so always from the standpoint of the great constitutional tradition of American religious pluralism, never from a narrow or exclusive standpoint. His distinguished career, combining the strands of devout Catholicism and the broadest patriotism, helped to pave the way for later figures, such as Governor Al Smith and President John Fitzgerald Kennedy.

But it may have been in his tenure on the Electoral Commission of 1877, an office which some held accountable for denying the White House to another worthy Democrat, that Kernan performed his most valuable service to the nation. This episode, lasting barely more than a week—and then after all the important votes had been taken—might be regarded as no more than a footnote to Kernan's career, and indeed does not even appear in his entries in the *Dictionary of American Biography* or the *Biographical Directory of the United States Congress*. Yet the days that Kernan served on the commission have been described as one of the most dangerous moments in the history of the republic. By his presence on that body, ratified by the unanimous vote of every Democratic senator, Kernan bestowed upon it an appearance of legitimacy it could not have obtained otherwise. He protested the result of the commission, but he acquiesced in it. Although many in the party were willing to second-guess Kernan later, it seems clear that never were Kernan's level-headedness, wisdom, and patriotism employed to more valuable effect.

In the end, what Kernan chiefly contributed to the politics of his era was character. Few qualities during the Gilded Age were in shorter supply or in greater demand.

The Last of
the Oneida County Trio

*The last of the trio of great and honored men, whose lives have shed a
luster over the name and history of our city, has passed away.
Seymour, Conkling, and Kernan are no more.*

THE UTICA JACKSONIAN CLUB

ONEIDA COUNTY PRODUCED an exceptional group of lawyers, statesmen,
and politicians who directly connected its proud citizens to state and national councils, to economic opportunity, and to a front row seat at the major debates of the
19th century. Utica's three most notable native sons were nicknamed "The Oneida
County Trio." Horatio Seymour, Roscoe Conkling, and Francis Kernan each lived a
long life in public service, and in their final years continued to advise local, state, and
national leaders.

Seymour's health began to decline noticeably in 1875. Even so, he went to
Albany in the depths of winter that year to see the fight for Kernan's senatorial
election through. The effort cost him a bad cold and his health continued to suffer.
By the autumn of 1875 the six-time governor of New York State felt "too ill and
too old to do much" to help with Governor Samuel Tilden's reform efforts. The following summer, a sunstroke removed him from the national campaign. Even so, the
state convention in 1876 nominated him to succeed Tilden. Having learned his les-

son in his embarrassing presidential nomination in 1868, this time he was firm in his refusal to accept a nomination. He notified the chairman of the state committee that while he would "cheerfully sacrifice" himself to the campaign, his recent illness made him unable to perform the duties of governor.

Seymour's health prevented his taking any active part in Tilden's 1876 presidential campaign, other than corresponding with the candidate and agreeing to press interviews. On election eve he shared a platform with Kernan in Utica, having to sit down until the uproar caused by his arrival was over. Later, before the Electoral Commission vote gave the presidency to Rutherford Hayes, Seymour spoke in Albany, suggesting that the proper resolution of the crisis would be to appeal respectfully to the Republican party, on whose shoulders rested the responsibility for an honest outcome. The Republicans would bear the consequences of fraud.

He spent most of his retirement years on his farm. However, Grover Cleveland's 1882 campaign for governor stirred him to a last effort. While visiting with relatives in Cazenovia that autumn, he addressed the local Democratic club, laboring up the long flight of stairs to the halls to say, "I love the State of New York and want to see its dignity preserved. . . . I am an old man; it concerns me no longer. My days have gone by, but I want to die with the conviction that the prosperity of the state will be sustained."[1] It was his last official public appearance.

In January 1886, Seymour's wife fell ill. Unable to manage alone, in the fierce midwinter, the elderly couple was taken to the Utica home of Seymour's sister Julia (Mrs. Roscoe Conkling). There, Seymour also became ill, and after several episodes, succumbed on February 12. In less than a month, his wife was buried beside him.

Samuel Tilden died later that same year. Tilden's associates noticed a pronounced physical decline after his presidential campaign in 1876. Sickly throughout his life, he suffered an apoplectic stroke that partially paralyzed one leg, one arm, and one eye. Shaking palsy affected his hands, and he suffered greatly from pulsing headaches. According to his biographer, Tilden was a "confirmed hypochondriac . . . everlastingly diagnosing his condition; . . . in his last years [he] spent a small fortune consulting specialists in America and Europe." He died at his Graystone residence on August 4, 1886. President Cleveland journeyed to Yonkers for the simple funeral three days later. His remains were buried in a cemetery in New Lebanon, which he often called "the beautiful valley where I was born."

Senator Roscoe Conkling, who had always regarded New York patronage as his special privilege, ended his long career in public office after a bitter fight against reform. After the election of Hayes, New York's senior senator became progressively

The Oneida County Trio

Utica's foremost statesman: six-time governor Horatio Seymour, 1810–1886,

Senator Francis Kernan, 1816–1892, and Senator Roscoe Conkling, 1829–1888.

[Seymour] From Vignettes of Old Utica by John J. Walsh, reprinted with author's permission. [Kernan] From a photograph belonging to
co-author John D. Kernan. [Conkling] From a Mathew Brady daguerreotype, permission of the National Portrait Gallery.

more isolated in his battle. Unlike Grant, who favored Conkling, the new president was unwilling to concede control over New York patronage. In the 1880 campaign (as in 1876) Conkling prevented the Republican party's nomination of James G. Blaine and had the satisfaction of seeing his stalwart lieutenant, former New York Collector Of Customs Chester A. Arthur, elected as vice president with James Garfield. Conkling's frustration knew no bounds when, after Garfield's assassination, Arthur became president and appointed an anti-Conkling man to his old customs house post. Furious, Conkling resigned his Senate seat in protest, and was soon joined in this pointless gesture by his devoted follower (and Kernan's successor), Thomas "Me Too" Platt. Conkling expected a triumphant vindication from the New York legislature; but that body failed to see the thwarting of his will as the matter of transcendent principle that he did, and both Conkling and Platt found themselves rejected for reelection with no hope of ever returning to the Senate. (With Conkling defeated, Blaine was finally able to win the Republican nomination in 1886.) Conkling returned instead to the private practice of law, and secured a tidy fortune before his peaceful death in 1888.

Francis was the longest surviving member of the Oneida County Trio. After his senatorial term ended in 1881, he continued to devote himself to his law profession, to his family and, increasingly, to his faith, taking part in political movements only as adviser and occasional campaign speaker. He passed his interest in politics along to his son John D. Kernan.

Like Seymour, Francis and John D. were ardent supporters of Grover Cleveland. John D. was among the reform organization of Democrats of western New York ("the County Democracy") who were instrumental in Cleveland's nomination in 1882. Members of that organization wanted a candidate who was free from political antagonisms with New York and King's County. Confronting the power of Tammany Hall, "the County Democracy, inspired by men of iron nerve, went to Cleveland in a body, making the hall resound with cheers."[2] Once governor, Cleveland rewarded John D. for his support in the campaign with a five-year state appointment as the Democratic member of the bipartisan railroad commission.[3]* Cleveland offered Francis a minor appointment as well, which he turned down, either for lack of interest or because of his age.

Father and son continued to work for the popular governor's presidential nomination in 1884, with John D. actively helping to enroll 250,000 Cleveland supporters. A large contingent packed the state convention in Albany that year and, according to the *Utica Daily Observer,* "as one man" selected John D. as chairman. "His speech on taking the chair and his subsequent efforts in the campaign, were vital in swinging New York's support for Cleveland." Although the local paper may have exaggerated John D.'s influence at the convention, events were to prove the value of that influence later on: Tammany delegates, led by Honest John Kelly, were not happy that Governor Cleveland kept his campaign promises of governmental reform. Francis attended the Chicago national convention in the unofficial capacity of elder statesman, while John D. attended as a delegate. During the convention, Tammany members of the New York delegation launched a dirty, whispering campaign against Cleveland, accusing him of being a drunkard and an anti-Catholic; but the New Yorkers' coarse behavior only enhanced Cleveland's reputation as a man above politics. Francis took the opportunity of inviting the nominee to visit his home during his next summer vacation.

After the convention the whispering campaign continued. Francis Kernan joined two of Cleveland's Irish-Catholic managers, John McCall and James Shanahan, calling on newspaper offices around the state, following the visits of Tammany operatives pronouncing Cleveland a "Presbyterian bigot," to tell the truth to editors and offering themselves for cross-examination.[4]

The Republican nominee, James G. Blaine, might well have won the crucial New York vote were it not for a disastrous remark by a New York City clergyman, who opined to Blaine that the antecedents for the Democratic party were "rum, Romanism, and rebellion." Blaine had not commented, but his lack of response allowed the Democrats to turn the insult into high outrage, making sure the voters saw the insult on posters, handbills, and banners throughout the urban Irish precincts.

On July 13, 1887, President Cleveland and his new bride, Frances, visited Utica

---

* Grover Cleveland appointed John D. Kernan railroad commissioner of New York State in 1883. In 1894, during his second term as president, Cleveland appointed him as one of two commissioners charged with investigating the famous Pullman strike

as Kernan's guests. The presidential party arrived at the train station by private railway car shortly before six o'clock. The crowd surged up to Kernan's carriage as it began its progress from the station, and a score of people walked beside it with their hands on the outside, until a special guard from the Jacksonian Club was detailed to march along side instead. Many in the crowd followed the carriage over the entire dusty route as Francis pointed out to his guests some of the principal residences of Utica. Homes and businesses (and the entire Devereux Block) were decorated with bunting and lanterns and large pictures of Cleveland. The president responded to the clouds of waving handkerchiefs with waves of his hat. After an hour and a half the entourage arrived at Chancellor Square, where the Jacksonians presented arms and then cheered as Cleveland stood in the carriage and made a short thank-you speech. The guests were welcomed at the door by Kernan's son Francis and his wife, along with other family members. Following the dinner with the family and friends, a "private" reception was held at the Butterfield House. An estimated 5,000 people shook the hands of their new president and his wife. The receiving line went on until after midnight.[5]

The Clevelands stayed overnight at the Kernans' house, and then went on the next day to Alder Creek, to visit family. The visit was described in the Kernan family's Springbank Record, showing the time the various members spent with the Clevelands.[6]

Kernan meanwhile was gradually retiring from public view. A newspaper interview published after he left the Senate, described him as "a relic of the days when Governor Seymour and the Democratic party ruled New York by the aid of the Catholic Church."[7] Kernan spoke proudly of Utica as "the home of statesmen," but when the reporter asked about Roscoe Conkling, Kernan responded tactfully, leaving the impression that "the Senator was scarcely more acquainted with him than if they were not fellow townsmen." The reason apparently given by Kernan for his inability to provide any details about his lifelong rival was that Conkling had been in Utica very little since he had entered public life, and scarcely at all since he had reentered the practice of law after leaving the Senate.

As for Horatio Seymour, Kernan gently defended the name of his mentor against the recently published memoirs of Senator Blaine, saying that Blaine "had retained a little too much of the old war spirit in reviewing Governor Seymour's action."

Concluding the interview, the reporter noted "a quiet remark . . . [that] impressed me forcibly as characterizing the integrity of all of them." As Kernan observed, "In all that has been said of Utica politicians and statesmen, there remains one striking thing. We never had any canal contracts at Utica. There was a sort of feeling among the leaders, both the Democrats and the Republicans, that the contracts were not to be desired, and we never even sought any for our friends. It is a point that can be made with great force for the credit of Utica in the history of the canal frauds."

Another, more personal image of how Francis spent his last years appears in a news article written the year before his death. Headed "He Is The Sage of Utica,"[8] it reads, "He is rarely seen in public now. . . . Most of his time is spent in his magnificent mansion in Chancellor Square. From his library window he looks out upon the fleeting show daily and passersby often see him as he sits in the window perusing some law volume. Every Sunday he goes to 10 o'clock mass in St. John's Church, which is but a block away from the house." And later the same article continues, "The home life of Senator Kernan is charming to behold. His sons and daughters and their sons and daughters all live within a short distance of Chancellor Square. They call in and see him almost daily. Mrs. Kernan and her daughter Miss Lizzie, who is well remembered in Washington society, are ever with the ex-senator. Mr. and Mrs. (Francis) Kernan attend church together on Sundays and can be seen daily in the summer time walking in their beautiful garden in the rear of their home, which is filled with choice fruit trees, vines, flowers and shrubs, in which he takes great delight."

Kernan's interest in his alma mater, Georgetown, continued to the end of his life. He served as vice president of its Alumni Society in 1880, and on June 27, 1880, he was given the honorary degrees of Doctor or [sic)] Master of Laws. They were awarded, according to the Latin citation, for his "outstanding knowledge of laws," to make it evident "among cultivated people . . . [t]hat rewards are not lacking for serious study and additions to knowledge for their own sake." [See Appendix X.] On November 11 and 12 of that same year, Kernan was Georgetown's delegate to the American Catholic Congress, held in Baltimore, and his son Nicholas was one of the many vice presidents. The congress was sanctioned by James Cardinal Gibbons of Baltimore with the blessing of Pope Leo XIII "to counsel and deliberate upon subjects and affairs of common Catholic interest, and for the mutual social benefits to be derived from the intercourse and opportunities afforded by such a meeting." It was attended by men from all over the country, including Hoguets from New York, friends of the Kernan family, and Jenkinses and Shrivers from Baltimore, connections by marriage. The topics covered by the papers presented to the meeting were widely varied and included, for example, Lay Action in the Church, Education in the United States, Temperance, Sunday Observance, Labor and Capital, and Church Music.

On the first day of the Congress, Francis was invited to deliver a brief address. "The man who is loyal to the teachings of the Catholic Church," he began, "must always be loyal to his country. He will be an honest voter; he will be an honest official. . . . Our mission will be to make us better Christians and therefore better citizens."

Following an interruption occassioned by the arrival of Cardinal Taschereau of Quebec and Cardinal Gibbons, he continued:

> Why should not we Catholics love the political institutions of these United States? There is no country in the world, Catholic or Protestant, where our church is as free from persecution and as free from harsh treatment as in these United States. We will be faithful to these institutions where every man has the right and is respected for fearlessly on all proper occasions avowing what he believes to be his duty to his God by practicing that religion which he thinks is the correct one, and which he thinks he ought to practice.... I do not desire to coerce any person of a different creed to worship God as I think is right. I desire to encourage him to examine for himself, and I respect him when he has so examined, for teaching his children and worshipping God according to what he believes is right for himself, and not according to what I believe is right.[9]

Francis Kernan enjoyed good health for most of his life, but in 1889 he began to fail, suffering from rheumatism and difficulty walking. Several years of reduced activity passed until, on August 13, 1892, he "took a chill." He was prostrated the next day, and suffered another relapse 24 hours later. The daily newspaper carried the smallest details: "He improved somewhat until the twenty fourth, when he suffered another relapse. Since then he improved again but gradually fell away. During all his sickness he has suffered no pain.... He was conscious to the last, and death marked its victim silently and painlessly. It was like the dying of a bright day; his great light dropped behind the mountains of the hereafter."[10]

The Oneida County Bar met on September 10 to take appropriate action on his death. Chairman, Judge M. H. Merwin testified to Kernan's integrity as lawyer, saying,

> [Francis Kernan] occupied at the Bar of this county, State and nation, a commanding position; still he held it not by favor, but by right, for he honestly acquired that position by his industry, his ability, and his integrity.... When he rose in court to argue his case, the court expected it would receive aid in the investigation and decision of cases. True, his side would be fully represented, because he was faithful to his client, still he was exceedingly fair in the presentment of a case. He was unusually correct in his statement of principles and when he cited cases which were in point, it became important, if not necessary, not only for the opposing counsel, but for the Court, to look at those cases and see where they stood....[11]

His kindness and cordiality toward younger members of the profession were proverbial. The minute passed at that meeting attested to his impact on the Onieda bar:

He was a peacemaker … uniformly courteous to the opposing counsel, adroit in management, persuasive to the jury, his success *nisi prius* was great… Perhaps his masterly intellect shone most brilliantly before the court in banc …In short he was a great lawyer, not surpassed by any of that galaxy of legal luminaries who made the Oneida bar famous throughout the country. His intercourse with his professional brethren was of the most pleasant nature. He was always easy of approach. The younger men who came to him for advice and counsel always found him ready and willing to assist them and those who chanced to be opposed to him in court remember with gratitude the kindly manner in which he treated them.

The Honorable W. A. Matterson shared a personal memory from his own youth, saying,

In 1863, when on my way to Whitestown Seminary, I looked out of the car window and saw a distinguished looking gentleman. It was Francis Kernan. Some years after that I resolved to enter on the study of law. I had no friend among the profession, but I remembered his kindly face. I went alone to his office and sought his advice. I remember well his cordial reception and felt when I went away that I had left the presence of a great, good, and kind-hearted man—my friend. When he told me he had decided to give me a desk in his office he never knew how I blessed him for tendering me that opportunity.

The regents of the University of the State of New York, took note of his demeanor at the bar:

Mr Kernan had a logical mind with unusual powers of statement and analysis, united with rare gifts of persuasion. … In the examination of witnesses he displayed rare knowledge of human nature. … His language as well as his bearing toward the jury were such as to create the belief that he was absolutely honest and sincere. He treated the court with uniform respect and seemed only desirous that it should comprehend his views and receive fitting impression from their statement ….

The Utica Jacksonian Club at a large meeting held the day after his death declared in a resolution, "The last of the trio of great and honored men, whose lives have shed a luster over the name and history of our city, has passed away. Seymour, Conkling, and Kernan are no more."[12]

Francis's oldest son, John Devereux Kernan, writing in the *Springbank Record* on September 11, put it more simply: "Father, aged 76 yrs., 7 mos., 23 days, died peacefully and happily on Sept 7th at 4:30 P.M. … He indeed died full of years and honors! '*Requiescat in pace!*'" These few words reflect the happy home life lauded by others at the time of Francis's death.

Of Francis's funeral on September 10, his oldest son continued in the *Record:* "The funeral was held yesterday at 10 A.M. at Saint John's Church. Nick, Frank, Will, Joe, my Frank and myself carried his remains out of the house.[13] Walter is detained in Quarantine on the cholera stricken ship '*Normania*' with Will Quin." (The pall-bearers named were all sons except "my Frank," who was a grandson, Francis Kernan Kernan, 1875–1945. Will was a nephew and law partner, who had been on a European trip with Francis's son Walter.)

The family members then walked in procession from the house to Saint John's Church, the church where Francis had been married, where all his children had been baptized, and from which he would be buried. The celebrant of the High Pontifical Mass was the Right Reverend Bishop Ludden of Syracuse, and one of the assisting deacons was Francis's nephew, the Reverend George Quin, S. J. Some 16 other priests, including the Right Reverend Bernard McQuaid, bishop of Rochester, and the Reverend Doctor J. S. M. Lynch of Saint John's Church, were in the sanctuary.

Francis was buried in Saint Agnes Cemetery, Utica, with his father, mother, and many other members of the family. A marble pulpit dedicated to his memory was given by his son Nicholas in 1892 to Saint John's Church, which Francis had attended faithfully, and where for many years he was a trustee elected by the pewholders.[14]

The will and the handling of his estate were so satisfactory to all concerned that it never became necessary for the executors to file an accounting in the Surrogate's Court.[15] Thus, there is no simple way to know its size, but there is no doubt that it was large. One clue is that in the 1860 federal census, more than 30 years before his death, his real property was valued at $40,000, and his personal property at $15,000, which together would have a present-day purchasing power of over $5 million.

Francis had been a loving husband, and surely the "faithful friend and protector" that his mother-in-law hoped for before the wedding. For more than a decade the family had annually celebrated the wedding anniversary of Francis and Hannah. Francis died the year before their golden anniversary. Hannah lived another ten years after her husband and died on September 30, 1902, at the age of 82.

_A_ Personal Afterword

by John Devereux Kernan

THE FOREGOING PAGES reveal much of Francis Kernan. But for all that we have been able to discover and reconstruct of our patriarch, we are grieved to have so few of the hundreds of the personal letters left from those he daily sent to Hannah. What did he report of his days in the state Assembly as the nation headed for war, or while he sat in the U.S. House of Representatives during that conflict? We regret not learning, from his own words, how he felt about the unrelenting, charges of being a "Copperhead" as he fought for constitutional law and helped to forge the new American tradition of "the loyal opposition." From his lost letters we might know his personal thoughts about President Lincoln, and learn of any conversations they might have had, or learn the subject of his consultations with Lincoln's cabinet members Seward and Chase. Kernan's failure to applaud the Emancipation Proclamation or to vote against the Thirteen Amendment is deplorable, especially in the light of present-day perceptions, although his stand in that regard was widely held at the time. It is hard for a modern reader, post-civil rights era to comprehend the political and social realities of the years in which the entire nation wrestled with the issue, and honorable people on all sides went to war against one another.

What were his impressions of America's West as he toured to support Horatio Seymour for president? Did slander against his war record, his faith, and his Irish heritage extract a personal price during the months of his gubernatorial race in which he broke new ground against religious prejudice in American politics and paved the way for later politicians such as Al Smith and John F. Kennedy? What burden of responsibility did he feel for the unity of the Democratic party—both in New York and in Washington—upon his election to the Senate? And how did he reconcile his bitter disappointment when his highest hopes for an honest administration were dashed in an election stolen by the Republicans for Rutherford Hayes?

In a bibliography of Tilden there are frequent footnotes referring to the Kernan papers owned by the family in Utica.[1] But such a collection, if it still exists, has not been found: if it should be, might it also tell us of other aspects of his character—for example, how he spent his leisure, whether he enjoyed hunting and fishing, or had a favorite horse. We know he liked an "innocent" game of cards, probably whist or euchre, and that he liked to read, but what? His son John D. wrote that Francis took no pleasure in the theater, opera, or club life, but did he sing, as did his oldest son? Did he smoke? Did he know a foreign language other than the Latin he loved to quote, or know enough French to chat with Hannah? The few letters from Washington that have been preserved reveal their continuing tenderness for each other, but what private impressions did they share of the old Washington society? The flaws in his makeup—being a man, he must have had some—are not obvious from what he left behind or what others wrote of him.

Whatever of Francis Kernan has been lost in the century since his death, we hope in these pages to have restored a sense of his warmth, his moral integrity, and his part in our national story, and to pass this along to all his descendants.

The log house at Tyrone is gone, and William Kernan's many acres are now owned by several different individuals. The family graveyard is in sad condition, at one point having served as a lane for cows to pass between their barn and their pasture; not a gravestone is still upright, and the stones that once formed its wall are dismantled and scattered about. William's homestead farm now comprises only a 100 acres and is farmed by a Mennonite from Lancaster, Pennsylvania, who occupies the old house, minus its two chimneys, with his wife and four children. Wayne no longer has churches, feed mills, saw mill, basket factory, hotels, or a local school, and a number of its houses are derelict.

Georgetown is now a great university with an enrollment of 12,600 students, with a four-year college of 3,153 students, and several graduate schools, including a law school of its own. It is still run by the Jesuits, and has many new buildings and all modern amenities. Its students arrive by plane, train, or automobile, rather than by horseback. Dancing is no longer taught, and no lectures are given in Latin. The students no longer march in line to meals, and trips to the Congress or anywhere else are unchaperoned. Fencing is a sport only, and the university has all the usual teams—football, basketball, swimming, and so on. The cost for one year is $25,000.

Catharines, Jefferson, and Watkins have become Watkins Glen, which is now the seat of Schuyler County. Virtually no one "reads law" any longer. All aspiring lawyers have to take bar exams, which in some states may last as long as four days. Some of the questions now struggled over seem as odd as those posed to George

Templeton Strong in 1841, and questions asked at the personal interviews are equally surprising.[2]

Utica is no longer growing in population. It has no aldermen under a new charter. Its schools include several institutions of higher learning. Its position as a railroad center is much reduced, and of its canals only the Erie's replacement, the Barge, is still used for transportation. The houses on Kent Street and Chancellor Square are no more, that area of the city being no longer residential. The Devereux Block was demolished many years ago, replaced by a small park.

The New York State Assembly still meets in Albany. The House of Representatives and the Senate still meet in Washington, but for much longer periods so that the legislators live there for much of their terms. Its members still battle with and malign their president. Senators, of which there are now one hundred, are elected by popular vote, not by the state legislators. The political prejudices against Roman Catholics have all but disappeared: several have been elected governor of New York and one has been elected president of the United States.

What today of the law firm that Francis Kernan started in 1853? It is now a firm of five practicing lawyers at 258 Genesee Street, still called Kernan and Kernan, but with no active lawyers of the name. Thomas Spratt Kernan, a great-grandson, and James Sedgwick Kernan, a great-nephew, are of counsel, and in effect retired. There are several young Kernan lawyers, but they practice in Rochester, Buffalo, and Newark, New York, Washington, D.C., and in Doylestown, Pennsylvania. Several descendants have studied law but never practiced..

Kernan's Reports, which originally appeared in full leather bindings with KERNAN'S REPORTS embossed in gold at the top and NEW YORK COURT OF APPEALS near the bottom of the spine, now appear in reprint in anemic cloth bindings called 11 through 14 New York. The reporter's name still appears but in much less conspicuous lettering. Copies in their original bindings are hard to locate, most having been discarded to make space for their thin reprints, or rebound.

And what of the Utica Kernans? Although there are almost 400 descendants of Francis Kernan living today, only about 70 bear the name, and only 9 of these live in Utica or near enough to be actual Utica Kernans. The rest live throughout the United States and Europe, and one is frequently in Africa. Whereas in the old days their families were large, now they are more apt to be of two or three children, with one glaring exception of 14 (Elizabeth Cook [Kernan] Dore's), and several have none at all. Most of them manage to get good educations, and they, both boys and girls, go to dozens of different colleges and universities, not just Georgetown and Seton Hall. Many, especially among the younger, are no longer Roman Catholics, having melted into the American pot.

They have, and have had, many and varied occupations, professions, and avocations. Besides lawyers, doctors, nurses, writers, poets, foresters, photographers, businessmen, journalists, builders, capitalists, musicians, teachers, museum executives and curators, fund raisers, social workers, couturières, etc., *ad infinitum;* some of course have humbler occupations.[3] But none could now cut a pen as Francis did for his Hannah. Only one has ever followed Francis into the political world: Michael Jenkins Kernan, 1884–1954, a grandson, who served in the New York State Assembly 1923–1924, and in the New York State Senate 1933–1935.

Avocations have included horse racing, singing, antique silver, gardening, farming, camping, exploring, sailing, skiing, languages, traveling, fishing, and hunting. Only two still have farms: Gilbert Butler, in addition to his other interests, has a game farm in Boonville, which at times has specialized in alpacas, North American wapiti, fallow and sika deer, the last a Chinese breed; and Ben Kernan has a farm in Shoreham, Vermont, where he raises cattle for sale to dairy farmers. Neither, according to the best reports, is a plain dirt farmer who hoes potatoes in his bare feet.

Many served with honor and distinction in the Second World, Korean, or Vietnam Wars, in the Army, Navy, Marines or Air Force. At least three have attended the United States Naval Academy, and two of these are brothers and great-great-grandsons of Francis: Captain Robert Furey Kernan, a flyer and at the moment of writing, commanding officer of Barbour Field on Oahu, and Commander Joseph Devereux Kernan, who has recently finished a two-year term as skipper of Seal Group Two at Virginia Beach, and is now on special assignment in North Carolina working with the United States Army.

Members of the family meet, of course, for funerals and weddings. But there are gatherings at other times as well, such as bashes at Alder Creek on the Fourth of July, one very memorable occasion being at Springbank in 1984 on the 100th anniversary of its purchase, where some 178 kissing cousins were in attendance. Francis Kernan's distinctive nose and the striking Nordic fold of his eyes appear in all their glory only in his most fortunate descendants, and at gatherings we occasionally dispute in good humor as to who is the most "Kernan" looking among us. None of us sports Francis's trademark collier.

Surely we must all agree that Francis Kernan is our most distinguished ancestor since the days of Bryan Mac Thighearnain of the Conflicts, Dux of Tullyhunco.[4] Let us hope that Francis's character, achievements, public spirit, and example will inspire us to strive for a better world.

NOTES

1. See Mitchell.

2. One question on my Connecticut Bar Exam was: If a man standing on my land shot a rabbit that ran over the property line onto your land, and then died on a third man's land, to whom does the dead rabbit belong? I was able to answer that at the time, but alas, I have forgotten and can no longer tell you! The questions asked of me at my personal interview for the New York Bar by "Holy Joe" McKee, Jimmy Walker's successor, were, much to my surprise: a. How many judges are there on the Appellate Division of the Supreme Court of New York (in whose courtroom with about five seats for the judges we were seated)? b. Who is first baseman on the Yanks? and c. Who discovered the circulation of the blood? c. was the only one I was able to answer— Harvey.

    As to Strong the diarist's experiences, see Chapter 4.

3. "Rich men may have very poor devils for second cousins," George Eliot somewhere in *Middlemarch*.

4. For whom see *MacKernan of Tullyhunco*.

Author's Note

by Karen Kernan

IF A FAMILY is fortunate, it will have a member such as my father-in-law, John Devereux Kernan, who has cared enough about our history to devote an exceptional number of evenings, weekends, holidays, and vacations to uncovering and preserving that past. Often at the risk of pestering or boring those less concerned with their legacy, John had spent over 30 years compiling and maintaining the genealogical records for the clan when the possibility of writing this book first came up for discussion. Very little was known about the political career of our most eminent member and patriarch—few knew that he had run for governor of New York, or even that he had served in the House of Representatives during the Civil War. There were some letters John had transcribed years earlier, and some old, often inaccurate, stories were shared on rare occasions at family gatherings. Without John, this book could not have been written. Another generation and the thin thread he had preserved would have been lost and I could not have begun this long journey backward to reconstruct the life of Francis Kernan. This note is in appreciation for John's dedication to preserving and sharing the Kernan family's unique history.

OTHER WORKS BY JOHN DEVEREUX KERNAN

Notes on the Descendants of John Kernan of Ned, County Cavan, Ireland, and of Jane Brady His Wife. 1949

The Utica Kernans, Descendants of Bryan Kernan, Gentleman, of the Townland of Ned. 1969

Devereux of the Leap, County Wexford, Ireland, and of Utica, New York Nicholas Devereux. 1791–1855 (with Clifford Lewis 3rd). 1974

Chinese Export Silver 1785–1885 (with H. A. Crosby Forbes and Ruth S. Wilkins). 1975

The Chait Collection of Chinese Export Silver. 1985

Supplement to the Utica Kernans 1968–1993. 1993

MacKernan of Tullyhunco. 1993

ℐioneer Life in 1816

THE FOLLOWING DESCRIPTION from McMaster's *History of the Settlement of Steuben County, N.Y.* is so similar to what William Kernan's circumstances must have been like in about 1816 when he is reported in Everets and Ensign's *History of Tioga,* at page 680 to have entertained three travelers that it is given in extenso. Make the host ten years older, put shoes—for the sake of family pride—at least on the wife, make the oldest child a boy, and the travelers coming to Tyrone, and one could accept it as being about William.

> As I was travelling through the county on horseback on a summer day in an early year of settlement I fell in company with two gentlemen, who were going in the same direction. . . . . We had followed in Indian file a mere path through the woods for several miles, . . . when having passed the outskirts of settlement and penetrated deep into the woods, our attention was attracted to the tinkling of a cow bell, and the sound of an axe in chopping. We soon saw a break in the forest, and a log house. As we approached we heard the loud barking of a dog. . . . A shrill whistle from within called off the dog. We proceeded to the house. A short distance from it, standing on the fallen trunk of a large hemlock, that he had just chopped in two, was a fine looking young man four or five and twenty years of age, with an axe in his hand. He was dressed in a tow frock and trousers, with his head and feet bare. The frock, open at the top, showed that he wore no shirt, and exhibited the muscular shoulders and full chest of a very athletic and

powerful man. When we stopped our horses he stepped off the log, shook hands with the agent, and saluting us frankly, asked us to dismount and rest ourselves, urging that the distance to the next house was six miles, with nothing but marked trees to guide us a part of the way; that it was nearly noon, and that he could not promise anything very good to eat, yet he could give us something to prevent us from suffering from hunger. He had no grass growing as yet, but he would give the horses some green oats. We concluded to accept the invitation and dismounted and went into the house.

Before describing the house I will notice the appearance of things around it, premising that the settler had begun his improvements in the spring before our arrival. A little boy about three years old was playing with the dog. . . . A pair of oxen and a cow with a bell on, were lying in the shade of the woods; two or three hogs were rooting in the leaves near the cattle, and a few fowl were scratching the soil. There was a clearing, or rather chopping around the house of about four acres, half of which had been cleared off and sowed with oats, which had grown very rank. The other half of the chopping had been merely burnt over and then been planted with corn and potatoes. . . . The chopping was enclosed with a log fence; . . . a small brook ran down across the clearing, along the borders of which a few geese were feeding.

When we entered the house the settler said, "Wife, here is the land-agent and two other men," and turning to us said, "This is my wife." She was a pretty looking young woman dressed in a coarse loose dress and bare footed. When her husband introduced us, she was a good deal embarrassed, and the flash of her dark eyes and the crimson glow that passed over her countenance, showed that she was vexed at our intrusion. The young settler noticed her vexation and said, "Never mind, Sally, the Squire (so he called the agent) knows how people have to live in the woods." She regained her composure in a moment and greeted us hospitably, and without any apologies for her house or her costume. After a few minutes conversation, on the settler's suggesting that he had promised "these men something to eat to prevent their getting hungry," she began to prepare the frugal meal. When we had first entered the house she sat near the open door, spinning flax on a little wheel, and a baby was lying near her in a cradle formed of the bark of a birch tree, which resting like a trough on rockers, made a very smooth, neat little cradle.

While the settler and his other guests were engaged in conversation, I took notice of the house and furniture. The house was about 20 by 26 feet, constructed of round logs *chinked* with pieces of split logs, and plastered on the outside with clay. The floors were made of split logs with the flat side up; the door, of thin pieces split out of a large log, and the roof of the same. The windows were holes unprotected by glass or sash; the fire place was made of stone and the chimney of sticks and clay. On one side of the fire place was a ladder leading to the chamber. There was a bed in one corner of the room, a table and five or six chairs, and on one side a few shelves of split boards, on which were a few arti-cles of crockery, and on one of them a few books. Behind the door was a large spinning wheel and a reel, and over head on wooden hooks fastened to the beams were a number of things, among which were a nice rifle, powder horn, bullet pouch, tomahawk and hunting knife—the complete equipment of the hunter and the frontier settler. Everything looked nice and tidy, even to the rough stones which had been laid down for a hearth.

In a short time our dinner was ready. It consisted of corn bread and milk, eaten out of tin basins with iron spoons. The settler ate with us but his wife was employed while we were at dinner in sewing on what appeared to be a child's dress. The settler and the agent talked all the time, generally on the subject of the settlement of the country. After dinner the latter and his companion took their departure, the one making the little boy a present of a half dollar, and the other giving the same sum to the baby.

The above is soon followed by this description of the friendliness of the pio-neers:

The social relations and neighborly intercourse of the settlers were of the most kind and friendly character, and proved the truth of the common saying that "people were much more friendly in new countries than they were in the old settlements." It was no uncommon thing among them to comply literally with the injunction of scripture which requires us "to give to him that asketh and from him that would borrow to turn not away." Their kindness and sympathy for each other was indeed most extraordinary, and showed a degree of sensibil-ity which we look for in vain in a more cultivated and enlightened state of soci-ety. At the commencement of the sugar-making perhaps, someone in the settlement would cut his leg badly with an axe, making a deep and ghastly wound, which would render him a cripple for weeks and perhaps for months. The neighbors would assemble, that is, make a bee and do all his work as far as it could be done at that time, and then, by arrangement among themselves, one would go every afternoon and gather the sap, carrying it to the house where it could be boiled up by the settler's wife. Again, one would be taken sick at har-vest time: his neighbors would make a bee, harvest and secure his crops, when, at the same time, their own grain would be going to waste for want of gathering. In seed time perhaps a man's ox would be killed by the falling of a tree: the neighbors would come with their teams and drag his wheat when they had not yet sown their own. A settler's house would be accidentally burned down—his family would be provided for at the nearest neighbors, and all would turn out and build and furnish a house in a day or two so that the man could take his family into it. . . .

William Kernan's Land Purchases

THE TITLE DEEDS to William Kernan's homestead in the Town of Tyrone suggest that when he arrived in Steuben County in 1802 he did not have sufficient funds to buy the land outright. Presumably he contracted to buy it, and acquired title when he was in a position to pay for it; hence the late dates of the deeds that are referred to below, long after he had cleared the land and had been farming it for some years. No contracts have been found; but the deeds were recorded at Bath in Steuben County near their dates of execution and transcribed to the books at Watkins Glen in Schuyler County when that county was set off from Steuben. The deeds for a total of 455¾ acres are the following:

1. On January 8, 1811, Nicholas Low and Richard Harrison conveyed to William Kernan, for $372.00, 123¾ acres, being part of Great Lot 49 in Township Number 5 in the First Range of Townships, recorded in Liber 5 of Deeds, Page 57, in Steuben County.

These same 123¾ acres are the subject of a similar deed dated January 28, 1811, between the same parties, for $372.00, transcribed to Liber 1 of Deeds, Page 163 in Schuyler County.

2. On November 27, 1818, Nicholas Low conveyed to William Kernan, for $210.00, 80 acres, being lot number 1 in Great Lot 49 in Township Number 5 in the First Range of Townships, recorded in Liber 1 of Deeds, Page 605 in Steuben County, and transcribed to Liber 9 of Deeds, Page 355 in Schuyler County.

3. The deeds to the 200 acres in Great Lot 56 are somewhat more complicated:

On February 8, 1819, Thomas O'Connor, of New York, gentleman, mortgaged to William Kernan, of Wayne, Esquire, 200 acres of land in Great Lot 56 in Township Number 5 in the First Range of Townships, the mortgage being in the sum of $500.00 and recorded in Liber 3 of Mortgages, Page 398 in Steuben County, and transcribed to the records of Schuyler County. These acres had been bought by O'Connor from Low and Harrison by deed dated June 30, 1815.

On June 15, 1830, O'Connor conveyed to Kernan that same 200 acres by deed recorded in Liber 17 of Deeds, Page 324 and 325 in Steuben County and transcribed to Liber 3 of Deeds, Page 262 in Schuyler County for a consideration of $1500.00; $500.00 being paid by satisfaction of the 1819 mortgage recorded in the margin of Book 6 of Mortgages, Page 398 in Steuben County; another $500.00 by the satisfaction of another mortgage, apparently unrecorded, from O'Connor to Kernan dated November 3, 1820, and the last $500.00 in lawful money of the United States. This land was sold in 1831 for $2000.00.

4. On June 9, 1829, Cornelius and Nicholas Low conveyed to William Kernan, for $128.00, the west 52 acres of Subdivision lot number one in Great Lot 50 in Township Number 5 in the First Range of Townships, recorded in Liber 3 of Deeds, Page 264 in Steuben County, and transcribed to Liber 17 of Deeds, Page 343 in Schuyler County.

These lands were all contiguous. William Kernan built his house on the land in Great Lot 49 and he eventually sold it for $11,340.00 to William Houck by deed dated March 23, 1865, recorded in Liber 18 of Deeds, Page 452 in Schuyler County. The portion south of the road to Dundee, containing 100.44 acres, was owned and farmed, and the house lived in, in 1995, by Ammon Hoover, a Mennonite from Lancaster County, Pennsylvania. The family graveyard lies at the southeastern corner of Hoover's land, and just outside it, but we have been told that he has surrounded it with an electric fence to keep out large, destructive animals.

At various times William Kernan bought and sold land in several nearby Great Lots and Townships. When his friend Patrick Quin got into financial difficulties in 1818, William bought his land in nearby Reading at a sheriff's public vendue, and sold it back to him in 1820.

On August 20, 1842, William took title from Cornelius Covert and Wife to 28 acres of land in the Town of Wayne, in Great Lot 3 in township Number 5 in the Second Range of townships, the deed being recorded in Liber 38 of deeds, Page 118 in Steuben County, and conveyed it to his son Edward on August 25, 1851, that deed being recorded in Liber 38 of Deeds, Page 140 in Steuben County, and transcribed to Liber 96 of Deeds, Page 416 in Schuyler County. Edward presumably sold it when he moved to Whitesboro.

Among the papers at Cornell University, we found a deed dated August 23, 1823, to William for "the one equal and undivided third part of Pew or Slip No.

Five" in the United Presbyterian and Baptist Meeting-House at Wayne for the consideration of thirteen dollars and sixty seven cents. Neither that meeting-house nor either of the congregations any longer exists. We have found no document, letter, or family memory to explain such a purchase by a man we have always regarded as a staunch Roman Catholic. We can venture to suggest that either he availed himself of what other religious services were at hand on the frontier (as did Nicholas Devereux in attending Episcopalian services in Utica until there was a Catholic church) or, in an early and happy instance of ecumenism, he did it to help a struggling congregation, a not uncommon gesture, we have been told, at least among the Protestant sects. If this is so, William's gesture was repeated years later when Francis bought and gave to a Methodist Episcopal congregation in Utica a plot for its new church.

Letter from Francis Kernan about the McLeod Case Addressed to L. A. Marsh, Esq., New York

Utica Oct 1, 1859

My Dear Sir

I am gratified with the just & kind mention you make of Mr. Spencer in your forthcoming life et c of Mr. [or Mrs.?] Stewart. I admired him as a lawyer & loved him as a man; and it is a pleasure to hear him spoken of as Mr. [illegible].

I have filled up the time of his death—It was in 1857—I have made one or two suggestions in pencil—You might add that he read & practiced law many years in Madison Co before coming to Utica in 1829—In reference to the McLeod defense I have changed a few words to express the idea that he was employed by the Gov of Great Brit. with the approbation of that of the U. S. He was not employed by the U. S. Govmt; but at the time of the trial he was U S atty for the Northern Dist of N.Y. and the U S Govt approved of his defending McL as counsel for him & was gratified at his success —

'Tis true as I have heard him try important causes in every county of this state but two or three.

I shall be gratified to see your book when and I doubt not it will be interesting—

Yours truly
F Kernan

N.B. The original of this letter was given to Francis Kernan Kernan (1903–1986) by a friend who serendipitously found it in a bookstore. It bears the notation: "A letter of Francis Kernan's written in 1859; bought in a collector's office." Searches by the reference librarian at Yale's Sterling Library, and in the Library of Congress database and the RLIN joint university database failed to turn up any book by L. A. Marsh.

The Law Firm Kernan and Kernan 1853–1963

THE FOLLOWING LETTER was written by Warnick Joseph Kernan, nephew of Francis Kernan, to Francis's great-grandson, also named Francis Kernan. It is on the letterhead of the firm, of which Warnick was then the senior partner.

Mr Francis Kernan   February 6, 1963
White, Weld & Co
10 Broad Street
New York 5, NY

My dear Francis:

A little while ago I was looking over some old papers and I found a copy of a letter written by your great grandfather Francis Kernan to his brother-in-law George Quin, a photostat copy of which is enclosed herewith.[1] The letter tells of the completion by your great grandfather of the arrangements for the opening, in July, of their partnership office in the law, and the letter is of interest for such reason as well as for its date—February 10, 1853—which means that July 1st of this year will mark the firm's one hundred and tenth birthday.

The William mentioned in the letter was my father—living as he then was with his brother Francis while attending school in Utica—and Winny was their sister, the wife of George Quin.

It has been suggested that I tell something of the little I know about the firm which explains why I am writing this letter.

Your great grandfather Francis Kernan had come to Utica shortly after his graduation from Georgetown in 1836 and he studied law in the office of Joshua A. Spencer,[2] an outstanding lawyer of that day, eventually becoming his partner. In 1853 the firm Spencer and Kernan was terminated by your great grandfather, his brother-in-law, George Quin coming as he did to Utica from Tyrone in that year at which time, as evidenced by the latter, the firm of Kernan and Quin was started. In 1857 my father William Kernan was admitted to practice and thereafter the name of the firm was changed to Kernan, Quin and Kernan. Thereafter, in 1865, your grandfather John D. Kernan[3] was admitted to practice and the firm name was changed to W. and J. D. Kernan. In the early eighteen eighties—having served a term as Railroad Commissioner by appointment of Governor Cleveland—your grandfather left Utica and opened an office in New York. Thereupon the firm name was changed to W. and N. E. Kernan, your [great] uncle Nicholas Kernan having entered the office, and becoming a partner, shortly after his brother John.

Other members of the family who entered the office and became partners in the eighteen eighties and eighteen nineties, but without their initials appearing in the firm name, were your great uncles William J. and Walter N. Kernan and my brother Leslie W. Kernan.[4]

In June, 1902, your [great] Uncle Nicholas died—your uncle William having died a few years prior thereto—and this was followed, in September, 1903, by the death of my brother Leslie. Francis Kernan having started the firm in 1853, fifty years before, it was now saved by another Francis—your father.

With the death of your uncle Nicholas and of my brother Leslie, there were left the two surviving partners, my father and your Uncle Walter. Father was well over seventy years of age and had already started to lessen the burden he was carrying. Your Uncle Walter's interest was business. He did no court work, either trial or appellate, and the court work in that day—I think it no exaggeration to say—was the important work in any office. Corporate work, as we know it today, was in its infancy.

It was at this critical time that your father started to commute from Buffalo, spending a few days in the office each week. In the following year, 1904, your father and mother moved to Utica, bringing you and Moll.

After your father's move to Utica he was in complete charge of the office and did practically all of the trial work. He was helped, in various matters, by my father and your grandfather, who was moving, or had moved from New York to Utica at about that time. Also, of course, there were some young lawyers in the office. It was your father, however, who carried the burden. Your Uncle Walter was chiefly acquiring the local street railways in Rochester, Syracuse, Rome and Utica, eventually organizing as he did the New York State Railways of which your Uncle Walter became the General Counsel.

In June 1904, I completed my law studies at Cornell, being admitted to the bar and entering the office in the fall. After a few years, I was literally pushed into court work by your father—how he did it is too long a story to be told at this time—and by 1910, or a little after, he was able to ease his way out. This enabled him to give all his time to the Bossert Company, the Skenandoa Rayon and his other business interests, not forgetting the organizing and development of Donnaconna Paper Company, the successful sale of which, effected by him in 1928, was to such great advantage to those who were so fortunate as to hold its stock.

I sat by Mr. Henry Taft one night at a dinner in New York. He had just written an account of his firm[5] and he asked about our Utica office. The little I told him amazed him and he said its history should be written. On my return I repeated the conversation to your grandfather and he was greatly interested, giving me to understand that he might undertake it. A few days later he died.

I neglected to say when it was decided that your father would come to Utica the firm name was again changed to Kernan and Kernan. It was not because of running out of initials—rather, I imagine, it was thought that initials and the frequent change in the firm name, were too confusing to the public.

The announcement card of the change in the firm name bears the date December 1, 1903.

It is too bad that your great grandfather Francis—when he started the firm in 1853—could not have foreseen how fruitful was to be the seed which he was planting.

I am writing this same letter to Dick, Walter, and John,[6] knowing that they will be interested.

My best as always.

NOTES

1. The enclosure appears in part in Chapter 4.
2. Francis, as noted in Chapter 2, did not graduate; he left after three years with no degree, and he first read law in the office of another brother-in-law, Edward Quin, in what is now Watkins Glen.
3. This was John Devereux Kernan, 1844–1922.
4. Cousin Warnick must have forgotten to mention that William Patrick Quin, the oldest son of George and Winifred (Kernan) Quin, was also a member of the firm in the 1880s and 1890s. He was my godfather and was referred to in my youth as "Judge Quin."
5. Cadwalader, Wickersham and Taft, in New York.
6. Dick and Walter are Richard Dickinson and Walter Avery Kernan, the addressee's younger brothers; John is your humble servant. Dick was treasurer of the Equitable Life Assurance Society of the United States; Walter and John were lawyers in New York City.

*W*ynehamer versus The People
3 Kernan 378

THE KERNAN REPORT cited so many times over the years is in fact two: Wyne-hamer against the People, and The People against Toynbee, argued in Albany in March 1856 and reported in 3 Kernan 378. They dealt with the constitutionality under the state constitution of a statute designed to "prevent intemperance, pau-perism and crime" by making the sale of alcoholic liquors a crime, and that pro-vided that the trial of an alleged offender could be in a court without a jury. In one case, Wynehamer was indicted for selling liquor, "to wit, a gill each of rum, brandy, gin, whiskey and strong beer," tried before a jury and found guilty; that judgment was affirmed by the New York Supreme Court, but reversed by the Court of Appeals on a writ of error. In the other, Toynbee was tried for selling brandy and Champagne by a court without a jury, and was found guilty; that judgment was reversed by the New York Supreme Court and the reversal upheld by the Court of Appeals.

The ten of the eleven printed opinions were most learned: in one hundred five pages, they discussed the Magna Carta, a statue of King Edward III, pronounce-ments by Lord Coke, Blackstone, Chief Justice John Marshall, and Chancellor Kent; they cited cases in the Supreme Court of the United States, and opinions by the chief judges of Pennsylvania and North Carolina, and, of course, many earlier New York cases. One judge dissented in part, and two dissented wholly from the major-ity, and wrote separate opinions. Three opinions were delivered in the Wynehamer case, seven in the Toynbee case, and one in both.

The basic holdings of the cases were that the statute destroyed Wynehamer's property in the liquor legally owned before the enactment of the statute by making him unable to sell it legally, and it was therefore a taking of property without due process of law in violation of the due process clause of the state constitution; and that it violated Toynbee's right to a trial by jury guaranteed by the state constitution.

The report is a good example of exactly what a court reporter has to do. It opens with Kernan's headnotes summarizing the court's holdings and the important points of law involved. This is followed by a three-and-a-half-page summary of what happened in the lower courts and in the earlier appeals. Then follow ten opinions, which he had to check for accuracy of citations and prepare for printing. Finally, he wrote short statements of the important points of the two cases for the twenty-six-page index at the end of the volume under the general heading "constitutional law" with cross references from headings such as "Courts of Special Sessions," "Excise Law," "Jury Trial," and "Property." This process would have been followed in all one hundred sixteen cases reported in this volume. All cases were indexed by name in the front of the volume. Finally, if the court had not itself ordered the case to be reported, Francis would have had to decide whether nonetheless it was important enough to report. Clearly, the position of court reporter was no sinecure.

Francis's analyses of hundreds of cases during his tenure is what the law student is now taught to do in the case system of study used in the leading law schools. It must surely have developed his analytical skills and thus account in large measure for the success of his later professional life.

ﬤtudents in the Kernan Law Firms

In addition to Roscoe Conkling and Richard H. Moore, who, as we have already mentioned, read law in the Kernan firms, the following also read law there:

John C. Churchill
S. J. Barrows
Josiah K. Brown
Eugene H. Hastings
J. F. Hurley
William Kernan
John Devereux Kernan
Nicholas Edward Kernan
Smith N. Lindsley
Theo. P. Cook
William Patrick Quin
William A. Matteson
John E. Curran
Francis M. O'Neil

Charles B. Mixer
Engelhardt C. Dieffenbacher
William Townsend
John F. Shrader
Johnson L. Lynch
John E. Brandegee
Henry A. Doolittle
James Conkling
Herbert M. Tufts
William J. Meltcrow
C. S. Kent
Reese F. Thomas
William Joseph Kernan
Thomas E. Kinney

This list may not be complete.

$\mathcal{F}$rancis and Hannah Kernan's Children

THE NAMES, BIRTHDAYS, and christening dates of Francis and Hannah's children and of their godparents are given as they appear in the church records, with the godparents' relationship and other data gleaned from other sources. The list illustrates the closeness of the parents to their relatives. The mother's relatives, Butlers, Clapps, Pierreponts, and Newberrys, are missing because they were not Roman Catholics and therefore ineligible. Mary Dolbeare (Butler) Devereux and Mary Rice (Colt) Devereux appear as godmothers only after their conversions to the Catholic Church.

1. John Devereux, born February 25, 1844, baptized April 7, 1844, John Devereux Junr. and Catharine Devereux, maternal uncle and aunt.
2. Edward Nicholas, born July 10, 1845, baptized July 13, 1845, William and Rosanna Maria (Stubbs) Kernan, paternal grandparents.
3. Mary Devereux, born June 5, 1847, baptized July 20, 1847, John C. and Mary (Colt) Devereux, maternal great uncle and great aunt by marriage.
4. Rosanna Maria, born July 15, 1849, baptized July 22, 1849, Nicholas and Mary Dolbeare (Butler) Devereux, maternal grandparents.
5. Elizabeth Butler, born March 23, 1851, baptized March __, 1851, Owen and Mary O'Neil, family friends.
6. Francis, born May 28, 1853, baptized June 3, 1953, William Kernan and Mary Devereux, paternal grandfather (or uncle) and maternal aunt.

7. Thomas Philip de Neri, born September 3, 1856, baptized September 7, 1856, Richard W. and Cornelia (Devereux) Lalor, maternal aunt and uncle by marriage.

8. William Joseph, born August 23, 1858, baptized August 29, 1858, Michael J. and Alice Kernan, paternal uncle and aunt.

9. Joseph, born April 29, 1861, baptized May 5, 1861, Thomas Butler Devereux and Rosa Kernan, maternal uncle and paternal aunt.

10. Walter Joseph, born March 21, 1864, baptized March 27, 1864, William, Jr. and Frances (Warnick) Kernan, paternal uncle and aunt by marriage.

Other records show no. 2 as Nicholas Edward, no. 3 as Mary Agnes, no. 4. as Rosa, no. 9. as Joseph Francis, and no. 10 as Walter Newberry. Uncle Nick, Aunt Lizzie, Uncle Tom, and Uncle Joe will be easily recognized. The dates given above do not always agree with other family records.

The oldest daughter, Mary Agnes, was the first to leave the hearth—in 1867 she entered the Order of the Sacred Heart, Kenwood, in Albany, and died three years later. She was then the only nun in the immediate family, but was followed in a few years by several Devereux cousins, and later by several Kernans.[1] Many others have been educated at the Order's convents and colleges in New York, Albany, Purchase, and in Connecticut. It was Madam Kernan's mortal illness in 1870 that occasioned the letter written by her brother Nicholas to their brother, "Jack," asking that he return from his grand tour of Europe; Francis's postscript reveals his fatherly concern and strong family feelings.

The two oldest sons went to the newly founded Seton Hall College in South Orange, New Jersey, rather than to their father's alma mater, in all likelihood because of the threat of Confederate attacks on Washington, at least one of which got as far as the outskirts of Georgetown. John D., the eldest, won several gold medals for excellence and passed his Latin books on to Nicholas. Francis's younger sons went to Georgetown, all graduating (as he did not), and only one, William, appearing to have had any problems with studies. His father's letter of September 6, 1875, to Father Healy, the president, indicates the possibility of his having to repeat a class. It revealed that William had spent the summer studying "some," in the hope that a further examination would allow him to be promoted; the letter asked no favors, but only that Father Healy do what he deemed best for William.

His daughters went to the Sacred Heart Convent at Albany. While none of them had had the wide travel and sophisticated social life of the young Newberry girls, it is hard to believe that Elizabeth was "rude, ill bred and ignorant of the world," as Julia described her in her diary. Perhaps this judgment was merely an instance of Julia's sharp pen, or the result of a teenage tiff.

The first to marry was Nicholas, whose bride was Harriet Anne Jenkins of Baltimore, Maryland, "Aunt Hattie." She was a cousin of Ellen Jenkins, the wife of Hannah's brother, John Corish Devereux Jr., and presumably they met through that connection. The marriage was an impressive one, the ceremony having been performed on June 1, 1871, in the cathedral at Baltimore in the presence of Cardinal Gibbons, a friend of the Jenkins family. In January 1900, he came to Utica to marry their oldest daughter, Isabel, to Clifford Lewis, of Philadelphia. Nicholas's marriage was fruitful and produced 13 children—not the largest in the family. Uncle Nick is reputed to have said when there were only ten alive, in response to the usual inquiry after their health: "Six have the measles, and the other four are fine, thank you." They lived in the landmark house designed by Philip Hooker for Rutger Bleecker Miller in 1830 as the centerpiece of Rutger Park, and once owned by Roscoe Conkling. It was bought by Francis Kernan Kernan, 1875-1944, after Aunt Hattie's death in 1923, but is no longer in the family.[2]

The marriage of Rosanna Maria Kernan to Thomas MacCarthy, of Syracuse, followed on April 23, 1873, in Utica. Her grandmother wrote in her diary that "she is extremely lovely in person and character. She will be a treasure to her affianced." The marriage was short-lived, for she died on June 11, 1874, in Syracuse, leaving no children. There are windows in the little church in Forestport given by their brother John in memory of Rosa Kernan MacCarthy and Madam Mary Agnes Kernan.

Later the same year, on October 1, Francis's oldest son, John Devereux Kernan, was married in New Castle, Pennsylvania, by his Seton Hall classmate Father Brann to Katherine Peebles, who was known as "Kate," "Kathleen," or "Aunt Kate," and to many as "Grandmother Kernan." The two had met while Kate was in Utica visiting Sue Rockwell, with whom she had been at school in New York.[3] That marriage too was fruitful, producing six children. The family lived first in Utica, and later in Springbank in Alder Creek, New York, in Rutherford, New Jersey, at 307 West 102nd Street, New York, and finally in the Devereux house on Chancellor Square, Utica, until that was sold in about 1920.

The last fruitful marriage was that of Francis Kernan, who married Henrietta Warnick, of Utica, on November 23, 1880, in Utica. "Aunt Etta" was a younger sister of Frances Warnick, the wife of William Kernan, 1831–1916, who were "Aunt Fannie" and "Uncle Will." This family, with its seven children, lived in Utica, and later in Syracuse.

Of Francis's other sons, Thomas, after a spell of studying with the Jesuits for the priesthood in the 1870s, which his health did not allow him to pursue, married Regina Paul, the widow of George Cornelius on May 29, 1899, at Utica. They visited us in the summer of 1925 when we occupied Springbank for several months.

He was then suffering from what I suspect was Alzheimer's, and I remember his wandering off and the worried search made to find him.

Walter was first engaged to marry Susan Sicard, who died. He ultimately married Sophia Swan, of Utica, on November 23, 1898, but the marriage ended in divorce, the first in the family. He later married Ruth Pelaw. Neither of these unions produced any children.

Francis and Hannah's other daughter, Elizabeth, was her father's hostess when he was a senator in Washington. Her scrapbook, now at Cornell, contains numerous invitations to governmental and diplomatic parties, newspaper clippings, and miscellany, suggesting an active social life.[4]

With three fruitful marriages, it is hard to believe that only one of Francis Kernan's descendants still lives in the city of Utica, and that with the flight to the suburbs there may be none in the next generation.

NOTES

1. Margaret Agnes Brent Kernan ("Cousin Marge" or "Margery") as Mother Saint Thomas and Charlotte Stewart Kernan as Mother, then Sister, Charlotte entered the Society of the Holy Child Jesus; several others have joined and then withdrawn from other orders.

2. From JDK: "I remember staying there the night before my grandfather's funeral, in a huge bedroom that had a prie-dieu in one corner, the only one I have ever had a chance to check out."

3. From JDK: "We remember her as "Auntie Sue," who, with Grandmother Kernan, was an avid bridge player, but "never on Sundays" in Springbank. There is no official proof of this marriage because, as I have been advised by a prominent Pennsylvania genealogist, Catholic marriages were not recorded by the state. However, there are family letters describing the ceremony that took place in her father's house."

4. From JDK: "I was told years ago by a lady I once met, an Outerbridge with connections to Bermuda, that she remembered hearing her forebears talking fondly about Senator Kernan, whom they had known years before in Washington. I conclude that he must have made a notable impression outside the Senate if he was still being talked about so long after."

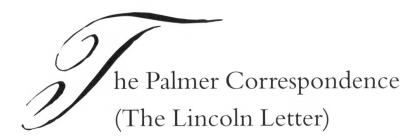

The Palmer Correspondence (The Lincoln Letter)

Vernon N.Y.
13 Feb 1865

Hon. Francis Kernan
Washington

Dear Sir

The bearer is the wife of Luther T. Palmer a Private in the 5th N Y Artillery who now lies at Harpers Ferry under sentence of death for desertion. He is to be shot on the 17th Feb. She wishes an immediate interview with the President, that she may make a personal appeal for pardon.

She claims that, his only object was to see his family, from whom he had not heard in three months, owing to mis-carriage of letters.

Palmer, I do not know. I do know that Mrs. Palmer belongs to an excellent & worthy family, who deeply feel the disgrace of the desertion—and hopes to be spared the further degradation of an execution.

I could not, my dear Sir, do otherwise than ask you to exercise your kindness of heart by helping her to produce an early interview with the President—with whom she can make her own pleading.

Resp'y
A. P. Case

This letter from Francis Kernan to President Abraham Lincoln, written from the House of Representatives, reads "Sir, I know well Mr. Case the writer of the conveyed Re is a most estimable & reliable citizen and his statement can be implicitly relied upon I commend the unhappy wife who presents this to your kind consideration. Very Respect'ly, Francis Kernan."

The above correspondence is in the Robert Todd Lincoln Collection of the Papers of Abraham Lincoln (1809-1865) in the Library of Congress. The Case letter is endorsed in the handwriting of President Lincoln: "13 Feb 1865/ Letter of A. P. Case/Vernon, / In behalf of Luther/ T. Palmer sentenced / to be shot on Feb/ 17th 1865." What follows is in the index to the collection:

Major Gen'l Sheridan   Executive Mansion
&c &c   Washington, 15 February, 1865
Suspend execution in case of Luther T. Palmer 5th N.Y. Artillery for fourteen
(14) days and send record to me for examination.
John Hay A.A.G.   A. Lincoln

General Sheridan replied to Lincoln's telegram in the same day: "Dispatch in the s\case of Luther T. Palmer received and order issued suspending the sentence."

Commanding Officer   Executive Mansion
Harpers Ferry VA   Washington, 28 February 1865
Let the sentence in case of Luther T. Palmer be suspended until further order. A. Lincoln

It is noted in the index to *The Collected Works of Abraham Lincoln,* edited by Basler, that on April 10, Lincoln pardoned Private Palmer, but that the record is missing from the file. Lincoln's telegrams are in the handwriting of John Hay, who was Lincoln's secretary—hence his signature as shown above.

Four days after the pardon was granted, on April 14, 1865, Lincoln was shot at Ford's Theater, and died the following morning.

The originals of the two letters above are in the Robert Todd Lincoln Papers in the Library of Congress.

$\mathcal{R}$egents of the University of the State of New York

W<small>HEN WE BEGAN</small> this project, we were aware that Francis Kernan had been a regent of the University of the State of New York, but had no idea what the regents did. Assuming that many of our readers may wish to be enlightened, we add this further explanation.

Francis was elected to be a regent by the state legislature on February 10, 1870. The original bill establishing the university was passed on February 10, 1784. With a few later changes, the amending bill, passed on April 13, 1787, is still in force and forms the basis of the present-day system of collegiate and academic education within the state. Initially, the University of the State of New York included only one institution, Columbia College (previously King's College), but growth in the number of public schools kept pace with the exploding population of the state. The board's official records indicate that, from its beginning, it fulfilled its functions extraordinarily well. Today's 20 campuses of the City University and the 64 campuses of the State University, together with all the state's other universities, colleges, academies, and schools, are monuments to its guidance.

The university was made a corporation with the power, exercised by the regents, to visit and inspect all colleges and academies (which are roughly equivalent to today's high schools) and examine the state of education and discipline, and to make an annual report thereof to the legislature, to grant degrees above that of master of arts and charters of incorporation to colleges and academies, and to grant charters to such academies as may grow to be worthy of it. To these ends, the university was empowered to hold property to the amount of the annual income of 40,000 bushels of wheat. While at first the regents' chief business was the government of Columbia College, their labors were lessened by later provisions that all colleges and academies were to have their own boards of trustees to manage their individual affairs.

From its beginning, the board attracted leading statesmen; along with John Jay and Alexander Hamilton, other members in the early years included George and DeWitt Clinton, Pierre van Cortlandt, James Duane, Philip Pell Jr., Lewis Morris, Morgan Lewis, John B. James, Gilbert and Brockholst Livingston, and Baron Frederick William de Steuben [*sic* in the official list].

Francis Kernan served for 22 years. From his first year on the board, he served on the Standing Committee for the Incorporation of Colleges and Academies, obviously a basic committee with the job to see that the applicants for corporate status had the financial and physical means and the personnel to fulfil their functions. For most years of his service, he also was on the standing committee that prepared the annual report required to be made to the legislature on the condition of the educational institutions throughout the state; these were based on the institutions' reports and the board's inspections. He also served for short periods on the Standing Committees for Appropriations for Books and Apparatus (maps, globes, etc.), for Visitation of Colleges and Academies, for Legislation and Printing, for Inspections and Reports, for Degrees, of the State Museum, and on a special committee on Higher Examinations.

In 1863 the regents instituted the practice of holding a yearly convocation under their direction in the state capitol at Albany of the officers, professors, and teachers of the state's colleges, academies, and schools, whose purpose was "[t]o secure an interchange of opinions [among the regents and instructors, officers and trustees of the several colleges, academies and other seminaries] on the subject of education and of literature, science and art, and to advance their standard in this state." The convocations were popular with the elite of the state's leading institutions and they fulfilled at least in part their stated purpose. Those attending heard papers on learned subjects such as A Method of Integrating the Square Roots of Quadratics, Points of Scholastic Philosophy in Relation to Modern Science, and Cypriot Inscriptions, and on pedagogical problems such as Industrial Drawing in Public Schools, The Metric System (which the speaker was against), and Ethical Aspects of Science. The regents were not usually among the speakers, although Governor Cleveland once offered a few formal words. None of the regents, Kernan included, was conspicuous for faithful attendance at these meetings—he was present only twice.

Along with his committee work, Francis no doubt took special interest in the regents' granting of a provisional charter in 1875 to Saint Bonaventure College in Allegany, Cattaraugus County. This institution, which opened as a private academy, had its beginnings in 1854, when Kernan's father-in-law, Nicholas Devereux, was visiting in Rome and prevailed upon the Brothers of the Minor Order of Saint Francis to come from Italy and open a mission, by proposing a gift of 200 acres of land and $5,000. The full charter was granted in 1883, following an inspection for which the committee of the regents noted that "The [Franciscan] Order insures the college a perpetual succession of competent teachers. Its buildings are commodious and in all respects fitted for the uses of the College. Its library and philosophical apparatus are very respectable. All necessary revenues for the use of the College are assured. We see no reason why the petition [for a full charter] should not be granted." The Saint Bonaventure charter was made absolute on that day, and "Saint Bonnie's" subsequent growth and progress to its status as a university can be traced in its annual reports to the regents.

Kernan was unable to maintain his record of attendance during his final years. However, at the January 30, 1890, meeting, he received a number of votes to be elected vice chancellor, even after he asked that his name not be used. Nonetheless, he was made chairman of a special committee to inspect Saint John's Catholic Academy in Syracuse. This he was able to do and, finding the property satisfactory but with title in the church corporation, he suggested that the academy be chartered on the condition that the Church give it a long-term lease. At the July 10, 1890, meeting, probably the last one he attended, he reported that the Church had signed a 50-year lease, and the charter was granted for that period.

In its 106th report, January 9, 1893, the regents noted with profound regret the deaths of its two oldest members in terms of length of service, Francis Kernan and George William Curtis. In the resolution relating to Kernan, they recorded that "in the discharge of all his civic duties he brought to his work such integrity, wisdom, and faithfulness as entitle him to the lasting remembrance of the citizens of this state." The resolutions were transmitted to his family. The report also alluded to "The eloquent addresses [that were] suitably published in a memorial pamphlet."

Prior to Kernan's membership, the board had chartered most of the state's major educational institutions, which are still functioning today, and since many of Kernan's descendants are familiar with the state's schools, they may enjoy knowing this history. The first institution the regents chartered, in July 17, 1787, was an academy, the well-known Erasmus Hall in Flatbush. Academies in East Hampton, North Salem, and Canandaigua and elsewhere soon followed. The regents' first college was started in 1793 as Hamilton-Oneida Academy and incorporated as a college in 1812. Geneva College, which had operated since 1806, was incorporated as a college in 1813 and has become the present Hobart College. The first medical colleges (for which special empowering acts were passed by the legislature) were The College of Physicians and Surgeons in New York in 1807, and The College of Physicians and

Surgeons for the Western District of New York at Fairfield, Herkimer County, in 1812. Doctor Joseph White of Cherry Valley (where his descendants, the Cannons, still live in his house) played an important part in the founding of the latter college. The first school of science was Rennselaer Polytechnic Institute in Troy, in 1826; and the first law school was the Albany Law School, in 1851. The first funds for these institutions were raised by lotteries; and the legislature made grants in after years from the so-called Literary Fund, the principal of which derived from tracts of public lands expressly reserved for educational purposes. The first institutions granting degrees to women were Elmira Female College in 1855, Ingham University in 1857, and Vassar College in 1865. The regents also founded a state library in 1844, a state museum in 1845, and the Normal School at Albany for the training of teachers in 1844.

Francis Kernan, LL.M., LL.D., 1880

IN 1880, GEORGETOWN conferred an honorary Doctor or Master of Laws degree on Francis Kernan. The citation reads as follows:

> *Quum perspectum Nobis planeque cognitum sit Franciscum Kernan, virum inter Reipub-licae Senatores gravitate et eloquentia clarissimum, praestantem sibi legum peritiam comparasse: aequum censemus ut Ei illud honoris insigne et laudis monumentum tribuatur quo apud excultas gentes cautum est ne sua desint ingenuis studiis praemia neve scientiis incrementa.*
>
> *Quamobrem copia per summam Reipublicae auctoritatem Nobis ad id facta, Eidem meritam Jurisprudentiae Lauream quaeque illam sequuntur jura et privilegia libentes conferimus, Eumque Legum Doctorem seu Magistrum pronuntiamus.*
>
> *Utque haec jura sarta Ipsi tectaque adserventur, liberas hasec Collegii Nostri signo notatas et manu nostra rite subscriptas Ei dedimus.*
>
> *Ad diem V. Kal. Quint. anno a Partu Virginis MDCCCLXXX*

In translation it reads:

Inasmuch as it is well known to us and clearly recognized that Francis Kernan, a man most distinguished among the Senators of the Republic for his dignity and eloquence, has acquired for himself an outstanding knowledge of laws, we deem it proper that this sign of honor and mark of praise be bestowed upon him, by which among cultivated people it will be made evident that rewards are not lacking for serious study and additions to knowledge for their own sake.

Wherefor pursuant to the highest authority of the republic granted to us for this purpose, we are herewith pleased to confer upon him the well-deserved laurel wreath of jurisprudence, along with the rights and privileges pertaining thereto, and we pronounce him to be Doctor or Master of Laws.

So that these prerogatives might be retained in good order and protected, we give him letters duly sealed by our college and signed by our hand on this fifth day before the Kalends of the fifth [month] in the year 1880 of the Virgin's giving birth.

The date in modern terms is June 27th, 1880, the fifth month in the Roman calendar being July, the Kalends of July being the first day of that month, the fifth day before that, in the Roman way of figuring, being June twenty-seventh.

We are advised by Father Curran of the Jesuit Community of Georgetown University that it is no longer the practice to give Doctor *or* Master degrees, but rather to grant one or the other. Under the then-practice, Francis was entitled to use either set of initials after his name. The whereabouts of the original document is not known.

As an example of his "dignity and eloquence" and his "outstanding knowledge of the law," we append a summary of his speech delivered in the House of Representatives on February 4, 1864, in opposition to a proposed act of Congress to confiscate the property of rebels and other purposes:

On the joint resolution to amend the act of Congress to suppress insurrection, to punish treason and rebellion, to seize and confiscate the property of the rebels, and other purposes, FK's opening words stated that there had been objections by someone other than himself to closing the debate to the end that he might state his views as he had desired to do earlier. This suggests that he was in effect selected by some member or members of the House to make the arguments on their side of the question.

FK spoke specifically to the confiscation provision. He addressed those who believed that the federal government could forfeit the lands of people in rebellion under the Constitution; those who believed that, though it cannot constitutionally forfeit their lands in fee, it can in some other way than by trial and conviction so punish them; and those who believed that the law had nothing to do with treason but that the Congress was dealing not with traitors in the eyes of the law but rather with belligerents, and that by the law of nations, it could confiscate the lands of such forever.

First he pointed out that, when the Constitution was adopted, there were but two modes by the law of England by which a man's property could be forfeited in punishment of treason: one, by a bill of attainder by act of Parliament which condemned a man and forfeited his estate without allowing him to be heard in a court of justice; and two, by trial and conviction in a court of justice. He then stated that, by a statute of Queen Anne, Parliament abolished forfeiture for treason beyond the life of the offender.

FK argued that 1) the Constitution provided that "[n]o bill of attainder or *ex post facto* law shall be passed"; and that an act of Congress to forfeit a man's property for treason without a trial is a bill of attainder, and as such is expressly forbidden; and 2) that the Constitution defined treason and declared that no person shall be convicted of that crime unless on the testimony of two witnesses, or his confession in open court, and that "no attainder of treason" (i.e., the consequence of judgment pronounced by the court against a person who had been tried and convicted of treason, citing Blackstone) shall work corruption of blood or forfeiture of estate except during the life of the person attainted. Hence, FK concluded, an act of Congress proposing to forfeit a man's property for treason without a trial would be void.

NOTES

1. See Lynch, *Grover Cleveland,* page 445.
2. *Ibid.*

otes

CHAPTER I

1. William V. Shannon, *The American Irish: A Political and Social Portrait,* 2d ed. (Amherst: University of Massachusetts Press, 1989), 6–7.

2. For this and other statements about the forebears of Francis Kernan, and their lands, see *MacKernan of Tullyhunco, The Utica Kernans,* and *Supplement to the Utica Kernans,* a monograph about the Stubbs family written by Alice Kernan (Francis's sister), *Rooney's Genealogical History,* and a letter from Edward Mac Lysaght to John D. Kernan.

3. Calendar of Close and Patent Rolls of Chancery, page 143.

4. See lease dated June 20, 1747, from Martin Armstrong, Esq., to Bryan Kiernan [sic], gent, No. 86581, Book 127, page 227, *Registry of Deeds,* Dublin (limited to 31 years under the Penal Laws because he was a Catholic); John Kiernan [sic], gentleman, *Catholic Qualification Rolls,* 1778, Public Record Office of Ireland.

5. Francis in his holographic will (Hall of Records, New York, New York, Liber 56, Page 353) referred to Charles O'Conor of Mount Allen as the "friend and fosterer of my youth." William must have been known to him also, for he was named as the life that measured a Mount Allen lease to one Thomas Flynn.

6. So described by Sir George Macartney, an Ulster-born diplomat. See Macartney, "Extract from an Account of Ireland in 1773" in J. Barlow (ed.), "Some account of the public life . . . of the Earl of Macartney" (London, 1807), i, 116, cited in *Endurance and Emergence.*

7. Andrew Parks, "Emigration to America," 1798, cited in David A. Wilson, *United Irishmen, United States: Immigrant Radicals in the Early Republic* (Ithaca: Cornell University Press, 1998), epigraph.

8. *Ibid.*

9. Quoted in Art McDonald, *How the Irish Became White,* website, http://www.pitt.edu/~hirtle/uujec/white.html (accessed December 31, 1998).

CHAPTER 2

1. What did they want in the way of amenities? An 1804 map of Bath, the nearest sizable settlement where William had to go for his mail, shows a "theatre"! See Hake, opposite page 109, but also Appendix I, infra.

2. See Everets and Ensign, page 679.

3. His original commissions were in the possession of William Kernan, 1913-1994, of Utica, and now of his widow.

4. The full title is *"The Complete Military Tutor containing a system of Modern Tactics applicable to Infantry; in Company, Regiment, or Line. As laid down by the most approved authors, and now in practice by the Armies of the United States—Illustrated by Sixteen Copperplates, together with a Variety of Reports. The whole carefully prepared for the press by Thomas Town, Philadelphia, 1809. "*

5. An 1876 letter from Charles O'Conor, quoted in Everets and Ensign, at pages 678-679, mentions "a widow named Kernan with many grown-up boys" among the settlers in his father's colony.

6. 18th-century letters at Cornell show that Margaret had relatives at Navan.

7. Stubbs is said to derive from Saint Aubin.

8. From JDK: "There has been no contact with her Stubbs relatives for many years, and, but for one branch—that of her generous uncle, Edward, in the person of his descendant, Lawrence of Gaithersburg, Maryland—they have been lost sight of."

9. So reported by John Devereux Kernan, (1844–1922) 80 years later in the family's *Springbank Record* on June 24, 1892. He refers to the Stubbs house as the "old Knox house."

10. From JDK: "In about 1926, my father took my brothers and me to visit the Kernan farm and we camped on the Stubbs property. I recall speaking to some local people who showed us documents of a legal nature bearing William's signature. Unfortunately I paid too little attention. Perhaps some of these papers are of record, but the only one I have been able to find is a power of attorney dated June 25, 1816, from John Hendrix of the county of Richland, state of Ohio, to William empowering him to take possession on Hendrix's behalf of a 60-acre tract of land in Steuben County." See Deed Book 11, pages 47–48, Steuben County Clerk's Office at Bath.

11. Found in the Kernan Papers, Division of Rare and Manuscript Collections, Cornell University Library, Ithaca, N.Y.

12. See deed from William Kernan to William Bouck, dated March 23, 1865, Liber 18, page 452, Schuyler County.

13. For this and all other figures relating to present-day values, we are indebted to Professor William Nordhaus, of Yale University.

CHAPTER 3

1. From a letter written by Charles O'Conor introducing John Devereux Kernan, 1844–1922, who was about to leave on a grand tour of Europe, to his relatives in Ireland, the O'Conor Don and Thomas Ryan MacDermot of the Coolavin family. See also Alice Kernan's life of her father, *Supplement to the Utica Kernans,* and Appendix I.

2. From JDK: "Perhaps he was severely spanked by his father for playing in the pail of drinking water he was set to guard, as was his son John Devereux Kernan, 1844–1922, in the summer of 1850. The latter never forgot it, and told his son, Devereux, 1878–1961, who told his son, Henry Sherrill Kernan, 1916–."

3. See Everets and Ensign at page 680.

4. For further information on education, see Pulliam at pages 12 ff, 18 ff, 43 ff, 49; Glenn at pages 3, 8 ff, 179; Griffey at page 55; Finegan at page 34.

5. See Ryan in Chapters 1–3.

6. As told by John Devereux Kernan, 1878–1961.

7. The information about Francis's sojourn at Georgetown comes from Father Daley's book and its archives.

8. Daley, at page 266, note 66.

9. The *Ratio Studiorum* is the Jesuit curriculum and methods guide that grew out of the process begun by Saint Ignatius de Loyola in the 16th century. Its successes have been considered to be due to four characteristics: careful preparation of the teachers and their inspiration with an apostolic dedication; lack of tuition fees for the students; careful organization of the pupils' studies and activities to promote learning in graduated steps; and its continual revision by adaptation to varying places, times, and persons. The aims were moral formation in prime place of honor and intellectual formation receiving most attention. Students were motivated primarily by attraction of honor and the rewards of scholastic success. For further information, see *New Catholic Encyclopedia under Ratio Studiorum* and the bibliography given there.

10. "1833 [sic; 1835] Bill of Sale for Negroes of the Maryland Mission," http://www.georgetown.edu/departments/amer_studies/conditn.html *Jesuit Plantation Project* (accessed December 28, 1998).

11. Transcriptions and digitized images of the original documents are available at the *Jesuit Plantation Project Home Pages,* http://www.georgetown.edu/departments/amer_studies/cover/jpp.html (accessed December 28, 1998).

12. Cited in William Lee Miller, *Arguing About Slavery: The Great Battle in the United States Congress* (New York: Alfred A. Knopf, 1996), 77.

13. XV *Journal of the American Bar Association* for 1893 at page 453.

CHAPTER 4

1. Alexis de Tocqueville, quoted in Stevens, at page 6.
2. See Chroust, vol. 2, at page 174.
3. See McManis, at page 605, note 52.
4. *Noble & Eastman* v *Holmes,* 5 Hill 194, 1842.
5. Quoted in Walsh, at page 31.

CHAPTER 5

1. We are indebted for this information to Professor Paul Carrington, of Duke University Law School, and to Professor Robert Gordon of the Yale Law School. The practice was followed in many jurisdictions after it had died out in New York. New York was one of the fussier states in its requirements for admission to the bar. The Constitution of 1777 required that rules be adopted for admission of attorneys, but it was not until 1797 that any were adopted. It was then provided that a candidate for admission must have served a regular clerkship with a practicing lawyer of the court for seven years, the time not exceeding four years devoted to classical studies after the age of fourteen years being accepted as part of the required period of clerkship. Only in 1829 was it first required that an attorney "be found to be duly qualified."

2. See *Yale Law Journal* (1907); See Chroust, vol. 2, pages 250–252. Law schools were specifically recognized only in 1837. In that year, any portion of time, not exceeding two years, spent in regular attendance upon the law lectures in the University of New York was allowed to a law student in place of an equal amount of time in a clerkship. In 1845, this provision was extended to time passed in attendance upon law lectures at "Cambridge University [Harvard] or the law school connected with Yale college."

3. His story and all quotations are from the diary identified in the bibliography.

4. Walworth, a cousin of Doctor Benjamin Butler through his, i.e., Butler's, mother, Diadema Hyde, wrote the Hyde genealogy.

5. See Strong, page 81. See also pages 156 and 175.

6. See *Cookinham,* vol. 1, pages 234–235; and letter of Francis Kernan, dated October 1, 1859, in Appendix III.

7. See Strong, page 81. See also pages 156 and 175.

8. Richard H. Moore, a clerk in Spencer's office, was the origin of the report. See Cookinham, vol. 1, pages 234–235.

9. The report in the edition we consulted actually says "J. Kernan," but this must be a misprint.
10. See Jones, at pages 48–49.
11. The information in this paragraph is from Ryan, chapters 1–3. The quotation is on page 153.
12. See Chidsey, page 8.
13. See Bagg, *History of Utica,* page 91.
14. Letter dated September 12, 1892, to the editor of the *Utica Morning Herald.*

CHAPTER 6

1. Their careers and antecedents are discussed more fully in Lewis and Kernan, and in *The Irish Genealogist; The Official Organ of the Irish Genealogical Research Society,* vol. 4, no. 5, November 1972.
2. See Richard Roche, "*Forth and Bargy—A Place Apart,*" in Whelan, page 111.
3. See *Connecticut Courant,* September 26, 1796, where his name is given as "Devero."
4. A picture of this house appears on the sixth page of illustrations following page 114 in Walsh.
5. Beach Street is a five-block street a few blocks south of Canal Street, running east from the North River past the south side of Saint John's Square to what was Chapel Street and now Church Street. The area is now occupied by warehouses and commercial buildings
6. The quotations and information given in the foregoing and succeeding paragraphs, and much more, are to be found among the letters and documents in the Kernan Papers at Cornell.
7. This house, located on Kent Street on the east side of Chancellor Square, was rented from Edward Cook by lease dated April 19, 1843. Until 1848, no street number is given in the city directory, but in that year, Francis is listed at number 2, Kent Street. Chancellor Square was named for Chancellor James Kent, an appropriate place for Francis to live, since he read his *Commentaries on American Law,* first as a law student and every year thereafter.
8. Julia Clapp, Hannah's first cousin, was engaged to marry Walter Newberry of Chicago. The bulk of his fortune eventually founded the Newberry Library in that city after the legal disputes over his will in which she was represented by Francis Kernan. These resulted in her being given the equivalent of her dower rights. Upon her death in Paris, with no survivors, her personal property passed to her brother, James Clapp, and finally to their cousin, John Devereux Kernan (1844–1922). This accounts for so many of the beautiful objects in the way of paintings, silver, china from the Tuileries, and linen that were in Springbank before they were divided among six Kernan children in 1925. The diary of Julia's daughter, Julia, and her portrait came

to Springbank in the same way. The diary is now in the New York Public Library, the gift of J. Kernan Slingluff.

9. The deed, Charles A. Mann to Francis Kernan, is recorded in the county clerk's office in Book 135 at page 462. An 1850 map of the city locates the property on the east side of Kent Street, about one-third of the way north from Elizabeth Street toward Bleecker Street and running eastward to Second Street. The property comprised lots 6 and 11 of the original Rutger Bleecker lands. There are no longer any private houses on Kent Street.

10. In 1855 his listing was changed to 5 Kent Street, possibly a renumbering rather than a move, for the land records do not show the purchase of another house until 1882. After his mother-in-law's death in that year he bought her house on Chancellor Square, which had been built by Nicholas Devereux in 1840.

11. From JDK: "Kernans have tended to be taller with each succeeding generation, our tallest, Richard Sessions Slingluff, now being six feet six and one-half inches, and they do not run to flesh. Francis had the typical, sizable Kernan nose, a long, oval face, and the Nordic fold about the eyes that seems to have come from his mother."

CHAPTER 7

1. The salary was raised to $2000 when the original ban on the simultaneous practice of law was removed in 1849. See Moore. This article was called to the authors' attention by the present state reporter, Frederick Muller. We are grateful for the copy he sent.

2. See Moore, page 293.

3. *Dictionary of American Biography,* vol. 5, page 356.

4. Francis and his wife's brother, John C. Devereux Jr., were executors and there was much correspondence between them. There is no question but that Francis gave satisfaction, for on Saint Patrick's Day, March 17, 1856, his mother-in-law wrote:

> My dear *Son* Francis,
>
> Allow me to call you by that endearing name, to thank you for all yr great kindness & consideration for me, since God took my Beloved. How much trouble you have spared me, and how many annoyances, perplexities & sorrows have you averted from me, for which accept my heartfelt thanks.
>
> My children also are under the greatest obligation to you for the valuable time & thoughtful labour given to the successful settlement of the Estate; and for constant acts of personal kindness.
>
> John, Thomas, Cornelia & myself request yr acceptance of the enclosed, to furnish a library, or in whatever way will add most to your own *personal gratification & comfort.*
>
> Accept a Mother's blessing. May God bless you, yr Wife and Your Children.
>
> Mary D. Devereux
>
> [The enclosure was a check for $1,000.]

5. See Torrey.

6. See Chidsey, at page 390.

7. *Douglass* v *Ireland,* 73 N.Y. 100.

8. A matter of family interest is the litigation in which the Colvill family, grandchildren of William Kernan's sister, Margaret (Kernan) McKeon, were represented by Kernan Brothers and Quin, as the firm was then known. The case turned on the mysterious disappearance of John Colvill, as told in *Cambreleng* v *Purton* in 12 New York Supplement 741, and its affirmance in 125 New York 610. The facts were that John Colvill, his sisters, Mary Margaret (Colvill) Cambreleng and Euphemia (Colvill) Purton, and his brother Alfred, had inherited from their father, Alfred Colvill, a valuable building on lower Madison Avenue, in New York City. Some years later, John's siblings agreed to sell the property for $24,700, but, in the partition proceeding, the buyer asked to be relieved of his contract on the ground that the Colvills could not give a marketable title without proof that their brother had died intestate, or leaving no wife or children.

   It appears that John, melancholic because the young lady to whom he was engaged to marry had broken the engagement, but who was also intemperate and unhealthy, walked out of his father's house at 251 Fifth Avenue one rainy day in June 1874, wearing a one-button gaiter and a shoe, took a Fifth Avenue stage, and was never heard of again. The family endeavored to find him in vain, and his sister Euphemia eventually took steps to settle his estate, and on proof of these facts, his property was distributed among his siblings. The lower court held that the buyer had to complete the purchase of the Madison Avenue property because the Colvills could give good title, and the decision was affirmed ultimately by the Court of Appeals.

   [From JDK: "Eurphemia Purton is the lady known as "Cousin Effie Purton." She made her cousin John Devereux Kernan (1844–1922) her residuary legatee, and pieces of her silver and other mementos are still scattered around the family and elsewhere. One, a 1790 silver teapot engraved with her maiden name but that must have belonged to a forebear, may be the one lent to the Metropolitan Museum of Art in 1911 by R. T. Haines Halsey. She was known for her luxurious living and the elegant parties in New York attended by her Utica relatives. Her early religious connections were with Old Saint Patrick's Cathedral, Mulberry Street, but her funeral was at the High Anglican Saint Mary the Virgin."]

9. See volume 15 of the *Journal of the American Bar Association.* Reports at page 456. Although the two cases mentioned seem to have been important, we have been unable to find any full report of them. The litigation in the Beehive Bank case appears to have ended in a no-opinion affirmance in the Court of Appeals, in which Francis's brother William, appeared for Buchanan.

10. III *Journal of the American Bar Association* at Page 658 et seq. and page 689.

CHAPTER 8

1. David S. Reynolds, *Walt Whitman's America: A Cultural Biography* (New York: Knopf, 1995), 117.
2. *Utica Daily Observer,* June 2, 1848.
3. See Douglass, vol. 2, page 71.
4. See Morison, page 61.
5. Blue, *Free Soilers,* 85.
6. *Utica Daily Observer,* July 28, 1848.
7. *Utica Daily Observer,* June 1, 1848.
8. See Douglass, vol. 2, page 73.

CHAPTER 9

1. *Utica Daily Observer,* May 24, 1848.
2. A letter from Mary D. Devereux to her sister Elizabeth Butler, dated October 20, 1856.
3. In a letter from Julia Clapp (later Newberry) to her aunt Elizabeth Butler in the spring of 1842, which begins "You and Mary are one, therefore I will answer her profound letter to you."
4. See Mitchell, page 158.
5. September 20, 1856.
6. *Utica Daily Observer,* July 24, 1860.
7. *Utica Morning Herald,* September 18, 1860.

CHAPTER 10

1. *Utica Daily Observer,* January 28, 1861.
2. See Mitchell, page 225.
3. *Utica Daily Observer,* February 19, 1861.
4. *Ibid.,* February 9, 1861.
5. New York State Assembly Journal, 1861, page 96.
6. See Ellis, page 352.
7. See Johnson and Smith page 457.
8. *New York Tribune,* September 5, 1861.
9. See DeAlva, vol. 3, page 17.
10. *Utica Daily Press,* September 6, 1861.
11. *Ibid.*
12. *Utica Daily Observer,* October 28, 1861.
13. *Utica Daily Observer,* April 17, 1861.

CHAPTER 11

1. *Utica Daily Observer,* July 17, 1862.
2. See Johnson and Smith, page 462.
3. An unidentified newspaper clipping from a family album lists the "Honorable A.D. Barber, P.V. Kellogg, Mr. Ferry, and others," as the local Republicans ready to campaign for Kernan.
4. See Mitchell, page 382.
5. See Donald, page 319.
6. See Mitchell, page 382.
7. *Ibid.,* page 302.
8. See Lynch, *Boss Tweed* page 246.
9. The definitive work on the draft riots is by Iver Bernstein, *The New York City Draft Riots: Their Significance for American Society and Politics in the Age of the Civil War.* New York: Oxford University Press, 1990.

CHAPTER 12

1. Franklin [Pennsylvania] *Valley Spirit,* April 17, 1861, p. 1.
2. Description of Washington and the opening day of the Thirty-eighth Congress is drawn from John C. Waugh, *Reelecting Lincoln,* pages 66–67.
3. *Congressional Globe,* 1864.
4. Francis Kernan, Washington, to Henry G. Stebbins, [no destination], February 7, 1864, Samuel L. M. Barlow papers, Henry E. Huntington Library, Box 52, folder 32.
5. See Rhodes, page 209.
6. *Ibid.,* page 208.
7. *Congressional Globe,* March 9, 1864.
8. *Congressional Globe,* March 10, 1864.
9. *Congressional Globe,* March 14, 1864.
10. See Donald, page 509.
12. *Congressional Globe,* March 28, 1864.
11. See Rhodes, page 273.
12. See Sibley, *Respectable Minority,* page 128; also see Francis Kernan Papers, Division of Rare and Manuscript Collections, Cornell University Library, Ithaca, New York; and the *New York Herald,* August 28, 1864.
13. See Chidsey, page 44.
14. See Klement, page 295.
15. *Congressional Globe,* 1865, page 219.
17. *Ibid.,* page 242.
18. Letter, Samuel S. Cox to Manton M. Marble, December 21, 1864, Manton M. Marble Papers, Library of Congress.

19. Michael Vorenberg, email correspondence to Robert P. Forbes, September 18, 1998.

20. See Blaine, vol. 1, page 537.

21. See also Curtis, pages 296–297, for slightly varying reports of this incident. There are numerous newspaper reports many years after the Civil War that Kernan was often consulted by Lincoln, but we have found no evidence to support these statements.

22. The president's actual words on this occasion were classified as of "more than average doubt as to ... authenticity" by Virginia Fehrenbacher, co-author of "*Recollected Words of Abraham Lincoln,*" because, she explained in a letter to us on January 16, 1997, the very numbers of stories relating to deserters who returned to see their dying mothers make them all suspect. On a credibility scale of A to D, she put these words, along with four other reports of such words, in grade D. The recent discovery of a trove of Lincoln papers in the National Archives was reported in the *New York Times* on March 14, 1998, right before this manuscript went to press, so the authors were not able to discover any connection to those new findings and this story.

23. See Blaine, page 546.

CHAPTER 13

1. See Foner, *Reconstruction,* page 187.

2. Speech at the state Democratic convention in Albany, New York, September 14, 1866, *Utica Daily Observer.*

3. *Ibid.*

4. See Chidsey, page 195.

5. Kernan spoke in a major outdoor rally in September to support the Democratic state ticket.

6. *Utica Daily Observer,* September 26, 1866.

7. *Ibid.,* November 1, 1866.

8. See Flick, *New York,* vol. 7, page 201.

9. *Ibid.,* page 202.

10. *The Amended Constitution of the State of New York adopted by the Convention of 1867–'8, together with the Manner and Form of Submission and an Address to the People,* Luther Caldwell, Secretary, (Albany: Weed, Parsons and Company, 1868).

11. As noted in the Memorial Address of Hon. William H. Watson, presented to the regents of the University of the State of New York, December 14, 1892.

12. See Lynch, *Boss Tweed,* page 192.

13. Over the next two decades, in addition to his house on Kent Street and the Devereux house on Chancellor Square, Kernan also bought farmland in Whitestown, New York Mills, and North Bay. One piece was gotten solely as a gift to the Cornhill Methodist Episcopal Church. The conveyance was made for a nominal one dollar, in trust that the property be maintained as a place of divine worship. All these lands were disposed of in the course of the years; however, the property purchased for the church, on

Nichols Street at the corner of Rutger Street, is now occupied by the Asbury Methodist Church. [See the Deed of Francis and Hannah D. Kernan to the Cornhill Methodist Episcopal Church, April 7, 1883, recorded in Book 422, page 435.]

14. Samuel Tilden's convention speech was afterward printed in a pamphlet entitled "*The Republican Party Irritating.*"

15. *The Herald,* March 12, 1868.

16. See Klement, page 307.

17. *New York Post,* July 6, 1868.

18. See Bigelow, page 231.

19. *Official Proceedings . . . National Democratic Convention,* pages 154–155.

20. See Klement, page 307.

21. See Flick, *Tilden,* page 179.

22. *Ibid.,* page 184.

23. See Lynch, *Boss Tweed,* page 293.

24. *Ibid.,* page 295.

25. See Cook, page 95.

CHAPTER 14

1. See Mandelbaum, page 164.

2. Exact source has been lost. The story is likely from Bigelow's biography of Tilden.

3. September 29, 1870.

4. See Cook, page 123.

5. See Tilden, vol. 1, page 274.

6. *Ibid.,* page 125.

7. See Breen, page 355.

8. See Alexander, page 267.

9. *Ibid.,* page 267.

10. *Ibid.,* page 218.

11. *Ibid.,* page 267.

12. *New York Tribune,* October 6, 1871.

13. See Tilden, vol. 1, pages 284-285.

14. See Flick, *Tilden,* page 236.

CHAPTER 15

1. See Alexander, vol. 3, page 276.

2. *New York Tribune,* April 13, 1872.

3. See Alexander, vol. 3, page 286.

4. From a newspaper obituary (source unknown) in the Kernan papers at Cornell University Library.

5. *New York Tribune,* January 4, 1868.

6. See Alexander, vol. 3, page 290.

7. See Mitchell, page 513.

8. See Schauinger, page 2.

9. See Tilden, page 311.

10. *New York Times,* September 6, 1872.

11. *Ibid.,* September 9, 1972.

12. *New York Times,* September 29, 1872.

13. *Ibid.*

14. September 9, 1872.

15. See Henry Scott's *Distinguished American Lawyers—With Their Struggles And Triumphs in the Forum,* page 548.

16. *New York Times,* October 27, 1972.

17. From a newspaper clipping (missing source and date) in a family scrapbook.

18. See Flick, *New York,* vol. 3, page 360.

CHAPTER 16

1. See Allen, pages 128-29.

2. See Flick, *Tilden,* page 243.

3. See Mitchell, page 508.

4. See Flick, *Tilden,* page 242.

5. *Utica Daily Observer,* October 29, 1874.

6. *Ibid.*

7. See Flick, *Tilden,* pages 251-252.

8. From the Tilden papers, at the New York Public Library, Box 8, page 1, November 13, 1874.

9. See Flick, *Tilden,* page 254.

10. See Allen, page 148.

11. See Mushkat, *Wood,* pages 238-239.

12. See Mitchell, page 512.

13. *Utica Daily Observer,* January 16, 1875.

14. *Ibid.*

15. *Troy Press,* cited in *Utica Daily Observer,* January 18, 1875.

16. Cited in the *Utica Daily Observer,* January 18, 1875.

17. *Ibid.,* January 16, 1875.

18. *Ibid.*

19. *Utica Daily Observer,* January 21, 1875.

20. *Ibid.,* January 22, 1875.

21. *Ibid.,* January 16, 1875.

22. *Ibid.,* January 18, 1875.

23. Cited in the *Utica Daily Observer,* January 18, 1875.

24. *Utica Daily Observer,* January 18, 1875.

25. *Harper's Weekly,* February 6, 1875, page 1.

26. *Utica Daily Observer,* January 18, 1875, page 1.

27. Quoted in the *Utica Daily Observer,* January 18, 1875.

28. *Utica Daily Observer,* January 16, 1875.

29. Jonathan M. Sewall's "*A New Epilogue to Cato, Spoken at a Late Performance of that Tragedy*" had been delivered at a performance of Addison's popular tragedy at the Bow Street Theater in 1778.

CHAPTER 17

1. From Tilden letters, New York Public Library, May, 24, 1875, Kernan to Tilden.

2. From Tilden Letters, August 30, 1875, Kernan to Tilden (Utica).

3. *Ibid.,* September 20, 1875, Kernan to Tilden.

4. *Utica Daily Observer,* September 30, 1875.

5. From Tilden Letters, February 28, 1875, Tilden to Kelly.

6. See Flick, *Tilden,* page 262.

7. *Ibid.,* page 160.

8. On Tilden's dangerous delays, see Mushkat, *Reconstruction,* pages 181–182.

9. *New York Times,* November 30, 1875.

10. Kernan to Tilden, November 5, 1875.

11. James P. Sinnott to Tilden, February 2, 1876.

12. *Utica Daily Observer,* June 29, 1876.

13. See Flick, *Tilden,* page 299. 15. *Ibid.,* page 302.

14. *Ibid.,* page 302.

15. *Ibid.,* page 309.

16. *Ibid.,* page 317.

17. *Ibid.,* page 328

18. See Randel, page 227.

19. *Ibid.,* page 330.

20. *Ibid.,* page 357.

21. *Journal of the Senate,* February 24, 1877.

22. See Flick, *Tilden,* page 398.

23. See Watson, page 10.

24. See Flick, *Tilden,* page 408.

25. *Ibid.,* pages 407–408.

26. *Ibid.,* 398.

27. See Schauinger, page 159.

28. See Robert H. Wiebe, *The Search for Order, 1877–1920* (New York: Hill and Wang, 1967).

29. See Schauinger, pages 160-161.

30. *New York Times,* October 31, 1878.

31. *Congressional Record,* February 24, 1876.

32. *Congressional Record,* June 30, 1876.

33. *Congressional Record,* 46th Congress, 2nd Sess., page 1402.

34. See Gouverneur, pages 360-361.

35. *New York Times,* October 31, 1878.

CHAPTER 18

1. See Mitchell, page 571. Also see the *New York Sun,* February 14, 1886.

2. See Alexander, page 493.

3. The Pullman railroad strike began in May 1894, when four thousand workers in a plant that manufactured railway cars in Pullman, Illinois, protested the abusive policies of their employers, including a 20-percent wage reduction and an increase in company housing costs. The American Railway Union, headed by Eugene V. Debs, supported the strikers with a sympathetic boycott, which soon spread to Chicago and threatened the delivery of the U.S. mail. The Pullman Company received the support of the General Mangers' Association, which was made up of officials from twenty-four railroads. In the major struggle between organized labor and organized employers, Cleveland unhesitatingly used the tremendous power at his disposal for the employers. Cleveland approved the use of federal troops to insure order, and stood behind his attorney general's federal court order directing Debs and his associates to cease their support of the boycott. The strike formally ended on August 6 (the federal troops had been withdrawn eighteen days earlier). Although the strikers had returned to work, Debs was arrested for violation of the federal injunction. He refused to give bail pending the outcome of an earlier contempt order. On July 26, Cleveland appointed a committee to investigate. Debs received the news of the appointments as an indication of belated fair play, and expressed confidence in the outcome: "The men chosen were assurance of a dispassionate finding" (see Lynch, *Grover Cleveland,* page 445). Carroll D. Wright, of the United States Commission on Labor, was chairman; and his associates were John D. Kernan and Nicholas E. Worthington. Cleveland directed them to "visit the State of Illinois and the city of Chicago and other such places in the United States as may appear proper.... [Make] careful inquiry into the causes of any pending dispute ... and hear all persons interested therein." While Mr. Debs and his fellow prisoners awaited trial, the commission examined over one hundred witnesses regarding the property destroyed, the expenses of the employers in hiring marshals, and their loss of income. Employees gave witness to the loss of life and wages. The investigating committee exonerated the American Railway Union and condemned the Pullman Company and the twenty-four railroads; but this did not

absolve Debs and his companions of the indictment and contempt charge, and, after a vain appeal to the United States Supreme Court, they were found guilty. Debs was sentenced to six months' imprisonment, and his associates to three months each.

4. See Lynch, *Grover Cleveland,* page 172.

5. At the dinner, besides the family, were Col. Lamont, N.E. Kernan, Mr. and Mrs. Francis Kernan, Walter Kernan, and James Clapp (of Luzerne). After the dinner, William J. Bacon, Edward Kernan and family (of Whitestown), William P. Quin, and a few others called and met President and Mrs. Cleveland.

The reception at the Butterfield House began as a private affair. Then, after the town's leading citizens had been presented to the distinguished guests, the doors on Devereux Street were opened to admit the public. An estimated 5,000 citizens had come to shake the hand of the president. The receiving line included T.R. Proctor, Mr. Bailey, and W. P. Quin. Miss Kernan with William Kernan stood beside Mrs. Cleveland at the top of the grand stairway. An hour later, with some struggle, the doors were closed against the crowd. But learning of the disappointment, Mrs. Cleveland insisted they be reopened, and the line continued until the last person had been satisfied, half an hour past midnight.

6. Entries by John D. Kernan in the *Springbank Record,* page 187, note Mr. Cleveland's visit to Forestport and to Springbank:

July 14. President and Mrs. Cleveland arrived at 10 am. Ed Thorp drove them by at 10:30 in his light wagon with Mr. and Mrs. Wm. Cleveland [Grover Cleveland's brother, William, was the minister at Forestport]. Jim and Kathleen met them with Billy [a family horse] at the Depot. Uncle Frank Peebles, Devereux, Rosa, Robert, Herbert, and I cheered the party as it passed. The President & Mrs. C. returned our salute. Poor Frank is sick upstairs and in bed—his mother with him. He has conflagration of the bowels. Mamma and I called and saw the Pres. and Mrs. Cleveland this evening.

July 15. Called on the President and Mrs. Cleveland—arranged to drive this afternoon and to have them take tea with us, then to have reception at Rev. Wm. Cleveland's in the evening. Pres. taken sick last night & In bed today. 5pm. Called & brought the two Mrs. C's up to tea. Pres better but not up & resting for evening reception. Everything mighty grand at tea! 7:30 to 9:30 pm grand reception at which about 1000 attended at Rev. Wms.

July 16. 9AM. Mamma & I went to the St. Lawrence with the Presidential party for the day. A lovely day. Dinner & supper on boat. Accident on the way home. Side rod broke on locomotive. Engineer Riley jumped or fell from Engine and was killed. Reached home at 12 o'clock at night.

July 17. Mamma took the Pres & Mrs. C. to the Presbyterian church. In the afternoon Frank Peebles, Kathleen & I drove the Pres to White Lake Corners to church thence to Lake [illegible]. In the evening the Pres came up with Mr. Spinney of N.Y. Times & sat with us on the front porch for three hours. He went up past Frank & looked over the house. Pres sat in one of the red chairs—the one without rockers, in one of the wicker chairs with rockers, [I]n my desk chair while writing autographs! [The] night turned out dark it began to rain. We sent for George who drove him home in buggy.

 July 18, 9AM. The Pres & Mrs. C. just drove by with Ed Thorp out of the wilderness. We cheered them & were saluted! *Vale! Vale! Longe Vale*"

7. Source and date unknown, perhaps the *New York Enquirer,* sometime between 1887 and 1890.

8. *Utica Daily Observer,* December 27, 1891.

9. See *Official Report of Proceedings of Catholic Congress* pages 13–17.

10. *Albany Times-Union,* September 8, 1892, deriving its report from the *Utica Daily Press.*

11. From an unidentified Utica paper of 1892 pasted in a family scrapbook.

12. *Utica Daily Press,* September 8, 1982, page 4.

13. The custom of having members of the family carry the coffin in and out of the church has continued up to the present time, the only difference being that now some female members take part. The latest instance was at the funeral of Leslie (Hadden) Kernan, "Coupie," at Saint Ignatius' Church in New York, where thirteen male members of the Kernan and Hadden families served first as ushers and then as pallbearers.

14. During his years of service, the Orphan Asylum was enlarged several times and the Assumption Academy was built.

15. About a year before his death, on February 14, 1881, Francis had signed his last will and testament with William and J. Kernan as witnesses. His first clause was a devise to his beloved wife, Hannah D. Kernan, of the Devereux house on Chancellor Square, with all its contents, which he had bought of her mother's estate. He bequeathed to his four lawyer sons equally the library and furnishings of the law office of W. and N.E. Kernan, and left $5,000 to his unmarried and only surviving daughter, Elizabeth Butler Kernan (who was the godmother of the co-author of this book, John D. Kernan III). This was followed by a bequest of $10,000 in trust for his son Thomas, with remainder to Thomas's children (of which he had none) or next of kin. He left the entire residue of his estate in trust to his sons John, Nicholas, and Francis, the executors, to pay the income to his wife during her life in lieu of dower, and upon her death to divide it among his surviving children, John, Nicholas, Elizabeth, Francis, William, Joseph, and Walter, with provision that the share of any child dying before his wife be paid eventually to his child or children, if any. He empowered his executors, during the life of his wife and with her consent, to advance to any of his children his or her share of his estate.

Bibliography

The Albany Law Journal: A Weekly Record of the Law and the Lawyers. Conducted by Irving Browne. Vol. 26. From July 1882 to January 1888. Albany: Weed, Parsons and Company, 1888.

Alexander, De Alva Stanwood, A.M., LL.D. *A Political History of the State of New York.* Volumes 1–3. New York: Henry Holt & Company, 1905.

Allen, Oliver E. *The Tiger: The Rise and Fall of Tammany Hall.* Reading, Mass.: Addison-Wesley, 1993.

The Amended Constitution of the State of New York adopted by the Convention of 1867-68. Together with the manner and form of submission and an Address to the People. Published under the direction of Luther Caldwell, Secretary. Albany: Weed, Parsons and Company, 1868.

The Amended Constitution of the State of New York, adopted by the Convention of 1867-68, with the corresponding provisions of the Present Constitution. Also Manner and Form of Submission, As Proposed. Brooklyn, N.Y.: The Standard Press, 1869.

American Bar Association Reports, various.

Articles Proposed to be Inserted in the New Constitution of the State of New York and Respectfully Submitted to the Consideration of the Members of the Convention which assembled June 4, 1867. New York: Herald Book and Job Establishment, 1867.

Atlas of Schuyler County, New York, from actual surveys by and under the direction of Beach Nichols. Philadelphia: Whitman & Co., 1874.

Bagg, Moses M., A.M., M.D. *The Pioneers of Utica: with Sketches of Its Inhabitants and Its Institutions, with the Civil History of the Place, from the Earliest Settlement to the year 1825—the Era of the Opening of the Erie Canal.* Utica, N.Y.: Curtiss & Childs, 1877.

————, ed. *Memorial History of Utica, N.Y. from Its Settlement to the Present Time.* Syracuse, N.Y.: D. Mason Co., 1892.

Basler, Roy P., ed. *The Collected Works of Abraham Lincoln.* New Brunswick, N.J.: Rutgers University Press, 1955.

Bates, William Alan. *Tiger in the Streets.* New York: Dodd, Mead & Company, 1962.

Bigelow, John, LL.D. *The Life of Samuel J. Tilden.* Vols. 1–2. New York: Harper Brothers, 1895.

Blackstone, Sir William. *Commentaries on the Laws of England in Four Books with an Analysis of the Work with References to American Cases by a Member of the New York Bar,* New York: W. E. Dean Printer and Publisher, Collins, Kane & Company, 1836.

Blaine, James Gillespie. *Twenty Years of Congress, from Lincoln to Garfield.* Norwich, Conn.: The Henry Bill Publishing Company, 1884-86.

Boller, Paul F. Jr. *Presidential Campaigns.* Rev. ed. New York: Oxford University Press, 1966.

Brandon, Edgar Ewing, ed. *A Pilgrimage of Liberty; A Contemporary Account of the Triumphal Tour of General Lafayette Through the Southern and Western States in 1825, as reported by the Local Newspapers.* Athens, Ohio: The Lawhead Press, 1944.

Breen, Matthew P. *Thirty Years of New York Politics.* Published by the author, 1889.

Bridgewater, William and Elizabeth J. Sherwood, eds. *The Columbia Encyclopedia.* New York: Columbia University Press, 1950.

Brookhiser, Richard. *Founding Father; Rediscovering George Washington.* New York: The Free Press, a division of Simon & Schuster, Inc., 1996.

Bruce, Anthony Peter Charles. *The Purchase System in the British Army 1660–1871.* London: The Royal Historical Society, 1980.

Calendar of the Close and Patent Rolls of Chancery in Ireland from the 18th to the 45th of Queen Elizabeth. Dublin, Ireland: HMSO, 1862.

Callow, Alexander B. Jr. *The Tweed Ring.* New York: Oxford University Press, 1966.

Chidsey, Donald Barr. *The Gentleman from New York: A Life of Roscoe Conkling.* New Haven, Conn.: Yale University Press, 1935.

Chroust, Anton-Hermann. *The Rise of the Legal Profession in America, The Revolution and the Post-Revolutionary Era.* Vol. 2. Norman, Okla.: University of Oklahoma Press, 1965.

Civil List and Forms of Government of the Colony and State of New York: Containing Notes on the Various Governmental Organizations; Lists of the Principal Colonial, State and County Officers, and the Congressional Delegations and Presidential Elec-

tors, with the Votes of the Electoral Colleges. The whole arranged in constitutional periods. Albany: Weed, Parsons and Company, Publishers, Printers and Stereotypers, 1869.

Clayton, Professor W.W. *History of Steuben County, New York, with Illustrations and Biographical Sketches of Some of Its Prominent Men and Pioneers.* Philadelphia: Lewis, Peck & Co., 1879.

Coke, Sir Edward. *The First Part of the Institutes of the Laws of England: or, A Commentary upon Littleton. . . .* 19th ed. London: J. and W.T. Clarke, 1832.

Coleman, Charles H. *The Election of 1868: The Democratic Effort to Regain Control.* New York: Columbia University Press, 1933.

Conkling, Alfred R. *The Life and Letters of Roscoe Conkling, Orator, Statesman, Advocate.* New York: Charles L. Webster & Company, 1889.

Cook, Theodore P. *The Life and Public Services of the Hon. Samuel J. Tilden.* New York: D. Appleton & Company, 1876.

Cookinham, Henry J. *History of Oneida County, New York from 1700 to the Present Time.* Illustrated. 2 vols. Chicago: S. I. Clarke Publishing Company, 1912.

Corey, Albert B., Hugh M. Flick, and Frederick A. Morse., eds. *The Regents of the State of New York 1784–1859.* Published in Commemoration of the Establishment of the Regents by Law on May 1, 1784. Albany: The University of the State of New York, The State Education Department, 1959.

Cremin, Lawrence Arthur. *Traditions of American Education.* New York: Basic Books, Inc., n.d., c. 1977.

Curtis, William Eleroy. *The True Abraham Lincoln.* Philadelphia: J. B. Lippincott Co., 1903.

Daley, John M., S.J. *Georgetown University: Origins and the Early Years.* Washington, D.C.: Georgetown University Press, 1957.

Donald, David Herbert. *Lincoln.* New York: Simon & Schuster., 1995.

Donovan, Herbert D. A. *The Barnburners.* New York: The New York University Press, 1925.

Douglass, Frederick. *The Life and Writings of Frederick Douglass.* Edited by Philip S. Foner. Vol. 2. New York: International Publishers, 1950.

Durant, Samuel W. *History of Oneida County, New York, with Illustrations and Biographies of Some of Its Prominent Men and Pioneers.* Philadelphia: Everets and Fariss, 1878.

Durkin, Joseph Thomas, S.J. *Georgetown University: The Middle Years.* Washington, D.C.: Georgetown University Press, 1963.

Ellis, David M., James A. Frost, Harold C. Syrett, and Harry J. Carman. *A History of New York State, A Revision of A Short History of New York State.* Ithaca: New York State Historical Society in cooperation with Cornell University Press, 1967.

Ellis, Elmer. *Henry Moore Teller, Defender of the West.* Caldwell, Idaho: The Caxton Printers, Ltd., 1941.

Everets and Ensign. *History of Tioga, Chemung, Tompkins, and Schuyler Counties.* Philadelphia: Pierce and Hurd, 1879.

Fehrenbacher, Don E. and Virginia Fehrenbacher. *Recollected Words of Abraham Lincoln*. Stanford, Calif.: Stanford University Press, 1996.

Filby, P. William, ed., with Mary K. Meyer. *Passenger and Immigration Lists*. Vols. 2, 3 and 1982 Supplement. Detroit: Gale Research Co., 1981.

Finegan, Thomas Edward. *Free Schools A Documentary History of the Free School Movement in New York State*. Albany: The University of the State of New York, 1921.

Flick, Alexander Clarence. *History of the State of New York*. 10 vols. New York: The New York State Historical Society and Columbia University Press, 1935.

Flick, Alexander Clarence, assisted by Gustav S. Lobrano. *Samuel Jones Tilden, A Study in Political Sagacity*. New York: Dodd, Mead & Company, 1939.

Franklin, John Hope. *The Emancipation Proclamation*. Garden City, N.Y.: Doubleday & Company, 1963.

General Register of Georgetown University. Washington, D.C.: 1916.

Georgetown University Alumni Directory. Washington, D.C.: Georgetown University Alumni Association, 1957.

Glenn, Charles Leslie, Jr. *The Myth of the Common School*. Amherst, Mass.: The University of Massachusetts Press, 1988.

Gouverneur, Marian. *As I Remember; Recollections of American Society during the Nineteenth Century*. New York: D. Appleton and Co., 1911.

Griffey, Carl Hayes, Ph.D. *The History of Local School Control in the State of New York*. Teachers College, Columbia University, Contributions of Education, No. 683. New York: Bureau of Publications, Teachers College, Columbia University, 1936.

Hakes, Harlo, ed. *Landmarks of Steuben County, New York*. Assembled by L.C. Aldred and others. Syracuse, N.Y.: D. Marm and Company,

Hall, Florence Howe. *Julia Ward Howe and the Woman Suffrage Movement*. New York: Arno and the New York Times, 1969.

Harper's Weekly; a Journal of Civilization. New York: Harper Brothers, October 1872 and others.

Hastings, Hugh, state historian, compiler and ed. *Military Minutes of the Council of Appointment of the State of New York, 1783–1821 (Henry Harmon Noble, Chief Clerk)*. 4 vols. Albany: Published by the State of New York; James B. Lyon, State Printer, 1901–02.

Hoogenboom, Ari. *Outlawing the Spoils: A History of the Civil Service Reform Movement 1865–1883*. Urbana, Ill.: University of Illinois Press, 1961.

Hough, Franklin B., M.D., Ph.D. *Historical and Statistical Record of the University of the State of New York during the Century from 1784 to 1884, with an Introductory Sketch by David Murray, Ph.D., LL.D., Secretary of the Board of Overseers*. Albany: Printed by the Authority of the Legislature, 1885.

Hubbell, John T., ed. *Civil War History*. Vol. 12. Iowa City, Iowa: University of Iowa Press, 1966.

Instruction from the Regents of the University of the State of New York, to the several Col-

leges, Academies and other Literary Institutions subject to their Visitation, prescribing Requisites and Forms for Reports, Applications, etc. Rev. ed. Albany: C. Van Benthuysen, 1853.

Johnson, Willis Fletcher and Ray B Smith. *Political and Governmental History of the State of New York.* Vol. 2. Syracuse, N.Y.: The Syracuse Press, 1922.

Jones, Leonard Augustus, A.B., LL.B. (Harv.). *An Index to Legal Periodical Literature.* Boston: The Boston Book Company, 1888.

Jones, Pomeroy. *Annals and Recollections of Oneida County.* Rome, N.Y.: published by the author, 1851.

Journal of the Assembly of the State of New York, 83rd Session, Albany: Charles Van Benthuysen, Printer to the Legislature, 1861.

Journal of the Convention of the State of New York, begun and held at the Capitol, in the City of Albany on the 4th Day of June, 1867, Albany: Weed, Parsons and Company, 1867.

Kent, James. *Commentaries on American Law.* New York: O. Halsted, 1826.

Kernan, Francis. *Counselor at Law, State Reporter, Reports of Cases Argued and Determined in the Court of Appeals of the State of New York; with Notes, References, and an Index.* 4 vols. Albany: W. C. Little & Co., 1855-1857.

Kernan, John Devereux, (1911–). *MacKernan of Tullyhunco.* Hamden, Conn.: Printed for the author, 1993.

———. *Supplement to the Utica Kernans, 1969–1993.* Hamden, Conn.: Printed for the author, 1993.

——— . *The Utica Kernans, The Descendants of Bryan Kernan, Gentleman, of the Townland of Ned, The Barony of Tullyhunco, County of Cavan, Province of Ulster, Kingdom of Ireland.* Hamden, Conn.: Printed for the author, 1969.

Kernan, Thomas P. N. "Francis Kernan." *New Catholic Encyclopedia.* Vol. 8, page 168. New York: McGraw Hill Book Company, 1967.

Klement, Frank L. *The Limits of Dissent: Clement L. Vallandigham & the Civil War.* Lexington, Ky.: The University of Kentucky Press, 1970.

LaPiana, William P. *Logic and Experience: The Origin of Modern American Legal Education.* New York: Oxford University Press, 1994.

Laws of the State of New York passed at the Sessions of the Legislature held in the Years 1777–1784 inclusive. Vol. 1. Albany: Published by the secretary of state, 1886.

Levasseur, A. *Lafayette in America in 1824 and 1825 or Journal of a voyage to the United States: by A. Levasseur, Secretary to General Lafayette during His Journey, translated by John D. Godman, M.D.* 2 vols. Philadelphia: Carey and Lear, 1829.

Lynch, Denis Tilden. *"Boss" Tweed, The Story of a Grim Generation.* New York: Blue Ribbon Books, 1927.

———. *Grover Cleveland, A Man Four-Square.* New York: H. Liveright, Inc., c. 1932.

Mac Lysaght, Edward. *Irish Families, Their Names, Arms, and Origins.* Dublin, Ireland: H. Figgis, 1957.

——— . *More Irish Families.* Galway, Ireland: 1960.

Maguire, James K., ed. *The Democratic Party of the State of New York.* Vol. 2. New York: United States History Company, 1905.

Malone, Dumas, ed. *Dictionary of American Biography.* Published under the auspices of American Council of Learned Studies. New York: Charles Scribner's Sons, 1943.

Mandelbaum, Seymour J. *Boss Tweed's New York.* New York: John Wiley & Sons, Inc., 1965.

Manual of the Regents of the University of the State of New York. Albany: J. Munsell, 1864.

McCabe, James D., Jr. *Lights and Shadows of New York Life.* New York: Straus and Giroux, 1970.

McManis, Charles R. *"History of First Century American Legal Education: A Revisionist Perspective."* 59 Washington University Law Quarterly 597. St. Louis: 1981.

McMaster, Guy Humphrey. *History of the Settlement of Steuben County, N.Y., Including Notices of the Old Pioneer Settlers and Their Adventures.* Bath, N.Y.: R.S. Underhill & Co., 1853.

Mershkowitz, Leo. *Tweed's New York: Another Look.* Garden City, N.Y.: Anchor Press/Doubleday, 1977.

————. *The Reconstruction of the New York Democracy, 1861–1874.* Rutherford, N.J.: Fairleigh Dickinson University Press, 1981.

Mitchell, Stewart. *Horatio Seymour of New York.* Cambridge, Mass.: Harvard University Press, 1938.

Moore, John H. *"One Hundred Fifty Years of Official Law Reporting and the Courts in New York."* 6 Syracuse Law Review 273. Syracuse, N.Y.: 1954.

Morison, Samuel Eliot. *The Oxford History of the American People.* New York: Oxford University Press, 1965.

Morrison, Chaplain W. *Democratic Politics and Sectionalism: The Wilmot Proviso.* Chapel Hill, N.C.: The University of North Carolina Press, 1967.

Muir and Company, compiler, editor and producer; historical research by Leslie W. Devereux, *Utica and Its Savings Bank 1839–1939.* Utica, N.Y.: Published to Commemorate the One Hundredth Anniversary of The Savings Bank of Utica, 1939.

Mushkat, Jerome. *Fernando Wood: A Political Biography.* Kent, Ohio: The Kent State University Press, 1990.

————. *The Reconstruction of the New York Democracy, 1861–1874.* Rutherford, N.J.: Fairleigh Dickinson University Press, 1981.

Near, Irvin W. *History of Steuben County.* Chicago: Lewis Publishing Company, 1911.

Newberry, Julia. *Julia Newberry's Diary.* With an introduction by Margaret Ayer Barnes and Janet Ayer Fairbanks. New York: W.W. Norton and Co., Inc., 1933.

New Century Club. *Outline History of Utica and Vicinity.* Prepared by a Committee. Utica, N.Y.: L.C. Childs and Son, 1900.

O'Conor Don, the Right Honorable Charles Owen. *The O'Conors of Connaught:*

An Historical Memoir. Compiled from a MS. of The Late John O'Donovan, LL.D. With Additions from the State Papers and Public Records. Dublin, Ireland: Hodges, Figgis and Co., 1891.

O'Donnell, Thomas Clay. *The Sapbush Run, An Informal History of the Black River and Utica Railroad.* Introduction by Walter D. Edmonds. Boonville, N.Y.: Black River Books, 1948.

Official Report of the Proceedings of the Catholic Congress Held at Baltimore, Md., November 11th and 12th, 1889. Detroit: William H. Hughes, n. d.

Population Schedules of the Third, Fourth, Fifth, Sixth, Seventh and Eighth Censuses of the United States—1810, 1820, 1830, 1840, 1850 and 1860.

Porter, The Reverend J. Jermain. *History of the Presbytery of Geneva, 1805–1880.* The Geneva Courier Job Department, 1889. Reprint by the Reverend Andrew J. Mac Taggart. Lyons, N.Y.: 1993.

Proceedings of the Ninth Anniversary of the University Convocation of the State of New York, Held August 6th, 7th and 8th, 1872. Albany: The Argus Company, 1873. (N.B. All volumes of reports of the proceedings between 1870 and 1893 also consulted.)

Pulliam, John D., College of Education, University of Oklahoma. *History of Education in America.* Columbus, Ohio, Foundations of Education Series. Columbus, Ohio: Charles E. Merrill Publishing Company, 1968.

Randel, William Peirce, *Centennial: American Life in 1876.* Philadelphia: Chilton Book Co., 1969.

Rayback, Joseph G. *Free Soil: The Election of 1848.* Lexington, Ky.: The University of Kentucky Press, 1970.

Reynolds, Reginald. *Beards, Their Social Standing, Religious Involvement, Decorative Possibilities and Value in Offense and Defense Throughout the Ages.* Garden City, N.Y.: Doubleday and Company, 1949.

Rhodes, James Ford. *History of the United States; from the Compromise of 1850 to the Final Restoration of Home Rule at the South in 1877.* Vol. 5. New York: Macmillan Company, 1906–1907.

Rogers, the Rev. Patrick, M.A., D. Lit., Member of the Royal Irish Academy. *Father Theobald Mathew, Apostle of Temperance.* Dublin, Ireland: Browne and Nolan, Limited, 1943.

Rooney, John. *Genealogical History of Irish Families, with Their Crests and Armorial Bearings.* New York: 1896.

Rose, Charlie, Chairman. *History of the United States House of Representatives, 1789–1994, 103rd Congress, 2d Session, House Document No. 103–324.* Washington, D.C.: U.S. Government Printing Office, 1994.

Ryan, Mary P. *Cradle of the Middle Class; The Family in Oneida County, New York, 1790–1865.* Cambridge, England: Cambridge University Press, 1981.

Schauinger, J. Herman. *Profiles in Action: American Catholics in Public Life.* Milwaukee, Wisc.: The Bruce Publishing Company, 1966.

Sewall, Jonathan M. *A New Epilogue to Cato, Spoken at a Late Performance of That Tragedy.* Portsmouth, N.H.: 1778.

Sexton, John L. Jr. *An Outline History of Tioga & Bradford Counties in Pennsylvania, Chemung, Steuben, Tioga, Tompkins, and Schuyler in New York, by townships, villages, boro's, and cities.* Elmira, N.Y.: The Gazette Company, 1885.

Sibley, Joel H. *A Respectable Minority, The Democratic Party in the Civil War Era, 1860–1868.* New York: W.W. Norton & Company, Inc., 1977.

Sibley, Joel, ed. *The Congress of the United States 1789–1989.* Vol. 2. Brooklyn, N.Y.: Carlson Publishing Company, 1991.

Smith, Jean Edward. *John Marshall, Definer of a Nation.* New York: Henry Holt and Company, 1996.

Spalding, Lyman A. *Recollections of the War of 1812 and Early Life in Western New York.* Lockport, N.Y.: Niagara County Historical Society, April 10, 1949.

Stanton, Elizabeth Cady, Susan B. Anthony, and Matilda Joslyn Gage, eds. *History of Woman Suffrage.* Vol. 3. New York: Arno & The New York Times, 1969.

Stanton, Theodore, and Harriet Stanton Blatch, eds. *Elizabeth Cady Stanton.* New York: Harper Brothers, 1922.

Stevens, Robert Bocking. *Law School: Legal Education in America from the 1850s to the 1980s.* Chapel Hill, N.C.: University of North Carolina Press, 1983.

Strong, George Templeton. *The Diary of George Templeton Strong, Young Man in New York 1835–1849.* Edited by Allan Nevins and Milton Halsey Thomas. New York: Macmillan Company, 1952.

Tilden, Samuel J. *Letters and Literary Memorials.* Edited by John Bigelow, LL.D., 2 vols. New York: Harper and Brothers, 1908.

Torrey, E. Fuller, M.D. *Frontier Justice.* Utica, N.Y.: North Country Books, 1992.

Turner, Orsamus. *History of Pioneer Settlement of Phelps and Gorham's Purchase and Morris Reserve Embracing the Counties of Monroe, Ontario, Livingston, Yates, Steuben, Most of Wayne and Allegany, and Parts of Orleans, Genesee and Wyoming.* Rochester, N.Y.: William Alling, 1851.

University of the State of New York. *Official Minutes of the Regents of the University during the Secretaryship of Melvil Dewey.* Albany: University of the State of New York, 1900.

Wager, Daniel Elbridge, ed. *Our County and Its People, A Descriptive Work on Oneida County.* Boston: The Boston History Company, 1896.

Walch, Timothy, ed. *Early American Catholicism, 1634–1820.* Selected Historical Essays: (The Heritage of American Catholicism). New York: Garland, 1988.

Walsh, John J. *Vignettes of Old Utica.* 2d. ed. Utica, N.Y.: Utica Public Library, 1982.

Watson, Hon. William H. *Francis Kernan, LL.D. A Regent of the University of the State of New York, A Memorial Address by Hon. William H. Watson. Delivered at the Annual Meeting of the Regents of the University, Senate Chamber, 14 December 1892.* Albany: University of the State of New York, 1893.

Waugh, John C. *Reelecting Lincoln; the Battle for the 1864 Presidency.* 7 vols. New York: Crown Publishers, 1997.

Werstein, Irving. *The Draft Riots, July 1863.* New York: Julian Messnerr, a division of Simon & Schuster, Inc., 1971.

Whelan, Kevin, ed. *Wexford: History and Society, Interdisciplinary Essays on the History of an Irish County.* Dublin, Ireland: Geography Publications, 1987.

Williamson, Charles, Esq. of Bath, New York. *Observations on the Proposed Road from Hudson's River, near the City of Hudson, to Lake Erie, by the Oleout, Catharine's, Bath, and Gray's Settlement on the Western Bounds of Steuben County.* New York: 1800.

Zwierlein, Frederick. *The Life and Letters of Bishop McQuaid.* Rochester, N.Y.: The Art Print Shop, 1925.

COLLECTIONS AND MSS CONSULTED:

The Kernan Family Papers, #772, Division of Rare and Manuscript Collections, Cornell University Library, Ithaca, N.Y.

The Robert Todd Lincoln Collection of the Papers of Abraham Lincoln, The Library of Congress, Washington, D.C.

The Tilden Papers, the New York Public Library, New York, N.Y.

Collections of the Oneida County Historical Society, Utica, N.Y.

Collections of the Utica Public Library, Utica, N.Y.

The Archives of the United States, North Eastern Division, New York, N.Y.

The Library of Congress, Washington, D.C.

The Archives of Georgetown University, Washington, D.C.

The Archives of The Visitation Convent, Washington, D.C.

The County Clerk's Office, Schuyler County, Watkins Glen, N.Y.

The County Clerk's Office, Steuben County, Bath, N.Y.

The Devereux Papers at Saint Bonaventure University, St. Bonaventure, N.Y.

The Springbank Record, Alder Creek, N.Y.

$\mathcal{I}$ndex

C